AMBASSADOR
L. PAUL BREMER III
with Malcolm McConnell

MY YEAR IN IRAQ

THE STRUGGLE TO BUILD A FUTURE OF HOPE

SIMON & SCHUSTER

NEW YORK   LONDON   TORONTO   SYDNEY

SIMON & SCHUSTER
Rockefeller Center
1230 Avenue of the Americas
New York, NY 10020

SIMON & SCHUSTER and colophon are registered trademarks
of Simon & Schuster, Inc.

For information about special discounts for bulk purchases,
please contact Simon & Schuster Special Sales at
1-800-456-6798 or business@simonandschuster.com

Map © 2005 Jeffrey L. Ward

Designed by Karolina Harris

Manufactured in the United States of America

10 9 8 7 6 5 4 3 2 1

ISBN-13: 978-0-7432-7389-3
ISBN-10: 0-7432-7389-3

Photo Credits will be found on p. 418.

To the courageous men and women of Iraq struggling to build their future of hope;

and

To the brave men and women of the American military who have sacrificed so much to make it possible.

Contents

MY
YEAR
IN
IRAQ

TURKEY

IRAQ

Tigris

Salahuddin

Mosul • Irbil

Sulaymaniya

Kirkuk • Halabja

IRAN

SYRIA

Baiji

Euphrates

Tikrit • Ad-Dwar

Samarra

Ramadi • Kirkush

Baquba

Sadr City

Baghdad

JORDAN

AL-ANBAR

Fallujah

Karbala • BABYLON

Al-Kut

Al-Hillah

Tigris

Kufa

Najaf • Diwaniya

Amara

QADISIYA

MAYSAN

Euphrates

Nasiriya

Basra

Shatt al-Arab

Umm Qasr • Al Faw

Rumailah oil fields —

KUWAIT

Persian Gulf

Kuwait

0 Miles   100   200

0 Kilometers   200

SAUDI ARABIA

© 2005 Jeffrey L. Ward

■ONE

Chapter 1
CHAOS

Baghdad was burning.

As the Air Force C-130 banked above the curve of the Tigris River, I twisted in the sling seat and stared out the circular window of the cargo bay. The capital of Iraq stretched north beneath the right wing, dusty beige, sprawled in the shimmering heat. Dark smoke columns rose in the afternoon sun. I counted three, five . . . seven.

Beside me, my colleague, retired ambassador Hume Horan, was saying something. But his voice was swallowed by the engine roar. I took out the foam earplugs the crew had distributed when we'd boarded the plane that morning in Kuwait.

". . . government buildings," Hume shouted over the howl of the turboprops. ". . . Baath Party offices." He pointed toward the smoke rising above the arc of the river. "Most of the ministries were concentrated in that district. Saddam liked to keep a close eye on his people."

Ahead in the open compartment, Air Force General Richard Myers, chairman of the Joint Chiefs of Staff, and his entourage also peered down at Baghdad. Over the weekend, my small staff and I had flown nonstop with Dick Myers aboard a huge C-17 jet transport from Andrews Air Force Base in Maryland to Doha, Qatar, on the Persian Gulf. From there, we'd taken this C-130, first to overnight in Kuwait, and then this morning to Basra in southern Iraq. We'd been traveling almost forty-eight hours.

The smoke below in Baghdad held all our attention.

Clay McManaway, another retired ambassador, my old friend—and now my deputy—was seated nearby. "Industrial-strength looting," he yelled. "After they strip a place, they torch it. Lots of old scores to settle."

Hume nodded in agreement as I replaced my earplugs. He was one of the

State Department's leading Arabists, had spent much of his career in the Middle East, and knew Baghdad well. I did not.

Among my own assignments during almost three decades as an American diplomat, I'd been Secretary of State Henry Kissinger's chief of staff and ambassador-at-large for counterterrorism under President Ronald Reagan, jobs that had taken me to almost every capital in the region. Every one but Baghdad. While Francie, my wife of thirty-seven years, and I had served at the American Embassy in Afghanistan long ago, this was my first trip to Iraq, the country where I was about to face the biggest challenge of my life.

Less than a month before, I'd been just another former ambassador living happily outside Washington, working in the private sector. I ran the crisis management division of a large American company, Marsh & McLennan. Francie and I didn't miss the political pressure and crushing workload of high-level diplomacy. We'd recently bought an old farmhouse in New England where we hoped to vacation with our children and grandkids.

But on this hot afternoon above Baghdad, I was eight thousand miles away from suburban Washington and the mountains of Vermont. I was also back in the government, the recently appointed administrator of the newly formed Coalition Provisional Authority (CPA). Some press reports characterized me as "the American viceroy" in occupied Iraq.

As the senior American in Baghdad, I would be President George W. Bush's personal envoy. My chain of command ran through Secretary of Defense Donald Rumsfeld and straight to the president. I would be the only paramount authority figure—other than dictator Saddam Hussein—that most Iraqis had ever known.

Being a civilian, I would have no command authority over the 170,000 Coalition troops spread thin across Iraq, a country the size of California with a population of more than 25 million. But the U.S. Central Command (CENTCOM)—the Coalition's military arm, headquartered in Tampa, Florida—had orders from the president and Rumsfeld to coordinate their operations with the CPA and me.

The Coalition forces that had toppled Saddam after three weeks of intense combat were mainly American soldiers and Marines, but included more than 20,000 British and a much smaller number of Australians, as well as troops from NATO countries, including our new Central European allies.

The terrain they occupied was as varied as Iraq's human landscape. Coalition troops held positions in the marshy Shatt al-Arab delta of the Tigris and Euphrates, in the river towns and holy cities of the south where the Shiites, 60 percent of Iraq's population, were concentrated. Five hundred miles to the north, there were Coalition outposts on the pine-covered ridges in the homeland of the Kurds, non-Arabs who comprised about 20 percent of the population. And our units were also dotted across the flat, baking desert of central and western Iraq, the heartland of the minority Sunni Arabs who made up the 19 percent of Iraqis and had dominated Iraqi society for centuries.

The plane's whining engines dropped in pitch, and the bank angle increased to the left. A young crewman in a desert-tan flight suit strode through the swaying cargo compartment, flexing the fingers of his right hand.

"Five minutes," he called, "five." He then made a sharp cinching gesture at his waist to remind us to tighten our red nylon seat belts.

This model of the workhorse C-130 transport was called a Combat Talon and normally carried Special Operations Forces on low-altitude parachute drops or steep assault landings deep in enemy territory. We'd flown up from the southern Iraqi city of Basra at an altitude of only 200 feet, flashing above the mud-walled villages and date groves among the ancient skein of irrigation canals that had made Mesopotamia the Fertile Crescent for millennia.

The purpose of flying fast, "down on the deck," had not been to provide sightseeing for VIPs but to minimize the risk from ground fire. During the invasion a month earlier, automatic weapons and small arms had mauled U.S. Army attack helicopters passing over these sleepy farming compounds. Although President Bush had declared the end of "major combat operations" eleven days before, Deputy CENTCOM Commander General John Abizaid had conceded that the country was not yet fully pacified when he'd briefed us at CENTCOM's forward headquarters in Qatar.

In less than five minutes we'd land at Baghdad International Airport. Pulling my seat belt tight, I stifled a yawn and thought back over the events that had brought me here.

It was mid-April and Francie and I were leaving the Hartford, Connecticut, airport in a rental Ford Taurus, en route to Vermont to choose furniture for our farmhouse. Francie had bought one of those sticky buns at the airport and the smell of cinnamon filled the car as we pulled onto Interstate 91.

She seemed happy and turned to me. "Honey, I always feel I'm in good hands with you."

I glanced at her smiling blue eyes and hated to spoil that contentment. Not only does Francie have fibromyalgia, which often keeps her bedridden, but she had recently popped two discs in her back, which sent hot twinges down her sciatic nerve along the right leg. Still, she was temporarily free of pain and excited about furnishing our vacation home.

But I had to tell her what was weighing on my mind, and I had to tell her now. Washington couldn't wait any longer.

"We need to talk," I said gently. "About a job I may be offered."

"What job?" she asked quickly, the bun halfway to her mouth. Francie and I are so close that we sense each other's moods instantly, and the atmosphere in the car cooled at once. "What *job*?" she insisted. "Last time I checked you had a job."

She was right, of course. Running Marsh & McLennan's crisis management division for eighteen months had been engrossing work. But Francie knew I was eager to draw on my experience to help our country some way, *any* way, in the global war on terrorism. I had been fighting this battle for almost twenty years, most recently as chairman of the bipartisan National Commission on Terrorism. In our report to President Bill Clinton in June 2000, the blue-ribbon commission had predicted mass-casualty terror attacks on the American homeland "on the scale of Pearl Harbor." As with most such panels, our recommendations had been largely ignored until the attacks of September 11, 2001, proved our point.

And after that disaster, even at the age of sixty-two I just couldn't stay safe on the sidelines. Members of the Bush administration had discussed several jobs with me in the past months. But whenever the topic arose, Francie had opposed the idea, vehemently.

"I need you too much," she'd say. "I depend on you too much." And I knew she had a point.

Now as we drove north from Hartford, I raised the subject again. "This time it's a job where I can really make a difference. In a way, it uses all the skills I've acquired over a long career . . . diplomacy, insight into other cultures, management, and stamina . . ."

"*What* job?" Now she was curious. I knew Francie; if I could hook her intellect I'd be halfway there.

"Helping to put Iraq back together." Only a few days before, we'd sat in our suburban Washington home watching the CNN coverage as deliriously happy Iraqi men and boys had beat their shoes on the decapitated head of Saddam Hussein's statue that the victorious American Marines had just toppled.

"*You?*" She became quiet and just looked at me while I studied the road ahead with my heart pounding. I wanted this challenge. At least I wanted the chance to try. But I wouldn't do it without her blessing.

Slowly, as we drove north through the greening hills, we worked our way around the subject. I told her that I had been contacted by Scooter Libby, Vice President Dick Cheney's chief of staff, and by Paul Wolfowitz, deputy secretary of defense. The Pentagon's original civil administration in "post-hostility" Iraq—the Office of Reconstruction and Humanitarian Assistance, ORHA— lacked expertise in high-level diplomatic negotiations and politics. And, contrary to most media accounts, the White House had never intended ORHA's leader, retired U.S. Army Lieutenant General Jay Garner, to be the president's permanent envoy in Baghdad. I had the requisite skills and experience for that position.

"They're interested in my being considered for the job of running the occupation of Iraq."

Finally, after a long, thoughtful silence, Francie smiled again. "Okay, if anybody can do it, you can."

Now, I'm no softy, but her words brought tears to my eyes: I knew what it would demand of her as well as of me. But she patted my leg and said, "You better call whoever you have to call before I change my mind."

We both understood that the task of rebuilding Iraq would be difficult. But driving through the sunny foothills of the Green Mountains that April afternoon, neither Francie nor I could anticipate the true nature of the assignment or the strain it would put on both of us.

Ten days later, I was in the Oval Office.

Since my talk with Francie, things had moved quickly. Undertanding that I was willing to be considered for the job, Secretary of Defense Rumsfeld had asked me to meet with him. I had known him for decades, since the time we both had worked for President Ford. We had stayed in touch over the years, and I admired his patriotism, quick intelligence, and drive. We discussed the situation in Iraq, and I confirmed my interest. He said he would check with the other members of the national security team and get back to me. At 6:30 that night, his office told me we had a meeting with the president the next day at 10:00 A.M.

"Why would you want this impossible job?" President Bush asked me bluntly.

George W. Bush was as vigorous and decisive in person as he had appeared on television, trying to rally the country after 9/11. I had never met him before, although during my years as a diplomat I had come to know and respect his father and mother.

"Because I believe America has done something great in liberating the Iraqis, sir. And because I think I can help."

This first brief meeting was over, except for a message Francie asked me to give him. "Mr. President, my wife wants you to know that her favorite passage from your State of the Union speech is, 'Freedom is not America's gift to the world. It is God's gift to mankind.' "

The president smiled as he shook my hand, obviously moved by Francie's words.

Over the next two weeks, I had a frenzied series of meetings at the Pentagon, struggling to get "read in" on the situation in Iraq before my departure. Between sessions, I scrambled to assemble a staff. The Pentagon had already made available Air Force Colonel Scotty Norwood as my military aide. Scotty knew the ropes at the Department of Defense and immediately began serving me with extraordinary skill. The Navy offered up an energetic young lieutenant, Justin Lemmon.

On a visit to Vice President Cheney I learned that his special assistant, Brian McCormack, was interested in going to Iraq. I found him standing by the copy machine in Cheney's outer office at the White House and asked him if this was true.

"It is," Brian said with a confident smile.

"Are you married?" I asked. I wasn't eager to take people with young families to Baghdad.

"Not yet," he replied. "I can be ready to leave in a week."

This is the kind of enthusiasm I need, I thought, and hired him on the spot.

Realizing I would also need some wise, experienced counsel, I thought of my old friend and colleague, Ambassador Clayton McManaway. He had been my deputy twice in the State Department, had served in Vietnam, in the Department of Defense, and knew the intelligence community. After a tour as our ambassador to Haiti, where he'd managed a difficult "regime change" himself, Clay had retired and was living in South Carolina.

With the DOD's help, I tracked him down that Friday afternoon. Clay was on a train, on his way south to a vacation in Florida.

I described my concept of the job: "Lots of long days and nights, and there's bound to be frustrating negotiations. I'm going to need a lot of help, Clay. Please come join me."

"I'll get off at the next stop and be there tomorrow, Jerry."

Next, there had to be a senior person who knew the culture and language of the Arab world. I had worked closely a decade earlier with one of the State Department's very best, Ambassador Hume Horan. I found him in happy retirement in Washington.

My pitch to him also worked, and the next day he joined my briefings at the Pentagon.

Clay and I discussed the gigantic administrative job the Coalition Provisional Authority would face. The Coalition already had over six hundred civilian employees and the staff would undoubtedly grow into the thousands.

"I know only one guy who could handle such a management challenge," I said. "Pat Kennedy."

"Absolutely," Clay agreed. We'd worked with Pat for decades at the State Department, where he was recognized as the best administrator the modern Foreign Service had produced.

Pat was serving as a deputy ambassador to the United States mission at the United Nations in New York. Would he give that up and leave his family for the uncertainties and dangers of Iraq? Through the State Department Operations Center, Clay tracked down Pat, who was on his way back from a family vacation in Mexico.

After obtaining the blessing of his boss, Ambassador John Negroponte, Pat reported, "I'll be honored to serve."

There was one final gap to fill. I knew that my work would involve intense interaction with Congress. Someone suggested that congressional expert Tom Korologos might be interested in serving in Iraq. I'd known Tom for decades and knew he would make a strong addition to the team because of the high regard he commanded in both political parties. But I doubted that at this stage in his life he would want to leave the quiet security of his lobbying practice in Washington for the dangers of life in Baghdad. To my happy surprise, Tom immediately agreed to come along. Later, we added another former State Department colleague, Bob Kelley, to the team managing the hundreds of congressional visitors to Iraq.

Less than ten days into the job, I had my personal staff and senior deputies. But I was beginning to gauge the scope of the task we faced. A chaotic power vacuum prevailed in Iraq. When Coalition tanks rolled into Baghdad, they destroyed more than Republican Guard armor and artillery. Saddam Hussein's Baathist dictatorship, one of the world's most repressive totalitarian regimes, lay shattered, its leaders fugitives. And, while the American-led Coalition had accomplished half of its stated goal of regime change by ousting Saddam Hussein, we were far from identifying honest, energetic, and patriotic Iraqis who could govern post-Baathist Iraq.

As I was considering this situation, Jim Dobbins, a former diplomat and experienced analyst with the RAND Corporation, added another dimension when he came to my Pentagon office. "Jerry," he said, handing me a document, "you've got to see this." I knew RAND to be one of the country's most respected think tanks.

The paper was a draft RAND report estimating the troop levels that would be needed to stabilize postwar Iraq. The study was impartial, and unflinching. The professionals at RAND did not deal in rosy scenarios; they applied cold logic to problems.

The study examined the relationship between troop levels and stability during seven previous occupations, ranging from the Allies' post–World War II experience in Germany and Japan to Somalia in 1993, the Balkans later that decade, and our recent experience in Afghanistan. Although I was not a military expert, I found the conclusions persuasive. And troubling.

The historical record demonstrated that to achieve stability in the initial years after military occupation there should be twenty occupying troops for every one thousand people in the country occupied.

"The population of Iraq today," the report noted, "is nearly 25 million. That population would require 500,000 troops on the ground to meet a standard of 20 troops per thousand residents. This number is more than three times the number of foreign troops now deployed to Iraq."

The analysis was stunning. I agreed with Secretary Rumsfeld's efforts to transform the American military to meet the emerging challenges of the 21st century. Rumsfeld envisioned smaller, more agile units, augmented by "multipliers" such as precision weapons and Special Forces. And I also agreed that our forces were still better configured for the unlikely event of heavy land combat in Europe than for the contingencies we were likely to face in more remote corners of the world. Moreover, Rumsfeld's lighter and faster forces had certainly won a stunning short victory in Iraq. But did the situation on the ground in Iraq support the conclusion that we would need only a third of the occupation forces suggested by the RAND study?

That afternoon, I had a summary of the draft copied and sent it down the corridor to Don Rumsfeld. "I think you should consider this," I said in my cover memo.

I never heard back from him about the report.

The next day, Colonel Norwood and I were talking about our mission.

"You know, sir," he said, reading our staff roster, "all the civilians in Baghdad are volunteers. The job will be difficult and frustrating, and maybe even dangerous." He was right. The CPA couldn't hope to succeed unless I could inspire our people's optimism and loyalty. After mulling this over for a couple of days, I hit on a mission motto I hoped would instill optimism.

Scotty tracked down someone in the Pentagon who made the ubiquitous long hardwood desk plaques. On mine, the plaque maker affixed the phrase that visitors to my office would see for the next fourteen months: SUCCESS HAS A THOUSAND FATHERS.

During those months, I would tell my staff that I meant every word of it.

Meanwhile, there were the usual Washington leaks. News of my possible appointment had reached the media soon after my meeting with the president. Immediately the Beltway rumor mill went into high gear trying to assess my selection in relation to the ongoing turf war between Secretary Rumsfeld and Secretary of State Colin Powell.

Some stories pointed out that I had known Rumsfeld since we served together in the Ford administration. Noting that Rumsfeld had proposed me for the job to the president, they concluded that I must be "his man." Other stories, emphasizing my years in the diplomatic service where I had come to know Powell, speculated that I was really State's candidate.

President Bush was clearly aware of these rumors because the following week, just four days before I was to leave for Baghdad, he invited me to have lunch alone with him at the White House before a meeting of the National Security Council.

We ate in a small room off the Oval Office, the windows opening onto the White House lawn. We were both athletes; George Bush was a jogger and weight trainer, and I competed in triathlons and ran marathons. So we dined on a salad of pears and greens.

After a wide-ranging discussion of foreign policy issues, we focused on Iraq.

"What can I do to help you?" Bush asked.

"I need help in a couple of areas, Mr. President," I said.

First, I noted that my experience in government and the private sector made me a strong proponent of the "unity of command" principle. I could not succeed if there were others in Iraq saying they too represented the president. I was particularly concerned that a National Security Council official, Zalmay Khalilzad, who bore the title "presidential envoy," had visited Iraq in mid-April, helping Jay Garner contact political leaders. I had the impression he intended to continue visiting Iraq in his capacity as "envoy."

"Mr. President, this also means I must have full authority to bring all the resources of the American government to bear on Iraq's reconstruction."

"I understand and agree," he said immediately.

"This is going to be long and hard," I said, "a marathon, not a sprint. And I'll need your support to buy time to do a decent job."

Some people thought we could get away with a short occupation and quickly turn full authority over to a group of selected Iraqi exiles. In part, this optimism was based on the relative ease of a military campaign that had been described as "a cakewalk." And it appeared to be encouraged by the predictions of some Iraqi exiles. Just the day before, as I drove to work at the Pentagon, the lead story on the 6:00 A.M. news had been that Jay Garner had announced his intention to appoint an Iraqi government by May 15. I almost drove off the George Washington Parkway.

I knew it would take careful work to disabuse both the Iraqi and American proponents of this reckless fantasy—what some in the administration were calling "early transfer" of power—animated in part by their aversion to "nation-building." I mentioned to the president that giving Iraq a stable political structure would require not just installing democratic institutions, but also creating what I called the social "shock absorbers," institutions which form civil society—a free press, trade unions, political parties, professional organizations. These, I told the president, are what help cushion the individual from an overpowering government.

"I understand," President Bush said. "And I'm fully committed to bringing representative government to the Iraqi people. We're not going to abandon Iraq." He paused, and then added emphatically, "We'll stay until the job is done. You can count on my support irrespective of the political calendar or what the media might say."

"There's one other important issue, Mr. President," I added. "Troop levels. I'm a diplomat, not a general. But I just saw a pretty persuasive draft RAND report arguing that to stabilize Iraq we'll probably need an awful lot more troops than we now have."

Bush listened carefully and noted that Secretary Powell and the State Department were trying to enlist more troops from friendly countries. "But I'll mention it," he said.

After our lunch, the president led me into the Oval Office and asked the others to join us. As they filed in—the vice president, the secretaries of State and Defense, National Security Adviser Condoleezza (Condi) Rice, and Andy Card, the White House chief of staff—Bush waved me to the chair beside him and joked, "I don't know whether we need this meeting after all. Jerry and I have just had it."

His message was clear. I was neither Rumsfeld's nor Powell's man. I was the president's man.

True to his word, on May 9 President Bush gave me a letter with my appointment as Presidential Envoy to Iraq with full authority over all U.S. government personnel, activities, and funds there. Rumsfeld followed up, designating me administrator of the Coalition Provisional Authority, empowered with "all executive, legislative, and judicial functions" in Iraq.

Those two documents, stuffed into my overloaded briefcase on the C-130 sling seat, gave me the powers I needed to do the job, and I was impatient to begin.

The plane's engine noise softened again. We'd climbed to about 500 feet. Flaps whirred, and the deck tilted beneath our feet. Then the landing gear came thumping down. We were landing in Baghdad.

My party climbed into an armor-plated Chevy Suburban in the center of a small convoy that was guarded head and tail by armored Humvees mounting machine guns and grenade launchers. Two squads of security guards in flak jackets carrying submachine guns rode in SUVs ahead and behind us. As we rolled past the bullet-pocked terminal, an evil-looking Apache helicopter gunship clattered overhead, flying top cover.

The car's air-conditioning felt chill after the blasting heat on the tarmac. *Only May*, I thought. *What's August going to be like?*

Baghdad's Airport Road, a six-lane freeway, like so much else in Iraq, had been officially named to honor Saddam Hussein. The road was almost deserted as we sped toward the city center, five miles to the east. Abrams tanks and Bradley fighting vehicles guarded some, but not all, of the overpasses and exit ramps, heat waves rippling off their dusty brown armor. A column of Humvees rolled along the westbound lanes, but there were no Iraqi vehicles on the road, only the occasional blackened hulk of a truck or Russian-built jeep that had been destroyed in the brief, savage combat to capture Baghdad.

The green highway signs in Arabic and Roman letters announcing distances to exits gave the empty road a surreal quality. We could have been in a sci-fi movie about postapocalypse Los Angeles, a city which Baghdad rivaled in size and population. Nearer the heart of the capital, I gazed up empty intersecting boulevards through the oleander hedges screening the parallel service roads. No traffic on any of those streets either. But the smoke was denser here, boiling in gray or black clouds from the sooty windows of government buildings.

Then we heard the flat crack of small-arms fire off to the right. I caught a glimpse of a dirty white pickup careering around a corner, two men clinging to a lopsided pile of furniture in the truck bed. The truck disappeared behind a stand of palms along the road's right shoulder.

"Looters," Scotty Norwood said from the backseat. "The GIs call them 'couch pushers' because they usually don't have a vehicle. I guess those guys found a truck, but it sounds like someone's defending his property."

I nodded and shook my head at the irony, remembering the arson and looting in Los Angeles during the Rodney King riots of 1992. With that city's police department unable or unwilling to stop the anarchy, there had been calls for troops to restore order by force. Eleven years later in Baghdad, the Iraqi police and army had melted away, disappeared, "self-demobilized," in military jargon. And apparently, the more than 40,000 American soldiers and Marines occupying greater Baghdad didn't have orders to stop the looters.

We'd passed more than a dozen tanks and Bradleys along the Airport Road and seen other American armored vehicles and Humvees mounting machine guns parked in defensive positions north and south of the freeway. Yet we'd also just seen a pickup full of loot roaring away, challenged only by some hapless citizen firing an AK-47. One round from an Abrams tank's 120 mm cannon would have vaporized that pickup, along with the looters. But, according to the CENTCOM briefing in Qatar, we didn't yet have enough troops in Baghdad to "secure key tactical objectives"—traffic circles, bridges, power plants, banks, and munitions dumps—and also patrol the streets.

I remembered the words of the RAND report. *This has got to change. Fast.*

In many ways, it had been the initial wave of looting after Baghdad fell in April that had expedited my assignment as the Presidential Envoy in Iraq. No sooner had the euphoria among the Iraqi crowds that greeted the Marines' toppling of Saddam Hussein's statue in Firdos Square been broadcast worldwide than the international media switched to virtually nonstop coverage of the subsequent looting. It was as if the camera crews all abruptly shifted gears from images of victorious American tanks blasting through enemy positions to uninterrupted footage of ragged looters scrambling out of vandalized government buildings, hauling desks, chairs, air conditioners, crystal chandeliers, and rococo vases on their backs.

The competing cable networks, with their penchant for gripping "visuals," were pleased with their correspondents' feeds from the chaos in the streets of Baghdad. Secretary of Defense Rumsfeld was not amused. During a Pentagon news conference on April 11, he'd exploded.

"I picked up a newspaper today and I couldn't believe it," Rumsfeld had announced. "I read eight headlines that talked about chaos, violence, unrest. And it just was Henny Penny, 'The sky is falling.' I've never seen anything like it! And here is a country that's being liberated, here are people who are going from being repressed and held under the thumb of a vicious dictator, and they're free. The images you are seeing on television you are seeing over and over and over, and it's the same picture of some person walking out of some building with a vase, and you see it twenty times and you think, 'My goodness . . . is it possible that there were that many vases in the whole country?' "

But Rumsfeld's scorn concealed the first ripple of disquiet along the Pentagon's E-Ring, where the secretary's senior civilian and military staff responsible for postwar Iraq was beginning to confront the reality of occupying a large Muslim nation in the heart of the volatile Middle East.

Now, riding through the smoky afternoon heat into central Baghdad, I thought about the meeting I'd had with Jay Garner in Kuwait the night before. I had asked him and his senior staff to fly down from Baghdad and meet me at the Marriott hotel for dinner and briefings.

I took an immediate liking to Jay, an affable man with a relaxed manner, a ready smile and a Southern accent. But Jay wasn't smiling much that night. He was clearly upset by media accounts that he was being replaced because he'd mismanaged the three-week-old reconstruction. Lead stories in both the *New York Times* and the *Washington Post* that morning had reported that Washington was engaged in a wholesale purge of ORHA, including Garner.

"All these stories put me in a helluva difficult position, Jerry," Garner said.

"It's just the usual leaks, Jay," I reassured him. "People inside the Beltway with agendas and grudges."

I was sympathetic to Jay, a former soldier who had come out of retirement for no other reason than to serve his country again. I felt strongly that his service should be honored and that he deserved to be treated with respect.

But the relentless media focus on the "anarchy" in Baghdad had tainted Garner's image. It hadn't only been Rumsfeld's bugaboo—the stock footage of the young looter lugging away the tall blue vase—but also accounts of angry lines at gas stations and the "total" pillaging of Iraq's National Museum, where looters purportedly stole thousands of priceless antiquities dating from the dawn of civilization in Mesopotamia.

Garner and his staff might have made mistakes, but he had much more experience in Iraq than I did, and I wanted a smooth transition between ORHA and the new Coalition Provisional Authority.

So Sunday night in Kuwait, over lamb and stuffed grape leaves, I had emphasized how eager I was to have him aboard. Nonetheless, I was acutely aware of the fact that I was indeed replacing him, not for his management failings, but because the president and Rumsfeld wanted someone with more political experience in charge. As a practical matter, I knew I needed to keep him around until I could get my feet under me. At the end of dinner, I felt that Jay had recommitted to staying on in Iraq until his planned departure date of June 15.

Now, twenty hours later, our convoy was rolling down the empty Qadisiya Expressway toward the Tigris and Baghdad's Al-Karkh district, a sector that had been virtually the exclusive reserve of Saddam's regime. We were headed to the

ORHA headquarters Garner had set up in the sprawling Republican Palace that occupied an eighty-acre compound on a bend in the river. For better or worse, this would be the headquarters of the CPA as well.

The lead Humvee stopped at a sandbagged roadblock across the palace gate. As we crawled along the curved entrance drive between rows of unkempt royal palms, I squinted at the turquoise tile dome topping the central wing.

The structure wasn't a white elephant, as I'd feared in Washington, studying aerial photos of the site. It was a *turquoise* elephant.

Of the many decisions Garner had been forced to make on the fly those first days after Baghdad fell, the choice of this site was one I definitely regretted. The palace was not only impractical, being physically isolated from the professional and cultural life of the capital, it was also irrevocably associated with the Baathist regime in the minds of Iraqis. Baathist intelligence officers had tortured and executed an unknown number of dissidents in the cellars and outbuildings of this very compound. I learned that when the first group of Iraqi workers entered the palace after Liberation, they were in tears at the evidence of Saddam's profligacy.

The core of the palace was built in the 1950s, in a vulgar splurge of the country's burgeoning oil revenues. Later, Saddam Hussein had added twin crescent-shaped, colonnaded wings, tastelessly decorated in neofascist style with facing pairs of twelve-foot-high bronze statues of the dictator. These were topped with bizarre military headgear resembling the pith helmets of the British Raj.

We entered the echoing marble foyer, its gleaming floor crisscrossed with communication and power cables, and I caught a whiff of two distinct odors: diesel exhaust and overloaded portable toilets. "No electricity or running water, sir," said one of the burly security guards lugging my bags.

No air-conditioning, either. The only significant battle damage to the structure had been a direct hit on the air-conditioning plant from a heat-seeking warhead.

I was eight thousand miles and at least a century removed from home.

Later that evening, after shaking the hand of almost every one of the several thousand employees and troops stationed at the site—right down to the cheerful young servicemen in the sweltering kitchen—I attended an "all hands" meeting held in a vast hall in one of the palace wings.

There was no microphone, so as I stood beside Jay Garner at the head of the crowd I had to half shout to be heard. "First," I said, my words echoing off the shadowy alabaster ceiling, "I want to extend the president's deep appreciation to

General Garner and his colleagues for the extraordinary work you have accomplished under the most demanding circumstances imaginable. I look forward to working with all of you on the reconstruction of Iraq."

I meant those words, but I also saw the need to reassure these exhausted, frustrated ORHA people, many of whom felt that Washington bureaucrats were scapegoating them.

Next, Garner and I joined about thirty senior staff members in a small conference room whose windows opened onto an interior courtyard that radiated back the day's heat. This would be the first CPA briefing in Baghdad. Our "Senior Advisers" were the core of the CPA, assigned to the Iraqi ministries and to work with counterpart senior Iraqi civil servants to get those ministries running again. They were a dedicated group of men and women, all of them volunteers. The light from the chandelier would fade, then swell to a glare, according to the whims of a generator that was chugging outside near the filthy swimming pool.

I sat at the head of some folding tables that had been pushed into a square. Jay and his ORHA deputy, British Major General Tim Cross, were beside me.

"You know the size of this challenge better than I do," I told them. "America and its allies haven't taken on a job this big since the occupations of Germany and Japan in 1945."

Several of the tired, expectant faces in the room nodded in somber agreement.

"Establishing law and order will be our first priority," I stressed. "The media coverage of the unchecked looting makes us look powerless." I paused. "When the American-led forces occupied Haiti in 1994, our troops shot six looters breaking the curfew and the looting stopped."

Everyone around the table was staring at me.

"I believe we should do the same thing here, even if it means changing the military's Rules of Engagement."

The group was uncomfortably silent.

"Guarding Iraqi ministries buildings and commercial concerns is a matter of great urgency. We have to work hard to get local police back on the street."

Again, I paused and then softened my tone. These were mainly Garner's people. They'd worked full tilt for weeks. The media was describing their effort as a failure.

"I want you all to know how proud I am of your service to our country and to the people of Iraq," I began. "We have one hell of a job ahead of us. And now we have to look forward, not backward."

After that effort to boost their morale, I requested a "warts-and-all" briefing. During the frantic round of meetings I'd had in Washington, I'd been briefed by representatives from the departments of Defense, State, and Treasury, by the CIA, and by the Joint Chiefs of Staff. But nobody had given me a sense of how utterly *broken* this country was.

Peter Gibson, the ORHA Senior Adviser to the Electricity Ministry, began.

"In the whole country, sir," he said, "the power plants are only generating three hundred megawatts of electricity. That's hardly enough for a small city, but this is a country of more than twenty-five million people."

"What the *hell* happened?" I asked. "Coalition aircraft and artillery didn't attack Iraq's power plants."

"It's complicated," he explained, and several military officers observing the meeting offered details.

Before the war, Iraq never produced enough electricity to meet demand. So the Baathists simply rationed power. Naturally the Shiites in the south and the Kurds in the north got the short end of the stick. And during the three-week campaign, Baathist officials and Republican Guard officers had used rolling, wide-area blackouts as a warning system that streams of American attack helicopters were flying north at night. When the electricity surged and then was cut, loyalist forces knew to fire their weapons blindly into the dark sky. These surges had severely damaged the power grid.

"And we've got a big-time looting problem," Gibson added.

Looters had ransacked power plants and substations to steal controls, gauges, and electronics. They also knocked down transmission towers for the copper cable, which, melted into ingots, sold well on the black market in Kuwait.

"Sewage?" I asked. "Water treatment?"

Equally grim. Other essential services, including trash disposal and firefighting, were spotty.

"Most schools and universities are closed," Drew Erdman, the Education Ministry adviser, added.

"Supplies of potable water are very low," Steve Browning, the CPA Health Ministry adviser, said. But he offered a more positive note. "Fortunately many hospitals and clinics are still functioning, though the lack of power hampers surgery."

One after another, the staff gave their bleak reports.

"Okay," I said. "Let's talk about the police."

Bob Gifford, adviser to the Interior Ministry, which oversaw Iraq's police, spoke in an unemotional tone. "Whatever law and order existed under Saddam has broken down completely." Three weeks of largely unchecked looting— spurred by long-suppressed rage against the regime, or conducted as sabotage by Baathist "dead-enders"—had destroyed many of the government buildings in Baghdad. Only the Oil Ministry had been spared, because American troops had been ordered to guard the site. It contained archives and data on the southern and northern oil fields—the patrimony of the Iraqi people.

The targets of the looting were widespread. All across the country, buildings associated with the army or Saddam's multiple intelligence agencies had been flattened—in many former army barracks, not a single brick stood upon another. Several dozen state-owned enterprises, especially those that had been part of the Ministry of Military Industries, had been looted down to the bare walls, even to the plumbing inside those walls.

"Where are the *police?*" I asked.

Gifford, a State Department expert on policing, with experience in Afghanistan, looked around at his colleagues. "In theory, there are about four thousand poorly trained officers on duty in Baghdad. But they're armed only with pistols. Most of them have just disappeared, like the army. The looters have AKs, some machine guns, and even RPGs [rocket-propelled grenades]. The cops are home guarding their families. Violent street crime is way up . . . armed robbery, kidnapping . . . and murders."

We were also getting many reports of sexual assault. Rape had been one brutal tool Saddam had used to control the population. In almost every police station, there'd been a rape room, and one of the busiest had been at the Baghdad Central Police Academy.

We've got to have a lot more well-armed American MPs patrolling these streets, I realized, and made a note to call General Abizaid in Qatar.

Before the session ended, I told the group that I was going to issue an order on de-Baathification soon. "And I hope to set up an Interim Iraqi administration by mid-June. But we're not going to rush into elections because Iraq simply has none of the mechanisms needed for elections—no census, no electoral laws, no political parties, and all the related structure we take for granted. We've also got to get this economy moving and that's going to be a helluva challenge. A stable Iraq will need a vigorous private sector."

They all understood the scale of the task, but perhaps this was the first time it had been delineated so frankly.

"Let's keep in mind the relevant lessons of Germany and Japan. Democracies don't work unless the political structure rests on a solid civil society . . . political parties, a free press, an independent judiciary, open accountability for public funds. These are society's 'shock absorbers.' They protect the individual from the state's raw power."

President Bush and I shared these goals for a free Iraq. It was just as important for all of us here to keep focused on them as it was to solve the welter of immediate crises.

"Finally," I said, closing my briefcase, "we all have to avoid arrogance, either individual or institutional. Yes, we're an 'occupying power.' No getting around that. But we must never forget that this country belongs to the Iraqis. Our goal must be to help them get their nation back on its feet as soon as possible."

Some of the men and women at the table looked inspired, some faces showed no emotion, and a few seemed dubious.

"Thanks, everyone," I said. It was late, and I needed a couple hours of sleep to fight jetlag. "We'll have a full staff meeting at 7:00 A.M. tomorrow."

Donald Rumsfeld's special assistant, Larry Di Rita, and I had been assigned a small bedroom adjacent to the temporary "Boys' Dorm," an area for senior civilian staff on the second floor. I had a cot with a mosquito net mounted on a frame above it. A powerless fan stood at the open window and effectively blocked the weak breeze. But we were lucky: the junior military were billeted, stubbly cheek by sweaty jowl, in brown general-purpose tents that sat sagging in rows on the shadeless palace grounds.

Standing beside my cot, I looked down and noticed that my black dress shoes were covered with the tan dust deposited across Baghdad by the last *shamal* sandstorm. The cuffs of my dark suit trousers were also dusty. Most of the men and women in the senior staff had been dressed casually, a concession to the sand, heat, and primitive laundry facilities. (We had to deposit our laundry at a pickup table—"Remove Ammunition from Pockets," the sign read.)

But I intended to continue wearing a dark suit, white shirt, and tie. I was the president's personal envoy to the people of Iraq, not a technician in a rumpled safari jacket and a baseball cap. From my assignments in Asia and Africa as a young diplomat, I'd learned that local officials—even village schoolteachers in threadbare suit coats and frayed neckties—dressed according to their position in society. I felt strongly that it was a mark of respect for the Iraqi people that I also would dress in the manner demanded of my position.

Even though my suits would survive the dust, dress shoes wouldn't make it in Baghdad. Tired as I was, I suddenly realized, as I prepared for bed, that I had a solution.

I had been thinking about our family farewell party three days earlier. Our kids had driven down to join us for Maryland blue crabs on our terrace, site of so many birthdays and Fourth of July gatherings. Sitting beside me were Paul, his wife, Laura, and our first grandchild, Sophia, who was just a year old. Our daughter and her husband were on either side of Francie. We were up to our elbows in crab shells, and the cold beer and white wine flowed. Little Sophia's gurgling enthusiasm lightened the underlying sadness of the occasion.

It was hard to accept that I would be away from my beloved family for so long. The baby would be talking the next time I saw her. Often I had to close my eyes to hold back the tears.

The only thing that made leaving them bearable was knowing they would hold me in their prayers, just as I would hold them, and the assurance in our faith that God, who had asked us to make this sacrifice, would give us the strength to endure it.

After the crabs, the family gave me gifts. One was a photo of Sophia in a colorful frame. When I squeezed the edge, her lilting giggle sounded from a microchip embedded in the picture.

Then Paul handed me a box and said, "These'll come in handy."

Inside were a pair of tan Timberland boots and a note reading: "Go kick some butt, Dad."

I'll start wearing those boots tomorrow, I thought in the heat of my first Baghdad night.

Before turning in, I sat down at my desk, opened my battery-operated laptop, and began my first e-mail to Francie in the glare of the fluorescent camp lantern. Over the coming months, I would send Francie an e-mail each night, no matter the hour or how tired I was. It was one way to keep us connected despite the distance that kept us apart. On this first night, I had no way of knowing if this message would make it through the unfamiliar maze of military communications.

After summarizing the kaleidoscope of impressions that I'd had over the previous fifty-six hours, I closed with a note on my new home.

Apparently, the palace conditions are much better than a week ago. We have some electricity (generators), a few bathrooms with a periodic trickle of running water (mostly it is porta-potty town). No air-conditioning, which will be a problem in about a month (it was 115 in Basra today). They have begun to bring in small trailers with running water and air-conditioning, each of which sleeps four, and had planned to put me into the first one, which was installed today. When I heard this last night in Kuwait, I gave orders for the Chief of Staff to choose four people who had been here longest and put them into the first trailer. I will bunk in where I am for the time being. It's primitive living, but not half bad compared to what it was just a few days ago . . . or to what the troops face.

I have begun issuing directives to sort things out. It is a managerial nightmare, but I have to move carefully so as not to offend Jay (I cannot afford to lose him now, as he would also take several key people with him). But I will gradually start up a parallel management structure to run alongside his and shift over to that in the weeks ahead.

I yawned and the words on the laptop screen blurred.

"That is about all I can manage tonight," I typed. "Love to both my blondes!"

The second blonde in my life was our Maltese dog, Minny.

I pulled aside the mosquito net and stretched out on the damp sheet. Although my head sagged into the lumpy pillow, sleep did not come as quickly as I'd expected. Instead, I lay in the stifling darkness, listening to the unfamiliar sounds of the compound. Static from a military radio. The rumble of the generators. A huge truck engine starting.

The blast of small-arms fire ripped the night. A string of loud single shots across the river, the noise echoing off the walls . . . an even louder burst of a weapon on full automatic. Lighter taps. Another jackhammer blast of the machine gun.

I pulled back the mosquito net and groped for the earplugs from the C-130 ride. With the foam jammed into my ears, the noise of the gunfire was tolerable.

What's going on? I wondered. *Looters . . . criminals?* It was impossible to tell from this dark, isolated room.

Then I remembered a reassuring phrase from the military briefings I'd received in the past couple of weeks. "There is no indication of 'organized' resistance to the occupation, no evidence of 'command and control' among the handful of Iraqis who are shooting at our troops."

And with that comforting thought, I slipped into exhausted sleep.

Chapter 2
TAKING CHARGE

■ BAGHDAD
MAY 13–16, 2003

I managed four solid hours of sleep my first night in Iraq before snapping awake in the relative cool before dawn. The muezzin in a nearby minaret was calling the faithful to morning prayer, the *salaatus subh*. Without scratchy loudspeakers—one result of the power shortage—the chant was pure in the half-light.

There was no treadmill for exercise, so I pulled on shorts and running shoes, joined my bodyguard, Erik, and ran a couple of quick kilometers along the gravel paths through the weedy garden and palm grove behind the palace. My hopes for a shower ended with a couple of feeble dribbles of rusty water in the ornate bathroom. So I bathed by dumping a plastic bottle of water with one hand and scrubbing with the other. I looked ridiculous in the big gilt-frame mirror.

Ten minutes later, Clay and Hume entered my office. We did not yet have a direct communication connection to Washington, so I had to forgo the Foreign Service tradition of reviewing the overnight cables.

Clay, too, was frustrated. ORHA and the new CPA mission had been flooded with unauthorized volunteers who'd simply been appearing unannounced in Baghdad, straining our already overburdened infrastructure. We needed to control this flow of people, so I'd asked Clay to send Washington a cable that no one was to come to Baghdad without our prior approval.

"No way to send an official cable from this place, Jerry," Clay said.

"I know. We'll have to improvise."

We'd soon learn that hundreds of civilians working for CPA did in fact have unofficial e-mail connections from their laptops through the military's uplinks and to the bureaucracies in the States. Veteran ambassador that he was, Clay recognized the inherent disorganization—and potential ill discipline—of this improvised system.

Clay and Hume now handed over a stack of reports, maps, and satellite pictures collected from ORHA's makeshift offices scattered around this huge building.

I knew we could learn more about the organization's true nature and track record by culling its "in-country" documents than we had from consulting ORHA's patrons and detractors eight thousand miles away in Washington.

"You asked us for a quick analysis," Clay said, tapping the papers on my desk. "There it is."

"As they say," Hume added, "things haven't exactly gone 'according to plan.'"

"Lots of fundamental misconceptions, Jerry," Clay said.

Although there would later be widespread acrimonious speculation about what went "wrong" after the collapse of the Iraqi military, we learned that morning that there was no mystery about the actual sequence of events.

I scanned a summary of the preinvasion planning.

Before the Coalition had launched the ground war on March 19, 2003, responsibility for "post-hostility operations" had been removed from General Tommy Franks and assigned to the Pentagon's new Office of Reconstruction and Humanitarian Assistance, ORHA. In January 2003—late in the planning process—Rumsfeld appointed retired Army Lieutenant General Jay Garner to lead ORHA.

The organization's initial *raison d'être*, as its name implied, was to oversee repairs to vital war-damaged Iraqi infrastructure such as oil fields, hospitals, roads, and telecommunications networks. Another priority was averting a humanitarian disaster—starvation and epidemic—among the millions of internal refugees expected to flee what might be months of combat. Although an adjunct of CENTCOM, the organization reported directly to the Office of the Secretary of Defense in the Pentagon.

Garner had led the emergency humanitarian operation in 1991 that saved thousands of refugees in the snowy mountains of northern Iraq after Saddam Hussein unleashed his army against the rebellious Kurds following the Persian Gulf War cease-fire. To prepare for initial reconstruction and humanitarian assistance in 2003, Garner had been authorized to recruit about three hundred administrators and experts. ORHA was meant to be a civilian rapid reaction force, a fire brigade, responsible for meeting immediate needs. If Saddam Hussein sabotaged Iraq's oil fields, ORHA had specialized teams to douse the fires and cap the wells. If prolonged fighting drove throngs of refugees out of the cities and into the empty desert, Garner's people were prepared to house and feed them in tent cities.

"Looks like Garner and his folks started working around the clock as soon as they hit the ground in Kuwait in February," I said.

Beyond oil field repair crews and refugee workers, ORHA's team included civil engineers as well as administrative and infrastructure experts. ORHA also had a few political experts in a "governance" team, led by Ambassador Ryan C. Crocker, a deputy assistant secretary of state for Near Eastern affairs. Ryan was an experienced career Foreign Service officer (FSO), having served as ambassador to Syria, Kuwait, and Lebanon. A fluent Arabic speaker, he had also spent several years at our Baghdad embassy in the late 1970s.

Although many press stories alleged that the Pentagon had "shut out" the State Department from participation in Iraq's reconstruction, the presence of hardworking Crocker and dozens of other career FSOs, as well as my own senior staff, shows that State officials were deeply involved after the fall of Baghdad.

Sometime after arriving in Baghdad, I read press reports about a State Department study on the future of Iraq, claiming that it provided a full plan for postconflict activities in the country. Crocker had been deeply involved in the study, so I asked him if it provided a practical "plan" for postwar Iraq. "Not at all," he told me. Its purpose was to engage Iraqi-Americans thinking about their country's future after Saddam was ousted. "It was never intended as a postwar plan," Crocker noted. When I eventually had a chance to read the fifteen-volume study, I agreed.

Beyond the State Department, Garner had also hoped to be able to tap into the resources of other American government agencies when and if the job required.

"The one problem Garner couldn't solve was the unknown," Hume said.

And the biggest unknown back in February had been whether there actually would *be* a war followed by an occupation. The widely accepted assumption — that Iraq had developed and stockpiled weapons of mass destruction (WMD) in defiance of multiple United Nations resolutions — was the crucial issue before the war, the *casus belli*. Many senior members of the Bush administration, including Secretary of State Powell, sincerely hoped that international diplomacy would prevail in disarming Iraq and deposing the Baathists.

If Saddam Hussein, his sons Uday and Qusay, and the other senior Baathists with bloodstained hands could be toppled by Iraqi dissidents or forced into exile without an invasion, ORHA's task would be greatly reduced. No war, no battle damage or refugees. In this optimistic projection, the post-Liberation

Iraqi government, centered on a group of exiles that took over from the Baathist regime, could govern the country immediately.

So when Jay Garner had solicited people and money from government agencies in early 2003, the bureaucrats politely told him, "Come back and see us when you have specific requests."

When the war began on March 19 and Saddam's regime fell just three weeks later, Garner and ORHA found themselves orphans, thrust into responsibilities they had never anticipated, and without sufficient resources, whether human or financial.

I pulled out a couple of satellite pictures from the pile of documents. The huge Rumailah oil fields in the south, which the Baathists had targeted for destruction, had escaped with only minor sabotage because CENTCOM troops had seized the booby-trapped wells before the Iraqis received the order to blast them.

Elsewhere, battle damage to infrastructure was relatively minor because the enemy Republican Guard had chosen to fight along the rivers and canals south of the capital—and not to turn the city into Fortress Baghdad as some military planners had feared. As I had heard in the first CPA senior staff meeting, the Coalition did not attack power plants. But Iraq's power grid had been failing from years of neglect, and most recently from the attempt to use surges and rolling blackouts as a primitive weapon.

With the "large unit" combat lasting only twenty-one days, not months, and with Coalition forces bypassing towns and cities and moving so fast on Baghdad, the flood of refugees never materialized. Saddam Hussein had also ordered before the war that all Iraqis be issued a three-month supply of basic rations (flour, rice, beans, cooking oil), so famine was not an immediate threat either.

"Guys, in a nutshell, it's not that we didn't plan. The problem is that we planned for the *wrong* contingency," I said.

"Well, there's nothing like twenty-twenty hindsight," Clay said.

"That wasn't the only best-laid plan that went astray," Hume said, handing me a red-bordered classified file folder.

The Pentagon had also anticipated that most of the Iraqi army of 715,000 men, 400,000 of whom were Shiite conscripts, would surrender *en masse*. Units would remain intact and so the soldiers could be employed on ambitious reconstruction projects that paid a steady living wage. General Franks had ordered Iraqi troops on April 10 to "remain in uniform at all times. Maintain unit integrity and good order and discipline in your units."

But those plans had not taken into account the harsh reality of life for the

Shiite draftees, who had endured Spartan rations, token pay, brutal hazing, and arbitrary execution at the hands of their mostly Sunni officers. These soldiers felt no allegiance to their hated commanders and had little incentive to maintain unit integrity. Under relentless bombardment from precision-guided weapons that struck their targets unerringly on the darkest night or during the fiercest *shamal* sandstorm, they shouldered their rifles and trekked home to their farms, villages, and cities across Iraq. At Liberation, there was not a single Iraqi military unit standing intact anywhere in the country. And, as U.S. Central Command confirmed after the fall of Baghdad, the Iraqi Army no longer existed as an organized force. In Pentagon terms, it had "self-demobilized."

So Jay Garner and his small team had neither a refugee crisis to resolve nor a willing workforce of Iraqi soldiers to employ on the WPA-type reconstruction projects many in the Pentagon had envisioned. All the government's ministers, deputy ministers, and thousands of top Baathists had fled, too. So Garner had encountered a political power vacuum, a lack of experienced Iraqi leaders, from village headmen to town mayors to administrators in the ministries of Baghdad.

Running through my mind this first morning in Baghdad was the much-quoted remark from 19th-century Prussian Field Marshal von Moltke, "No battle plan ever survives the first contact with the enemy." As we reviewed the reports, I thought, *No civilian plan survives the first contact with reality.*

Hume drew my attention to another problem that he'd noticed from long experience in the region. As Coalition military commanders had liberated Iraqi towns, their civil affairs officers, few of whom spoke Arabic or understood the dynamics of Iraqi society, had hastily assembled village councils or appointed mayors and even governors. This was a reasonable reaction to our military's need for "points of contact" in the local population.

"From the looks of it," Hume said, "many of the commanders made these decisions without considering the political consequences. They seem to be acting without critical information about these guys. It'll be a miracle if we don't end up with a bunch of Baathists, criminals, or both."

Most of those sitting around the tables for the 7:00 A.M. senior staff meeting were obviously weary. Their fatigue was written in unshaven chins and dark sunken eyes.

I sensed wariness, as well. Under Jay Garner ORHA had been relatively informal and with few regularly scheduled meetings because people were usually scattered, facing the multiple crises of the moment. Jay was a likable guy, rather easygoing for a senior military man, and he had many loyal friends in this room. I was replacing him. Naturally his people wanted to see more of me before shifting their allegiance. Fair enough. But part of my job was to instill discipline and a sense of purpose in a dispirited organization, so that we could plan for the long haul.

I listened to the morning situation reports, and then announced that I wanted to focus the rest of the session on the economic troubles average Iraqis were facing.

"Beyond security, we've got to solve bread-and-butter problems. That has to be our immediate priority," I told them. "All the way from macro issues like what to do about the subsidies, the state-owned enterprises and the currency, down to the price and availability of rice and beans . . . of—"

"—LPG . . . cooking gas," our oil adviser Gary Vogler interrupted, completing my list of vital household commodities now in short supply. "And the gasoline situation is bad and getting worse."

Under the Baathist command economy, with state monopolies controlling distribution of cooking gas and gasoline, subsidized prices were kept artificially low. We had inherited a structural crisis.

Beyond the near-term shortage of gasoline and LPG cooking gas lay a deeper problem. Iraqi refineries, which produced fuels of all types as well as LPG, had been antiquated relics before the war—largely because Saddam deprived them of adequate funding. Iraq had been able to swap crude oil with the Turks for LPG, but now we faced a daily shortfall of at least 150 truckloads.

In two weeks the country would run out of cooking gas.

And my advisers told me that Iraq's three major refineries were so old and poorly maintained under Saddam's command economy that this critical component of the energy industry might soon cease to function altogether.

But fuel was not our only problem. My adviser to the Finance Ministry, David Nummy, said we were facing "a major budget crisis" unless we could generate some revenue. He noted that 98 percent of the state's budget came from oil revenues, but these could not be quickly ramped up while UN sanctions, imposed after the 1991 Gulf War and forbidding such sales, were still in place. The measure had been designed to stop Saddam from using oil sales to rebuild his military or to obtain WMD.

In 1996, the UN established the Oil for Food (OFF) program, under which limited oil sales were permitted. The revenues, deposited in UN-controlled accounts, were supposed to be used to import food and medicines. But the program had been corrupted and there were reports that some countries, including France and Russia, may have been involved in shady OFF dealings. Saddam himself had not only skimmed off his share, he'd used a lot of the funding for a nationwide building binge, constructing *fifty* palaces. This was what General Franks called the "Oil for Palaces Program."

Another problem concerned the purchase of the Iraqi wheat and barley crop, which under Saddam the Ministry of Trade bought at an artificially low price. Buying the crop would cost us over $130 million, according to Ambassador Robin Raphel, our adviser to the Trade Ministry.

"Where are we going to find that?" I asked.

She noted that we might be able to get it from the UN's World Food Program. "They're sitting on about five billion dollars in OFF funds," she told me. But the UN was worried about security at the collection points. I told Robin to pull together materials and we'd go call on the head of the UN mission.

During the session, I also learned that the Education Ministry was planning elections for the administration of Baghdad University the next day, to allow the school year to finish on time. Our education team was uneasy because the best-organized group on campus was likely to be Baathists. I told them to let the elections proceed, but we would consider anybody elected to be "interim" until we had a chance to vet them.

After almost an hour, I ended the meeting. I'd made my point: The staff had to become more decisive, to focus on practical solutions, and not indulge in pessimistic rambling. It was always easy to be negative, especially with the news media carping at us. But I couldn't allow pessimism to slide into inaction. I might not have won a popularity contest, but as my kids had suggested, my desert boots had encouraged me to start kicking some butt.

"Better look at this, sir," my military aide, Colonel Scotty Norwood, said. It was 6:15 the next morning, Wednesday, May 14. He handed me a Web printout of a *New York Times* article.

"Damn it to hell," I said, and read the headline aloud. "NEW POLICY IN IRAQ TO AUTHORIZE G.I.S TO SHOOT LOOTERS." I slammed the page onto the inlaid rosewood on my desk. "When did this come in, Scotty?"

"Around 0600, sir."

Patrick Tyler, the *Times* reporter, must have filed the story from Baghdad Tuesday afternoon. Tyler's unnamed sources quoted directly from my staff meeting the first night. I read further into the story. " 'They are going to start shooting a few looters so that the word gets around,' that assaults on property, the hijacking of automobiles and violent crimes will be dealt with using deadly force," Tyler quoted his sources.

Referring to unnamed "officials," Tyler noted my "tougher approach" appeared to be "at the core of Mr. Bremer's mandate from President Bush to save the victory in Iraq from a descent into anarchy" and cited the risks of "the possible killing of young, unemployed or desperate Iraqis . . ."

The leakers had also taken it on themselves to try to drive the CPA's agenda. "Another tough measure that the officials said Mr. Bremer was eager to make public is a decree on de-Baathification . . ." Although the information was accurate, it concerned major policy, and I certainly did not want Iraqi political leaders and average citizens to hear about this on Al-Jazeera television, via the *New York Times.*

The busy rumor mill inside the palace now had it that Garner would be leaving sooner than expected and would take several of his loyal staff members with him. I wanted Jay's expertise in logistics, but I wouldn't be sorry to see the leakers go.

Later I was sitting in a communications center at the headquarters of the Coalition's ground commander, Army Lieutenant General David McKiernan, near Baghdad International Airport. We were in the middle of a secure video teleconference linking Baghdad, CENTCOM forward headquarters in Qatar, and Secretary Rumsfeld at the Pentagon. Before we hooked up on the satellite phone, I had congratulated McKiernan, a blond Irish-American, on the wonderful Coalition victory, but his blue eyes betrayed deep exhaustion.

Don Rumsfeld was philosophic about the leaked story. He had certainly put up with more than his share of leakers. "Sure the article was unhelpful," he said with typical sardonic understatement. "But what I'm more concerned about is that the ROE are getting diluted as they're passed down the chain of command."

The Rules of Engagement (ROE) under which our troops dealt with Iraqis had been steadily eroding. During the invasion, which saw widespread attacks from Fedayeen Saddam—irregular forces in civilian clothes—our units were authorized to defend themselves by firing on any civilian bearing arms. Now there were militias and armed criminal gangs prowling the streets of many Iraqi cities, and Coalition forces and their commanders were not certain how to respond.

Lieutenant General John Abizaid, CENTCOM's deputy commander in Qatar, agreed with Rumsfeld about the weakening of the Rules of Engagement. "As of today, I'll reenergize the chain of command to ensure we have robust ROE in place and that every soldier and Marine understands them," he said.

No one mentioned shooting looters because there was a disciplined restraint to these teleconferences. "We need to review the tasking to see what makes sense," Abizaid continued, referring to the detailed web of missions, objectives, and orders that controlled all aspects of military operations.

"What have you concluded so far?" Rumsfeld asked him, his insistent tone coming through clearly over the satellite link.

"Where we've had active security patrolling," Abizaid explained, "conditions have been fairly calm."

"Active?" Rumsfeld asked. His aversion to obscure military jargon was well known.

"Mounted patrols, Mr. Secretary," the general explained, then hastened to clarify. "Armored vehicles, armed Humvees, foot patrols . . ."

"What we civilians call a show of force," I added.

"We soldiers like to think there's a little more military science to it, Jerry," Abizaid said, lightening the tone. "Whatever you call it, a more active troop presence on the street makes an impression. It's not so much a question of force levels as it is what procedures and priorities the troops follow."

I remembered the clusters of armored vehicles around traffic circles and highway overpasses on my drive in along the Airport Road. An Armored Cavalry unit comprised of tanks, Bradley fighting vehicles, and Humvees mounting machine guns could certainly guard a fixed objective. But two blocks away, looters or armed robbers might be sacking a government food warehouse or a merchant's store with impunity.

"Mr. Secretary," Abizaid said, "perhaps it's time to redistribute the forces."

Now we're making progress, I thought, jotting this on my notepad.

"One thing's certain," Abizaid said. "No forces will be released for redeployment out of Iraq until we have security in place."

This was the first admission that military force needed to be applied to stop the lawlessness in the streets.

Later, in my office, I spoke to Abizaid at his headquarters in Doha, Qatar, via secure telephone.

"Thanks for your support with the secretary, John," I said. "It helps a lot to know none of the troops are going home while the security situation is still shaky."

"We're working on more robust ROE and more vigorous patrolling right now," he said. "McKiernan will have something for you by tomorrow."

"I appreciate that," I said. "I don't want to look a gift horse in the mouth, but CENTCOM doesn't have enough Abrams tanks or Bradleys to guard every police station in the country. We need to convince Iraqi cops to return to their posts. I need as many American Military Police as you can get me as fast as you can get them here."

Abizaid was silent a moment. "I might be able to scrape up about 4,000 more." He added that he thought they could start flying them into Iraq from the States and Europe within forty-eight hours.

There were around 14,000 Iraqi policemen missing from their posts in Baghdad. Replacing them with 4,000 American Army MPs in Kevlar helmets and vests, toting M-16 rifles or poised at the machine-gun turrets of Humvees, was bound to dampen the enthusiasm of the looters.

"Thanks, John."

The phone hissed, and went silent.

A strange turn of events. Disgruntled staffers had leaked chapter and verse from a confidential meeting with me to the *Times*. The story had prompted Rumsfeld and CENTCOM to patrol Iraq's streets more vigorously. And now the military had agreed to provide needed MPs to bolster and train Iraqi police.

I'd heard criticism of the ORHA staff not getting out of the Republican Palace enough. To fight that image, I planned to visit at least one Iraqi institution each day, first in greater Baghdad and then farther afield.

On Thursday morning, CPA Health Ministry adviser Steve Browning and Said Hakki, an Iraqi-American physician who'd come to Baghdad with ORHA in April and knew the ministry well, met me at the Central Children's Hospital. Hakki was one of almost two hundred expatriate Iraqis from all walks of life and from all over the world who came to serve their native country in an organization called the Iraqi Reconstruction and Development Council. The group was headed by a talented Iraqi-American, Emad Dhia, who reported to me.

Set in the middle of Medical City, the multistory hospital's tan, concrete-slab style evoked 1970s oil-boom Baghdad. The interior did not match the modern façade.

The hospital director, Dr. Nazar al-Anbaky, met us just inside the dusty glass doors of the entrance. If anything, it was hotter in the spotty shade of the foyer than it had been on the drive outside. The air was thick with sharp odors: disinfectant, sewage, sweat, and fumes from a generator.

"Welcome, Ambassador," the doctor said, taking my hand.

His white coat was clean, his mustache well trimmed, and his eyes bright. He looked every bit a competent, caring physician.

"*Sabah al-khair*," I said, using the formal Arabic greeting that Hume had drilled into my head that morning.

My attempt at speaking their language drew fleeting smiles from the senior staff assembled to meet us. But they looked anxious. Iraqi civil servants like these doctors never knew what lay in store on such occasions. Like all Iraqis, they had lived in a universe of one man's often brutal whims. Part of my job now was to convince them, through example, that times had indeed changed. But soothing their anxiety as long as Saddam and senior Baathists remained at liberty would not be easy.

"*T'fadl,*" Dr. al-Anbaky said with an openhanded sweeping gesture of hospitality, leading us to the stuffy VIP visitors' room where a sun-faded tablecloth was laid out on a conference table. There was the expected array of bottled water, warm lemon soda, and tulip glasses for tea.

After the requisite small talk required in any Arab culture, I spoke slowly and clearly in English, having been told that the director and his senior staff seated around the table knew the language. "What are your immediate needs, doctor? What can we do to help you and your patients . . . this week, next week . . . next month?"

"Well, Ambassador, our needs are many, and we know you have just arrived . . ."

"How can we help you *now*, doctor? Please speak freely."

Expressing one's honest thoughts, of course, was a new and worrisome experience to them. But al-Anbaky tried. "Ambassador, the city is not safe, either night or day." He pointed out the open glass doors, across the hospital grounds toward Rashid Street, Baghdad's commercial heart. "My staff reported for work every day during the war. We operated at night when the bombs were falling. We walked many kilometers to come here even as the American tanks were shooting. Now . . ."

". . . Now the streets are too dangerous, sir," a woman doctor said. She was in her thirties, slender, a silk scarf complementing her white medical coat. "My female staff do not dare report for the night shift. The criminals are . . . *taking* any women they find alone in the dark. I have a few doctors and nurses living here now. But we all have families. Ambassador, the streets are impossible."

"I promise you that the security situation will improve. Thousands of well-armed American Military Police will arrive within days. What are your other problems?" I asked, turning back to the director.

Again, he spread his hands. "Our ambulances cannot get gasoline because of the current shortage. We need diesel for our generator and it's not working properly. We have delayed needed repairs, since long before the war. We lack basic medical supplies and equipment . . . syringes, drip tubes, bandages . . . certain antibiotics. We have been working without rest since March, and we will not stop. But we do need help."

ORHA had reserves of medical supplies in Kuwait for the refugee camps they never had to build. And I was sure I could squeeze some gasoline and diesel fuel out of David McKiernan and CENTCOM. Not only would helping this hospital and its heroic staff foster goodwill toward the Coalition; assisting them was simply the only moral option.

"I'll send our experts over right away to look at your generator's problems. Please give me a list . . . a complete, detailed list of your other needs," I said. "We'll do everything possible."

The director smiled his appreciation, but then twisted his fingers again. "Our salaries . . . the money we are paid, nothing has come for almost two months. Ambassador, our pay is low. But when we have nothing, it makes life impossible. All of us support large families, parents, uncles, cousins . . . so many children."

I nodded gently to spare this gracious man the indignity of begging. "We hope to announce soon the payment of all back salaries to every civil servant in Iraq, and the Ministry of Health is one of our top priorities." A visible wave of relief swept their faces.

Now, I thought, *we've got to deliver.*

I then toured the hospital. I had braced myself to see sick children, but nothing could have prepared me for the rows of cribs and battered incubators. Because the hospital generator ran only at night, and then only periodically to save fuel, the air-conditioning plant was not working. The air was oppressive and stale. Flies swarmed through the open windows and clumped on the chipped metal bars of the cribs. Distressed mothers, half-shrouded in black *abaya* robes, waved cloths or squares of cardboard to keep the flies from their children's faces.

The stench of diarrhea took me back to my service in Afghanistan and Africa thirty-five years earlier. But Iraq had enjoyed an admirable public health system before Saddam and the Baathists had looted the country's oil wealth and squandered billions of dollars, first on the futile, eight-year carnage of the Iran-Iraq War in the 1980s, and then on the invasion of Kuwait in 1990.

This hospital had been in an especially precarious position when UN sanctions took hold in 1991. The official Baathist propaganda line was that the sanctions had caused widespread malnutrition and premature death among destitute Iraqi children. But much of the decline in health occurred when the regime had skimmed off medications and hospital equipment obtained under the Oil for Food program, diverting it to clinics reserved for the party elite and Republican Guard.

Malnutrition had principally afflicted dispossessed Shiite children, whose families had suffered the brunt of assassinations and massacres carried out by Saddam's Intelligence services, as well as by the Republican Guard. Shia families were often denied food ration cards. So their children starved and died. The ones who lived found their way to hospitals such as this, where the international news media captured their plight on videotape, "shocking examples of the cruel, misguided sanctions policy"—just as the Baathist propagandists had intended. I'd seen a World Bank study before I left Washington estimating that Iraq now had the shortest life expectancy and highest infant mortality of any country in the region.

In the neonatal ward, I bent to read the stainless-steel model tag on an incubator. It had been built in "West Germany" in 1962, forty years before. The tiny baby inside wore a ragged cloth diaper. I touched the chipped glass. Fierce sunlight from the open windows provided the only warmth. The nurses shifted the powerless incubators from sunlight to shade, improvising to maintain an even temperature.

In the next ward, we stopped at the crib of a shriveled infant, so small I was sure she was a preemie. No shrouded woman fanned the air at her bed.

"Why don't you put her in an incubator?" I asked the attending pediatrician, a tall young man with stooped shoulders and a two-day growth of beard.

"Because she is not one of the premature," the doctor said. He glanced at the child's chart. "Little Khadija is actually . . . *seven* months old. She is just badly undernourished."

I studied the feeding tube in her crusted nostril. The child stared back at me with unblinking liquid eyes. I had to look away. Was she a war orphan or a victim of Baathist repression and mismanagement? It didn't matter. Like millions of other Iraqis, she needed help. Seeing this suffering baby, it hit me like a thunderclap: I was responsible for her, and for thousands like her. Having authority as administrator meant nothing if I couldn't bring some improvement in the lives of ordinary Iraqis. Before it was too late.

Later that morning, Robin Raphel and I climbed into my armored Chevy Suburban for the ride to the UN office at the Canal Hotel across the river. I had alerted the press to the visit and there was lots of interest. That was fine with me because I intended to get the UN to pay for the wheat and barley crop one way or another.

We arrived at the walled UN compound at about 10:00 A.M. Ramiro da Silva, an engaging UN official from Portugal, met us in his large conference room, accompanied by several of his colleagues.

"We need money to buy the national grain crop," I told da Silva. "Ambassador Raphel will explain."

No sooner had she presented a précis of the crisis than da Silva and his colleagues began picking away at her arguments in tones that indicated they didn't want to give us one dinar, as Robin had foreseen.

"Mr. da Silva," I interrupted, "this is a vital matter for Iraqis. We've got to start the economy moving and buying the crops is a good way to pump lots of money quickly into people's hands."

"But, Mr. Ambassador," he said, "the OFF money belongs to the Iraqi government and I can't release it without the approval of their government."

"I *am* the Iraqi government for now," I replied. "And on behalf of that government, I am asking the United Nations to release these funds immediately."

Then one of da Silva's colleagues shifted the argument. "The grain purchase program is the responsibility of the Iraqi Ministry of Trade. And we don't know what that ministry's position is on the matter."

We'd anticipated this argument. Robin, looking earnest, said, "As the Senior Adviser to that ministry, I am here to tell you we want this done and quickly."

We had made the point that the Coalition was in charge and needed the UN's help. We'd left the UN little maneuver room.

But to seal the deal, I rose and shook da Silva's hand. "The press are standing by outside. Why don't you come downstairs with me and say a few words?"

From the shade of the lobby I made my announcement to the press: I was delighted to report that the UN was prepared to spend more of the Iraqi people's money on their immediate needs by agreeing to use OFF funds to purchase the grain crops. The purchases would start the next week. Da Silva stood silently beside me with a tight smile pasted on his face.

We began to buy the grain the following week.

That evening, I held another impromptu historical seminar with Clay and Hume. It began when Hume handed me a copy of one of the new uncensored Iraqi newspapers that had mushroomed up in Baghdad during the first burst of freedom after Liberation.

"They're calling you the 'MacArthur of Baghdad,' Jerry," he said with a grin. "Where's your corncob pipe?"

My new assignment did combine some of the viceregal responsibilities of General Douglas MacArthur, de facto ruler of Imperial Japan after World War II, and of General Lucius Clay, who led the American occupation of defeated Nazi Germany.

The heat in the small office was oppressive, and the sputtering pedestal fan, connected to a generator, wasn't very effective. "I don't think it ever got this hot in Tokyo or Berlin," Clay said. As the darkness deepened, we heard small-arms fire from across the river.

"I'd settle for MacArthur's problems," I answered. "Conditions weren't this complicated for him."

Then over tepid bottled water, we compared the occupations after World War II with our own challenge.

By 1945, the United States had spent more than three years planning the postwar occupations. And, although German and Japanese cities lay in ruins, the U.S. government had accomplished detailed postwar planning, right down to stockpiling freight cars with the correct wheel gauge to run on the foreign rails. In Iraq, the Coalition had avoided widespread destruction of infrastructure and civilian casualties. But the speed of the war had left us with little time to plan for the ensuing social upheaval, while decades of chronic mismanagement had left Iraq's economy devastated.

America had had no embassy in Baghdad for over a decade. Moreover, economic statistics normally available in an open society were treated as a state secret in Saddam's Iraq. In this regard, Iraq did indeed follow the model of the former Soviet Union, which eventually imploded even while many in the West believed there were inherent strengths in its economic system.

As we talked in the gathering dusk, we discussed a vital political and psychological difference with this occupation. At the end of World War II, the United States and the other Allies had clearly defeated the countries we had occupied. The entire nations of Germany and Japan had been mobilized to fight long, relentless wars. They had lost and surrendered.

"The Germans and Japanese may not have liked being occupied," Hume said, "but they knew occupation is what happens when you lose a war."

"But here," I said, "we've defeated a hated regime, not a country."

The vast majority of Iraqis were delighted to have Saddam and his henchmen thrown out, but few were happy to find a foreign, non-Muslim army occupying their country.

And, Clay added, with the Soviet Red Army occupying eastern Germany and Japan's northern offshore islands, the countries we had defeated in World War II had a strong motive to cooperate with us—nobody wanted the American Army replaced by the Red Army.

Although Germany and Iraq were both relatively young nations, German unification had come about by the efforts of Germans, particularly Germany's 19th-century leader Chancellor Otto von Bismarck. While there were religious differences between the Protestant north and the Catholic south, Germans spoke one language and shared a common culture.

Hume noted the difference with modern Iraq.

After World War I, the British had cobbled Iraq together from three provinces of the former Ottoman Empire, an ally of Imperial Germany. The disparate people of Iraq formed a patchwork with sharp ethnic and sectarian differences. In the south, the Shiite Muslim Arab majority had strong religious ties to Iran. The Sunni Arab minority, about 20 percent of the population, was anchored on tribes and clans of central Iraq. And for hundreds of years, first under the Ottoman Turks, then under the Baathists, the Sunnis had ruled Iraq. Kurds and Turkmen, also Sunni Muslims, but not Arabs, dominated the north. And there were yet other minorities, such as Christians and Yazidis.

The Baathists came to power in Iraq through a coup d'état in 1968. Saddam Hussein ruthlessly eliminated his party rivals and seized personal control of the state. By the time he was driven out in April 2003, Saddam's Baathists had been in power three times longer than Hitler. The effects of his ruthless dictatorship were deeply woven into the moral and psychological fiber of Iraqi society.

The economies of the two occupied countries also presented a contrast. For almost a century before World War I, Germany had built a strong, diverse industrial base. The rapid recovery of German industry after World War I showed its resilience. At least until the mid-1930s, Germany had a robust private-sector economy relatively free from state control.

Iraq had been almost entirely dependent on a state-owned oil industry. And Saddam's vicious brand of socialism had all but destroyed the country's middle class and private sector.

Saddam had copied Josef Stalin's practice of using forced population resettlements to inflame underlying ethnic and religious tensions. The Iraqis had settled thousands of Sunni Arabs onto Kurdish lands in and around the key northern city of Kirkuk.

In many ways, the Baathist Socialist Party of Iraq had been a throwback to the 20th century's totalitarian "isms."

But the senior Iraqi Baathists were about to become officially extinct.

For almost three decades, the Baath Party had subjugated Iraq. Like the Nazis and Soviet Communists, the Iraqi Baathist Party—dominated by Saddam and other Sunni Arabs—had controlled not only political life, but Iraq's entire society through a combination of police state terror and toadyism, while mismanaging a corrupt command economy.

Baath Party members were required to attend weekly indoctrination meetings where they had to memorize the latest party slogans eulogizing Saddam, his sons, and Hussein family cronies. Members were expected to recruit children, first as informers (many of whom betrayed their own families) and then as party members. As in both Nazi Germany and Stalin's Russia, party members were required to spy on their family, friends, neighbors—and fellow Baathists. These dehumanizing practices, combined with Saddam's and his sons' capricious brutality, had created an atmosphere of pervasive fear and mistrust throughout Iraqi society.

Like Adolf Hitler, Saddam was convinced destiny had chosen him for greatness. He believed in this grandiose mission so firmly that he had ordered top Baathists—including hundreds of Mukhabarat intelligence officers posing as diplomats abroad—to study Hitler's *Mein Kampf*.

On May 9, my last day of preparation at the Pentagon, Don Rumsfeld had given me my marching orders in a memo. Among all my other instructions, Rumsfeld's memo emphasized: "The Coalition will actively oppose Saddam Hussein's old enforcers—the Baath Party, the Fedayeen Saddam (the irregular fighters that had harassed our forces on the march to Baghdad), etc. We will make clear that the Coalition will eliminate the remnants of Saddam's regime."

That morning, Under Secretary Douglas Feith had shown me a draft order for the "De-Baathification of Iraqi Society." He had underscored the political importance of the decree. "We've got to show all the Iraqis that we're serious about building a New Iraq. And that means that Saddam's instruments of repression have no role in that new nation." Although there was no mention in the draft of the regular army, I knew that Walt Slocombe, the Coalition's senior adviser for Defense and Security Affairs, had begun discussing the army's future with Feith now that it was clear the force had broken ranks and disappeared.

I had scanned the decree. General Franks had already outlawed the Baath Party in his "Freedom Message" of April 16. This more sweeping order was to rid the Iraqi government of the small group of true believers at the top of the party and those who had committed crimes in its name, and to wipe the country clean of the Baath Party's ideology.

"We're thinking of having Jay issue the order today," Feith had said.

"Hold on a minute," I said. "I agree it's a very important step, so important that I think it should wait 'til I get there."

Feith agreed to hold off but encouraged me to issue the order as soon as possible after my arrival in Baghdad. He underscored another point in Rumsfeld's memo stating that the decree was to be carried out ". . . even if implementing it causes administrative inconvenience."

The Baath Party boasted it had over two million members. Many people had joined the party because it was often the only way to get a job as a teacher or civil servant or because the person or a family member had been coerced. The Coalition had no gripe with them.

Our concern was only the top four levels of the party membership, which the order officially excluded from public life. These were the Baathist loyalists who, by virtue of their positions of power in the regime, had been active instruments of Saddam's repression. Our intelligence community estimated that they amounted to only about 1 percent of all party members or approximately 20,000 people, overwhelmingly Sunni Arabs.

But I realized that the "administrative inconvenience" Rumsfeld mentioned could prove a lot more than inconvenient. Senior Baathists had formed the leadership of every Iraqi ministry and military organization. By banning them from public employment, we would certainly make running the government more difficult. On the other hand, I was somewhat comforted by the knowledge that apolitical technocrats were usually the people who made organizations work.

I had told Feith I would discuss the timing of the decree with Ryan Crocker and our CPA Governance Team—which was responsible for guiding a free Iraq toward self-government—after I got out to Baghdad. The leaks to the *Times* now made this urgent.

I met with Ryan, his designated successor, Scott Carpenter—deputy assistant secretary of state for humanitarian affairs—and two of our governance officials, Meghan O'Sullivan and Roman Martinez, later that Thursday evening.

My cubbyhole office facing the back of the palace was crowded and hot with five of us jammed inside. We each had a copy of Coalition Provisional Authority Order No. 1: "De-Baathification of Iraqi Society."

Ryan held the official Arabic version beside the English text to check that each word had been properly translated.

"The White House, DOD, and State all signed off on this," I explained. "So, let's give it one final reading and, unless there's some major screw-up in the language, I'll sign it."

I noticed that Meghan, who was always well organized, had highlighted her copy with different colored markers and neatly printed points in the margins. She was a personable young woman, Boston Irish, with red hair and a cheerful laugh. A brilliant State Department official, she had earned a Ph.D. in political science from Oxford University and had written two well-received books on the role of sanctions in the age of international terrorism.

Roman Martinez, a young Cuban-American raised in New York, was educated at Harvard. He always seemed to have a wry comment to enliven the most turgid meeting. Roman had spent months in the Pentagon's Office of Special Plans working on the structure of the new Iraqi government in 2002. Like Meghan, he had a nimble and creative mind, and was intimately familiar with the de-Baathification order.

Ryan Crocker called these two young deputies his "Brainiacs" and I was grateful to have them on board.

"Ryan," I said, "we've all read the text several times. Are you guys sure that the order accomplishes its objective?"

Once more we each reviewed the six concise paragraphs of the order.

After recalling that General Franks had "disestablished the Baath Party of Iraq" in mid-April, the order implemented that declaration "by eliminating the party's structures and removing its leadership from positions of authority and responsibility in Iraqi society." This was intended to ensure that the new representative government of Iraq was not threatened by Baathists returning to power.

The next two paragraphs delineated those members of the Baath Party who were "removed from their positions and banned from future employment in the public sector." They included the four ranks officially known as "Senior Party Members." Further, these party members would be evaluated for criminal conduct or as security threats to the Coalition and detained or placed under house arrest if required.

Already, the Coalition had issued the famous deck of playing cards bearing the names and photographs of the fifty-five most-wanted Baathist regime leaders, starting with Saddam Hussein, his sons, and senior leaders. But these fifty-five represented a fraction of the Baathists who had to be removed from public life. The order supported this effort by offering rewards for information leading to the capture of senior members of the Baath Party and "individuals complicit in the crimes of the former regime"—who in many cases were the same people.

Further, the order stated that the top three layers of management in every national government ministry, affiliated corporation, and other government institution, including universities, institutes, and hospitals, would be reviewed for possible connection to the Baath Party. Any of these managers found to be "full members" of the party would be removed from their government positions, though they would be free to work elsewhere.

"That aspect of the order is going to upset some of our own ministry Senior Advisers," Meghan said. Those Senior Advisers had been working for almost a month with the managers of their ministries, some of whom would likely be banned from public office when I signed this order.

The order also prohibited the "image or likeness of Saddam Hussein" or other identifiable members of the former regime from public display. In this regard, de-Baathification was similar in its intent and scope to de-Nazification in postwar Germany, which banned the swastika and portraits of Hitler, and MacArthur's decrees in occupied Japan that removed the trappings of the militarist regime.

"The last paragraph is critical," Ryan said.

I read it aloud. "The administrator of the Coalition Provisional Authority or his designees may grant exceptions to the above guidance on a case-by-case basis."

In other words, we had the flexibility to judge if individual Baathists had joined the party only to be able to practice their profession.

Meghan looked up from her notes. "The education advisers are going to have to sort out some Baathists over at the university," she said.

As expected, because Baath Party members had presented the best-organized slate of candidates, their ticket had just won the elections at Baghdad University. But allowing these elections to go ahead had been an expedient so that the semester could conclude on schedule.

When the order took effect, I explained, we could sort out "the sheep from the goats." But we'd have to move quickly to quash the impression that the Coalition had toppled Saddam only to hand power to the next level of Baathists.

Although the order would bar only about 1 percent of Baath Party members from public service, I wanted to be sure we were focused on the right people. Everyone agreed that this was difficult, given the sorry state of our intelligence.

"We don't know Iraq as well as the Iraqis themselves do," I said. So we had to engage responsible Iraqis from the start in the de-Baathification process. Further, we had to admit our order wasn't perfect, but contained a degree of flexibility.

I had another important political matter to discuss.

"I met with the Principals Committee of the National Security Council last week," I said. "The whole crew was there in the SitRoom [White House Situation Room] . . . the VP, Powell, Rumsfeld, Condi Rice, George Tenet. The agenda included the exiles and the new government of Iraq."

The "exiles" comprised the small Iraqi Leadership Council (ILC) who had been selected during a conference of several hundred Iraqis in London in December 2002, which in turn had been a product of the Iraqi Liberation Act that President Bill Clinton had signed into law in 1998. This law made it U.S. policy to support efforts to ". . . remove the regime headed by Saddam Hussein."

The exiles were dissidents living abroad, men who had opposed Saddam Hussein's regime for years and received varying levels of support from the West and moderate Arab states, usually through intelligence agencies. It seemed to me that Feith's office, the CIA, and ORHA had been talking to the exiles in an unstructured fashion for several months. We needed clarity about our intentions in setting up an Iraqi government.

I had lived in three countries occupied by the Germans during World War II and knew that "governments in exile" tend to be viewed with suspicion by those who had remained. Focusing solely on the ILC as the presumptive nucleus of a new representative Iraqi government was going to create similar concerns among average Iraqis who'd stayed and suffered Saddam's brutality.

Moreover, the ILC lacked a proper balance between Sunni and Shia, was overly weighted toward Kurds, and had no Christians, Turkmen, or women.

When I'd arrived in Baghdad on that Monday, I'd learned that Garner had scheduled me to chair a meeting with the ILC on the very next day. I had postponed that meeting because I wanted to have time to consult with my political advisers before plunging into delicate discussions about our plans for the interim government. Also, I wanted to signal to the Iraqi political figures that I was not in a hurry to see them. And finally, I wanted to show everybody that I, not Jay, was now in charge.

Despite the heat, I now had the attention of everyone in my office. "Let me read some of what the Principals had to say about the new Iraqi government."

"First, the important takeaway is that the president insists that since the interim Iraqi government will have to write a new constitution, a legal code, and oversee Iraq's economic reform, that governing body *has* to be fully representative of all Iraqis, north and south, Sunni, Shia, Kurd, Turkmen, and Christian. And it's *not* going to happen overnight, despite what the exile leaders hope or even believe. Here's what Colin Powell said: 'The president's guidance is to take our time on setting up an Interim Iraqi Administration so what we get is a representative group.' And here's Colin's personal view: 'We should focus on the conditions for the political process, especially security. We should let Iraqi leaders emerge.' "

"Do the Principals have a good grasp of the political reality here on the ground?" Roman asked.

"Here's the vice president," I said, reading from my notes. " 'We're not at a point where representative Iraqi leaders can come forward. They're still too scared. We need a strategy on the ground for the postwar situation we actually have and not the one we wish we had.' " This didn't sound like an open endorsement of the exiles.

I flipped through my wilted notes. "Okay, in summary, the Principals of the NSC agree that we need time, we need more balance than what we have in the small group of exiles we've dealt with to date."

"When are you going to break the news to them, Jerry?" Ryan asked.

"Tomorrow afternoon," I said. "In the morning, I'll be good cop when I sign the de-Baathification order. Then, during my five o'clock meeting with the leadership crowd, I'll let them know that we're not about to turn over the keys to the kingdom."

Naturally, the exiles wanted to establish themselves as the government quickly before locally based political leaders could get organized. And they also realized that their influence in London, Washington, Tehran, and Riyadh would diminish unless they accrued political power on the ground in Iraq. Following the president's instructions, the CPA wanted to be certain that we put together an interim government broadly representative of the Iraqi people.

In short, we wanted more control over creating the interim government than the ILC wanted us to have. The situation was complicated by the fact that in his last meeting with the council two weeks earlier, then "Presidential Envoy" Zal Khalilzad had left them with the impression that we would turn over governing power to them by mid-May. This statement apparently fit the "early transfer" of power scenario that the Pentagon was pushing. But the guidance from the Principals meeting foresaw a process that at best would take months.

So, going into Friday afternoon's meeting, I would be in the awkward position of having to assert that we wanted to build on the "progress" we'd already made with the ILC, while essentially disavowing what Khalilzad had told them.

Early Friday morning, May 16, 2003, with Ryan, Scott, the Brainiacs, Hume, and Clay wedged into my office, I signed Coalition Provisional Authority Order No. 1.

Scott took a picture. The photo looks like the inside of a rush hour subway car.

"The Iraqi press and television will be running this story nonstop," I said.

Hume smiled. "The news is already out in every village *souk* and tea shop from Basra to Irbil."

"Good," I said. "That'll make my job this afternoon a little easier."

Before meeting the Iraqi delegation that afternoon, I discussed the de-Baathification decree with the press. "The process will be guided by three principles,"

I announced. "It will be fair, transparent, and consistent. We will seek to ensure that those who joined the party under duress can still put their talents to work for the Iraqi people. And we are prepared to accept that the policy will result in some temporary inefficiency in the administration of the government."

This statement was intended to address grumbling among ORHA staffers as much as among displaced Baathist technocrats.

As it turned out, most senior Baath Party members affected by the order had left their ministries after the fall of Baghdad. Many had even fled the country. But implementation of the decree would still be difficult.

I reiterated that the Coalition would make mistakes in selecting which Iraqis must go and which could remain in their jobs. Iraqis, I added, would be better able to make the fine distinctions necessary for a fair policy. "So as soon as possible we will turn the implementation of the de-Baathification process over to an Iraqi interim government."

After a twenty-minute backgrounder with the press, I had a meeting with the ORHA senior ministry advisers, which I described to Francie in my late-night e-mail:

> There was a sea of bitching and moaning with lots of them saying how hard it was going to be. I reminded them that the president's guidance is clear: de-Baathification will be carried out even if at a cost to administrative efficiency. An ungood time was had by all.

I sent the advisers off to their respective ministries to brief Iraqis on the pending changes. One of them immediately told the *New York Times* that my order was "fascist."

Since the objective of the order was to dismantle an avowedly fascist party, this comment struck me as particularly stupid.

On the plus side, the reaction of the Iraqi people to the de-Baathification decree was overwhelmingly favorable. Literally hundreds of times over the next fourteen months I would hear that Order No. 1 was the single most important step I had taken as administrator. It clearly demonstrated that we intended not just to throw out the brutal tyranny of Saddam, but also to establish in its place a new political order.

On Friday afternoon, we were expecting seven Iraqi representatives to meet us in the palace conference room where I held staff meetings. The group, whom we had come to refer to as the G-7, included:

• Ahmad Chalabi, of the Iraqi National Congress, a Shiite. He had been something of a child prodigy, completing his Ph.D. in mathematics from the University of Chicago at a young age. From one of Iraq's wealthiest families, he had fled Iraq and made a fortune in business dealings about some of which there hung a cloud of suspicion. Chalabi enjoyed close personal ties on Capitol Hill and with some Pentagon civilians but not at the State Department and CIA.

• Ayad Allawi, leader of the Iraqi National Accord, also a secular Shiite, was Chalabi's chief rival. Allawi, a physician, had escaped a brutal assassination attempt in 1978 while in exile in Britain when several of Saddam's thugs tried to axe him to death in his bed. In the following years, Allawi had worked closely with Western and Arab intelligence organizations.

• The two Kurds were Massoud Barzani, head of the Kurdish Democratic Party, and his sometime ally and sometime rival, Jalal Talabani of the Patriotic Union of Kurdistan. Both groups had provided effective militias to fight alongside Coalition Special Forces in northern Iraq during the invasion. The feisty Peshmerga militias made up of tribal freedom fighters had earlier fought each other during internecine Kurdish conflicts in the 1990s.

• The ILC also included Naseer Chaderchi, a respected seventy-year-old Sunni lawyer, who led the small, secular National Democratic Party. The party had its roots in the abortive attempt to establish democracy in Iraq but was crushed by the Baathist junta in the late 1960s.

• Ibrahim al-Jaafari, like Allawi a medical doctor, was the principal representative of the Shiite Islamic Dawa Party, which had fought an open insurrection against the Baathist regime beginning in the late 1970s, before both the party and Jaafari were forced into exile.

• The other Shiite Islamist party, the Supreme Council for the Islamic Revolution in Iraq (SCIRI), was represented by Dr. Adel Mahdi and Hamid al-Bayati, reportedly because the party's most senior leader in Baghdad, Abdul Aziz Hakim, was ill. I suspected Hakim's illness might be "diplomatic," since he was known to be distrustful of the Coalition's motives.

We hoped to use the ILC to create a steering committee that would convene a larger group, which would in turn choose an interim government. But we knew the Iraqi exiles had bolder ambitions.

When we convened a little after 5:00 P.M. on Friday, May 16, the palace conference room was even hotter than it had been Monday night. There were lots of small bottles of lukewarm mineral water on the large table. We all drank practically nonstop in the heat. As usual, the light of the chandelier swelled and dimmed with the surging generator.

Representing the Coalition were Lieutenant General David McKiernan, the military commander in Iraq; the British special envoy, Ambassador John Sawers, a seasoned Arabic-speaking diplomat; Jay Garner; Ryan Crocker; Hume Horan; and myself. General Abizaid had flown up from Doha at my invitation to underscore the political-military coordination within the Coalition. The Iraqis sat along one side of the table facing the CPA group, with their deputies behind them.

I made some opening remarks, introducing our delegation and employing the forms of Arab politesse in which I personally thanked each "guest" for accepting our invitation. I didn't want to overdo the formalities, but I wanted the Iraqis to know that the CPA had leaders like Hume and Ryan who knew their culture well.

"I want to stress the importance that the Coalition attaches to the partnership between the CPA and your council as we move toward representative government," I said, speaking slowly so that those who required translation could follow each word.

To emphasize this point, I added, "We expect progress along this path to be incremental." Obviously, this wasn't going to be the immediate transfer of power that some had desired. "But we *are* prepared to cede increasing responsibility to responsible Iraqi leaders."

Dr. Jalal Talabani, the gray-haired Kurdish leader, was the first to reply. He was a short, rather plump, cheerful man, with round owlish glasses and a neatly clipped silver mustache. "I must say, Ambassador Bremer," he commented in urbane English, "that I am personally delighted at attending a meeting with the Coalition in one of Saddam's former palaces."

Ahmad Chalabi echoed Talabani's remarks. Chalabi was of medium build with a smooth, even sleek look about him. Unusual for an Iraqi, he had no mustache. He spoke fluent English.

First Chalabi turned toward Garner. "General," he said, "we all thank you for the hard work you have done for the people of Iraq." Chalabi then faced me. "And we welcome Ambassador Bremer and his associates."

Massoud Barzani was the leader of an important Kurdish tribe in the far northeast of the country and a hardened warrior. Short and compact, his receding hairline made his head look like a projectile. His small dark eyes were watchful. Barzani was much less at home in such settings than his colleague Talabani, but people paid attention to him.

"Ambassador Bremer, General Garner," Barzani said in Arabic, "I speak for all Iraqis when I thank the Coalition for the Liberation of Iraq."

"I want to talk about the security situation," I then told them. "And I'd appreciate learning your opinions. Security is the cornerstone of all of our efforts in building a new Iraq, including the eventual creation of a representative government."

Ayad Allawi squared his stocky shoulders and spoke decisively in fluent English. Like Chalabi, Allawi had neither mustache nor glasses. "There is a security vacuum. Lawlessness, street crime that we have never experienced before." He continued to describe the chaos we had all witnessed. "The people need more protection," Allawi concluded.

General Abizaid fielded that comment. "I'd like to organize a meeting early next week with my senior commanders and the members of this council to discuss practical solutions to the security problem."

That seemed to resonate well with the group.

We next discussed the de-Baathification decree I had signed that morning. Each of the seven made a short statement heartily welcoming the order. Then Dr. Ibrahim al-Jaafari, whose Shiite Dawa Party followers had suffered so grievously under Saddam's regime, voiced a fear that Talabani and Chalabi echoed. "Ambassador, we are all concerned about signs that the Baath Party is regrouping." Jaafari spoke broken English. Gesturing frequently and speaking even more rapidly, he often jumped between languages and among subjects, to the despair of our interpreters. "The Coalition must never let this happen. We all hope that you act decisively to nip this resurgence in the bud."

"I urge the Coalition to go beyond the decree issued today, to conduct even more aggressive de-Baathification," Chalabi said.

Draconian measures would benefit the Shia. But surprisingly, Chalabi undercut his own comment. "However," he said, wagging his right index finger in the Arab gesture of caution, "we must also realize that many Iraqis have been forced to join the party." I noted that our policy was designed to recognize that fact.

The first half hour of the meeting had been cordial if formal. The atmosphere cooled when we turned to the political process.

"I want to reemphasize that the path to representative government will be incremental," I told them again.

The council members now spoke more assertively, beginning with Talabani. "While we sincerely thank the Coalition for all its efforts, we have to warn against squandering a military victory by not conducting a rapid, coordinated effort to form a new government."

Hamid Bayati, representing the Shiite SCIRI, spoke for the first time. "Ambassador, you *must* hasten the political progress. The 'street' is waiting for the freedom you promised." I would learn that Iraqi politicians love to invoke the mystical "Arab street" on almost any argument.

"With respect, Ambassador Bremer," Chalabi said, "I must remind the CPA of the promises made in this past month about the establishment of a transitional government in a few weeks' time." He smiled benignly at Jay Garner.

"It is the Coalition's intention to establish a transitional government as soon as it can be done," I said, keeping my tone even. I looked directly at Chalabi. "But I reject the idea that the Coalition is stalling. As I have said, the process will be *incremental* and must have as its goal a truly representative group. This body is not representative. There is only one Arab Sunni leader among you." Everyone looked toward Naseer Chaderchi. "There are no Turkmen here, no Christians, no women."

I was exerting the authority President Bush had granted me, "putting down the hammer." These were educated leaders. I did not have to articulate the fact that, with the exception of Chaderchi, they were all exiles, recently returned to Iraq. "Surely a representative government will have to include many Iraqis who lived here and suffered under Saddam for decades. This is not to detract from the exceptional efforts that the parties represented here this evening have made for years to free your country." This last compliment might have mollified some sensitive feelings. Then again, it might not have. I wasn't running in a popularity contest with either my staff or the exiles.

It was time to make them think and work. After all, we needed their help in rebuilding their country. "The Coalition respects the role each of you and your organizations have played opposing Saddam for so many years. And we see a role for all of you in the interim government we intend to establish soon. But to play that role, you're going to have to make yourselves into a body much more representative of all the streams in Iraqi society. I'd like to meet you again in two weeks, and during that time, I hope you'll find a way to broaden yourselves into such a group."

At the conclusion of the meeting, I announced that the press had been invited to greet the Iraqi Leadership Council. Even now we could hear the reporters and camera crews clamoring in the hallway outside the conference room. "I'm going to make a few comments and I suggest that you nominate a representative to speak after me."

My request provoked animated confusion. Despite the public posture of cooperation, this ethnically, spiritually, and politically disparate group was not accustomed to cooperation. It took them more than twenty minutes to select the Kurdish leader, Massoud Barzani, as spokesman. This was a harbinger of the difficulty the group would have making even simple decisions.

Chapter 3
REPAIRING A
SHATTERED NATION

■ AL-HILLAH, IRAQ
MAY 22, 2003

A backhoe had scraped away several feet of earth, exposing a mass grave the size of a football field.

Although hundreds of men and women were working in the dust, the scene was strangely quiet. The men dug with their bare hands, while the women, most wearing black *abayas*, gathered clusters of bones into neat piles and wrapped them in plastic.

Ryan, Scott, and I had driven down the potholed highway beside the Euphrates to this killing field sixty miles south of Baghdad late that morning. The heat reflecting off the baked mud wasteland was intense.

"Take a look over there, sir," one of the Marines with us said, pointing to the left.

Men handed clumps of bones—many tangled in shreds of *dishdashas* (long collarless garments often worn by Arab men) or *abayas*—to people searching for massacred relatives. The flesh of the dead, of course, was gone, except for a few leathery sinews, but there was still a surprising amount of hair among the white bone.

Sometimes the skeleton of a man or woman could be identified by a distinctive garment, a faded ration card, or a prominent gold tooth. One murdered family's identity often led to another's beside it, and then to that of an entire village. As the women wrapped the bones, I saw what the Marine had noticed: the palm-size skull of an infant, a wisp of black hair still clinging to the skull, was visible through the plastic. I felt sick.

Al-Hillah is in the heartland of Shia Islam in Iraq, near the pilgrimage cities of Karbala and Najaf. Like so many other towns and villages in the region, Al-Hillah had suffered horribly during the abortive 1991 Shiite uprising against Saddam Hussein when his battered army retreated from Kuwait. Acting in part on vague promises from the victorious Gulf War coalition, the Shiite rebels, led by lightly armed army deserters, seized towns and cities, executed Baathist officials, and seriously threatened Saddam's regime.

Saddam's retaliation had been rapid and brutal. Forces loyal to the regime—Sunni-dominated Republican Guard units and paramilitary formations of the intelligence services—ripped into the Shia south. Men of military age were hunted down and shot. Helicopter gunships had strafed and rocketed villages. And entire communities—men, women, and children—had been driven on trucks to secluded sites like this one and machine-gunned, their bodies piled into pits and bulldozed over.

"It's like the Einsatzgruppen during the Holocaust," I said.

"Yes, sir," the young Marine said uncertainly.

"Hitler's mobile killing squads, army, and police massacred over a million people at isolated places like this . . . Jews, Gypsies, prisoners of war, Catholic clergy . . ." I explained.

As we made our way back to the SUV parked in the shade of some eucalyptus trees, a man in a muddy plaid shirt waved me down. He led us to five stacks of bones, laid neatly on sheets.

"Mother," he said in broken English, pointing at one skull, tears streaming down his dirty cheeks. "Sister . . . sister . . . daughter . . . son." His fists gripped an invisible machine gun. "Army kill."

We met with the district *mokhtar* or headman, who showed us recently taken photographs documenting the excavation of the Al-Hillah graves. "Please, Ambassador," he said. "Take this evidence to Jacques Chirac. It was the French who kept butcher Saddam in power."

"Instead of me bringing these pictures to Jacques Chirac," I suggested, "why don't you and the mayor of Al-Hillah invite him to come see these graves for himself?"

That killing field was the face of the old regime, which our military had defeated in three weeks.

Later that day, in the town of Al-Hillah, I got a glimpse of the new Iraq when I met Sheik Farqat al-Qizwini. The sheik was an imposing figure, who stood six feet, three inches. But he seemed even taller because of his thick black turban, signifying that he was not only an imam, a Muslim cleric, but also a descendent of the Prophet Mohammed, which entitled him to the honorific "Sayyid." After the fall of Saddam, Sheik Qizwini "liberated" a mosque in Al-Hillah that Saddam had ordered built to glorify himself.

Over a warm Pepsi in Qizwini's office, he spoke expansively of his dream for that mosque.

"Ambassador," he said, gesturing dramatically, "I intend to create a university here. I will have Muslim, Christian, and Jewish students and teachers at this university to demonstrate that the New Iraq belongs to all Iraqis."

The sheik described his gratitude to America for freeing Iraq from Saddam's tyranny. "I deeply admire democracy." He leaned forward, eyes warm with excitement. "Iraq should become America's fifty-third state," the sheik bellowed.

His sentiment was clear, even if his math was a bit fuzzy.

I wondered what would become of Sheik Qizwini's dream. It would be my great joy to visit the sheik again on my last day in Iraq fourteen months later and find out.

Leaving Al-Hillah, we thought it appropriate to visit Babylon since our road passed the site. There was no evidence of the Hanging Gardens when we ventured out in the midafternoon sun to view the travesty Saddam had made of the ancient city.

"Looks like Disney World East," I said, squinting up at the brick ramparts and gaudy paintings on Nebuchadnezzar's rebuilt palace.

The massive russet brick walls could have enclosed a steel mill. Saddam had intensified his ambitious reconstruction of Babylon in the 1990s after his army had been routed in the Gulf War. Despite protests from foreign archaeologists, the regime had built directly atop the ancient ruins after only cursory excavation, burying untold artifacts and cuneiform tablets in the process.

Saddam had built yet another personal palace, high on a nearby hill and visible through the arches of the ersatz monstrosities that rose around us.

In the 7th century B.C. Nebuchadnezzar, the emperor who had conquered so many kingdoms, had himself rebuilt Babylon to reflect its past glory under Hammurabi, and ordered his own name stamped on each brick. Now the hundreds of thousands of bricks in the walls of this Babylon were inscribed with Saddam Hussein's name, noting that they had been laid to "the glory of Iraq."

The masons had set those bricks while thousands of bodies rotted in the graves of nearby Al-Hillah.

"Let's get the hell out of here," I told the team.

• • •

The killing fields of Al-Hillah brought me face to face with one of the most difficult challenges for the Coalition: how to lay the foundation for Iraq's new security forces, the army and police.

President Bush had made it clear to me that we were going beyond regime change to help create "a New Iraq," freed from Saddam's brutality. For more than three decades, the dictator had used the Baath Party, the army, and the intelligence services to inflict torture, misery, and death on Iraqis and their neighbors. That had to change.

But for generations, many Iraqis had served honorably in the armed forces. Despite decades of repression, Iraqi Shiite soldiers had bravely defended their homeland against Iranian Shiites during the long, bloody Iran-Iraq War of the 1980s. The old army had some true professionals and, partly for that reason, was distrusted by Saddam. Consciously copying Hitler's system, Saddam kept the force under close control through multiple overlapping security services and frequent purges of senior commanders to ensure the military leadership's loyalty to him. And he had perverted the army's purpose, turning it into an instrument of repression.

Over the years Saddam's army had slaughtered thousands of Iraqis. In the late 1980s, the army had conducted a brutal campaign of repression in the North, killing both Peshmerga resistance fighters and harmless civilians. In the Kurdish town of Halabja one sunny day in March 1988, Iraqi military planes had dropped nerve gas bombs while army helicopters sprayed poison gas on villagers. More than 5,000 Kurds died that morning. Thousands more were scarred for life. The mass graves of Al-Hillah were also mute witnesses to the army's role in the ruthless suppression of the 1991 Shia-led revolt. In the minds of Kurds, as among Iraqi Shia, Saddam's army was the tool of a cruel regime.

By the time I arrived in Iraq, the old army had long since disappeared. When Iraqi draftees had seen which way the war was going in 2003, they simply deserted and went home to their farms and families. General Abizaid had told a high-level teleconference on April 17, according to a report in the *New York Times*, that not a single Iraqi military unit remained intact. So the issue was not whether to use an existing force, but whether, as some American military and intelligence officers had discussed, we should try to recall units of the old army to "stand up" the new one on the pattern of the old.

Any idea of recalling the former force, or part of it, however, ran up against major policy and practical obstacles.

To help untangle these problems, I was fortunate to have Walt Slocombe as Senior Adviser for defense and security affairs. A brilliant former Rhodes Scholar from Princeton and a Harvard-educated attorney, Walt had worked for

Democratic administrations for decades on high-level strategic and arms control issues. Most recently, he'd been undersecretary of defense for policy for six years under President Bill Clinton. The fact that he was a moderate Democrat shielded him from the neocon label put on so many of Rumsfeld's advisers. Slocombe was a pragmatist with keen historical insight and a broad global perspective.

In early May, before we left for Iraq, Slocombe had begun discussions with top Pentagon officials, including Deputy Secretary of Defense Paul Wolfowitz, about the policy implications of Saddam's army having melted away. It was clear that Iraq would need an army and that we would have to find some place in Iraqi society for former soldiers. The question was how to accomplish these goals.

On May 9, 2003, the day before our departure, I sent a memo to Secretary Rumsfeld, copied to Wolfowitz, DOD's policy office and the General Counsel, summarizing these discussions and the tentative conclusion that we should formally dissolve Saddam's army as well as the security and intelligence services as a prelude to establishing Iraq's new security services. I attached to the memo a draft order doing that but told the secretary, "I will show the draft order to CENTCOM this weekend and send back any suggested changes."

One evening after we arrived in Iraq, when the breeze off the river actually gave a hint of coolness, Walt, Clay, and I had another meeting on the issue. We'd been discussing it for days, and as our thinking evolved, we continued discussions with Pentagon officials including Under Secretary of Defense Douglas Feith. Now it was time to come to some conclusions so I could make a recommendation to Secretary Rumsfeld.

"First, let's get straight what our objectives are," I said. "It's absolutely essential to convince Iraqis that we're not going to permit the return of Saddam's instruments of repression—the Baath Party, the Mukhabarat's security services, or Saddam's army. We didn't send our troops halfway round the world to overthrow Saddam only to find another dictator taking his place."

And because we had to take account of the ethnic make-up and the history of the country, assembling a New Iraqi Army (NIA) would not be easy. It would have to represent the entire nation: Shia, Kurds, and Sunni Arabs. This had certainly not been the case in Saddam's army. Its officer corps had been overwhelmingly Sunni Arab, with almost all senior positions assigned to Saddam loyalists. The rest of the army had been made of up draftees, the vast majority Shia, most held in the ranks through brutality and extortion: Not only was a deserter punished, but so was his family. So, few draftees of any description and virtually none of the Shia would return to the military voluntarily. "To get them back we'd have to go into their homes and drag them out," Walt said.

"Not on my watch," I responded. Slocombe added that "recalling" the old army would therefore mean, at best, trying to construct some new units commanded by Sunni officers with the lower ranks, too, dominated by Sunnis loyal to them personally, potentially another set of warlords and militias. Moreover, even if we could find some Sunni officers who we were satisfied were uncompromised to lead such a force, most Iraqi Shia and Kurds would see this as the Coalition trying to restore Saddamism without Saddam.

For a dozen years after the first Gulf War, the Kurds had enjoyed considerable autonomy, protected from Saddam's forces by American airpower. And in early meetings, Kurdish leaders Jalal Talabani and Massoud Barzani made it clear to me that the Kurds would "never" accept a formula to reconstitute and re-arm units of the former Iraqi army.

The distrust the Shia population and leaders felt for the old army was, if anything, even deeper. They remembered the slaughter carried out by Saddam's army after the Gulf War, and many Shia felt lingering anger that America had not intervened then to stop the killing. Nonetheless, since Liberation, Shia leaders, including Grand Ayatollah Sistani, had encouraged their followers to cooperate with the Coalition. We couldn't risk losing that cooperation.

There were also significant practical difficulties with recalling the old army. Any army needs barracks, bases, and equipment. But when Saddam's military melted away, barracks and bases had been demolished, stripped not only of all usable arms and equipment, but down to the wiring and plumbing, even the bricks themselves.

"There's not a single unit or barracks left intact," Clay underlined. "So it's not a question of 'standing up' a few old battalions." Even if we could find a way to bring back some all-Sunni units, there was no place to put them. New facilities and equipment could not have been provided for a "reconstituted" old army any faster than they could be built for a wholly new one.

Walt noted that some might argue that bringing back vetted Sunni officers would co-opt the old officer corps to support the Coalition. But as Walt pointed out, this argument ignored the problem posed by the enormous size and top-heavy structure of Saddam's army. Sitting atop the 400,000 largely Shia draftees had been an officer corps of several hundred thousand, mostly Sunnis. Saddam's army had been about the size of the American army. But America was a country with more than ten times the population of Iraq, and the Iraqi army had 11,000 generals, whereas America's had only 300.

So even if we had ignored the political objections to an all-Sunni force and could somehow overcome the equipment and basing problems, we would not have been able to offer command positions to more than a tiny percentage of the old officer caste. This would leave the others as disgruntled as they already were, probably more so for seeing a few of their old comrades back in power.

Shortly after arriving, I had told Generals Abizaid and McKiernan that the president wanted an Iraqi military adequate for national defense. But we would not countenance a huge, unrepresentative force that repressed Iraq's citizens and threatened her neighbors. Any army that appeared to hand power back to a group of Sunni officers from the old days would surely be rejected by the Kurds and Shia who made up 80 percent of Iraq's population. It was a recipe for civil war.

Still, we had to find some place in Iraqi society for former soldiers. So Slocombe's proposal provided that we would welcome into the all-volunteer New Iraqi Army carefully vetted officers from Saddam's army, the only automatic exclusion being against those at the very top ranks of the Baath Party and those who had served in the inner circle of the security forces. Former soldiers, too, were welcome to join as enlisted men.

Otherwise, applicants for officer positions would be judged on their individual merits. We believed that many Iraqis would be proud to serve in the NIA, once they were properly trained, led, and equipped. And this proved to be the case; in practice, virtually all officers who would serve in the new army over the next year had served in the old force or in one of the anti-Saddam militias.

We also had to deal with the reality that, since the NIA would necessarily be only a fraction of the size of Saddam's bloated force, very few of the old ranking officers could expect to resume military careers in the new force. So, besides making clear that former vetted officers willing to work in the new system would be welcome, we had to find a source of income for hundreds of thousands of former soldiers and to begin their integration back into Iraqi society. To some, we could offer employment as paramilitary government security guards to free up Coalition troops for more aggressive patrolling. Some had worked in military organizations such as the medical corps and engineering and could be transferred to civilian ministries. Others would resume a civilian life that the last war had disrupted.

To launch this delicate process, we had first formally to abolish the old regime's intelligence and security services. Doing so would not send home a single soldier or disband a single unit. All that had happened weeks before. But it would formally dismantle the old power structure and signal that the fall of Saddam and the Baathists was permanent.

We carefully coordinated this critical process with the Pentagon. On May 19, I sent a memo to Secretary Rumsfeld detailing our recommendations for the dissolution of the Iraqi Defense Ministry and its "related entities," including Saddam's intelligence, security, and propaganda services as well as the army, other military units, and paramilitary forces. The action, I said, would be "a critical step in our effort to destroy the underpinnings of the Saddam regime, to demonstrate to the Iraqi people that we have done so and that neither Saddam nor his gang is coming back."

I also advised Rumsfeld that we proposed to offer severance payments to hundreds of thousands of former soldiers, excluding only the most senior Baathists and intelligence and internal security types, many of whom had in any case fled the country. This meant we would be paying people who had only weeks before been killing young Americans, but that was a cost that had to be borne. Before sending this message to the Pentagon, Slocombe and I discussed the plans with the appropriate Coalition military commanders and civilians, including McKiernan in Baghdad and CENTCOM forward headquarters in Qatar.

At the Pentagon on May 22, Feith carefully reviewed our draft order, which would formally abolish Saddam's security and intelligence services. He asked us to clarify some of the wording, which we did to his full satisfaction. My press spokesman, Dan Senor, stayed up the entire night coordinating the text of the announcement and press plans with Rumsfeld's chief of staff, Larry Di Rita. Later that day, when Rumsfeld authorized me to proceed, I informed the president of the plan in a video teleconference.

On Friday, May 23, 2003, I signed CPA Order No. 2, "Dissolution of Entities." These included the Defense Ministry, all related national security ministries and offices, and all military formations, including the Republican Guard, Special Republican Guard, Baath Party Militia, and the Fedayeen Saddam. The order terminated the service of all members of the former military, noted that payments would be made, and announced that the Coalition planned to create a New Iraqi Army "as the first step in forming a national self-defense capability for a free Iraq." Under civilian control, the force would be "professional, non-political, militarily effective, and representative of all Iraqis."

Once this plan had been approved by Washington, CPA and CENTCOM units focused on a two-phased approach to reintegration of demobilized Iraqi soldiers. We sought out former conscripts, especially in the Shia heartland, for public works programs. Then Slocombe announced that we intended to have a full division NIA of about 12,000 soldiers trained and operational in one year, and three divisions a year later. We would recruit officers and noncommissioned officers from the old army, as well as from Kurdish and Shia anti-Saddam militia resistance groups, to command these new units.

Within weeks, we announced a program of transition payments to former soldiers. We started paying a monthly stipend to all former career Iraqi military men except for the most senior former Baathist officers (about 8,000 of hundreds of thousands of officers on the rolls). These payments continued up to and past the return of sovereignty in June 2004. We also made a one-time payment to all former conscripts.

In the announcement calling for the reintegration of Iraqi ex-soldiers, I added a personal message: "The Iraqi army had a long tradition of service to the nation, and many, perhaps most of its officers and soldiers, regarded themselves as professionals serving the nation and not the Baathist regime. We have always said that former military personnel, except for those most deeply involved in the regime, would be part of the future of Iraq."

Optimistic words. Iraq was a badly wounded society, and distrust was deep. The training would take longer and prove more difficult than we had expected. The Baathists had transformed Iraq into a zero-sum society. A person considered himself fortunate if Saddam's intelligence services, the Mukhabarat, raided his neighbor's house and left him alone. In the past, for many Shia and Kurds, avoiding execution was a small daily victory. Now we were asking these same people to put on their country's uniform and defend the homeland side by side.

Still, it was the only option we had.

Months later, as I was preparing to leave Iraq, Kurdish leader Jalal Talabani told me that the decision formally to "disband" the old army was the best decision the Coalition made during our fourteen months in Iraq.

Soon after issuing the order, I called on Sayyid Abdul Aziz Hakim, one of the leaders of the Shiite Supreme Council for the Islamic Revolution in Iraq (SCIRI). We hoped to draw some of his party's 10,000-member Badr Corps militia into the New Iraqi Army.

Hakim, a slender, bearded man in his early fifties, was not popular among his fellow Group of Seven, or "G-7," members. His father had been the grand ayatollah of Iraq's Shia until he died in 1970, and a brother, Ayatollah Sayyid

Mohammed Baqir al-Hakim, was one of the country's most senior Shiite leaders and the official head of SCIRI. Over the years, Saddam had killed eight of
Hakim's nine brothers, so even though Hakim had spent twenty years in Iran,
he commanded some respect among Islamist Shia.

But the leaders of SCIRI had a reputation among the other Iraqi parties for
being difficult to deal with. They were masters of brinkmanship, usually making their threats to walk out at the last moment. We would see a lot of this tech-
nique in the months ahead.

"Tell me, Ambassador," he said, watching me closely through his tinted
glasses. "You say the battalions of this new army will be commanded by Iraqi officers. And who will these officers be?"

"I promise you this, Sayyid," I said, using his honorific title. "The commander of the first battalion will be a Shiite."

The Coalition kept that promise.

Within days of signing the order on the former security services, I visited
Massoud Barzani at his mountaintop home near Salahuddin in the Kurdistan
Autonomous Zone.

Barzani, whose family and clan had suffered for decades under Baathist
forces, met me at the chopper pad on a mountain a few miles from his home. As
we climbed the curving road to his house, he pointed out a large field just to the
north of the road, which ran all the way up to high mountains.

"That's where we finally defeated Saddam's army in 1991. We couldn't stop
their T-72 tanks down in the valley, but when they came up here we destroyed
them," he said with grim satisfaction.

The hardened mountain warrior swept his hand to encompass the steep
ridges, some still with traces of winter snow. This had been the stronghold of his
people for centuries, and his pride in the spectacular landscape was palpable.

As our motorcade of armed pickups and white SUVs moved on, Barzani,
still gazing over the fields of battle, grasped my hand and said, "Congratulations
on formally abolishing Saddam's army. It's a wonderful thing you've done. It
proves that the Coalition is serious about creating a new and united Iraq."

"You know, some were encouraging us to reconstitute a smaller version of
Saddam's army," I said.

"That would have been a big mistake," Barzani said. "We Kurds would have
left Iraq, seceded. We've fought the Baathists' army from the beginning. For
twelve years, we've enjoyed autonomy. If they returned, we'd fight again . . . a
civil war."

Now I gestured toward the ring of mountains. "Syria," I said, pointing west. "Turkey, Iran . . . and here we are in Iraq, all countries with Kurds. That civil war would have become a regional war."

"But now we have escaped this disaster," Barzani smiled.

"*Insh'allah*," I replied, "God willing."

At 10:30 A.M. on May 26, I received the first of many congressional delegations (CODELs in Washington lingo). This was led by Congressman Duncan Hunter, a California Republican and chairman of the House Armed Services Committee.

That hot, dusty morning in Baghdad, we established a pattern for briefings that would be followed for the next year. For security reasons, the Pentagon had ruled that no congressmen could stay overnight in Iraq, so they flew in on C-130s from Kuwait or Jordan and came straight to CPA headquarters. There Lieutenant General Ricardo Sanchez, incoming Coalition Joint Commander, my CPA colleagues, and I briefed them on the security, political, and economic situation.

These visits demanded a lot from all of us. But almost invariably, members from both political parties came away with a better impression of the situation on the ground than they had had before arriving. And so it was always worth the time.

Over the next fourteen months, we would host 239 members of Congress— a record for a U.S. government post in the Middle East.

The overall pace of work at CPA headquarters rose with the rising heat of the season. One day in early June, the temperature hit 138 degrees, which to a New England boy felt pretty hot. Until an Iraqi friend warned, "Wait 'til summer comes."

With no air-conditioning at Coalition headquarters, the office I'd inherited in the palace was like an oven. The room was dominated by a very low octagonal marble table—coffee table height, but perhaps eight feet in diameter, around which visitors and staff met, sitting on tatty chairs that had been left behind in the palace. As my advisers educated me about Iraq's immense economic problems, I gradually accumulated quite a collection of maps and charts—a map showing all the oil fields and oil and fuel pipelines, a chart of the entire electrical grid network, a map of the railroad system, and another showing major agricultural areas. I would often rummage through this stack of maps and charts to illustrate a point to visiting Iraqis, a congressman, or my own staff.

One of our first economic priorities was getting crude oil and fuel production running again. But that posed a difficult challenge.

The control room of Daura oil refinery on the outskirts of Baghdad reminded me of the phony rocket ship cockpits on the *Flash Gordon* TV shows I watched as a kid: levers, steam gauges, and hand cranks. This stifling room exemplified the difficult economic challenges we faced. The manager, a soft-spoken, competent engineer named Dashar Khashab, pointed out the broken window at the acres of rusty, cracking towers and piping. "The Americans built this in 1955," he said, "during the time of the old king. Almost nothing has been replaced . . . repaired, yes, but not replaced."

Nineteen fifty-five . . . almost fifty years of neglect.

Gary Vogler, one of the CPA's Oil Ministry advisers, expanded on Khashab's statement. "Usually refining capacity should be steadily upgraded to stay ahead of production. But the Baathists invested only what they absolutely had to, almost nothing once they nationalized Iraq's oil industry."

The plant was operating far below capacity and demand, which explained the shortages of refined products—gasoline, diesel, and kerosene—we were experiencing. It was a tribute to the exceptional engineering skills of Khashab and his Iraqi workers that they had kept the machinery going decades beyond its useful life.

And they had more than technical skill. Khashab smiled as he described the tense days and nights in mid-April when looters had swarmed toward the refinery, seeking wiring, pipes, and what they hoped might be valuable electronics.

"I issued my workers Kalashnikovs. Together, we defended the refinery until your soldiers arrived," he said proudly. "I didn't sleep for three days and nights."

"When the 101st Airborne took control," Gary explained, "the plant was intact."

"You're a brave man," I told Dashar Khashab.

But we'd need more than just such stubborn courage. The oil industry was the blood of Iraq's economy. If it did not flow, the economy would die. Iraq has the second-largest supply of proven reserves in the world, some 112 billion barrels. But during Saddam's rule, oil production, like so many other industries, had suffered from chronic under-investment. Production had peaked at about 2.5 million barrels per day before the war. At Liberation, production had essentially ceased, largely because workers were afraid to come to work. Iraq was not exporting any oil when I arrived, which meant that the country I was supposed to administer had no revenues—but lots of expenses.

Other industrial sites were equally decrepit, as I discovered on an early visit to Al-Hillah's textile factory, another relic of Saddam's economic mismanagement, lack of investment, and cockeyed socialist economic theory.

The woven cloth was filthy; swallows flitted through the broken windows of idle spinning rooms to build mud nests in the rafters.

"We only have a few thread mills and looms operating," the manager apologized.

A plaque on one of the looms indicated that it had been built in Sheffield, England, in 1963. Most of the machines were repaired with ragged lines of welds or bolted plates. But the antiquated gear wasn't the mill's most serious problem. The plant was making products nobody wanted.

"We're weaving low- and medium-grade white cotton," the manager explained. "But people want bright polyesters for dresses and scarves."

"Can't you buy polyester?" I asked.

The man shrugged. "We did, several years ago. And we sold our production well. But then the government issued new orders."

The Industry Ministry, their owner, had forced them to shift to cotton fabrics. This was because the Baathist government had started a cotton project in the north, found that the cotton grown was of poor quality, and so with the devastating logic of socialism, forced the Al-Hillah textile plant to buy the cotton above world price and also required them to buy three years' inventory in advance. So now the place was run-down, in the wrong business, and deeply in debt to the state bank, which had been ordered to extend a loan that could never be repaid. Each mistake had bred another.

I ruminated on the Daura refinery and the Al-Hillah textile mill as the car bumped along the road north. From a purely economic point of view, we should let such now-idle state enterprises sink. But these enterprises employed over a half million Iraqis and unemployment was already over 50 percent.

If the war that toppled Saddam had done minor damage to Iraq's infrastructure, that could not be said of the Baathists' rule. Thirty-five years of mismanagement and outright theft, combined with a decade of sanctions, had crippled the nation's economy. We had to move quickly to restart it, and to begin the long-term process of reform.

Before Saddam wrecked it, Iraq had been one of the region's more successful economies. The country was earning $75 billion a year in the early 1970s from oil exports (in 2003 dollars). Per capita income had peaked at over $7,500 in 1980, which, with free education and subsidized health care, made Iraq a respectable middle-income country. But over the following twenty years, Saddam and his cronies had largely destroyed both the economy and the middle class. He squandered Iraq's riches on wars like the eight-year bloodbath against Iran, and palaces like the pseudo-Babylonian fortress beside the Euphrates.

In early June, our new top economic adviser, Peter McPherson, a former deputy secretary of the treasury and director of the U.S. Agency for International Development (USAID), on leave as president of Michigan State University, summed up the challenge: "The electricity system is substandard, marginal and erratic; the supply of water in one of the most fertile areas of the world is unreliable; the health system is a disgrace; and the communications and transportation system is of fourth-world quality. Overall the quality of the infrastructure of Iraq is much worse than that in the other countries that have successfully managed transition."

As the bad news piled up, I told Clay one night that we faced a crisis as serious as the one America experienced in the Great Depression.

One morning Peter popped into my office with some papers. His team had been scouring the Finance Ministry for budget figures for days and finally found some useful information. He showed me a printout which revealed that for decades the Baathists had diverted a staggering one third of the country's gross domestic product to the military.

The economic "system" the Baath Party had adopted combined the worst of socialism—utopian faith in bureaucratic guidance and state-owned enterprises—with the corruption characteristic of tyrannies. The result was a spectacular and persistent misallocation of Iraq's capital resources. The new Iraq needed a modern economy.

"You're an educator, Peter," I said. "Do you think we can teach influential Iraqis the basics of a free-market economy?"

"We certainly can try."

So began two months' of Monday night economic seminars that became quite popular among people from the ministries, Iraq's nascent "private sector," and younger potential political leaders. I hoped that these sessions would evolve into a sort of Council of Economic Advisers to the interim government we intended to set up.

At one of the early seminars, the overflow crowd sat at a large rectangular table in a room in the Convention Center, about a mile from the palace. Peter, as an esteemed American university president, held the Iraqis' attention as he presented the stark details, information that would have been a state secret before Liberation.

"We should all understand how bad the situation is," Peter said, "so that we can plan the way ahead."

During the 1990s, he noted, speaking from a chart, annual per capita spending on health care had fallen from the equivalent of $17 to about 50 cents. Half of the country's primary health-care facilities had closed in that decade. Iraq's infant mortality rate was five times that of neighboring Saudi Arabia. Life expectancy in Iraq had fallen to 61 years, compared to a regional average that had risen to 67 years.

"Education fared no better," Peter said. "According to UNICEF, 80 percent of Iraq's 25,000 schools are in poor condition. At least half of them need to be completely rebuilt."

Schools were chronically overcrowded; sometimes as many as 180 students were crammed into a room. There was an average of one book for every six students.

"And here in ancient Mesopotamia," he said, "the 'Land Between the Rivers,' there's a water crisis."

As elsewhere, underinvestment and mismanagement were to blame. Peter's experts and their Iraqi counterparts estimated that over half of the pumped water was lost due to leaky pipes, most of which were at least forty years old. Availability of drinkable water had fallen by 60 percent in Baghdad during the 1990s.

Half of Basra's water treatment plants were not operating when Coalition forces arrived. Only 20 percent of Iraq's population, almost all of them in Baghdad, had access to closed sewerage systems. Not one of Baghdad's three sewage treatment plants was operational—even though none had suffered battle damage. The sewage plants had been undercapitalized and then looted.

"We estimate that every day 500,000 tons of untreated human waste is being discharged into the Tigris and Euphrates rivers."

Around the table several Iraqis nervously fingered the bottled water.

At one Monday night seminar, David Oliver, the CPA's director for management and budget, had more grim news.

"Most of the country's 192 state-owned enterprises are operating at a loss, with a direct cost to the government of about a billion dollars a year. The indirect costs through the inefficient allocation of capital and labor are incalculable."

As the participants absorbed this, David added the coup de grace: "The banking system is bankrupt."

The six state-owned banks had made loans according to political guidelines. This was crony "capitalism" familiar to students of the Soviet Union. While there were about a dozen private banks, these were more family trusts than valid commercial institutions. At Liberation the entire banking system, including the politicized Central Bank, was closed down.

"So," David said, "we also face a liquidity crisis: how are we going to get money into the hands of the Iraqi people to start the economic motor running again?"

One day after returning from a visit to a Baghdad school, I asked Phil Carroll, my recently arrived senior Oil Ministry adviser, to come by. Phil, a tall, balding man with a Texas drawl, was a respected retired Shell Oil executive whom I came to rely on heavily for advice in the vital oil sector.

"Phil, on the way back to the palace this morning, I noticed that the gas lines are getting longer."

"Yeah, well, it's not surprising," he said. "We've got problems producing enough gasoline at the refineries. There's been a flood of cars coming into the country since Liberation. And the price of gas is about a nickel a gallon."

"Huge subsidies distort activity," I said. "Economics 101."

"Sure, but the problem is worse," he said. "You know you can get up to forty times as much for a liter of gas just across the border in Turkey? Even worse for other fuels. A liter of LPG cooking gas goes for 150 times over the line in Syria. So we've also got a major smuggling problem. It's going to cost us billions."

"Well, we've got to do something," I said. "We can't just sit here and watch this stuff exported while Iraqis stand in line for gas."

I asked the military to give me recommendations on dealing with the smuggling.

Distorting subsidies were woven throughout the economy. At a morning staff meeting, McPherson drew attention to one of the most destructive examples. "Iraqis paid nominal fees for electricity," Peter explained. "But under Saddam the billing system was sporadic at best, and corrupt at worst. Industry, too, paid noneconomic costs for power. For instance, Iraq's cement plants were charged next to nothing for the electricity they used."

This had allowed the plants to ask submarket prices for their cement. That in turn meant that the construction industry was built on the false premise of low-cost materials. And so on down through the economy.

"The World Bank estimates that the costs of these energy subsidies topped $5 billion a year," one of Peter's economists added.

There was even worse news. In 1995, Saddam had begun a system of food rationing. Each head of household was given a ration card, which entitled his family to a monthly "food basket," doled out through some forty thousand retail stores around the country.

"The UN believes that over half the Iraqi population depends on this monthly ration," Peter told me after the staff meeting. "But there's also an active gray market in buying and selling the commodities, so who knows? The food subsidies cost the government—that's us these days—another $3 billion each year." In all, subsidies gobbled up 65 to 75 percent of all state revenues.

And rationed rice, flour, beans, and cooking oil also distorted economic activity. The Trade Ministry had the exclusive right to import the food products destined for the basket. The ministry owned thirty-six huge silos to store barley and wheat. It had almost three thousand trucks to distribute the commodities. All of this suppressed demand for domestic agriculture and discouraged private sector warehousing and distribution activities. To keep the farmers—mainly Shiites—on the farm, the government resorted to still more subsidies, selling seed, fertilizer, and pesticides for as little as 25 percent of cost.

One busy afternoon in late May, a budget meeting I had scheduled for fifteen minutes with David Oliver stretched to over an hour.

"Central budgeting became chaotic," he explained, "because the Baathists subverted normal fiscal procedures." He put a bar graph on the marble table to illustrate the next point: "As far as we can tell only about 8 percent of the government's spending was channeled through the Ministry of Finance."

"That's nuts," I said. "Where the hell did the rest go?"

"Well, it looks like the vast majority of government spending was controlled directly by various offices attached to the presidency . . . and Saddam's hand-picked party cronies. And under Saddam the budget was a state secret—just like the Russians'. We can't find any useful records of this massive 'off budget' spending."

"Saddam was no economist," Peter said one afternoon when I'd been mulling over his team's work.

"I'm beginning to feel like you guys are ganging up on me, Peter," I joked, taking yet another printout.

To cover government expenditures, which throughout the 1990s far outran revenues, Saddam just printed more money. At the end of 2002, annual inflation was running at over 100,000 percent and unemployment was at 50 percent. Hyperinflation hit the middle classes, and civil servants, particularly hard. The Iraqi dinar had depreciated dramatically.

"Our most immediate need is to put money into the hands of ordinary Iraqis in order to prime the economic pump," he said.

He was right. The question was how to do it.

This was a complex task because Iraq's ministries had very limited budgeting capacity and in effect there was no banking system to distribute funds. So we focused first on government employees, people like the staff of the Children's Hospital. We estimated that there were about 1.5 million civil servants. They had not been paid since the start of the war in mid-March. We also needed to get money to the hundreds of thousands of Iraqi pensioners who had received nothing for months.

As Peter and David's colleagues dug deeper into the matter, they found a remarkably chaotic civil service pay system. Any coherence that had existed in the salary scales had been destroyed over the years by a web of special pay deals paralleling official government salaries. Sometimes these were "bonuses" for performance. Some were rewards for helping senior Baathists. Some were bribes disguised as commissions.

We agreed that we couldn't delay paying salaries until we had rationalized the wage system. We had to move fast. So I instructed them to come up with a straightforward plan to start paying government employees quickly while we worked with Iraqis to design a rational salary system. On May 18, I approved a simplified four-grade pay scale for the millions of civil servants. I raised the government pension, which had been the equivalent of two dollars a month, to $20.

"It's a rough and ready solution," I admitted. "But it's better than doing nothing and leaving all those people with empty pockets."

We skewed the wage scale to give the two lower grades more money and the upper one a bit less. All in all, our monthly payroll was more than $170 million. This would help stimulate consumption. Meanwhile, we initiated an urgent professional study with Iraqi and foreign experts to come up with a modern multigrade pay scale.

"You know, it's not going to be easy to actually pay the people," David warned.

And it wasn't.

•   •   •

We needed personnel records, which were difficult to obtain in some ministries, unavailable in others, and padded in most. The salaries and pensions had to be paid in cash, but since we had a shortage of Iraqi dinars, we had to pay in U.S. dollars. And we had to provide security to transport and distribute hundreds of millions of dollars around a country still insecure from terrorists and armed criminals. On May 24, under the vigilance of Coalition troops, we made our first payments to government employees.

Our next effort at economic stimulation was completing the deal I'd brokered with the UN to buy the wheat and barley crop. Cereals were already being harvested in the south and we would soon be faced with angry farmers, mainly Shiites, if we did not act quickly.

"Now that we've shaken loose some Iraqi money out of the UN," Robin Raphel said as I met her team, "we recommend jumping the price to $105 per ton."

"Let's do it," I told them.

Buying grain at this price would allow us to pump another $150 million into the economy while beginning to move toward market prices.

Meanwhile we searched for additional ways to stimulate the economy. The cascading bad economic news forced me on May 31 to put aside my conservative economic instincts. I told McPherson's team to come up with "WPA-type" spending projects. Soon, we announced a major stimulus program centered on an emergency $100 million public works program.

In the coming weeks, the acting minister of irrigation, Mohammad Dhari al-Shibli, and senior CPA adviser Gene Stakhiv developed a plan to refurbish the canal system in the Shia south and provide work for people there. The project would also spread goodwill and badly needed money among demobilized soldiers — essentially the type of postwar civil operation ORHA had envisioned.

The ancient network of irrigation canals connecting the Tigris and Euphrates was in bad condition because, among Saddam's many brutal punishments of the Shia in the 1990s, he forbade all work on their canals. They soon silted up. Normally fertile irrigated alluvial soil had reverted to desert. When I visited the ministry, Gene and the minister told me they could hire "tens of thousands of men" to clear the canals with hoes and shovels.

"We just need $20 million for the payroll," Gene said.

I thought the minister was holding his breath. Under Saddam, a mere minister did not ask for money, especially to hire Shiite workers.

"Do it," I said. *But where in the hell will I find the money?*

On the way to my car, the minister pointed to a couple of rusty iron cages in the courtyard.

"That's where my Baathist predecessor threw recalcitrant officials," he explained. "Or just ones he didn't like. He was one of Saddam's favorites."

Imagine a country where the minister of irrigation has his own prison cells, I thought.

Over the next three months, the project cleared 20,000 kilometers of canals and created more than 100,000 jobs — and helped win the Coalition the respect of moderate Shiites.

Peter and his economic advisers also developed a robust program to restore Iraq's essential services as quickly as possible. His goal, he reported, "is to get standards well above prewar levels." I approved a 3,200 percent increase in health-care spending, raised doctors' monthly salaries by 800 percent, and ordered the purchase and distribution of over 22 million doses of vaccines for children.

I told CPA's senior advisers that we also had to work on the educational deficit. So we set a goal of rehabilitating a thousand schools and distributing more than a million kits for individual schools by September 30.

We also increased teachers' salaries from the equivalent of $3 to $150 a month and started to purge textbooks and curricula of Baathist propaganda. This meant printing and distributing over five million books before schools reopened in October.

Meanwhile, CPA experts and contractors identified dozens of urgent projects to improve water systems, telecommunications, ports, and electricity. Before the war, Iraq had generated about 4,000 megawatts (MW) of power, though demand was estimated to have been at least 6,000 MW. For years Saddam had masked this shortfall by robbing provinces of power to give Baghdad 16–18 hours of electricity a day. I learned my first night in Baghdad that all of Iraq was generating only 300 MW, about what a small American town needed.

"With luck, we should be able to increase power generation tenfold by July 4," Peter Gibson, our electricity adviser predicted, "and I recommend we set a goal of reaching prewar levels by September 30."

"Go for it," I told him. "Just get Oliver an estimate of what it'll cost." Another demand for money . . .

We also began work on a system to spread the available power on the national grid to ensure a more just distribution among the regions.

•   •   •

Air Force One rolled to a stop at Qatar's Al-Udeid Air Base on the steamy evening of Wednesday, June 4. I'd driven out to the huge military airfield with American Ambassador Maureen Quinn. CENTCOM commander General Tommy Franks, due to retire soon, and Lieutenant General John Abizaid, his deputy and about to assume command, joined us and a retinue of Qatari dignitaries in the receiving line at the base of the plane's stairs. Here on the lower Gulf, it was as hot as Baghdad and as humid as a steam bath.

On the drive from Doha, the capital, you couldn't miss the conspicuous opulence of the oil-rich emirate. White marble mansions were scattered like gravestones across the tan desert. Every other car on the wide expressway seemed to be a BMW or Rolls. There were 160,000 native Qataris and about 700,000 expats living in the country: South Asians who did the menial work, Palestinians and Egyptians who handled commerce, and Europeans who managed the oil fields and banking, and kept the planes flying. Because of the country's huge gas reserves, most Qataris didn't have to work. This pattern was repeated up and down the Gulf. I'd found Iraqis of all ethnic and sectarian groups to be grittier, more substantive, and a lot tougher. Yet the Qataris I'd met at meetings earlier that day displayed a condescending attitude toward Iraq's Shia majority, whom they clearly considered devious, misguided peasants. When I'd pointed out that there was a robust Shiite professional class in Iraq, my hosts, in their gossamer summer robes, seemed dubious.

One day, I thought, *a free Iraq with its educated, hardworking people will help transform this region.*

President Bush, who was returning from an Arab-Israeli summit in Aqaba on the Red Sea, bounded down the staircase. He looked fit and seemed in great spirits as he made his way along the receiving line.

"Bremer!" he said, grabbing me by both shoulders. "How're you holding up? Come on back to the hotel with us and smoke a few cigars."

Colin Powell and Condi Rice followed the president to his armored Cadillac as I returned to the embassy's vehicle far back in the motorcade. I'd just climbed in when one of President Bush's aides jogged over. "Sir, the president wants you to ride with him."

I had to sprint back along the parked motorcade in the soggy heat.

"C'mon, Jerry," the president said with a grin. "You gotta bring us up to date on Iraq."

I sat on a jump seat opposite the president. Condi Rice was next to me on another, and the secretary of state was beside the president in the backseat.

The president and I conducted a fast, far-ranging conversation as the limousines and motorcycle outriders sped toward the Ritz-Carlton hotel on Doha's gaudy Corniche.

"Let's start with security," I said. "The situation in Baghdad is improving. But we've still got problems. The violence is coming from three sources: looters, die-hard Baathists—who include Fedayeen Saddam—and Mukhabarat paramilitaries. The Iranians may be playing around a bit, too."

"What do the Iraqis think of that?" the president asked.

"Based on my talks with Shiite tribal leaders in the south and others, they don't want those guys from Iran mucking around in Iraq."

"How about security elsewhere in the country?"

"We've got a lot more to do in the area west and north of Baghdad in the Sunni homeland. Lots of sore losers. And I've seen some reports of Saudi Wahhabi extremists coming into that area." That seemed to surprise the others.

I added that before the invasion, two full Republican Guard divisions—the Nebuchadnezzar and the Adnan—had been dug in north of Baghdad to defend against the expected attack by the U.S. 4th Infantry Division moving south from Turkey, the attack that never came because the Turks denied the Coalition permission for these troops to transit the country. The enemy's armor had been bombed, but most of the Iraqi troops had dispersed into the Sunni towns like Tikrit, Samarra, and Fallujah—and Baghdad. "We've got to do more to track them down."

"How's the overall situation?" Bush asked.

"I'm optimistic for two reasons, Mr. President," I answered. "First, Iraq has excellent resources, plenty of water, and it's fertile, besides the huge oil reserves. And, the Iraqis are energetic and resourceful folks."

I described my visit to the Daura oil refinery.

"On the other hand," I added, "it's hard for us to understand how psychologically shattered the Iraqi people are. This was the most dramatic collapse of any regime in decades. Saddam held power almost three times as long as Hitler. Most Iraqis have had no experience with free thought. They vaguely understand the concept of freedom, but still want us to tell them what to do."

"Will they be able to run a free country?" he asked. "Some of the Sunni leaders in the region doubt it. They say, 'All Shia are liars.' What's your impression?"

"Well, I don't agree. I've already met a number of honest, moderate Shia and I'm confident we can deal with them."

"What about the economy?"

"Our most urgent problem is unemployment. We think it's about 50 percent, but who really knows? Also, Iraq's got a young population, with about half of them under the age of nineteen. That's an explosive combination."

I explained that Iraq had a dysfunctional Stalinist economy. We needed to get productive activity going to create jobs. I told the president that I intended to announce some emergency jobs programs later that week. Longer term, we would have to help Iraqis transform military industries into civilian enterprise activities. And corruption was sure to be a big risk.

"I read a report that there are 150,000 pensioners who haven't been paid," he said.

"The number's actually a lot higher, Mr. President. But we're working to get them paid, too."

"What about putting a new Iraqi army and police in place?"

"Our top priority. But ex-soldiers are not suitable or trained for police work." I added that former New York City police commissioner Bernard Kerik had just arrived as my adviser to the Iraqi police. He had a plan to stand up a professional police force. "We'll start very rudimentary training within three weeks." I added that we were recruiting the first battalion for the new army.

I also told the president that oil production was creeping back. "We're producing 700,000 barrels per day. We should be able to start exports next week through the Turkish pipeline. Tankers can begin to call at the ports in the south soon."

The motorcade pulled into the Ritz-Carlton's basement garage, amid trash bags and Dumpsters.

"Stick with me," the president joked. "And you'll see the underside of the world's best hotels."

The next morning, over breakfast in the president's suite, General Franks gave a briefing on the security problems north and west of Baghdad. Powell, Rice, and the president's chief of staff, Andy Card, joined us around a long rectangular table.

"Mr. President," Franks said, "as I've stressed to Secretary Rumsfeld, we've got to keep force levels consistent to meet our needs."

Using a map of Iraq, he indicated areas of the south where a new Coalition division-size force under Polish command that included other nationalities would be based.

"I'm no military expert, Mr. President," I said. "But I think we need to be cautious in assessing the value of non-U.S. forces. Our goal has to be to avoid any deterioration in our overall combat capability." Former Warsaw Pact troops might look good on paper, but they were neither as well trained nor as well equipped as U.S. or British forces.

"It's important above all that we maintain sufficient strength to deal with any opponents of the new Iraq." I was thinking of unrepentant Baathists, Saudi Wahhabis bent on Jihad, and meddling Iranians. "We still have some very hard fighting ahead of us," I said, "especially in the area west and north of Baghdad.

We lost a soldier from the 82nd Airborne yesterday on patrol in a city called Fallujah."

Secretary Powell had kept a thoughtful silence for most of the discussion. We'd known and respected each other for years—since he was U.S. Army V Corps commander in Cold War Europe and I was American ambassador to the Netherlands. Now he said, "Some assumptions, Jerry: Assuming the best case over the next few months and we get representative government in Iraq, that'll have a Shia majority. Will we also have Sharia law, as in Nigeria or Pakistan?" He referred to Islamic law based on the Koran.

"Mr. Secretary," I said, "it's my understanding that Sharia can exist side by side with Western secular law as it does here in Qatar as long as Sharia is limited to family issues."

"What's your best-case scenario for the next year?" Colin pressed.

"Within a year," I said, "we could have a constitution and more or less democratic elections. But it'll be very difficult to pull off in that time frame."

Condi Rice had been taking notes. "Could the Iraqi election system have vote thresholds that parties have to reach in order to be represented in parliament, as in some European countries like Germany?" She was thinking of ways to avoid a future Iraqi parliament splintered into bickering factions.

"I sure hope so," I said. "That's one way to improve the chances for a stable political environment."

"Pace yourself, Jerry," the president cautioned me before he and Franks left to greet the troops at nearby Camp As Sayliyah.

When my plane landed back at Baghdad that afternoon, I went straight into a series of meetings with the economic team over the looming dinar crisis. And the word "crisis," although sometimes overused at CPA headquarters, was not too strong a term. Saddam's practice of randomly printing money notwithstanding, there was not enough currency to meet the country's needs. So much for pacing myself.

The Coalition's dilemma was that we were paying Iraqi government expenses, on the order of several hundred million dollars a month, in dollars. This was eroding already low confidence in the "Saddam" dinar—bearing the dictator's portrait—that had been the official currency in the south of Iraq since the first Gulf War. Our currency problem was complicated by the fact that the Saddam dinar came in only two denominations: 250- and 10,000-dinar notes. At the prevailing exchange rate, this was like trying to run an economy on the equivalent of dimes and five-dollar bills.

Another complication concerned the Kurds. When they had broken away from Iraq in 1991 and formed the Kurdistan Autonomous Zone, the north had continued to use Iraq's previous currency, called the Swiss dinar because it had been printed by a Swiss firm. The Saddam dinar had greatly depreciated against the Swiss dinar and against all world currencies due to Saddam's practice of covering deficits by running the printing presses. Yet from the outset, I had decreed that the Coalition would recognize these older dinars as Iraq's legal tender. It was essential, I believed, that Iraqis have confidence in their currency as a store of value.

The latest crisis had been caused in part by burst pipes flooding the Central Bank vaults toward the end of the war. This had destroyed billions of Saddam dinars. The shortage of dinars made it difficult for the Coalition to stop using dollars to pay civil service salaries and pensioners, our biggest recurring expense. But we couldn't print additional Saddam dinars because the plates for the 10,000-dinar note had been lost—or stolen. Moreover, because people suspected that many 10,000-dinar bills were counterfeit, the note was accepted on the street at only 70–75 percent of face value.

We did have the plates for the 250 note. Our economists suggested that we print these and offer to exchange them at par for the 10,000 note to shore up the credibility of the 10,000-dinar note. So I reluctantly authorized printing new 250s. Since my de-Baathification decree had outlawed the public display of Saddam's portrait, I had to grant myself a waiver to print the "Saddam" notes.

But, as each day passed with more dollars on the street, the public's trust in the Saddam dinar fell further.

The crisis had built in late May when the dollar-dinar exchange rate began to gyrate wildly. Some of the volatility was no doubt due to currency manipulators and to the ease with which the Saddam 10,000-dinar note could be counterfeited. Whatever the cause, the steep currency swings made budgeting for the government, and also for private firms, very difficult. We knew that currency uncertainty would make it even more difficult to attract much-needed foreign investment.

Peter McPherson came to see me after meeting with his senior financial advisers. "My colleagues and I now foresee the possibility of a complete collapse of the Saddam dinar," he announced.

I nodded at the grim news. A worthless Iraqi currency was the last thing we needed. The event would have major social and political consequences because it would effectively wipe out what remained of the savings of millions of Iraqis. Peter said that a collapse could force the formal dollarization of the economy.

"That would be a disaster," I replied. It would send a devastating message to Iraqis and the world that the U.S. considered Iraq an American appendage and that the occupation was permanent. "We simply can't let it happen."

After much debate, we decided that the Coalition should introduce a single new currency to be used throughout Iraq, including the Kurdish zone. We also agreed that after fixing the initial exchange rate for the old dinars, we would let the new Iraqi dinar float freely against world currencies, thereby doing away with the corruption encouraged by Saddam's multiple exchange rates.

"Okay," I told my assembled senior advisers one baking morning in June, "this is going to be a massive undertaking, unprecedented in wartime. But we've got no choice. It's either that or see the whole damn economy dollarized."

The first problem was determining how much money was already in circulation. On most matters Central Bank figures were spotty and unreliable. We had no reason to think they would be any better in this area. Our initial estimate was that there was about a 4–5 billion dollar equivalent of Saddam and Swiss dinars on the street, in the souks, and under mattresses. Based on this calculation, we believed that we'd need to print and distribute about 2,200 tons of new dinars and collect and destroy some 2,800 tons of old dinars, an estimate which would prove dramatically low.

The security situation was much on our minds. By this time, a little over a month after my arrival, small-arms fire and even rocket-propelled grenade (RPG) attacks on Coalition troops, although sporadic, were on the rise. Before the invasion, Saddam had released tens of thousands of common criminals — rapists, murderers, bandits. And armed street gangs were becoming a problem. Criminal raids on banks distributing the new dinars would increase the challenge of pulling off the exchange.

"By any measure," I told the senior staff, "this is a tall order. Iraq's a country without an effective banking system, no telephone service, lousy roads, and worse security. And we've got to do the planning in secret to avoid further currency turbulence."

McPherson began secret discussions with several printing companies about the cost and delivery time for a new currency. We were told it would take a minimum of three months from the decision to the start of delivery of the new currency. There was not a day to lose.

"Let's get moving," I told McPherson.

•   •   •

On June 21, accompanied by an Iraqi delegation, I boarded a C-130 at the Baghdad airport for the ninety-minute flight to Amman, Jordan, to attend the World Economic Forum. As I'd said in an e-mail to my daughter the night before, the event "is a big clambake where all the politicians and businessmen who take themselves seriously get together and look serious as they ponder serious issues."

In Amman, I joined Colin Powell for a private meeting with King Abdullah II in his personal office. The room was decorated with model tanks, and the walls displayed racks of rifles, swords, and daggers, which reflected his earlier career as commander of the Jordanian special forces.

"Mr. Secretary, Mr. Ambassador," the king said, "I'm most interested how Jordan can assist you on security matters."

Jordan, a Sunni state with a Palestinian majority, already had helped us considerably during the invasion, allowing Coalition Special Operations forces to operate from its territory. Two days earlier in Baghdad, at the king's request I'd had lunch with Abdullah's chief of intelligence and our CIA station chief to discuss cooperation on training Iraq's new police force and Jordanian-Iraqi cooperation on border control.

As we reviewed that conversation, I saw that the king was receptive to the concept, but that he wasn't ready to commit himself or his country to a formal security relationship. I thanked the king for his offer and said we'd be back in touch.

From Amman, Colin Powell and I drove down to the Jordanian side of the Dead Sea.

"You know," Powell said smiling, "Don Rumsfeld called me in early May before the president announced your appointment."

"Well," I answered as the big, frigidly air-conditioned SUV crawled down the twisting escarpment road through the heat mirage, "he told me he was going to bounce my name off you, Condi, George Tenet, and the vice president before going to the president."

"I tried to keep my voice lukewarm on the phone," Colin admitted. "But when I hung up, I flat-out whooped with joy." He pumped his arm to emulate his gesture. "The people in my outer office thought I'd just won the lottery."

It was a comfort to know that I had another supporter among the top NSC officials.

Down at the huge tent beside the pewter-gray waters of the Dead Sea, I told the audience that the Coalition's strategic objective was to open Iraq's economy to the outside world, something that was possible now that UN sanctions had been lifted. I stressed the importance we attached to encouraging Iraq's private sector, and foreign investment, which Saddam had effectively excluded. "Just as forming a vibrant political climate in Iraq will entail many challenges, so too creating a vibrant economy in Iraq will not be easy."

I reminded the audience that Iraq under Saddam had been crushed by "militarized, misguided state planning, and outright theft." Unemployment had been at 50 percent even before the war. But as I'd told the president in Doha, Iraq's economic future was far from hopeless. The nation possessed a vast reserve of natural resources, I emphasized. "In my brief time in Iraq, I have been repeatedly impressed with the extraordinary technical capabilities of Iraqis working in government and industry. They just need the opportunity to put these skills to productive work. We will give them that chance."

I concluded by reminding the assembled international leaders, "It is an axiom that political and economic freedom go hand in hand."

On Monday, July 7, we took the first two major steps in our program of long-term economic reform. I announced that Iraq would begin the exchange of all old dinars for new currency during the three-month period beginning October 15. I also signed a law creating Iraq's first truly independent central bank, analogous to the U.S. Federal Reserve and an essential economic institution in any modern, stable nation.

Chapter 4
POLITICAL MINUET

■ BAGHDAD
SUMMER 2003

While our experts struggled to develop plans to reform the Iraqi economy, another CPA team worked hard to begin the process of political reform.

The UN Security Council had voted on May 22 to lift the sanctions on Iraq that were first imposed on Saddam's regime in 1990. UN Resolution 1483 called on the Coalition to work with a new special representative of the UN secretary general to "facilitate a process leading to an internationally recognized, representative government of Iraq," which the resolution labeled the "Interim Iraqi Administration" or IIA.

"This resolution leaves a lot of wiggle room," I told Scott and Ryan one steamy afternoon. "And the Iraqis will have both the UN special rep's shoulders and mine to cry on."

"That'll make life even more interesting," Ryan said.

Having a UN special representative in Baghdad could complicate the task of setting up an interim administration. The possibilities for the Iraqis to play the Coalition and the UN off against each other were troubling. So we began to refine our political strategy. We then decided to test it on Ibrahim al-Jaafari, the Shiite leader of the Islamic Dawa Party. We called on him in the pilgrimage city of Karbala.

As we and our shepherding Humvees drove south from Baghdad, passing flat brown farming villages, we discussed our evolving plan.

"The key is to move fast," I said, summarizing our discussions.

I felt we had to get the Interim Iraqi Administration in place quickly to show the Iraqis that the Coalition was serious about political reform and about giving them early responsibility for their own governance. But the IIA also had to be representative of all Iraqis. I had told the Group of 7 (the "exiles") that they just didn't fit the bill. Iraqis wanted wider representation. So did the president. And that was what the UN resolution sought.

But I wanted our Coalition, not the United Nations—with its murky political agendas—to take the lead in pushing this process forward.

If we could pressure the G-7 to expand into a more representative group of about thirty people as soon as possible, the Coalition could officially name the enlarged body the "interim administration" and then quickly give it ministerial power.

"But," I said as we bounced along, "we've also got to develop a good plan for the longer term."

This would take time.

As in the economic area, Baathist misrule had severely damaged Iraq's political structures. These would not be fixed overnight. The thirty years of tyranny had gravely distorted civil administration, jurisprudence, and any semblance of representative governance. Elections and the rule of law had been a cruel charade.

Iraq needed a new constitution, written by Iraqis, to replace Saddam's sham Baathist document. A modern constitution, I believed, was essential to define and set boundaries for political activity. By itself no document could guarantee Iraq's future. But a good constitution could help to shape the country's political life. It would provide essential checks and balances in the new political system. By establishing in law the basic rights and obligations of citizens and defining relations among Iraq's peoples and regions, the document could make a huge contribution to a stable nation.

All the Iraqis we had consulted agreed that a new constitution was vital. Most of them referred back to the country's original 1925 constitution that had been adopted under the British. Then, a selected group of about one hundred men—mainly Sunnis—had written the document, which had been approved in a referendum. But to repeat this process now in a representative manner would mean mobilizing a wide spectrum of competent Iraqis. These, we hoped, would encourage extensive discussion and debate among all elements of Iraq's mosaic population. They would draft a constitution to be approved by the Iraqi people through popular vote. This would be a complex, time-consuming procedure. The result would have to be an Iraqi product. I told my colleagues that no doubt Iraqi democracy would be different from America's or Britain's. But since the Iraqis would need time to design their system, the process of writing and ratifying a constitution would be the "slow" component of our strategy.

"I guess we'll call this our 'Fast-Slow' strategy, I told Ryan and Scott as the convoy entered the outskirts of Karbala. Quickly setting up the government, but allowing adequate time to write the constitution.

We met Dr. Ibrahim al-Jaafari in a stuffy Karbala office near the tile-and-gilt shrine of Imam Hussein ibn-Ali, Shia Islam's greatest martyr. Jaafari, a high-strung, slender medical doctor in his mid-fifties, had lived in England for years. He spoke rapidly, emphasizing his points with elaborate hand gestures.

"The Baathists believe they can regain power," Jaafari said, repeating the warning he'd raised during that emotional session with the G-7 my first week in Baghdad. "They must be stopped."

He's got accurate information, I thought. As I'd told President Bush in Qatar, Coalition intelligence had plausible reports that fanatical Wahhabi Muslims from Saudi Arabia had been infiltrating Iraq and linking up with former Baathists, often in mosques. These Wahhabi fundamentalists considered all Shiites to be "apostates" and the non-Muslim Coalition forces in Iraq to be a sacrilege. Indications were that these extremists might be trying to find common ground with secular Baathist remnants, an "unholy alliance" against their common enemies. I knew from my background in counterterrorism that extremist Wahhabis had great influence in Al-Qaeda.

Thinking of the piles of bones in Al-Hillah, I reassured Jaafari: "The Coalition will never allow the Baathists to regain control of this country."

As I sipped a glass of steaming tea, I outlined the Fast-Slow political process that would begin now that the UN resolution had passed.

Jaafari was wary. His Islamic Dawa Party had suffered horribly under Saddam for having taken precipitous action. Now that he'd returned from exile in Iran, he was solidifying his power base. He sounded as if he favored a "Slow-Slow" approach.

"Ambassador Bremer," he said through his interpreter, "you speak of days and weeks for us to make decisions that will affect our people for decades and centuries. We need to move very carefully."

Jaafari was an educated man who had received his medical degree in Mosul, the multiethnic city in the north. I was dealing with a complex politician. Though the name of his party could be translated as "The Islamic Call," Jaafari was not a religious zealot.

After the Islamic revolution in Iran in 1979, many in the West thought that all Shiites were primitive religious fanatics. Repeated television images of self-flagellating Shiite pilgrims circling the nearby shrine of the martyr Ali, blood soaking their shirts, had reinforced this mistaken belief. But there were probably at least as many secular as there were devout Iraqi Shiites. Ibrahim Jaafari had elements of both. I appealed to his secular side.

"Dr. Jaafari," I said, "in accordance with the United Nations resolution, the Coalition plans to form an interim administration as quickly as possible. We hope that responsible leaders in the Shia community will cooperate with this effort. It would certainly be a tragedy for the Shia to make the same mistake today that they did in 1920."

He nodded, acknowledging my reference. After World War I, when British forces moved into the defunct Ottoman Empire's provinces in Mesopotamia, the Iraqi Shiites had obeyed the fatwa (religious order) of their clerical hierarchy to resist cooperation with the "Crusaders." This decision further marginalized the Shia in the governance of their own country. Now eighty years later, Liberation was giving them a new opportunity.

By contrast, the Iraqi Arab Sunnis, who had enjoyed centuries of preferential treatment under their Sunni Ottoman Turkish rulers, had cooperated with the British occupation and remained the privileged caste, first under the British-installed monarchy, and later in the Baathist regime.

Jaafari became pensive. I had thrown down a gauntlet, effectively signaling that the train was leaving the station and it was up to Shiite politicians to climb aboard.

One of my late-night rituals was a secure phone call to update Secretary Rumsfeld. I sometimes used the calls to speak, some might say "vent," my thoughts. I had plenty on my mind.

One night, I described my "Fast-Slow" political strategy and my conversation with Jaafari. "I think he'll sign up, Mr. Secretary."

"I like it, Jerry," Rumsfeld said. "How will the others react?"

"Don't know for sure yet. But I think they'll jump on board as well."

"Excellent. What else you got?"

"You might be sorry you asked, Mr. Secretary."

"I'm listening." Rumsfeld's tone was neutral.

"The bureaucratic hamsters in your department are beginning to nibble us to death."

Defense wasn't the only agency to nitpick us, but much of the harassment reached us through the Pentagon.

Many of our proposals were getting nickel-and-dimed and bounced back. Clay had told me that he believed we'd be headed for the same train wreck that had hit Jay Garner if we let the "clerks" in Washington dictate what we could and could not do and the pace at which we could proceed. "We're working twenty hours a day out here in pretty rough conditions," I said, "and half that time seems to be spent answering foolish questions from Washington. People are starting to call it the '8,000-mile Screwdriver.' "

The line was silent a moment. *Good . . . let Don think this over.*

During my ten days in the department that May, as I'd been briefed on Iraq, people had told me that Rumsfeld had a penchant to micromanage matters and to "terrorize" his civilian subordinates. Deputy Secretary Paul Wolfowitz gave as good as he got, but other civilians were said to leave woodshed sessions in Rumsfeld's office visibly shaken.

"I'll take care of it, Jerry."

I hoped.

Sergio de Mello, the new United Nations special representative for Iraq, arrived on Tuesday, June 3, and almost immediately came to the palace to call on me.

"Damn," I told Clay as we waited for him. "I didn't think the UN would get its act together so quickly."

My plan was to cooperate with the United Nations as we worked toward expanding the G-7 into the larger interim administration. But the U.S. and the UN often looked at the world differently. And I knew many Iraqis believed that the UN had turned a blind eye to Saddam's brutality.

De Mello, Brazilian born, European educated, and a veteran of Third World conflicts, proved to be an urbane international civil servant, with superb English and French. And he was a skilled diplomat. I liked him immediately.

For an hour, John Sawers, my British colleague, and I ran through our economic and political plans with him.

"I want to be helpful, Ambassador Bremer," he said.

This was a relief to hear. The last thing we needed in the very complicated political minuet we were dancing was to have the Iraqis feel that they could play the UN off against the Coalition.

As I saw de Mello out to his car, he shook my hand. "We'll be able to work well together," he said. Sergio de Mello was true to his word, but some members of the G-7 worked to undercut our plan. For two of them, Ahmad Chalabi and Jalal Talabani, their decades of intriguing proved hard to set aside. The day after my first meeting with the exiles on May 16, an article had appeared in the *New York Times* noting that the Iraqis I had met were disappointed with what they heard. They felt the Coalition was backtracking on "agreements" earlier reached with the American government.

When I'd learned that the story was based on interviews with Talabani and Chalabi, I called them in, separately. I told each that we could not conduct serious business with their group if our confidential discussions were to be reported, in a distorted fashion, to the press. Talabani agreed that the Iraqis needed to work seriously and that the G-7 was not representative.

But Chalabi, whom I'd seen in late May, lectured me on the need to carry out the agreement to move immediately to a "provisional government," which he said Zal Khalilzad, then "presidential envoy," had promised would happen within four weeks after Liberation.

"That's simply unrealistic," I countered. "We need a government which is representative of all Iraqis. You guys can help us. But we intend to move quickly to set up the interim government that the UN resolution calls for."

In June, I met with other Iraqi politicians, including Adnan Pachachi, the elderly Sunni whom the G-7 had added to their group, to go over the same points. Pachachi had briefly served as Iraq's foreign minister forty years earlier and then gone into exile in the United Arab Emirates.

"We're willing to work with the G-7 and to give you a role in the new government," I told him. "But you'll have to show you're serious by helping broaden your group to include more Arab Sunnis, Christians, Turkmen, and above all, women."

Pachachi said he agreed.

Earlier, I'd had a bracing conversation with the Shiite SCIRI party's Abdul Aziz Hakim. The conversation had begun politely with Hakim expressing joy at our decisions on de-Baathification and the disbanding of Iraq's hated security services.

"Until you announced these decisions," he said, "many Iraqis questioned the Coalition's commitment to rooting out Saddam's instruments of terror."

This was encouraging. "So you'll help us expand the Group of 7 into the Interim Administration the United Nations has requested?"

Hakim was silent, and then said one word, "Impossible."

"And why is that, Sayyid?"

He let a silence stretch. Finally he described the vision of his party. "If the Iraqi people convened a national conference now, we could write a constitution within three months . . . without foreign assistance. We have a great tradition of scholarship, you know, Ambassador."

In other words, let Iraq's Shiite clerics manipulate the Shia majority to the detriment of other sectarian and ethnic elements of Iraqi society.

I explained calmly why his formula would not work. Our goal was truly "representative" government, with constitutional protection for all Iraqis. I did agree, however, that Iraqis should write their own constitution.

He listened coolly. "Whatever you choose," he said dismissively. "Just make it happen quickly."

That night I sent Secretary Rumsfeld a memo outlining the situation. I noted that the G-7 was not stepping up to the plate, that "even within the group there appears to be paralysis over how to expand their own group quickly, despite their recognition of the need to do so."

I told him that the Coalition would work to appoint an interim government with around thirty members broadly representative of all major strands of Iraqi society (internal and exiles, Shia, Kurd, Turkmen, Christian, tribal, men and women). When we announced the government, we would also launch a constitutional process, perhaps as early as the end of July.

"National elections might be held about a year from now," I told Rumsfeld. This assumed that the Iraqis could write a new constitution in six months, and that it would then be ratified. A tall order, but a worthy goal.

Meanwhile, the CPA staff continued its efforts to draw other parts of Iraqi society into the political process. One of my top priorities was to ensure that Iraqi women were a part of the new government. Judy Van Rest, a talented political officer whom I charged with women's affairs, worked with two Arabic-speaking women on our governance team—Lydia Khalil, an Egyptian-American, and British diplomat Jules Chappell—to organize a meeting on May 29 with thirty-four Iraqi women leaders. Jules was on loan from the British Embassy in Jordan. All three had had excellent contacts among Iraqi women.

I greeted the women in one of the palace's ornate conference rooms.

"I hope this will be the first of many such meetings," I told the group through my interpreter, adding that the Coalition's objectives were to provide security, establish the rule of law, and improve the country's economy.

"I'm aware of the important position women used to have in Iraqi society. Many Iraqi friends have told me, with passion, about how Iraqi women played a role here unique in the Muslim world in the 1940s and '50s. I expect to see women involved in the political life of Iraq and I count on you and your colleagues to help us identify women who could serve in the interim government."

Some of the women were seated around a long table and others stood behind them. Several said they were delighted with our emphasis on women's affairs. Others began to speak out about their concerns and hopes for Iraq's future.

Suddenly, after about twenty minutes, one of them, a member of the Iraqi Women's League, a communist organization alternately tolerated and repressed by Saddam, shouted, "There are two Baathists in this room!"

A woman standing at the opposite end of the room, the apparent target of this accusation, yelled back, "If this is the spirit of such meetings, it's bad for the future of Iraq!"

The meeting degenerated as everyone joined in the shouting. My interpreter couldn't keep pace with the outbursts. Eventually I was able to impose some order, and told the women that there would be plenty of opportunity to discuss this issue. But what they needed to do now was find a way to organize themselves, to put together a committee that could work with us to call a national women's conference.

Happily, after I left, the participants chose a steering committee that helped us prepare for Iraq's first women's conference on July 9. But this meeting showed, once more, how near the surface lay bitter emotions from the Saddam decades.

My early meetings with the G-7 continued to be discouraging. After my first session, I'd given them two weeks to come up with ideas of how to expand their group to make it more representative. In mid-June, I convoked the G-7 again and reminded them of the challenge I had posed to them. I learned that they had failed.

We sat once more around the large square table in the palace conference room.

"The Coalition is going to continue our own search for additional representatives," I said. "We intend to appoint an interim administration in the next four to six weeks." The train was picking up steam.

I described a host of issues bearing down on the Coalition on which we sought the views of responsible Iraqis. The Coalition had to make decisions about introducing a new currency. What were their opinions? We believed it vital to lift the restrictions on foreign investment. Did they agree? We wanted to encourage the early establishment of cellular phone service. What was their advice? We also faced issues such as reform of the judicial and educational systems, and how and when to take a census. Even more important, we needed informed Iraqi advice on the process of creating the New Iraqi Army and training adequate numbers of police.

"I would welcome this group's advice and assistance on the wide range of issues the Coalition is facing," I told the G-7 and their retinues of advisers. "These are vital challenges concerning your country's future." But few of them were accustomed to offering well-reasoned advice on serious issues.

As Ryan remarked after the meeting, "These guys are more used to seeing themselves as the opposition than deciding anything."

I wanted that to change. And if Iraq were to move forward, it would have to.

This was part of my "work-to-play" program for Iraqis: if they wanted to play a role in the country's political transformation, these politicians were also going to have to work.

"The intention," I told Francie in my e-mail that night, "is to show them that there are serious issues they need to address instead of fantasizing about which office they will hold during the transition or which make of car they will ask for."

But the G-7 had flunked the test again. They were simply unable to allow any diffusion of their power. And the group's stultifying need for consensus kept it from coming up with a single recommendation on any of the issues we put before them. This promised greater difficulties ahead.

It began to dawn on some G-7 members that we and the UN were serious about forming an interim administration and that their authority would be diluted in a broader council. Several members didn't like the prospect. Chalabi had told Scott in late May that he was going back to America for his daughter's graduation from Harvard. I anticipated that he would spend time in Washington lobbying to undo our plan to install a more representative government.

Meanwhile, I was getting to know and respect Sergio de Mello. He had a wry sense of humor and a warm laugh. I kept him abreast of our plans to establish an interim administration by the middle of July. He briefed me regularly on his own discussions with Iraqis. One day he invited me to lunch at the UN's headquarters in the Canal Hotel. Over well-spiced Iraqi food and good Brazilian beer, I brought Sergio up to date on our discussions.

"It's a good plan, Jerry," he said. "I won't do anything to obstruct the Coalition."

"But Sergio," I cautioned him, "the UN isn't universally loved here. Many Iraqis believe it supported Saddam and turned a blind eye to the corruption surrounding the Oil for Food Program."

He nodded. This was not news to him, I gathered. "Well, through words and deeds we'll just have to regain the people's trust."

Now it seemed that the UN and the Coalition were on the same track and that de Mello would not complicate the task of identifying an interim government.

As the full heat of summer took hold, our U.S.-U.K. political team worked day and night to find additional candidates for the new government. Several dozen American and British diplomats and experts, many with Arabic language skills and regional experience, traveled the country, canvassing a mix of tribal, political, religious, and minority groups for candidates to the interim government. Gradually, the team identified women, tribal, and religious leaders we could consider for the membership. We decided to name the interim government the "Iraqi Governing Council," or GC, in recognition of the powers we intended to give the group.

In late June, the pretender to the long-extinct throne of Iraq came in for a meeting. Iraq's monarchy, a creation of the British in the 1920s, had been in the Hashemite family (which still rules Jordan) until a bloody coup d'etat in 1958.

Sharif Ali bin Hussein was a thin, elegant man with slicked-down black hair and an Errol Flynn mustache. Now in his late forties, Sharif Ali had been hustled out of Iraq by his family as a child when the monarchy was overthrown. Since then, he had lived well in England, and it showed. Dressed in a Savile Row suit that must have cost thousands of dollars, with expensive Italian shoes and a Rolex watch, smelling of aftershave and speaking flawless English, he was not your typical Iraqi. He had returned to Baghdad on a private jet with a retinue of seventy.

Unsurprisingly, Sharif Ali agreed that the G-7 was unrepresentative and that early elections were neither possible nor wise.

"They would simply favor extremists," he told me, in the tone of a headmaster addressing a schoolboy. "But, mind you, Ambassador, I would favor an early referendum on the form of the government—a return to the monarchy or not?"

He added that the interim government would have "a difficult time."

"No, it won't be easy," I agreed. "But that's the way democracy works."

As June wore on, some members of the original G-7 continued to resist the broadening of the new government. We learned that at one of their meetings, Kurdish leader Jalal Talabani had prepared a plan to preempt our Governing Council by having the G-7 itself call a handpicked "national conference" to choose the new government. This might fracture the national unity we were struggling to achieve.

Meeting with me the next day, Talabani, an engaging if somewhat imprecise politician, pledged that he was with us "one hundred percent," despite his vigorous opposition behind the scenes the day before. We would later learn that it paid to pin Talabani down when you were doing serious business with him.

A few days later, senior SCIRI official Abdul Aziz Hakim invited me for lunch at his house on the banks of the Tigris. After an excellent meal, we repaired to his meeting room and as he chain-smoked Iraqi cigarettes, we sipped tea and talked politics.

At our previous meetings he had consistently opposed broadening the G-7 into a more representative Governing Council. This day he was ambivalent. My advisers and I wanted his party in the Governing Council. But if they were out, it would have to be their choice. We didn't want the Coalition to be seen as having excluded an important, if controversial, Shia group.

Hakim told me he agreed that elections were not possible at this point. "But I still prefer to have a national conference convened to elect the interim administration."

He nibbled some pistachio ice cream. "Or," he said as if in passing, "just let the G-7 choose the Iraqi government."

"That is impossible, Sayyid," I said. "We are not going to convene a national conference at this point: There's nothing approaching a national consensus on how to select, let alone elect, such a group on so short notice. Nor can we just allow the G-7 to transform itself into a larger interim government. The Coalition is now entering the final phase of pulling together the Governing Council. I hope you and your colleagues will be part of that process."

From Hakim's bored expression, I might have been discussing obscure mathematical theory, not the future of his party or his country.

"Well," he said, with a laconic wave as he signaled a servant to clear the plates, "I'm planning to leave for London on vacation in two days."

"I certainly understand and sympathize with your need to rest," I said. "But with all respect, I think leaving now would be unwise."

I reminded him that we planned to finalize the Governing Council in the next three weeks. "We would like to include all the important party leaders in the Council," I added. And, as I had reminded Jaafari, I cautioned him that it was important the Shia not commit the mistake they had made in the 1920s.

Hakim got the reference. He grumbled and agreed to cancel his vacation, but remained studiously noncommittal about his participation on the Governing Council.

On June 23, it was Chalabi's turn. He had just returned to Iraq, after ten days in Washington lobbying Congress and the administration against the Coalition's political plans. Chalabi was still an influential figure inside the Beltway. I'd heard that some of the intelligence about Saddam's ongoing WMD program had reached Washington via his Iraqi National Congress, though I myself had never seen it.

Chalabi had by now moved into open opposition to the Coalition, trying to persuade other G-7 leaders to boycott the Governing Council by assigning only deputies to the body. I had established a firm rule that groups serving on the Governing Council would have to be represented by their leaders. This was the only way to ensure that the parties themselves took responsibility for GC decisions. Otherwise, party leaders could put representatives on the Council while they sniped at decisions from the sidelines.

I did recognize, however, that Chalabi was one of the few Iraqi leaders who understood economics. He had used his influence with political supporters in Washington to encourage Saddam's overthrow. So, as with SCIRI, we would rather have him in the tent than outside. But not at too high a price.

In a difficult two-hour meeting in my office that day, Chalabi lectured me on all our "errors" and how we should "drop" our plans for the Governing Council. "Instead you must organize provincial elections."

Right, I thought. *Without a constitution, with the Baathist legal code still in place, no census, no electoral laws, and no laws on political party activities.*

I let him run his course and then recalled our first meeting in May. "I told the G-7 then that you didn't represent Iraq. You were exiles. I challenged you to broaden yourselves to include Iraqis who had lived here under Saddam, to add women, Christians, Turkmen, and tribal leaders. You agreed to do it, but you haven't."

Since the G-7 had flunked the test, I told him the Coalition had worked night and day for the past month, and while he was in the U.S., identifying candidates for the Governing Council.

"We've now found more than eighty men and women from all over the country that we think could be qualified," I said. "I've no intention of throwing all this hard work out the window."

I confirmed that we wanted him and the other party leaders to participate in the Council. It was where real political power would lie.

Chalabi was clearly unhappy that we were not going to simply hand over power immediately to the exiles.

"Mr. Ambassador," he said, "by slowing down this political process, you risk giving the impression that America intends to stay a long time in Iraq. That is not a good signal."

"Dr. Chalabi," I responded, "the president has been very clear. We will stay in Iraq until the job is done but not a day longer."

"I know he said that. But by going slowly, you give the impression to some people that America wants to stay in Iraq."

I stood and went to my desk and took the picture of my family that I kept there. I walked back over to where Chalabi sat, and showed him the photograph. "Well, if anyone should doubt it," I said, "here is their guarantee that I will not stay a day longer than necessary." I added that nobody was ever a more reluctant "occupier" than I was.

"I will certainly consider this," he said. On the way out, Chalabi bitterly noted to British Ambassador Sawers that from what he'd heard, we had far too many "Islamist" candidates for the Governing Council. He was a leading secularist, better known for his love of things Western than Islamic. At this point, Chalabi apparently saw his political future in a secular Iraqi government.

In the last week of June, I had a thorough discussion of the security situation with General Abizaid, the newly confirmed CENTCOM commander, and Lieutenant General Ricardo Sanchez, the new commander of Combined Joint Task Force 7: all Coalition forces in Iraq.

John was a friend whom I greatly respected, a Lebanese-American fluent in Arabic who knew the region well.

Rick Sanchez was quiet and thoughtful and would prove to be unflappable in a crisis. Recognizing the crucial importance of close civilian-military coordination, Rick and I agreed to co-locate our offices in the palace.

If the Pentagon gave the military team the support they would be bound to need, I thought, we might be able to control the mounting violence.

As part of our effort to find suitable tribal representation for the Governing Council, I had a meeting with leaders from the large Shammar tribe that same week. My years as a diplomat in Afghanistan and Malawi had shown me the important role tribes still play in many countries.

The tribes of Iraq reflect Mesopotamia's ancient civilizations. Thus a tribe can have both Shiite and Sunni members, and, in some cases, members of different ethnic groups.

Iraqi tribes are a paradox in other ways. On the surface, they would appear to be relatively unimportant because more than 70 percent of Iraq's population lives in urban areas. And it's true that tribal leaders have less authority than they did when the British occupied the country eighty years ago. Nonetheless, tribes still play an important role in the social and political life of the country. Even Iraqis who have been city dwellers for several generations need little encouragement to discuss their tribal ancestry. Many still proudly proclaim their tribe's roots as their official last name.

But the tribes also had a reputation for respecting power and had always been acutely aware of who was up and who was down. They were likely to support whoever exercised authority in Baghdad, until someone stronger came along.

My meeting June 24 at CPA headquarters with about a dozen Sunni sheiks of the Shammar tribe was a memorable encounter with this fact. The Shammar is one of Iraq's largest tribes and has both Shia and Sunni members, though the overall leadership is Sunni.

The members came to the session in their flowing and perfumed white robes. Most were over sixty, but among them was a younger member, Sheik Ghazi al-Yawar, whom we were considering as a candidate for the Governing Council. About forty years old, American educated, Ghazi was a successful businessman based in Saudi Arabia. His uncle was the paramount chief of the tribe, and lived just outside Mosul. In deference to his elders, Ghazi said nothing at this meeting. Lydia Khalil, with her fluent Arabic, joined us from Governance Team.

Like most tribal leaders, these men talked a lot. They were fond of their historic role in Iraq, recalling with pleasure the days when they had alternately fought and supported the British. Toward the end of the three-hour meeting, and after much tea and mutual congratulations on the liberation of Iraq, the ruling sheik spoke.

"Hakim," he said (using the Arabic term for "governor," for this is how the tribes saw me), "I want to assure you of the everlasting loyalty of the Shammar tribe to you and to the governments that have freed us." Murmurs of agreement from the others.

Warming to his theme, he continued, "Our loyalty is constant and unshakeable." Touching his chest, he added that this sentiment was in his mind, but more important was written on his heart and the hearts of his colleagues. Sage nods all around.

"Through the decades, we have always shown our loyalty and we will be faithful to this ancient tribal tradition." More sounds of agreement.

"If," he concluded, "we should ever decide to betray you, I pledge my word that we will give you a month's notice."

With this reassuring message written on my own heart, I returned to the north the next day to meet the Kurdish leaders.

Northern Iraq, the ancient home of the Kurds, is entirely different from the south. It is a region of dramatic mountains, rolling hills, deep gorges, rushing streams, and flowering slopes. The farms are generously planted with wheat, sunflowers, mustard plants, and varieties of fruit trees. The climate is much cooler than in the south. The last of the spring snow was gone, and the high pastures were rich and green. What a pleasure after the heat of the river valleys.

The Kurds pride themselves on their history and culture. Most of them speak a unique, poetic language, Sorani, which is closer to Persian than to Arabic. They have preserved their traditional music and dances. Kurds also love their food, which is the best in Iraq, a wonderful combination of Arabic, Turkish, and

Persian cuisine. Many are less fastidious Muslims than most Iraqis, and often make their own wines.

The Kurds are mountain people, tough-minded and independent. For the better part of a century, they were in rebellion against the rulers of Baghdad, whether British or Iraqi. The two leaders, Jalal Talabani, whose area was the northeast, and Massoud Barzani, in the west, had been at war with Saddam, and with each other, for decades.

My purpose was to persuade both to join the Governing Council. In our previous discussions in Baghdad, the Kurds had expressed reluctance to submit ever again to rule from Baghdad.

For years before 1991, the Kurds had insisted that a free Iraq must have a federal structure respectful of the unique Kurdish people. And the independence they had won after the first Gulf War—represented by the Kurdistan Autonomous Zone, which Coalition air power had protected for years from Saddam's army—symbolized their ambition for an autonomous state.

I knew from my earlier visit that both Kurdish leaders welcomed Liberation and the dissolution of the Baath Party and security forces. But neither wanted to be on the Governing Council. Talabani even had the madcap idea of rushing off to Asia and Europe for three weeks, at precisely the time we were to pull the Council together.

At his headquarters in Sulaymaniya, I told him that we were "determined to support the creation of a federal Iraq." Talabani was pleased that the Coalition now endorsed this long-standing Kurdish goal, but was still skeptical about serving on the Council.

"The Governing Council will have real political power," I emphasized.

After several hours of discussion, and later over a lavish Kurdish dinner, Talabani agreed to "postpone" the Asia part of the trip, though he still intended to visit Europe.

"Ambassador," he finally said over a glass of sweet local wine, "I will agree to serve on the Governing Council based on your personal appeal."

One down. One to go.

The next day I tackled Barzani. He was less urbane than Talabani, more a classic Kurdish tribal leader. Barzani dressed in traditional Kurdish clothing, was enamored beyond words with life at his lovely house atop the mountains at Salahuddin, surrounded by his tribesmen and apple trees. I couldn't blame him, especially when the temperature in Baghdad was in the mid-120s, while at Barzani's it was a "cool" 90.

"I hate Baghdad," Barzani told me. "I don't want to have to live or even travel there. But, if you insist, I will agree, with great reluctance, to serve on the Council."

"I do insist."

"Then I agree."

The pace now picked up. John Sawers and I started twice-daily meetings of our large Governance Team. We had announced a goal of establishing the Governing Council by July 15. There were plenty of candidates by now. The job was to winnow and sort them, bearing in mind the need for the Council to be representative yet small enough to be effective. We calculated that this would yield a Council of between twenty-five and thirty men and women. Because of the fragmented nature of Iraqi society, this was proving to be an extremely complicated task. Our team had been further strengthened by the arrival of Irfan Siddiq, an Oxford-educated fluent Arabic speaker from the British Foreign Office.

First, we assumed that the Shia would have to be a majority of the Council since they were believed to make up 60 percent of the population. Next, we wanted to ensure that women—downtrodden under Saddam as in many other Arab countries—were well represented. We also needed to find effective, patriotic Sunni members. Finding them brought us face to face with a major structural problem inherent in Iraq's post-Liberation politics: a lack of credible Sunni leaders. Almost all politically active Sunnis had been co-opted into Saddam's security services or Baath Party, or killed as traitors. The Kurds would require representation in rough proportion to the Kurdish/Arab population, about 20 percent. There were Christians, Turkmen, and other minorities whom it was important to include in some way. And as if this were not complicated enough, we hoped that each of Iraq's eighteen provinces could be represented, and we did not want Islamists to dominate the secular majority of the country.

In a message to President Bush, I described the process of choosing the Council as "a cross between blind man's bluff and three-dimensional tic-tac-toe."

While the staff struggled with the complex permutations, I continued to try to bring the G-7 leaders on board. I had another long meeting with SCIRI's Hakim on July 1: he indicated that he would cooperate as long as he had a glimpse at the overall list of the GC beforehand, to assure himself that it was in fact "representative." I figured he wanted to count the Shia to be sure they were a majority. I assured him that the end result would reflect "Iraqi society's balance," which was our formula for recognizing the Shia majority. I said that I would have Hume Horan show him the list of candidates for the Governing Council provided he told no one we had done so.

When Chalabi came in for another meeting on July 3, he was much subdued, having heard that I had persuaded the Kurdish leaders to join the Council. This impressed him, he said, because the week before they had both insisted to him that they would never serve. He realized he had to stay in the game or risk being marginalized.

Chalabi told me that he had recently met with Grand Ayatollah Ali Husseini Sistani, the most revered Shia cleric in Iraq, an Iranian. The Shiites had a clerical hierarchy who achieved prominence through theological scholarship and whose leaders, the *marjaiya*, spoke with authority for their followers. The Sunnis lacked this clear line of authority over their clerics. Sistani was reputed to be a true man of God, who lived a Spartan life and led his people by example. He had told Chalabi he did not care how the Council was pulled together, but insisted that Iraqis, not the Coalition, should write Iraq's constitution.

"Sistani has read that General Douglas MacArthur wrote Japan's constitution," Chalabi told me. "The Grand Ayatollah is concerned that the Coalition will do the same here."

Several days earlier, the ayatollah had issued a fatwa insisting that the constitution be written by Iraqis and that the constitutional conference must be elected, not appointed by the Coalition.

"The Coalition has no intention of writing the constitution," I told Chalabi, "and I'll make sure that Sistani understands this."

Chalabi said that de Mello had apparently told Sistani that he saw no reason elections could not be held soon in Iraq. After all, when he was the UN representative to East Timor, de Mello had noted, his organization had conducted elections soon after arriving.

I replied that de Mello's analogy with East Timor—a former Portuguese colony in the Indonesian archipelago—didn't fit. Iraq had some 25 million citizens to East Timor's 1,000,000, and a much more complex social structure. Holding elections in Iraq under the present circumstances was simply not possible.

After Chalabi left, I called Sergio and told him that I thought his meeting with Sistani, while helpful on the whole, had given the ayatollah a serious misunderstanding of the complexity of conducting elections quickly in Iraq.

"I'll try to correct the record with Sistani," he said.

But, as we were to learn, the damage had already been done.

As we worked to broaden the Governing Council the first week of July, the British came up with the idea of including someone from the Iraqi Communist Party. In the 1950s and 1960s, the party had attracted many Iraqi intellectuals and artists and it still had a following in these circles. Saddam had let the party stagger along, calculating that its avowed atheism would be a useful counter to Islamism.

Sawers asked me if I had any principled objection to the idea. I said I had none, provided we could find someone who had cast off communism's misbegotten ideas about how to run an economy.

So, on July 8, I was in Sawers's office facing the recently retired general secretary of the Iraqi Communist Party, Aziz Mohammed. He was a seventy-nine-year-old Kurd, who clearly felt and showed his age. After describing our plans for the Council, I asked him what he had learned from the fall of Soviet communism.

In reply, Aziz wandered off into a long rumination about how Brezhnev had received letters he never read and sent letters he never wrote.

His comments left me with the distinct impression that he thought Brezhnev was still running the show in Moscow. I didn't have the heart to tell him that Leonid had not been too well recently. We struck Aziz from the list.

Fortunately, a couple of days later, Sawers and I interviewed Aziz's replacement as party leader, Hamid Majid Moussa. He was an energetic roly-poly man in his mid-forties who clearly understood the need to encourage a private sector in Iraq. Moussa, a Shiite, was to prove one of the most effective and popular members of the Governing Council.

We were now in the last stretch but still had to finalize Shia representation on the Governing Council. On July 10, I had another meeting with Abdul Aziz Hakim, who was still playing hard to get. He desperately wanted to designate his deputy, Adel Mahdi, to represent SCIRI on the Council.

"I need to be available to serve my people," Hakim asserted.

In this regard, Hakim was following the self-protective "quietist" tradition of Shia Islam in the region. Until religious revolutionaries like the Iranian Ayatollah Khomeini appeared on the world stage in the 1970s, many Shia religious leaders focused their energies on theology and the spiritual and social and welfare of their people. By remaining off the secular stage, they could sometimes, but certainly not always, avoid Saddam's executioners.

"The Governing Council's the best place to serve your people," I countered. "That's where the power and responsibility will be."

I also noted in passing that there would be substantial Shia representation on the Council, with or without SCIRI, a clear message that we were moving ahead whatever he decided.

"Can't you make an exception for SCIRI? So we can have a deputy there?"

"No. All the other party leaders have agreed to serve personally. If you're not on the Council, SCIRI won't be represented."

"Well, I'd seriously consider it if you could give me some assurances."

"What assurances?"

Mahdi, who had been silent until this point, said that they would want "preferential treatment."

"That's out of the question. I have my responsibilities to all Iraqis to make the whole Council work. I'll be available to Sayyid Hakim or any member of the Council any time, twenty-four hours a day. But the essence of democracy is compromise and fairness. You and your colleagues on the Council will have to work hard to sort out your differences yourselves."

It was left that Hakim would review the proposed Council membership list and then decide. Hume later showed him the proposed list in confidence. As expected, Hakim objected to one opponent's name, which we had added at the last minute as a red herring. When I sent word that I would remove the name if Hakim agreed to serve, we had a deal.

The political team worked and reworked the names and composition of the Council late into the night of July 9, identifying two remaining problems. We still had only three women on the tentative list for the Council and had hoped to have a minimum of four. I had pressed the Kurds for weeks to come up with some candidates, reasoning that women had been far more active politically in Kurdistan over the past decade.

On July 10, the two Kurdish parties told us that they had been unable to agree between them on any additional female members. I gave them another twenty-four hours. They huddled, talked, and argued for a day and came up with nothing.

The second problem was corralling one of Iraq's most respected Shia imams, Sayyid Mohammad Bahr al-Uloum. He was a very senior Shiite cleric who had fled Saddam's dictatorship during the Shia uprising of 1991 and spent most of the next decade in London but spoke almost no English.

I had met him several times and we had approached him through numerous intermediaries, but he remained adamant about not serving on the Council. We needed one more Shia to give them a majority of the Council's twenty-five members. And we knew that Bahr al-Uloum would add significant weight to the GC.

It was now Friday night, July 11, and we were planning to unveil the Council on Sunday, July 13. Sawers and I concluded that we had to make a last-ditch effort in person to persuade Bahr al-Uloum to come on board. So Saturday morning we drove over to his modest home in Baghdad.

Bahr al-Uloum is a short, heavy-set man with a long flowing white beard, chubby cheeks, and thick round glasses. During the meeting, the imam had his sardonic humor on full display. For over three hours, he disputed just about everything John and I said. He was quick, argumentative, demanding, and mentally agile. It was all done with a twinkle in his eyes. He put me in mind of a Jesuit priest masquerading as an elf.

Bahr al-Uloum gave three reasons for his reluctance to serve on the Council.

"First," he said, holding up his right index finger. "You have come to me very late in the process and there are many people on the proposed Council I do not know." Now the right thumb. "Second, Ayatollah Sistani's fatwa makes it clear that the constitution must be written by an elected body. Finally, three Shia provinces in the south are not represented on the Council."

We offered abject apologies for not having sought him out personally sooner and said that nothing we proposed would contradict the fatwa. We hoped that one of the Council's first steps would be to appoint a Preparatory Committee to advise on how the constitution should be written. Further, we explained, we'd worked for two months to select the smallest Council that would also be representative. Fully ten of the twenty-five members were from the south.

We went around and around over numberless glasses of tea and, to our relief, a bowl of delicious pistachio ice cream. At one point Sawers noted that if the imam said "no," he would be the only person in all of Iraq to reject us. This set off a long tirade.

"I have not rejected you. I'm willing to work with you. But I can't serve on the Council myself." He wanted to designate his son to be the representative. We said no. We could not at this stage allow any exceptions to the "principals only" rule.

"Working with us isn't enough. If you want to serve your people, you should be on the Council where important decisions will be made," I told him.

We outlined the substantial authorities we proposed to give the Governing Council, making clear that the Preparatory Committee would only propose a process for writing the constitution. It would not write the constitution itself. The Council would have to decide on the process. He had not understood this and it seemed to make a difference.

He reflected a moment and then, raising his finger again, asked, "But what if the Council recommends a process for writing the constitution which contradicts Sistani's fatwa? Where will I be then?"

I replied that the best way to ensure compliance with the spiritual edict was for him to serve on the Council.

"Ah, yes. But what if a majority of the Council agrees to a process that is in opposition to the fatwa?"

Everybody admires the patience of Job, but it was beginning to take on a special meaning for me.

Sawers pointed out that nobody we had spoken to on the Council favored ignoring the need for an elected constitutional commission.

We spent the next hour discussing his desire to designate his son to serve in his place. We held firm.

"So, Mr. Ambassador, you insist that I personally serve on the Council, is that it?"

Out came my violins one last time. This was a "turning point" in Iraq's history. Important leaders from society had to take part on the Council to make it a success. The Shia leaders must not repeat the tragic mistakes of 1920. The Governing Council would be the best place to influence matters of interest to "his people."

After hearing me out, Bahr al-Uloum reverted to the alleged underrepresentation of the Shia provinces in the south. Couldn't we just add three more people from there? We said it was too late. We intended to announce the Council the next day.

"Perhaps," I added somewhat mischievously, "the Council will want to consider expanding itself in some proportionate way later. Of course, there are other provinces that may not feel themselves well represented . . ."

"Well," he said with a smile, "I intend to raise this matter in a rather persistent way. And," his smile widening, "since you had already persuaded me to join the Council, I just thought I'd see if I could get even."

So by midafternoon on Saturday, July 12, we had a twenty-five-member Council. But there were still a few stragglers we had to run to earth.

Talabani was leaving Moscow, on his way to London "for talks." I got a hold of Sawers and asked him to call the Foreign Office right away to ensure that Talabani was given no official meetings in London the next day, so that he would be free to return.

Even so, Talabani had no way to get back in time for the Council's unveiling the next morning. Pat Kennedy had to use his own credit card to buy Talabani a first-class air ticket to get him back from Europe by early Sunday morning.

Sergio de Mello was also out of the country, in Saudi Arabia. Sawers and I had been keeping him informed of the progress on the Council. We had persuaded Sergio to play master of ceremonies at the announcement of the Council. This would help with international opinion and lessen somewhat any accusation that it was the creature of the Coalition.

After the meeting with Bahr al-Uloum, I reached Sergio by phone in Saudi Arabia. He was pleased with the final list and said he would get a flight back Sunday morning, he hoped in time to make the announcement himself.

Then it fell to me to inform several candidates that they would not be on the Council. First was Archbishop Delly, leader of the Chaldean Christians. Iraq's small Christian community, like most sectarian splinters in the country, was fragmented. There were the Chaldeans, who appeared to outnumber the Assyrian Christians, but who were not as well organized and less active politically. In keeping with the objective of the smallest representative body possible, we had room on the Council for only one Christian.

We had chosen a representative of the Assyrian Christians and anticipated this would cause unhappiness with the Chaldeans. We were right, for that night the bishop's heart was not overflowing with Christian love. After grumbling about being left out, he departed in a huff.

Next was the pretender to the throne. Sharif Ali was very unhappy about being excluded from the Council. "You didn't even consult me about this Council," he complained.

Sawers patiently replied, "I have tried to see you for the past four weeks. But you were out of the country." Moreover, the pretender's colleagues had made clear that Sharif Ali was above serving on such a Council himself. And the rule was principals only.

I finally said, "Look, the Coalition takes no position one way or the other on the monarchy. That's a question for Iraqis to decide. This Council will go forward tomorrow. We hope and expect that responsible Iraqis will support it." On that note the frosty meeting ended.

Our political team reassembled late that night to review the plans for the next day. They told Sawers and me that the G-7 had caucused that afternoon and spent many fruitless hours trying to agree on who should be the spokesman for the Council the next day. I instructed our guys to stay out of this food fight. "Imagine what it will be like," I said, "when there are twenty-five of them in the room and they have to decide important matters."

Sunday, July 13, was a historic day for all Iraqis. But not without the last-minute hitches typical of the country.

Talabani arrived from London, tired but elated.

Chalabi pulled up at the Council building checkpoint with four assistants, despite the rule set by the security officials that each GC member could bring only two to the ceremony. No other GC member had tried to violate the rule. But Chalabi was threatening to go home if we did not let them all in.

I sent Scott Carpenter out to the sandbagged gate with a message. "The rule is two. Go home if you prefer." Chalabi dropped two assistants.

At midmorning, Sergio phoned from the airport to say he had landed late, but was on the way into town.

The choreography we had agreed upon with the U.K., UN, and GC members called for the twenty-five Council members to gather in a building not far from the palace, which Pat Kennedy had, by some miracle, restored to considerable elegance. The plan was for the group then to constitute themselves as the Governing Council. (This became known to us irreverently as the "immaculate conception" option.)

Then, the self-anointed Council would "summon" the UN, U.S., and U.K. for a private meeting at which they would inform us that they had formed the Governing Council. Following lunch, we would all repair to a large hall where they would present themselves to the world's press.

Sergio got to town about 12:30 P.M. and came straight to my office. He, Sawers, and I chatted until, about forty-five minutes later, we got the call that the GC was ready to receive us. Sawers and I rode to the Convention Center together so that Sergio could arrive separately.

Sayyid Bahr al-Uloum, our famously recalcitrant late entry, had been chosen by his fellow GC members spokesman for the day out of respect for his age. (Although Adnan Pachachi was older than Bahr al-Uloum, Pachachi was a Sunni.)

With the GC members seated around a large oval table covered in green baize, Bahr al-Uloum took note of the historic nature of the day. He informed us that the Council had already passed two resolutions. The first repealed all Baath Party holidays, including the upcoming July 17 anniversary of Saddam's revolution. And they had declared April 9, "Liberation Day," to be a national holiday.

Bahr al-Uloum asked if I would like to speak. I suggested he first give the floor to de Mello, who spoke briefly. Bahr al-Uloum then insisted I speak, so I agreed it was a historic day for Iraq and Iraqis.

"The Governing Council is the first step on a journey we'll travel together toward our mutual goal of a democratic and representative Iraqi government. The Council," I concluded, "will have real power and the Coalition stands ready to help in any way possible. Together we will succeed."

After a brief luncheon, we all traveled the two hundred yards to the Convention Center. De Mello, Sawers, and I were seated in the front row of the auditorium, facing the stage. After twenty minutes, the members of the Governing Council filed onto the stage and took their seats in a crescent of chairs. Behind them hung a simple map of Iraq and the words *Majlis al-Hukm,* Arabic for "Governing Council."

This little piece of stagecraft had cost my team hours the day before. Late Saturday afternoon, I'd learned that someone in the CPA planned to put a bunch of American, British, and Iraqi flags on stage. I vetoed all but a single Iraqi flag, both to downplay the Coalition's role and to keep the stage serene and dignified. The problem was there was no accepted version of the Iraqi flag. After the Gulf War, to curry favor with the Islamists Saddam had added to the old black, white, and red flag the words "God is Great" in his own calligraphy. The Council's dilemma was that they objected to using Saddam's flag, but the more devout members of the Council could not agree to remove the words from it. So in the end, there was no flag. Just a map of a unified Iraq.

At the press conference, Bahr al-Uloum read from the "political statement" that the GC had released that day. Noting that the Council had been "established through an Iraqi national initiative," the statement identified the Council's objectives as providing security for Iraqis, "eliminating the consequences of political tyranny . . . de-Baathification and uprooting of Baath ideology from Iraqi society."

The Council was dedicated, he announced, to "laying down the foundation for a pluralistic, federal, democratic system and respecting human rights." The diminutive mullah added that the Council represented all streams of Iraqi life and looked forward to the participation of all Iraqis in developing the political life of the country. The Council would begin the process of writing a constitution, leading to elections for a parliament.

Despite the Coalition's overall responsibility for Iraq, I had chosen not to make any remarks at this ceremony. I thought having the UN's special rep speak would help establish the legitimacy of the Governing Council. So, after Bahr al-Uloum finished, only de Mello spoke, and on behalf of the UN he welcomed the formation of the Governing Council.

Then came questions from the media, and the fun began.

First on his feet was a BBC reporter who facetiously asked, "Isn't it true that" the Council was just a creature of the Americans, had no powers, and was essentially useless?

Talabani grabbed the mike and chided the reporter for representing "our former colonial masters. BBC never tells the truth about Iraq," he continued. Warming to his subject, Talabani said, "The Council is the most representative government Iraq has ever had." He went on to enumerate some of its powers and suggested in no uncertain terms that the reporter didn't know what he was talking about.

Then a reporter from Al-Jazeera Television, always hostile to the Coalition, made a speech, thinly disguised as a question, along similar lines. This set off a chain reaction among Council members.

Pachachi with great dignity refuted the implication that the Council was a plaything and suggested that the Arab media would do well to pay attention to the real changes taking place in Iraq.

Not to be outdone, Naseer al-Chaderchi, the elderly lawyer from a highly regarded Sunni family who had stayed in Iraq throughout Saddam's tyranny, blasted Al-Jazeera. "I say this to the Arab media: stop advising the Iraqis to fight the Americans." There was loud applause from the audience, including, we noted, a number of Iraqi journalists.

This brought Bahr al-Uloum up out of his chair. "All Arab TV coverage of the war and Liberation had been one-sided, biased against the Iraqis," he practically shouted. "These media have been threatening us from the first day of the war until now!" As he took his seat, his passion provoked more applause. This inspired the elfish mullah to rise again.

"You people from Al-Jazeera and Al-Arabiya and others—you never covered the atrocities committed by Saddam! He killed hundreds of thousands of Iraqis! He gassed Iraqis! Why haven't you shown the mass graves to your audiences?" There was more applause as Bahr al-Uloum sat down once more.

But now, egged on by Talabani, who was seated beside him, up jumped Bahr al-Uloum again. He was unstoppable.

"The Arab press keeps talking about Saddam coming back. He is not coming back! He is in the dustbin of history! He will never return!" More applause and at last he sank back in triumph and satisfaction.

So it went for another forty-five minutes. Members of the GC parried each hostile question (and most were hostile) with skill and emotion. At the end of the session, a woman in the audience who said she represented some obscure nongovernmental organization rose and gave a long statement about American imperialism, America's genocidal war against the Iraqis, and so on . . .

Now it was the turn of one of the Council's three women, Dr. Raja Khuzai, a gentle, head-scarved ob-gyn from the southern Shia town of Diwaniya. She was normally bashful and unsure of herself. Not this day. Dr. Raja said:

"Over the past thirty-five years, I helped deliver babies for thousands of Iraqi women. Now, for the first time in Iraq's recent history, Iraqi women will have a place in society. I am honored to be playing a role in giving birth to a new Iraqi nation today."

It was a stunning performance.

As I said in a note I later sent President Bush:

"Sunday was more than the birth of a rudimentary representative government; the process brought forth strong expressions of Iraqi national pride."

Chapter 5
A DISTANT HOPE

■ BAGHDAD
JULY 14, 2003

General John Abizaid's image on the flat TV screen flickered and then disappeared. But the audio channel was unbroken.

"The Baathist insurgents are definitely stepping up their activity level, Mr. Secretary," John reported from CENTCOM headquarters in Tampa to Don Rumsfeld in the Pentagon.

I'd grown used to the unreliable technology of these secure video teleconferences (VTCs) we held most afternoons. Sitting before the screen in a cramped room on the second floor of the palace, I could see the participant speaking, while at the bottom of the image electronic windows revealed whoever else was on the loop. When the system worked, we had the illusion of meeting around a conference table.

But on this hot July afternoon, the VTC connecting Baghdad, Abizaid in Florida, and Rumsfeld was shaky.

"I just lost the video, John," I said. "Did you lose it, too?"

"Not again," Rumsfeld muttered.

The secretary was not known for his patience. And today a reliable picture would have been helpful because Abizaid was using charts and maps.

". . . and we can confirm that foreign jihadis are being trained in Syria and Lebanon," Abizaid added, concluding his opening presentation.

The picture flashed on, revealing the general's PowerPoint slide and map from CENTCOM headquarters. Since the collapse of Saddam in April, Iraq's long, porous border with Syria had offered the primary escape route for fleeing Baathists and Islamic extremist fighters' main infiltration vector into Iraq.

The jihadis' destination was what CENTCOM now called the "Sunni Triangle," the vast wedge of desert and Euphrates River valley west and north of

Baghdad. This was the sanctuary into which an unknown number of die-hard Baathists from two Republican Guard divisions—originally the target of the U.S. 4th Infantry Division, which the Turks had not allowed to enter Iraq from the north in March—had fled after Baghdad fell.

In cities like Fallujah and Ramadi, and in Baghdad itself, the Coalition was losing an increasing number of troops to roadside bombs, snipers, and RPG attacks. More than forty soldiers and Marines had been killed in action or accidentally died in Iraq since our troops had torn down Saddam's statue in Firdos Square in April. Some of these young men and women were from Reserve and National Guard units. Their deaths reverberated from Hometown, U.S.A., to Capitol Hill, to the Pentagon.

The United States had publicly leaned on Syria to suppress this activity. But Syria, ruled by its own Baathist Party, seemed immune to most diplomatic or economic leverage and might only be susceptible to direct military intervention. President Bashar Assad, son of Syria's late dictator Hafiz Assad, knew this was unlikely with U.S. forces engaged in Iraq and Afghanistan.

As Rumsfeld and Abizaid discussed options for "better control of the borders," I reflected on the mounting security crisis.

The Pentagon was hoping to replace the large combat formations that had crushed the Iraqi army with a combination of American and foreign "Coalition of the Willing" units. A Polish-led "division" was due to take over security in the Shia heartland between Baghdad and Basra from an American Marine division by September. Comprised of Poles, Ukrainians, and smaller units from Central America, it was actually a brigade-size force of fewer than 3,000 soldiers responsible for a division-size area of operations. But it was the largest such formation in the south other than the British contingent of about 11,000.

Now Abizaid stated that, even if the projected Polish-led Coalition troops did replace American combat units rotating out of Iraq, the total of 23,000 non-U.S. soldiers in the country would be "inadequate."

I shared John Abizaid's frustration. For weeks, I'd sensed that the Pentagon did not grasp the need to crush a mounting Baathist-jihadi insurgency, and to crush it early on. The sheer size and institutional inertia of the Pentagon were part of the problem. In mid-June, I'd participated from Baghdad in a secure VTC with the National Security Council, chaired by the president, in which we discussed security in Iraq.

"I'm concerned that we may be drawing down our forces here too soon," I'd said. "It's simply not enough to say that Army and Marine divisions will be replaced by forces from other countries."

I'd looked at the list of small units that had set up liaisons at CENTCOM's headquarters in Tampa and would send troops to Iraq. It was a hodgepodge, "penny packets," and they all came with their own Rules of Engagement as to how, where, and when they could fight. For example, the Lithuanians would contribute four doctors and a platoon, about thirty-five people, total.

"Filling in with foreign troops must not detract from our combat capability," I stressed. I noted that the war was not over yet. We risked giving the Iraqis the impression that we were not serious and if that happened, the security situation could deteriorate very rapidly.

I was trying to reach the president's ear, because I had the impression that the armed services, and possibly Rumsfeld himself, were in a hurry to get our troops home.

As always at NSC meetings, President Bush sat at the head of the table in the wood-paneled White House Situation Room.

"I agree with you, Jerry," he had said. "But I think you've misunderstood. The American forces being withdrawn will be replaced by other U.S. units."

From what I understood of the coming troop rotation, this was not the case, but I might have been wrong and in any event it was the job of the military to set the record straight. But Marine General Peter Pace, vice chairman of the Joint Chiefs of Staff, wound up confusing matters further by saying that when the 3rd Infantry Division (which had spearheaded the assault on Baghdad) rotated out in July, it would be replaced by the equally heavy 4th Infantry Division. But since the 4th ID was already deployed to Iraq, as I understood it our net combat strength was going to drop by about a division.

At the end of that meeting, the president added that he "agreed with Bremer" that other nations' forces would not be as aggressive as U.S. troops. Condi Rice tried to pin the military down on whether the British were in fact planning to withdraw their forces from southern Iraq in the fall. They danced around the issue. And then the discussion had faded off.

After that meeting, I had called Lieutenant General John Craddock, Rumsfeld's senior military aide, to make sure the secretary understood my concern about the troop drawdown.

Then I'd called Dr. Rice.

"In my view," I'd told her, "the Coalition's got about *half* the number of soldiers we need here and we run a real risk of having this thing go south on us." I had in mind the RAND study I'd seen before leaving for Iraq.

"Well I'm concerned, too," she said. "I've asked the chiefs to give me a detailed breakout of our troop strength that I can show the president."

Immediately after that call I'd asked Clay McManaway to meet with John Abizaid on his return to Qatar to thrash out the details of realistic troop levels.

We certainly didn't want to get crosswise with the military. But I was convinced that if we didn't maintain adequate American and Coalition military force—especially combat strength—in Iraq, we would encounter real problems rebuilding the country.

Another major concern was the lack of precise intelligence on the nature of the enemy. In early July, the CPA's new CIA station chief reported for duty. "Bill" was a lean, loose-limbed professional who had served years in the region and spoke Arabic. The Baghdad station was already the largest in the world, so this was a big job for him. As I saw it, part of the problem was that Washington had established the station's priorities as hunting for weapons of mass destruction and capturing the senior Baathist fugitives made notorious on CENTCOM's Most Wanted deck of cards.

Coalition forces had been searching Iraqi arms depots from late March, but so far had discovered no WMD. I knew Bill was being squeezed by CIA headquarters in Langley, Virginia. He oversaw the Iraq Survey Group, an intelligence organization under CIA official David Kay and Army Major General Keith Dayton, which had some 1,400 Coalition civilians and military personnel searching for WMD. This effort had to be a managerial strain on the Baghdad station.

"Okay, Bill," I'd said bluntly, "the hunt for WMD is important. And we sure as hell need to catch Saddam and his crowd. But we also need to go on the offensive against the guys who are blowing up Humvees and killing our soldiers—and the characters who are sabotaging power lines and oil pipelines."

"I'm just trying to spread the load among priorities," he sighed.

"Look," I said. "It's pretty unlikely that our troops will be killed by WMD. But every day they're being blown up by Baathist insurgents or terrorists. Finding and eliminating these guys has to be our No. 1 priority."

He didn't seem convinced. I reminded Bill that as the representative of the director of Central Intelligence, his responsibilities for intelligence in Iraq went beyond the CIA itself and its stake in finding WMD.

"I want you to call together all relevant intelligence assets here and within twenty-four hours give me a new plan to get after these bad guys."

While Bill's people were at work the next day, I announced a cash reward program for Saddam and his two sons, which Washington had already approved. The reward on Saddam's head was $25 million and safe conduct out of Iraq for the informant and his family, with $15 million each on his sons, Uday and Qusay.

• • •

Thursday, July 17, began with one of those airless Baghdad midsummer mornings when sunrise threatens to transform the city into a smoggy oven. Clay and I now shared an air-conditioned trailer, so—when we had electricity—the nights weren't too bad. But today I was tired. So was everybody else.

Given the eight-hour time difference with Washington, I'd often be called to the second-floor communications room after midnight. I'd pass offices full of people who had been at their desks since dawn.

Although the Coalition Provisional Authority had grown to almost 3,000 employees from twenty-five nations, we were stretched thin. For weeks we had no phones. And the ornate palace rooms were unnumbered. So convening a meeting involved sending a messenger out to alert people, hoping that they would be found in time. I told Francie that it reminded me of the way African tribal chiefs used to convoke their palavers by sending out runners clutching cleft sticks.

Most of us at the palace were working these crushing hours, seven days a week. The urgency was always present, underscored by the sapping heat, the frequent cuts of power and running water, and the rattle of firefights and explosions. The intensity was such that many experienced a sort of time warp. I was often surprised to learn that a meeting I thought had occurred several weeks ago had taken place only three days before. But we'd laugh off these lapses as "Baghdad time." We finally agreed that there would be only three days in the CPA week: yesterday, today, and tomorrow.

Often, we'd long for a simple comfort, a glass full of ice cubes, a dependable shower . . . a surface free of dust, Baghdad's omnipresent element. Dust was everywhere and in everything; and everything had a faintly dirty tinge. Even the palm fronds and eucalyptus leaves were tan with dust. However, when we saw our troops in full combat gear on a stifling Baghdad day, we had no complaints. How those brave young men and women withstood that heat was a wonder to us all. For them, a few minutes in the shade and a gulp of warm water was the only comfort they had for hours on end.

Strong espresso coffee provided my principal succor. After serving abroad for years, I'd become accustomed to drinking what I called "real coffee"—good Italian espresso. I had an espresso machine at home in Washington, and soon after arriving in Baghdad, I ordered two machines through the military postal system (the APO). My son and daughter had standing orders to keep the packages of coffee coming through the APO pipeline, but given the vagaries of the system, I never knew when it would arrive. If we ran out, it was a cause of serious concern. But it kept us all going eighteen to twenty hours a day and provided a good reason for CPA employees to "drop by" my office.

This Thursday morning at 7:30 the temperature in my office was already over 100 degrees when I met with Dave Oliver, our chief financial adviser. The subject was just as uncomfortable as the heat.

Like all the CPA staff, Dave Oliver worked virtually nonstop because he understood better than most the serious financial problems we faced. He was grateful for the morning espresso.

"Boss, we're going broke," he said after walking me through printouts and graphs he'd brought.

Dave was a dark-haired retired admiral in his late fifties with a sailor's weatherbeaten face. He had commanded nuclear submarines, and served as a high-ranking Pentagon technology and acquisitions official in the George H. W. Bush and Clinton administrations. He excelled at squeezing every dinar and penny out of our limited funds. If he said we were in financial trouble, I could bet on it.

"When?"

"Hard to say. Could be November, December. Anyway, not later than the first quarter of 2004. Depends on how quickly we can ramp up oil exports."

The prospect of any country going broke is unpleasant. But if we could not pay our monthly bills, including the salaries of millions of government workers and pensioners, it would have disastrous consequences in Iraq.

"Well, how's next year's budget look?" I asked, almost fearing the answer.

Ten days earlier, I'd asked the CPA's advisers to work with their Iraqi counterparts on estimating the country's revenues and expenditures for 2004, and to try to nail down just how big that year's budget deficit would be. The news was not good.

The ongoing sabotage of oil pipelines and the resulting sharp decline in anticipated oil-export earnings was a major problem. Iraq exported crude oil from the northern fields on a pipeline running through Turkey to the Mediterranean and from the southern fields along shorter pipelines to tanker terminals in the northern Gulf. In all, Iraq had over four thousand miles of pipeline, and protecting them from saboteurs was almost impossible. Moreover Phil Carroll, our oil adviser, confirmed that the entire oil infrastructure—wellheads, pipelines, pumping stations, and refineries—was as decrepit as the Daura plant I'd visited.

"We've got a one billion dollar shortfall this year," Dave said, tapping the chart on the marble table. "And the projected shortfall for next year is over one and a half billion."

"Just means we've got to accelerate getting contract guards on the ground,"

I said. "When the new Iraqi security forces come along, sabotage should drop off."

"Yeah," Dave quietly noted, "but even then we've got a helluva big job putting the oil industry right. We don't have firm estimates because the surveys haven't been completed, but Phil Carroll's team estimates we'll need about two billion dollars a year between 2004 and 2007."

Sabotage wasn't the only problem in the crucial oil sector. Under the command of Lieutenant General Sanchez's Combined Joint Task Force 7 (CJTF-7), the Army Corps of Engineers had been doing a great job rehabilitating oil facilities. But in mid-June, some bureaucrat in the Pentagon suddenly decided to transfer responsibility for the engineers' activities from the CJTF-7 to the CPA, cutting their funding to zero in the process. CPA certainly didn't have the money to support their work. So overnight we ended up with a couple of thousand Army engineers—equipped with the assorted mobile cranes, ditch-digging machines, and metalworking tools needed to increase oil production— sitting in their hot tents playing video games.

I raised hell with the Pentagon. Deputy Defense Secretary Paul Wolfowitz directed acting Army Secretary Les Brownlee to restore the funding and so we eventually received a budget for the engineers. But it was an early-warning sign of how Washington could complicate the reconstruction job.

I raised another issue with Oliver.

"Dave," I told him, "everywhere I go, Iraqis are telling me that money simply isn't getting to them. Not to other ministries after we've made allocations, not to the provinces, not to anyone. What the hell is going on?"

"There are several reasons," David explained. "First, this Iraqi bureaucracy is incapable of moving quickly. Saddam's brutality taught them that they should never ever make a mistake. Could be fatal—literally. So nobody'll make a move without the approval of dozens of other bureaucrats."

Moreover, since the Finance Ministry had controlled only 8 percent of the national budget, that key ministry was simply being overwhelmed as we tried to run the entire national budget through the organization.

"What we've got is the equivalent of fiscal constipation. They'll adapt," David thought, "but it'll take some time."

Like everything else in Iraq, I thought.

We now had a good estimate of the damage that fuel smuggling did to Iraq's economy. Saddam had encouraged smuggling to get around sanctions and illegally earn export revenue for the regime. Meanwhile, criminal gangs along the

Shatt al-Arab waterway in the south and at the northern refinery near the Kirkuk oil fields had diverted diesel fuel, kerosene, and gasoline from these refineries to their own fleets of tanker trucks—with the compliance of Saddam's police. The smugglers could sell the contraband fuel in neighboring countries at forty times the subsidized prices charged in Iraq. This kind of profit had attracted many of the tens of thousands of criminals Saddam had released from prison just before the war.

Diesel smuggling in the south was an elaborate affair. It was moved in tanker trucks to barges at clandestine docks, and transshipped to small tankers that took the fuel down the Gulf to ports like Abu Dhabi where profits were immense.

Since the fall of Saddam, the smuggling had grown exponentially due to lack of adequate guard forces at the refineries and lack of control of Iraq's borders. The illegal trade had three major negative impacts. First, Iraq's Oil Ministry was losing profits it should have been earning from the fuel. Moreover, the smuggling, which drained away the last stockpiled fuels, provoked shortages nationwide, which in the case of gasoline led to the long, angry, and politically volatile gas lines we'd seen in the major cities. Lack of diesel compounded the power problems, since stand-alone electrical generators needed diesel fuel.

Dave Oliver had done some calculations. "We're going to have to spend something like $250 million a month buying these fuels from Kuwait and Turkey."

Three billion dollars a year! Where in the hell are we going to get that, I wondered.

To compound the problem, all of Iraq's refineries had been out of service from March until midsummer. Under Saddam the refineries had used the summer months to build stockpiles of fuel oils to meet the increased demand of the colder autumn and winter months. But we were not building the inventories we'd need in the coming winter.

General Sanchez and I discussed this emerging crisis, and his officers came up with a plan of action called Operation Power Crude. It was designed to cope with two aspects of the smuggling. First, Coalition forces would intercept and confiscate the smugglers' tanker trucks, drive them to wherever diesel fuel shortages were the worst, and turn the trucks over to the Oil Ministry. I also asked General Abizaid to have CENTCOM's naval component start intercepting the smugglers' tankers. Eventually, if we could confiscate enough ships, the smuggling operation would become unprofitable.

A second objective of the operation was to deal with clandestine copper smelters belonging to the gangs that had been ripping down electric power lines since late March. When they tore down high-tension cables to harvest the copper, it not only exacerbated the country's electrical power shortages, but also caused some of the southern oil fields near Basra to shut down, costing Iraq 500,000 barrels of production or $10 million a day. The British forces who controlled the sector correctly complained they were too thin on the ground to patrol every mile of the grid. Iraq had almost twelve thousand miles of power lines.

I recognized that while these problems were not unsolvable, they seriously exacerbated the Coalition's challenge in Iraq. Every adult Iraqi had indeed been shocked and awed by the speed and precision with which the Coalition had crushed Saddam Hussein's vaunted Republican Guard and overthrown the Baathist regime. After such a display of superpower might, many expected us to work similar miracles once the tanks stopped rolling. If we could destroy individual artillery pieces at the height of a blinding sandstorm, why couldn't we provide reliable electric power or a steady supply of gasoline? And of course as each day passed with the heavily armed Coalition unable to correct seemingly basic economic problems, the resolve and confidence of Iraqi insurgents and foreign terrorists increased.

Reality on the ground made a fantasy of the rosy prewar scenario under which Iraq would be paying for its own reconstruction through oil exports within weeks or months of liberation. We were clearly involved in a long-term project of nation-building here, like it or not.

This gap between reality and expectations worsened the increasingly negative press coverage of post-Liberation Iraq. Although few Western journalists reported any bad news during the war, few now showed much interest in reporting the positive side of Coalition operations.

My senior press counselor, Dan Senor, was increasingly frustrated by this problem. One stifling afternoon in July he came to my office to discuss the situation.

"We've got to change our approach. Right now the press won't cover any 'good news' story," he said.

Dan was an energetic colleague with a unique combination of business and government experience. A graduate of Harvard Business School, he had spent some years in the private sector before deploying to Qatar to help with the press during the war. He came to Baghdad with ORHA in April and was one of the most talented communications experts I'd seen in forty years.

Dan was certainly on the money about press coverage.

We completed thousands of individual reconstruction projects all over the country, some big, like rebuilding the roads and bridges, or clearing the Gulf port, but most small, such as renovating a school or building an orphanage. But these projects too had a high impact.

Over the summer I had visited many reconstruction projects, but they got little press coverage. These stories apparently weren't as attractive to editors and producers as looting, power outages, gasoline lines—and eventually the mounting violence.

The result was that while Coalition troops and civilians worked hard under difficult circumstances and accomplished a great deal in many parts of Iraq, few outside the country learned of their work.

"The coverage portrays our troops as victims, rather than heroes," Dan complained, holding up several TV news transcripts. "There's no sense back home of the incredible work they're doing." He added that the big challenge was getting the press to the stories. One reporter had just made a rare visit to a town hall meeting in Tikrit. He'd told Dan, "If they can do democracy in Saddam's hometown, they can do it anywhere." "And somehow, Ambassador," Dan said, "we've got to find a way to transport the media out of Baghdad."

"I'll talk to the military about getting Black Hawks to send reporters around the country," I said.

We did get the choppers to carry the news media. But, sadly, the focus of their coverage remained death and mayhem, while they largely ignored progress on reconstruction and building the foundations of democracy.

Dave Oliver's grim budget prognosis at least gave me some solid figures as I prepared to return to Washington for consultations. There, I would have to lay the groundwork for what undoubtedly would be a massive supplemental appropriation to cover unanticipated expenses of reconstructing a very sick economy. And almost every day the advisers brought in more bad news. Whatever the bottom line, I needed to start softening up the White House, the administration's Office of Management and Budget (OMB), and Congress to the fact that we were going to need a lot more money out here before things got better.

I knew that the job of persuasion wasn't going to be easy. Since arriving in Iraq, I'd often run afoul of the bureaucrats in Washington who controlled our purse strings. It was a sad reality that, while the president had ordered me to act with decisive speed, I was often hamstrung by organizations like the OMB and the State Department's Agency for International Development (USAID).

In a more normal situation, OMB had an important role in assessing and approving the details of how appropriated funds were spent. That process always took time. But the situation in Iraq in 2003 was anything but normal. We didn't have a lot of time to kick-start this economy. At the meeting with the president in Qatar in early June, I'd taken his chief of staff Andy Card aside and asked for some relief from the usual bureaucratic cobwebs. He'd promised to help. But the small-change struggle with OMB bureaucrats was incessant and demanded constant attention.

During my first weeks in Iraq, I'd written Don Rumsfeld that we simply could not tolerate the foot-dragging approach we were getting from the Washington bureaucracy. Rumsfeld had asked John Hamre, a former deputy defense secretary under President Clinton, to come out with a team in early July to see what the Coalition was up against. In his private report to Rumsfeld, Hamre outlined the challenges the CPA was facing, stating that "the CPA is confronting a much more difficult problem than a traditional post-conflict reconstruction challenge. Iraq is also a completely failed economy. The CPA is confronting the equivalent of both a defeated Germany in 1945 and a failed Soviet Union in 1989."

The former Clinton administration official noted that despite these conditions, "the CPA is making astounding progress, but it lacks the forces, the money, and the flexibility to do the job." He emphasized that "CPA is badly handicapped by a 'business as usual' approach to the mechanics of government." He said that the rudimentary budget system CPA has put in place "is an incredible accomplishment this early in such a complex environment." But, Hamre told Rumsfeld, "I was astounded to hear the constraints your lower level folks live with to get money and contracts. It is taking up to ten days for OMB to approve fund requests after you [Rumsfeld] approve them. They are asking for a level of detail which, frankly, I think is indefensible." He strongly urged Rumsfeld to "take this opportunity to get OMB off your back now . . . to give the CPA Administrator all the flexibility he needs."

To which I could only say, "Amen."

On July 7, I sent Rumsfeld a memo confirming that OMB's procedures were "making efforts to speed up the rehabilitation of the Iraqi economy more difficult and time-consuming." I also reminded him that Washington was being extremely slow in assigning personnel needed by CPA: of 250 people I had requested weeks before, not a single one had yet arrived in Baghdad. Washington red tape would slow reconstruction funds and personnel for almost a year.

It was one thing to recognize our challenges. It was another to figure out what to do about them. Within weeks of arriving in Iraq, it was obvious that we needed a comprehensive plan of action, especially since Washington's prewar plans had been overtaken. I also realized that a coherent, detailed plan would give direction to the thousands of people working in the CPA who otherwise were being pulled in too many directions by too many urgent problems. Without a clear sense of priorities, we risked unproductive wheel spinning.

I wanted to lay out for my colleagues and to those in Washington a clear vision of what the Coalition needed to accomplish, with tools to measure how well we were meeting our goals.

So I asked Pat Kennedy and Clay McManaway to oversee the production of a strategic plan with clear mission objectives, metrics, and timetables. Senior USAID officer Dayton Maxwell formed a team in our new Office of Policy Planning to create a practical plan of action, one that would lay out specific goals for the myriad problems the Iraqi people and we faced.

"I'm interested in results," I'd told Dayton, "not theory or endless debate. I already get too much of that from the Iraqi politicians."

This was the genesis of our Strategic Plan, an ambitious vision of Iraq's future and the specific steps needed to transform the shattered country into a prosperous, equitable, peaceful, and civil society. The planning proved to be a huge, complex undertaking, which our team had to execute both quickly and expertly.

By early July, Dayton's office had produced a draft plan called "A Vision to Empower Iraqis." I forwarded it to Secretary Rumsfeld on July 4 as the first step to getting buy-in from the Washington bureaucracy, the White House, and Congress later that month.

We summarized the ultimate goal that we envisioned for Iraq as "a durable peace for a unified and stable, democratic Iraq," with a vibrant economy and a representative government which underpinned and protected freedoms.

"A helluva high bar," Clay noted.

"Better to aim too high than too low," I said, aware that we were setting difficult goals for both the Coalition and the Iraqis. But I also recognized the need to provide a positive vision, to Iraqis, to the CPA staff, and to the world. The alternative, surrendering to pessimism, would result in paralysis.

The plan identified security as our top priority. Iraq belonged to the Iraqis, and the sooner they had the ability to defend themselves, the better. So we needed to train a professional police force as quickly as possible and rapidly move ahead on recruiting and training a New Iraqi Army.

We also recognized that we had to show improvement in the everyday lives of Iraqis. So we set out a series of objectives in "Essential Services" to be accomplished in the next ninety days. By October 1, we planned to restore power generation to prewar levels. We would refurbish a thousand schools and reopen the country's 240 hospitals. We would distribute schoolbooks purged of Saddamist ideology.

We recognized that a full transition to a market economy was beyond the scope of the Coalition mission. Four decades of economic devastation were not going to be fixed in what was certain to be a short occupation. But we could get started and set Iraq on the path for sustainable growth while creating momentum toward a market economy. One goal was to have oil production back to prewar levels by October 1. The Coalition would issue a new currency to replace the devalued Saddam dinar. We would set up an independent Central Bank for the first time in Iraq. We would seek to liberalize Iraq's commercial and investment laws.

Finally, we would prepare the ground for representative government. This was a complex challenge and would take time because Iraqis had little experience in self-rule and the institutions that supported it. So we would have to instill an understanding of democratic principles, although no one thought that would be easy. We could, and would, put the Iraqis to work writing a constitution.

I worked with the planning team and the military to create specific goals to be reached in 90, 120, and 360 days based on our strategic objectives. It would be important to have visible progress on the ground when the White House went to Congress for the supplemental appropriation, and when Secretary Powell and I attended a conference the UN had called for October to solicit international donations to Iraq's reconstruction.

As Dave Oliver had made clear, oil revenues were not going to cover Iraq's governmental expenses. He predicted we would go broke early in 2004. Unfortunately, every item on our key priorities list, from police training to rebuilding schools, cost money.

Throughout the process of developing our plan and the request for supplemental funding, we needed to stay connected to the work of the World Bank. The bank had already sent fifteen "assessment teams" to Iraq, each charged with estimating how much money Iraq would need to rebuild its power, agricultural, or manufacturing sectors—and a dozen other segments of the battered economy. In late July, I discussed the process on the phone with Jim Wolfensohn, president of the World Bank.

"Jim, I know the bank usually allows six months for an assessment," I said. "But we've just got to get these done faster so we can use your expertise to pull together our supplemental proposal."

"Understand. When do you need them?"

"Well, in six weeks—instead of six months. Everything out here happens on 'Iraqi time,' Jim."

With a chuckle, Wolfensohn replied, "I'll do the best I can."

He did, too. Somehow the bank's teams telescoped a week's work into a day—no small achievement in the Iraqi summer. The bank eventually concluded that Iraq needed $55–75 billion for reconstruction.

After the call to Jim, as Baghdad's heat rose with the rumble of afternoon traffic along Abu Nawas Street across the river, I felt that we were finally making progress. A helicopter thumped by, flying low above the rooftops to avoid ground fire, right here in the city center. The threat of surface-to-air missile attacks had forced me to delay reopening Baghdad International Airport to commercial air service. Now, the landing C-130s spiraled sharply down to "spoof" potential heat-seeking missiles.

We're in a race, I realized. Economic recovery and reconstruction, as well as the creation of representative government, were intertwined with security. A solitary saboteur blowing a hole in an oil pipeline with a leftover grenade could stop fuel production, which would paralyze trucks in several provinces, cause a halt to school and clinic rebuilding, and a massive outflow of scarce dollars to buy fuel from Kuwait or Turkey. Deteriorating security, from roadside bombs to sniper attacks, was also making it more difficult and expensive to hire foreign contractors.

As the summer dragged on, I came to realize that some folks in Washington underestimated the complexity of the challenge and thought we could solve all our problems by simply transferring authority immediately to the Iraqi Governing Council, as if that group could somehow overcome the interconnected security-economic-political problems when we in the CPA could not.

That kind of wishful thinking did not augur well.

The wood-paneled White House Situation Room was even cooler than the Pentagon offices where I'd spent the long previous day conferring with Don Rumsfeld and his staff. It was Tuesday, July 22, and I was at an NSC deputy-level meeting chaired by the council's point man on Iraq, Rice's deputy, Steve Hadley. Paul Wolfowitz represented Defense, while Deputy Secretary Rich Armitage held State's chair and Marine General Pete Pace filled in for General Myers. We were hashing out details for the next day's NSC meeting, which the president would chair. The CPA's Strategic Plan and the tactics to present the supplemental request were the top items on the agenda.

Hadley, whom I'd known for twenty years, is a precise, lawyerly, and well-respected government official. He ran efficient, productive meetings. And he seemed satisfied with the degree of detail that the Strategic Plan offered. Plenty enough "for both sound bites and op-eds," he joked.

"I think we're going to have problems with the Democrats," I noted. "This morning I was on the Hill briefing a crowd of congressmen on our plan and Representative Nancy Pelosi lashed out, claiming, 'If we'd had a plan, our soldiers wouldn't be dying out there.' " She was House minority leader and a veteran California politician. I said that another congressman, Florida Republican Porter Goss, had dismissed this assertion by noting that I had come to the Hill to discuss the very Strategic Plan she claimed did not exist. And, Goss had added, soldiers would continue to die as long as we had an army deployed in Iraq.

Moving Iraq toward self-sufficient sovereignty was one of the plan's main goals. Armitage felt confident that State could continue twisting arms and leaning on both the UN and Iraq's less friendly neighbors—"extending demarches," in diplomatic parlance—which would help on both the political and diplomatic fronts.

We were about to discuss the nuances involved with winning support for a supplemental appropriation when Brian McCormack, my special assistant, quietly entered the SitRoom by a side door and slipped me a note.

"General Sanchez confirms numbers two and three are dead," I read.

Saddam's two sons, Uday and his younger brother Qusay, the overlord of Iraqi intelligence services, were dead. Great work by our military and the reward program had borne fruit.

The deaths of Qusay and Uday would ease some of the lingering fear that gripped so many Iraqis. Saddam's sons were monsters. A satyr, Uday had enjoyed raiding wedding parties and having his henchmen drag off the bride for him to rape. We had information that the Hussein sons were helping organize some of the anti-Coalition resistance.

The normally staid Situation Room reverberated with cheers when I announced the news.

I'd had a firsthand confirmation of Uday's sadism. One of my earliest projects in Iraq was to start rebuilding Iraq's sports infrastructure, which had been totally politicized by Uday. Our objective was to get Iraq readmitted to the Olympic movement in time for the Athens Olympics in a year. To spearhead this effort, I had enlisted Ahmed Radhi, Iraq's most famous soccer player. One day, when I had gone to the old Olympic stadium to join Radhi in passing out the first of sixty thousand soccer balls to Iraqi youngsters, Radhi had told me how Uday had regularly tortured members of the national soccer team when they "disgraced" Iraq by losing a match, once making Radhi kick a concrete ball for fifteen straight hours.

Now I hurried back to the Pentagon to hear the story of their deaths. Troops from the 101st Airborne and some Special Operations forces had been led by an informant to a large but ordinary-looking villa in Mosul where the Hussein sons were in hiding. When the troops surrounded the house and demanded their surrender, they refused and instead opened up with automatic fire and grenades, wounding several American soldiers. The American troopers responded with well-aimed TOW missiles and heavy machine-gun fire that blew the villa apart. The brothers' bodies were now at a facility at Baghdad Airport undergoing autopsies.

When General Sanchez announced the sons' deaths, and released videotape of the incident, the 24/7 news channels went into hyperdrive. Clay called late that night to tell me that when the Coalition's TV station announced the brothers' deaths, celebratory gunfire had broken out in all of Iraq's major cities.

"It's a good paper, Bremer!" President Bush said, closing the summary of our Strategic Plan. He sat at the head of the Situation Room table at the National Security Council meeting the next day. "Your folks are sure thorough."

I nodded my appreciation, but I didn't reply because I saw he had more on his mind. He tapped the plan with a pen. "Okay, what I want to know is how much more money we're likely to need."

Vice President Cheney, Don Rumsfeld, Colin Powell, Condi Rice, and Andy Card were watching me from around the table. In April, Congress had appropriated about $2.5 billion to help Iraq recover, but that would be spent by mid-August. An administration request for a supplemental appropriation, always politically sensitive, was looming. That much was certain. The tactics of how and when to make that request had not yet been determined. The biggest unknown was how much we'd need.

"Mr. President," I began, "on the basis of the very preliminary analysis from my Baghdad team, we're looking at a minimum of $5 billion." But I added that the final figure would depend on our further analysis and that of the World Bank teams.

Bush rocked back in his chair. The number didn't seem to faze him. His only reaction was, "Surprised it's so low." I remembered the president's assurance in May that his administration would do what was necessary and stay as long as needed to help create and sustain a free Iraq. Now, too, he assured me that we'd get what we needed to complete the job.

"Mr. President, we've also got to do something about debt relief for Iraq. Treasury estimates that they've got about $120 billion outstanding—six times GDP. We simply can't saddle the new Iraqi government with Saddam's massive debts. It'd be repeating the mistake the war reparations dumped on Germany at Versailles." Ten days before, I had recommended to Rice that the president consider appointing former secretary of state Jim Baker to undertake an international political effort to get Iraq relief from this debt burden.

The final item on the NSC agenda was whether the White House and the State Department should press the UN for another Security Council resolution, this one calling on member countries to contribute combat units to the Coalition forces in Iraq.

"I don't think it's necessary," Powell said. "It's clear from Resolution 1483 that UN members can send forces." He paused a moment to think the matter through. "On the other hand, a new resolution might help get the Indians and a few others on board. The question is, what price would we have to pay for a new resolution. The Russians will try to play a game by getting guarantees on their outstanding debts and the oil contracts they had with Saddam. The French will be a pain in the neck as usual. But I think we can manage both of them, and a clean resolution might be possible. We could have our ambassadors sound out their counterparts in New York and key capitals."

"Do it, Colin," President Bush said.

That afternoon, the Pentagon's legislative office hand-delivered copies of the fifty-seven-page Strategic Plan to all 535 members of Congress. Although every senator and representative received one, by the next year many of the president's foes in Congress were arguing that the Bush administration "never" had a plan for the occupation of Iraq.

"This *is* delicious, Dr. Jaafari," I said, dipping a sliver of tender chicken and flat bread into the sauce in my bowl.

It was August 1, and I was paying a call on Ibrahim al-Jaafari at his Baghdad home, which doubled as the capital's Islamic Dawa Party office. He had just assumed the first rotating presidency of the Governing Council.

Knowing my interest in cuisine, Jaafari had been promising me for weeks to offer me a refined Karbala specialty, *fesinjan*, a Persian delicacy in which chicken was braised for hours in a mixture of pomegranates, walnut powder, lemon juice, and sugar. The dish before us was a tangible example of the centuries-old link between Mesopotamia and Persia. Undoubtedly, Persian Shia pilgrims had carried this and other equally delicate recipes to Karbala and Najaf.

Once the plates were cleared and tea served, several Dawa Party officials joined us. Then Jaafari launched into one of his free-form, hand-waving, rapid-fire discourses on how the Governing Council should conduct its work.

"Above all," he said, rocking enthusiastically in his chair, "we must help Iraq's disadvantaged . . . the hungry poor, the families of the martyrs . . ."

These were the tens of thousands of men, mainly Shia, who'd died in Saddam's eight-year war with Iran.

"Saddam destroyed so many families who left behind countless orphans. Ambassador, helping them is our highest priority."

Jaafari came at the issue in two roles, as a physician and as a Shiite leader. Iraqi Shiites had long tried to shield themselves from persecution by avoiding politics and extending a cloak of charity to the faithful. But in the case of the Dawa Party, Saddam's persecutions had produced a horrific number of victims, so it was natural that Jaafari wanted to devote precious resources to these supporters.

"I fully understand, Doctor," I said, gently trying to guide him toward practical solutions. "But we must define the problem more precisely and propose concrete solutions."

"There is so much to do for so many," he said, his voice rising in emotion.

This was not an encouraging performance. We needed practical steps, not unbound emotion.

"Who specifically do you want to help?" I asked. "What system would you use for screening applicants? Who would perform that duty? How much do you anticipate paying these people and for how long?"

Jaafari and his colleagues looked uncomfortable. They had no answers.

"Dr. Jaafari," I said. "Why doesn't the Governing Council appoint someone to work with the Coalition's experts? Once they have defined the scope of the need, they can estimate the cost and then make proposals to the entire Council to decide which programs take priority. We simply don't have enough money for everything. Based on what we know, we will probably run out by early next year. So there are trade-offs. Do you establish generous pensions for a hundred thousand war widows, or do you repair the power grid?"

Jaafari and his men looked troubled. Governing a country was a complex business. *Cold shower time isn't far off for these guys*, I thought. *What would have happened if the U.S. government had turned over Iraq to the exiles in May, as some in Washington had wanted.*

Before leaving, I asked Jaafari for a minute alone with him to raise "a sensitive matter." Jaafari's associates left us alone in the dining room. I explained that we'd learned that Muqtada al-Sadr, a rabble-rousing Shiite cleric from Najaf, had recently published in a newspaper, known as his mouthpiece, a vitriolic attack on Iraqis cooperating with the Coalition and had listed 124 people by name, calling them traitors and stating that "hitting these people is a patriotic and religious duty."

Muqtada al-Sadr was a surviving son of Grand Ayatollah Muhammad Sadiq al-Sadr, Iraq's leading Shiite cleric whom Saddam's agents killed in 1999.

Muqtada was in his twenties or early thirties—an important theological point because Shiite clerical leaders advance along a hierarchy largely defined by age and time spent in devout study. For several weeks, we had become increasingly concerned about the young firebrand's activities. Two weeks earlier he had announced plans to form an "Islamic Army" independent of the government. Now he was threatening to kill Iraqis.

"I'm puzzled by this," Jaafari began.

I handed him a copy of the paper. "Since this was published," I said, "one Iraqi on the list has already been shot dead."

Muqtada al-Sadr was also a suspect in the early-April assassination in Najaf of the Shiite Grand Ayatollah Abd al-Majid al-Khoei, who had just returned from exile to assume the city's spiritual leadership.

"Muqtada is a growing danger," I warned Jaafari, who by now had called in several colleagues to confer on the matter.

In an attempt to change the subject, one of his aides, Ali Adnan, cut in. "Well, Ambassador, if the Coalition improved the economy, Muqtada would have less support."

"Please don't lecture me about the importance of improving the economy. I've got thousands of volunteers working night and day to fix the economy, not to counter Muqtada, but because it's the right thing to do for Iraq."

The discussion degenerated into a waving of hands, which I halted by speaking directly to Jaafari. "Doctor, you are both a senior Shiite leader and currently the president of the Governing Council. The Shia leadership has got to exercise some control over Muqtada soon . . . before things get out of hand."

He nodded, but said nothing.

Driving back to CPA headquarters, I decided to send Hume Horan to Najaf to give the same message to other ayatollahs down there. And I would raise the issue with Sayyid Bahr al-Uloum the next day. *Muqtada al-Sadr has the potential of ripping this country apart*, I thought. *We can't let that happen.*

By early August, I was increasingly frustrated by the inertia that had gripped the Governing Council. So, on Monday the 4th (which I learned from some sadistic staff member was the fifty-eighth straight day with the temperature over 100 degrees by 9:00 A.M.), I met with them to go over details of the 2003 budget.

Before we could address the budget projections, one Council member, Dr. Mowaffak al-Rubaie, an urbane, British-trained Shiite neurologist, asked a mischievous question.

"Ambassador Bremer," he said, "Baghdad is abuzz with a press story that you are planning to marry several Iraqi women."

I'd heard rumors about these articles from my staff but had thought they were pulling my leg.

"So, Ambassador Bremer," Rubaie said with a grin, "the Council would like to know if this is true."

I returned his smile. "No, it's not," I answered, "because I currently have the maximum number of wives allowed by my religion."

But the levity didn't last. When we completed the budget review, I got down to my main business.

Before the GC had been formed, I had asked my staff to come up with a long list of "early wins" for the Council. These were decisions they could announce quickly to show the Iraqi people that the GC was indeed assuming responsibility. For example, I had suggested that they publicly "demand" the Coalition to restore electricity generation to prewar levels by October 1 and also find urgent ways to deal with unemployment. Since we had these plans already in hand, this would be a win-win operation, in which the GC would get the public credit when it made the demand of the CPA and when we responded. In my first meeting, I had made clear that we wanted the Council to succeed in a manner the public would understand. But the Governing Council had not acted.

This day I reminded them that the Council had not reacted to a memo I'd sent them weeks before requesting that they help us institute a broad program to ease the reintegration of former army officers into Iraqi society. Here too our proposal had been met with silence.

The Council continued to be too disorganized to meet even these safe-bet requests of the CPA.

It was, I told Francie in an e-mail, like playing "tee-ball with players who couldn't hit the ball teed up for them."

The Governing Council's effectiveness was hampered, from the first day to the last, by lax work habits. They established a pattern of meeting Monday through Thursday, usually just in the mornings, but even then not starting until after 10:00 A.M. After treating themselves to a lavish luncheon, members would drift off to other activities or a long siesta in the baking afternoon.

"Look," I said, "you can't very well hope to run a country of 25 million people without working hard. The Governing Council works fewer hours in a week than the CPA works every day."

The members seated around the broad table stared at me in astonishment. Some turned to Ibrahim al-Jaafari. He appeared flummoxed.

The rotating presidency also hindered the GC's effectiveness. It had seemed a necessary compromise when the Council was formed in July. Members found that they could not agree on any one leader and instead, through a tortuous line of reasoning—emblematic of the sectarian divides within the body, and Iraq itself—wound up selecting a nine-man rotating presidency.

Originally, they had decided on a five-man executive, made up of three Shia, a Sunni, and a Kurd. This would allow the Shias to retain a majority, which was their central concern, while giving the Sunnis and Kurds equal representation. However, the two Kurdish leaders, Barzani and Talabani, had been unable to agree which of them should take the Kurdish seat. So they demanded they each be seated in the Council's presidency. This immediately provoked a demand by the Sunni Arabs for a second seat to equalize their weight with the Kurds. At this point, the Shia insisted they have a majority on the presidency as they did on the Governing Council. That meant that the number of Shia had to go to four, which would have resulted in an eight-man presidency. But how would ties be broken? Another Shia was added and the Council presidency wound up with an unworkable nine members—the "P-9," the latest addition to Baghdad's alphabet soup.

The one issue on which the GC did work quickly was paying itself. A subcommittee chaired by Chalabi had come up with an outrageous budget for the Council. Chalabi's proposal was that members be paid $50,000 a year, when ministers received about $4,000. They were to have a gasoline allowance, which David Oliver wryly noted would allow each member to drive fifty thousand miles a month in a country with poor roads!

This day I told the Council that the budget they proposed for the twenty-five-member GC was more than that of the Education Ministry, which had more than 325,000 employees. Chalabi protested that after all this was just a "draft" budget.

I got back to my office just as Condi Rice called with bad news from the United Nations Security Council. The Spanish UNSC president had tried but failed to obtain a statement welcoming the Iraqi Governing Council, even though it was the very "Iraqi Interim Administration" the latest Security Council resolution had itself sought.

"Our pals the Germans," Rice explained, "with the help of the French and the Russians, killed the welcoming statement."

"Well, I guess that means State's not likely to have much luck convincing the Europeans to help out on a new UN resolution calling for international troops to come here."

" 'Fraid not, Jerry."

We then turned to the vital issue of the supplemental appropriation. From the work our budget people had done, and what we had learned from the World Bank's teams, it was already clear to me that we were going to need many times the $5 billion I had mentioned to the president and that the administration couldn't follow the usual schedule for requesting money. Normally such a request would be submitted to Congress in January, so funds for projects wouldn't be available until late spring. We had to get reconstruction going before then. And without more money, Iraq would be broke by February at the latest.

"I need your help persuading the White House and OMB to separate our budget request from the rest of the government's."

"It's gonna be tough," Rice said. Moreover, she reminded me that Congress planned to adjourn the first week of November.

I was looking at my calendar. "Well, we've got this UN donors' clambake in late October. It'd sure be great to have a supplemental in hand by then to show other countries that the U.S. is pulling its end of the rope."

"I'll do what I can from here, Jerry," she said, chuckling now. "But since you have so little on your plate in Baghdad, we're going to need a lot more details from the CPA on this in the next few weeks."

By the next week we had forwarded our supplemental request to Rumsfeld. David Oliver's staff, working day and night and coordinating with the World Bank teams, had concluded that we needed to ask for $20 billion. In my cover memo I told Rumsfeld, "We have to bridge the gap between a dysfunctional economy and one where the private sector provides self-sustaining growth. Our task is to show the Iraqi people that political freedom also means a better life. Time is a wasting asset here. We need a 'whatever-it-takes' attitude."

I made sure to copy Condi Rice so she could run interference at the White House.

But those bureaucratic spiderwebs continued to tangle our work.

While I had been able to scramble around and call on former colleagues to be my immediate staff, filling out the rest of the CPA workforce was an unending problem. The good news was that thousands of Americans from all walks of life volunteered to serve in Iraq. The problem was that the process of bringing them onto the government payroll was very slow. As a result, we were unable to fill our provincial offices until the fall. And for the first critical months of the CPA's efforts, most of them came on very short tours of duty—sixty days, for example, for the head of the FBI unit. It would be months before people began to flow more smoothly, and only at the very end of the occupation that State Department assignments lengthened to a year. This made for thousands of disconnected assignments with a dearth of institutional memory.

•   •   •

On the afternoon of Thursday, August 7, I was about to leave CPA headquarters with several Senior Advisers to confer with officials at the Finance Ministry when Bernie Kerik, my senior police adviser, popped into the office. He was wearing a Kevlar vest, and had his helmet tucked under his right arm. Not a good sign.

"There's just been a big car bomb at the Jordanian Embassy in the Al-Andalus district," he said. "I'm on my way."

"Be careful," I said.

He shrugged. Bernie was a beefy, streetwise former cop who'd handled New York City's police response to the 9/11 attacks.

When I returned from the ministry several hours later, he was back with details on the bombing. "It looks like a professional job," he told a group in my office including Clay, Pat Kennedy, the station chief "Bill," and Tom Fuentes, the head of our FBI unit.

Two men had parked a nondescript car on the quiet street near the embassy and walked away. Several minutes later, the car exploded in a powerful blast that killed four Iraqi policemen guarding the entrance and seven people on the street. The explosion knocked down part of the outer wall, but caused little damage to the main embassy building.

"Our first car bomb," I told Bernie. "Do we have international terrorists to contend with now?"

"It's possible," he conceded. "But why'd they hit Jordan?"

"Everyone knows they helped us during the war," Clay, just back from another trip to Jordan to discuss police training there, replied. "And it's probably known in every souk that the Jordanians might give some other assistance."

That night, Bill came back to drink an espresso and go over the day's events.

"I agree with Bernie," Bill said. "That bomb was a professional job. But maybe it wasn't *international* terrorists . . ."

"The Mukhabarat?" Could the former intelligence service have been responsible?

"Let's review the bidding," he said.

About a week earlier, at my morning intelligence briefing, Bill and an astute Arabic-speaking Army captain named Julia Nesheiwat had shown me a water-spotted Mukhabarat document in Arabic—replete with stamps and signatures—and a verbatim English translation.

"It's dated 23 January 2003, Mr. Ambassador," Julia had explained. "One of our teams found it in a ransacked Iraqi intelligence office."

"Both the MI analysts, and the station people consider it authentic, sir," Bill had added, referring to Military Intelligence. "It's their equivalent of Top Secret/Sensitive."

The document was addressed, "To All Offices and Sections." To cover "an emergency" (the Coalition invasion of Iraq), the Mukhabarat listed orders for a point-by-point strategy to be implemented after the probable collapse of the regime. Beginning with the order, "Burn this office."

I read the translation. It did indeed call for a strategy of organized resistance, which included the classic pattern of forming cells and training combatants in insurgency. "Operatives" were to engage in "sabotage and looting." Random sniper attacks and ambushes were to be organized.

The order continued, ". . . scatter agents to every town. Destroy electric power stations and water conduits. Infiltrate the mosques, the Shiite holy places . . ." The document also ordered Mukhabarat agents to arm themselves and conduct assassinations.

"Could Mukhabarat operatives pull off a bombing like the Jordanian Embassy?" I asked Bill.

"Yeah, they probably could," he said. "They had a department, M-16 it was called, with lots of explosives experts. We know from our intelligence that these guys worked closely with department M-14. They were the Mukhabarat's Special Operations guys—professional killers to a man."

He explained that the CIA's analysts were pretty sure that these departments were capable of producing the type of explosives used for improvised explosive devices (IEDs) and vehicle-borne IEDs: roadside bombs made from surplus munitions and car bombs.

So the car bomb at the Jordanian Embassy could well announce the opening of the Mukhabarat's resistance campaign.

"Any idea who might run their operations?" I asked him now.

"Well," he said, "the director of Mukhabarat's M-14 Special Ops branch was a guy named Al-Halbusi al-Dulaymi."

"Is he still on the loose?"

"As far as we know."

Tired as I was, I didn't fall asleep easily that night. There was a significant firefight up the river. But it wasn't the pounding of the weapons or the coffee I'd drunk that kept me awake.

The Arabic words "To All Offices and Sections" floated in my mind. Saddam's security apparatus had contained a lot of offices and sections.

The next night I sat down with Kerik and his team to review where we stood on the crucial problem of police training.

From my first day in the country, when I'd seen looters roaming freely through the streets of Baghdad and suggested they should be shot, I had considered training professional, well-equipped Iraqi police to be our top priority. In the long run, Iraq's security, like that of any country, would depend on a professional police force, which could stop street crime, smuggling, and help channel potentially explosive unrest into peaceful protests. Having more dependable Iraqi police would also free Coalition combat troops to fight insurgents. But achieving this complex goal would not be easy, cheap, or quick.

After the large-unit ground combat phase of the war, the State Department had allocated $25 million to assess the Iraqi criminal justice system. Contractors from DynCorp had begun arriving to conduct the assessment by late May. After Kerik arrived, he had presented his plan for the Iraqi police service. The first step was calling back to duty Iraqi police who had served under Saddam. Kerik began a shoestring program to retrain these men in the basics of modern policing and respect for citizens' rights. It was a start, and by mid-July more than 15,000 had returned to duty.

I had allocated another $120 million from Iraqi government funds to begin training and equipping the new Iraqi police force. But this was obviously just an initial down payment in what would prove to be a very expensive program. This night the tough former New York police commissioner gave a no-nonsense briefing, which summarized the problems and solutions that we'd worked on since early July.

"Here's the deal, boss," he said. "For adequate security, a country needs a policeman for every 300 to 350 inhabitants. So Iraq needs something like 65,000 to 75,000 of 'em. And today we've got, at best, about 32,000." And he said these were of very poor quality, former police who'd answered the Coalition's call to return to duty in late June. "Some of these guys may be okay. But they don't have any real training, lack equipment, and sure as hell are not attuned to modern police techniques."

Now we would have to sign up and train raw recruits. "But if we have to train another 40,000 officers from the cadet level to the street," he said, "and do it here in Iraq, it'll take almost six years."

"That's impossible." I shook my head. "Why should it take that long?"

"Because there's simply no place left standing anywhere in the country where we can conduct the training. The facilities were all destroyed."

The looting again . . .

"Can we do it in two years?" I asked.

Kerik's team had identified a disused, Warsaw Pact air base at Taszar in Hungary that had adequate barracks, mess halls, classrooms, and firing ranges.

"We could train 16,000 policemen a year up there," Bernie said. "But there's no precedent for such a huge program. When I was responsible for police in New York, I ran the world's largest training program. But that was *only* 6,000 a year. You're looking at almost three times that many. And it'll also cost you about $750 million the first year."

I must have shown my shock because Kerik quickly explained. "The major cost is for international police trainers. Then we've gotta figure out where to get 'em."

I told him to pursue urgent negotiations on the Hungarian base and asked Dave Oliver to squeeze another $18 million from our strained budget to start refurbishing the facility. I also asked the State Department to sound out the Organization for Security and Cooperation in Europe to learn what trainers they might provide and at what cost.

In the meantime, Kerik's people on the ground in Iraq would continue training on a shoestring. It was obvious that we were going to need a sizable chunk of money for police training and equipment, which would have to come from the supplemental budget—and we had no guarantee of training enough police to meet the mounting challenges to authority.

While we struggled to prod the Governing Council into action and as we dealt with the huge challenge of building a national police force, I had to confront the growing challenge to the Coalition from the radical young Shiite cleric Muqtada al-Sadr.

I'd received increasingly disturbing reports about Muqtada from our able regional coordinator for the Center South, Mike Gfoeller. Based in Al-Hillah, Mike was fluent in Arabic and had also spent years as an American diplomat in the Soviet Union. He described Muqtada as a "Bolshevik Islamist" who understood only one thing, raw power, and who would stop at nothing to get it.

Mike's analysis was that while Muqtada currently lacked broad popular support, this was irrelevant. He relied on a small, fanatically loyal gang of armed followers, totaling no more than two hundred men. But he was using them to gain control of mosques in the south, which also gave him control of their monetary collections. The only way to deal with him was to put him behind bars as soon as possible.

Then our Justice Ministry Senior Adviser, Judge Don Campbell, told me that an Iraqi judge, Raad Juhi, had found convincing evidence of Muqtada's direct involvement in the April murder of respected Ayatollah Abd al-Majid al-Khoei. The magistrate had issued a warrant for the arrest of Muqtada and a dozen of his cronies. Campbell added that Marine lawyers in the holy city of Najaf, within the Marines' area of operations, had seen the evidence of Muqtada's involvement. I asked the Marines to bring that evidence to Baghdad so that I could review the matter.

But the Marines would not authorize their lawyers to come. So on August 4, I constituted a "Special Investigative Unit," comprised of two top attorneys from the CPA general counsel's office, one American, one Australian, and directed them to go to Najaf immediately to meet the Iraqi magistrate. If they found the case against Muqtada solid, they were authorized to ask the Iraqi police to execute the arrest warrants.

That afternoon, I briefed both General Sanchez and Secretary Rumsfeld on developments. They seemed to understand and agree that some action was necessary.

The next day the temperature in Baghdad was 131. And the Muqtada case was heating up, too. Magistrate Juhi told our team that he had two eyewitnesses prepared to testify that they heard Muqtada give the order to kill al-Khoei. But before asking the Iraqi police to make the arrest, the magistrate wanted to conduct an autopsy on the body and for that he would first have to obtain Grand Ayatollah Sistani's permission to exhume al-Khoei, who was buried at the Shrine of Ali, Shia Islam's holiest site. Juhi said that he expected this process to take several days.

This suited us because General Sanchez said he needed three or four days to make plans and position troops to backstop the Iraqi police if they ran into trouble during the arrest. We also wanted to avoid doing the operation on a Friday when Najaf was always full of worshippers. So we penciled in Saturday, August 9, for the arrest.

I informed a small team from our governance section about the plan and tasked them to come up with an information program to support the operation. We would need to communicate with Shiite leaders and with the broader public. I asked Hume Horan to prepare our coordination with the religious authorities in Najaf.

Then the exhumation was delayed for technical reasons, which put the planned arrest off a week to August 16. We used the time to come up with a detailed list of reconstruction projects we could put into effect quickly in Najaf and in the Shiite neighborhoods of Baghdad following the arrest.

But by now the U.S. military was beginning to get nervous about the operation. None of the officers with whom I discussed the matter would say so directly, but I got the definite impression they were concerned that the arrest might lead to unrest in the south and in the Shia sectors of Baghdad. This anxiety was compounded when there were serious riots in the southern Shiite city of

Basra on August 11 and 12. The British forces there had been caught by surprise by the unrest and seemed at a loss to explain it. And there was evidence that Muqtada had a hand in these disturbances.

Up to this point, both Abizaid and Sanchez said they were prepared "to fully support" the Iraqi police operation to arrest Muqtada. But then it became clear that the Marines were against the operation. In the second week of August, Clay came to my office with Judge Campbell.

"The wheels are starting to come off the operation," Clay reported. "The Marines are actively campaigning in Najaf and within the Coalition military command to prevent Muqtada's arrest." They were pressuring the Iraqi magistrate to forgo the arrest.

That afternoon I discovered that the Marines were also lobbying at the Pentagon against the arrest. The only explanation I could come up with was that the 1st Marine Expeditionary Force was due to rotate out of Iraq in three weeks — to be replaced by the Polish-led force — and didn't want any trouble before that.

"It's understandable," I told Clay. "No Marine wants to be the last man killed in Iraq. But Muqtada poses a *direct* challenge to stability."

The next day, the CIA headquarters in Langley, Virginia, sent the president what I considered to be a near-hysterical assessment about the "risks of action" against Muqtada. The Agency view was that we should ignore him and that his support, already weak, would gradually fade away. And when I asked Ambassador David Richmond, who had replaced John Sawers as the CPA's senior British official, for his government's position, he could only look at his shoes.

Solving the problem of Muqtada's nascent rebellion was temporarily suspended.

After a mid-August meeting of the Governing Council, Judge Dara Nor al-Din, a large-handed, heavy-set Kurd who was both a member of the GC and one of the country's most respected jurists, buttonholed me on behalf of a former colleague. The man was a seventy-six-year-old Sunni judge who'd been picked up by Coalition forces in July in Baghdad, then transferred to a holding facility at the stifling Gulf port of Umm Qasr, where daytime temperatures often reached 140 with high humidity.

"He's a good man, even though he was a judge in the court," Nor al-Din told me. "I give you my word that he won't be a problem. But he will not survive long down there."

"I'll do what I can," I told him.

The case of this judge put in stark relief the growing problem of the many

Iraqi civilian detainees the Coalition held in custody. Our overstretched military was having real problems identifying and tracking them. And we were detaining people in conditions that I had told Judge Campbell "are at the very margin of acceptable."

In early July, I had asked Campbell to come up with a plan to keep better track of detainees so that we could answer questions from family members about where someone was being held. And if a detainee was considered to be a criminal, we needed to provide him access to a lawyer and have him brought to trial in an Iraqi court as soon as possible.

Campbell and his colleagues in the military were working to establish a nationwide computerized tracking system to find out how many people were being held and where. With that information in hand, we could provide a system to answer relatives' questions. It was an exceedingly complicated problem. For example, there were many alternative ways to transliterate common Iraqi names into the Roman alphabet ("Mohammed," "Muhammad," etc.). And there was no uniform process for data entry at the point where the detainee was captured.

Colin Powell raised his concerns in e-mails in mid-August. He told me that some foreign governments had complained that Coalition forces and Iraqi police were indiscriminately arresting innocent suspects, holding them incommunicado, and depriving them of legal representation.

Ghastly green night-vision images of GIs leading off handcuffed and hooded prisoners while their wives and children wailed were flashing across the Arab world, CNN, and BBC International. "We're getting killed in the media," Powell wrote.

He was right. I told him of our efforts and noted that I was not happy about the slow progress. In the manhunt for important Baathists, during the arrest sweeps that had finally stopped the looting, and on hundreds of sweeps for insurgents and foreign jihadists, our forces had taken thousands of suspects into custody. I hated this necessity and knew the bad impression it conveyed both in Iraq and abroad. But I hated even more hearing that another young American had been killed by a sniper or had her truck blown apart by a roadside bomb. Some detainees could provide useful intelligence about the hard fighting that still lay ahead and perhaps save American lives.

At the same time, I didn't want our policy on holding detainees to erode the goodwill the Coalition had acquired by overthrowing Saddam. I hoped that the eventual sorting-out process, once we had enough Arabic speakers and Iraqi interpreters, would proceed quickly, so that detainees guilty of minor infractions, and those who were obviously innocent, could be released. But when I asked about the elderly Sunni judge's status, no one seemed to know anything about him. It took the military three weeks to locate the man and another ten days before I finally got him freed. I was furious.

I had a private talk with General Sanchez about the detainee problem and he promised to do what he could.

The next morning, Pat Kennedy gave me his analysis. "Look, it's not just Rick Sanchez," he said. "Nobody wants to take responsibility for releasing detainees for fear one of them will have been involved in atrocities, WMD, or is some really bad Baathist type. If a detainee were released and then found to have killed an American, the repercussions from the Pentagon would be terrible. Folks won't earn their next star, if you get my drift."

Indeed I did, and since I wasn't looking for a promotion, I thought I had a solution. A couple of hours later, after Sanchez and I briefed yet another congressional delegation, I pulled him aside again.

"Is there any way for me to assume the responsibility for the release of some of the detainees?" I asked. "We're already holding 4,000 of them. Many are probably of no interest to us. I'm fully prepared to take the heat if it helps."

Rick had that look of patient exhaustion I saw so often in our senior military commanders who faced endless days of hard decisions, and rarely enjoyed more than an hour or two of uninterrupted sleep.

"We're working the problem, sir," he said.

But I never got an answer to my offer.

The other problem we had with detainees was that we had no decent facilities to hold them other than our military facilities. Soon after arriving, Judge Campbell had scoured the country for acceptable Iraqi prisons and had come up dry. In early June he had recommended that I authorize the reopening of Saddam's notorious prison at Abu Ghraib, twenty miles west of Baghdad.

"Don," I'd told him, "I'm very reluctant to do that because the place has terrible connotations for all Iraqis and for the world at large."

I knew that few Iraqis would see even a remodeled Abu Ghraib as a positive step. Under Saddam, the prison had been controlled by his secret police, the Amn al-Amm. In 1984 alone, during the first bloody years of the Iran-Iraq War, Saddam's executioners had murdered at least 4,000 prisoners at Abu Ghraib. Over the years, thousands of Iraqis had been tortured there in the most barbaric, mutilating manner before being hung, strangled, or shot. With this history in mind, I had also transferred responsibility for Iraqi prisons from the Interior Ministry to the Justice Ministry. As far as I was concerned, the only benefit Abu Ghraib offered was its thick walls and space to house several thousand prisoners.

So I had sent Don and his team out on a second search.

Several weeks later, at a late night meeting in my office, Don reported, "Mr. Ambassador, we've been all over this entire country. There simply is no maximum security facility in the country other than Abu Ghraib."

"What about the smaller prisons and jails?" I asked. "God knows Saddam had lots of those."

"Yes, he certainly did," Don confirmed. "But they were all trashed after Liberation. There simply is nothing else out there."

With great reluctance, therefore, I had agreed to let the military refurbish the notorious Abu Ghraib to hold detainees. But on two conditions. They had to bring it up to international penal standards, and we would set aside the execution rooms as a museum to be run by an Iraqi NGO to remind people of Saddam's brutality.

Abu Ghraib Prison was renovated. Hundreds of detainees were moved into reasonably cool cell blocks. They had running water, overhead fans, and slept eight to a cell on clean steel-frame bunks, in a space where Saddam's guards used to jam more than fifty squalid, unwashed men, so tightly packed no one could sit. But many hundreds of others were still housed in tents while the renovation proceeded.

In late July, I'd taken Sergio de Mello to see one of the first refurbished wings at the prison. He seemed impressed that we'd set aside rooms for family visits and consultation with lawyers for detainees facing criminal charges.

As we drove away, I looked back at the high sand-colored concrete walls and shuddered. One of the old wings we'd visited held a multiple-execution room, a ramp leading to a platform with hooks in the ceiling to hold a row of nooses. It was this torture chamber which would be preserved as a museum to educate future generations of Iraqis.

Meanwhile, the problem of Muqtada al-Sadr was hanging fire. In the face of the Marines' growing nervousness, I decided to send Mike Dittoe, a trusted lawyer in the CPA's general counsel's office, to Najaf to see the Iraqi magistrate and find out his real intentions. If he was ready to enforce the law, we would back him up. I felt strongly that the longer we waited to move on Muqtada, the more difficult it would become. My senior staff was in unanimous agreement with this assessment; indeed they were dismayed with the delays and what they might portend.

On August 14, I traveled to the south, visiting the cities of Diwaniya and Amara. In both places, I found that Muqtada's supporters were agitating against the established authorities. They had sought to oust the governor in Diwaniya for cooperating with the Coalition. At a town hall meeting I attended in Amara, one of Muqtada's agents stood to deliver a bitter denunciation of the Coalition and to call for the immediate withdrawal of its forces.

The day I was in the south, an American helicopter accidentally knocked over a religious banner in Sadr City—Baghdad's sprawling Shiite slum named for Muqtada's martyred father—which set off riots and attacks on American troops there. We soon had intelligence that someone in the crowd had called Muqtada in Najaf and asked if he and his colleagues should fire on the Americans. Muqtada had replied, "Yes. It is your duty."

Now it was the turn of the British to get cold feet on the Muqtada operation. The evening I returned from the south, David Richmond told me that the Basra riots had "unsettled nerves" in London. They doubted we should allow the Iraqi police arrest to go forward.

"Now everyone has their ass covered in this operation except me—the U.S. military, the CIA, the British military and now Her Majesty's government," I said, adding that from what I had seen that day in Diwaniya and Amara, time was not on our side in confronting Muqtada.

At the end of this very long and frustrating day, I sent a memo to Rumsfeld acknowledging the risks of moving against Muqtada, but arguing that we could not very well stop the Iraqi magistrate "from enforcing Iraqi law." I said the issue went to the heart of our goal of establishing the rule of law in Iraq. We had to stop Muqtada before he gathered more strength.

On Friday, August 15, I e-mailed Francie that everybody in Washington was "now thoroughly spooked, first by the spooks themselves, who sent a totally irresponsible memo to the president yesterday, and now by the Brits, who have gone weak in the knees . . ."

Our military, too, was going wobbly. Sanchez's command had developed a good operational plan to support Muqtada's arrest by the Iraqi police. But the Marines' campaign was beginning to tell. Abizaid called me from Doha late that night to express concern. But he said he would support whatever I decided to do.

Meanwhile, Magistrate Juhi explained that he needed another three or four days before making the arrest. This slipped the operation to Monday, August 18, at the earliest. And word of the possible arrest was beginning to seep out, so we thought it wise to talk to the GC's president, Jaafari.

On August 17, David Richmond and I went to see Jaafari to alert him to the imminence of the arrest. He appeared to be well informed about the case against Muqtada. He was firmly in favor of the operation. "Arresting Muqtada is a fundamental question of justice," he said, relieved to hear that the plan was for the Iraqi police—not the Coalition military—to execute the arrest warrant against Muqtada. He added that in the New Iraq "no man should be above the law."

Then out of the blue, late on the 18th, we got word that Rumsfeld had given instructions not to execute the plan to arrest Muqtada until "further notice."

Under Secretary Doug Feith told Clay McManaway, "We just want to be sure you have thought this operation through."

Clay went through the roof, given the time and thought we had spent on the arrest, and the importance we attached to the operation.

Feith said we should expect a series of questions about the operation within a few hours. When the questions finally arrived after midnight, they repeated the same points we had already answered many times. The first question set the tone: "Who will arrest Sadr?" It was exasperating since we had repeatedly told Washington that the action was to be taken by Iraqi police in response to an arrest warrant issued by an Iraqi court. But now it was too late, because events in the next twenty-four hours postponed an inevitable confrontation with Muqtada, unfortunately not for the last time.

The CPA's television "studio" was a makeshift affair. In June I had begun a weekly TV broadcast to the Iraqi people as a way of spelling out our vision for the nation and informing them of our actions. When I taped the addresses, I stood in the corner of a large room with green walls across the rotunda from my office. The minicam and tripod looked like toys. My press counselor, Dan Senor, stood beside the camera holding up improvised cue cards printed in block letters with a felt pen on copy paper. As I finished reading each sheet, Dan dropped it, to flutter down, sometimes toward my feet—a distraction that often made me look shifty on the screen.

But I'd rehearsed my talk on Friday, August 15. The summer heat was un-remitting, sabotage of the electrical grid and the oil infrastructure continued, street crime was up, and violence between Coalition troops and combatants, whom we now recognized as organized insurgents, was slowly mounting. Yet I had decided to deliver an optimistic message to Iraq for everybody's sake.

I knew that the Iraqi people were impatient, just as Americans were, to fix all the problems inherited from Saddam, and to improve security, the economy, and the political situation as quickly as possible. But, as I had predicted to the president in May, there would be no quick fixes. I needed to convey this to the Iraqis while also encouraging patience and hope, something most of them had never had.

In a phone call in late July, Francie had given me an inspiration. She had met with her prayer group the day before and had mentioned that the verse

Jeremiah 29:11 came to the minds of several of the women while they prayed for the Iraqi people.

I looked up the citation and liked it, but I was uneasy about using a biblical verse. So I checked with my resident Arabist-Muslim expert, Hume Horan, who was also an elder of the Presbyterian Church. He said that since Jeremiah is accepted as a prophet by Muslims, it would be appropriate to use the verse. And Jeremiah said what I wanted to say much more beautifully, and more profoundly than anything I could devise. I gave the verse to my skilled speechwriter Don Hamilton, a retired diplomat from the U.S. Information Agency. And a few days later, I made it the centerpiece of my address to the Iraqi people.

The hot minicam lights snapped on, and I began to read:

Allah Bil Khair.

I am Paul Bremer, administrator of the Coalition Provisional Authority. The Prophet Jeremiah told us: "For surely I know the plans I have for you, says the Lord, plans for your welfare and not for harm, to give you a future of hope."

The present difficulties of the Iraqi people are manifest. The problems are there for all to see.

But things will not remain as they are.

- There is, before all Iraqis, a future of hope.
- You will live in dignity.
- You will live in peace.
- You will live in prosperity.
- You will live in the quiet enjoyment of family, of friends, and of a decent income honestly earned.
- You will live in an Iraq governed by and for the people of Iraq.

These things will come to pass.

Your future is full of hope and dignity. Dignity is hard to maintain when foreign troops, no matter how well intentioned, walk your streets. In the months ahead you will see fewer troops on your streets as Coalition soldiers are replaced by trained, effective Iraqi police. In time, the foreign soldiers will be replaced by a New Iraqi Army dedicated not to a single man, not to a single party, but to a constitution approved by you.

Your future is full of hope and peace. Peace is hard to imagine when a quarter century of continuous conflict has seared the memory of all Iraqis. But freedom from a tyrant bent on foreign adventure will bring peace, peace with your neighbors and peace with the world.

Your future is full of hope and prosperity. Prosperity is hard to imagine when you are beset by continuing shortages. But repair and expansion of the infrastructure, coupled with your own intelligence, your own energy, and your own perseverance will realize that prosperity.

Your future is full of hope and honest, productive employment. Quiet enjoyment of family, of friends, and of a decent income honestly earned are hard to imagine when jobs are few and so much time is spent seeking a way to pay for life's necessities. But Coalition programs now in place will increase employment. Money is beginning to move from Baghdad to all governates [provinces]. We are taking urgent steps to encourage the creation and expansion of productive business, which will generate even more jobs. To cite but one example, one Coalition program to clear irrigation canals has created over 100,000 jobs in the past five weeks.

Your future is full of hope and of government by and for the Iraqi people. An Iraq governed by and for the people of Iraq is hard to imagine when most Iraqis were born during Saddam's dictatorship. While Saddam and the Baathists were certainly Iraqis, they never governed on behalf of the Iraqi people. Right now the Preparatory Committee appointed by the Governing Council is seeking your views about the means by which your new constitution will be written. I do not know the final form of that constitution. It will be written by Iraqis. It will arise from the collective desires of the Iraqi people and intended for the benefit of the Iraqi people. And once written by the people, the constitution will be submitted to you, the Iraqi people, for your approval.

This better future for all Iraqis will come. Today there is much hard work for all of us. The sabotage Friday of the Kirkuk export pipeline is a strike against the economic well-being of the Iraqi people. The criminals who did this do not share our vision of the new prosperous Iraq. But this problem will be overcome as we work together to build a better Iraq.

I understand that many of you are frustrated and angry. The people of the United States or the United Kingdom or Poland or any of the other Coalition countries would be frustrated and angry in the same circumstances.

You will not live like this forever. Together the Iraqi people will recreate a magnificent country—one that all of you will be proud to bequeath to your children and grandchildren.

Tuesday, August 19, started as a normal day in Baghdad.

After the usual morning staff meetings, and several press interviews, the UN official charged with overseeing the Oil for Food (OFF) program, a

Cypriot Armenian named Benon Sevan, came in for a meeting. A middle-aged career UN employee based in New York, he wore rimless glasses and had a smooth Levantine manner. He was on a short visit to Baghdad. (Sevan reported to the UN Secretariat and later became a subject of the OFF fraud investigation.)

His office was causing problems for the Iraqi government. For weeks the CPA staff had been working with the Iraqi ministries to prioritize the many thousands of contracts signed by Saddam's regime under the OFF program. Those contracts that the ministries judged to be valid, the CPA had forwarded to Sevan's New York office, which was to authorize the contracts so that the goods and services could be delivered in Iraq.

By August 19, the Iraqi ministries had validated more than 2,500 contracts worth billions of dollars for badly needed goods and services. But the UN had authorized exactly one contract to be implemented and paid. "We simply can't wait for the UN to grind slowly through its normal bureaucratic process," I told Sevan. "We need to get these projects moving and fast. The Iraqi people expect nothing less."

We had another problem. In addition to the OFF contracts that had not been acted upon, Sevan's office was sitting on $277 million in escrowed OFF funds set aside for the UN to cover administrative costs until the OFF program came to an end in November. Iraq had the right to any of these funds that the UN did not use.

"It's *their* money," I reminded Sevan. "Not the UN's."

"I'll look into the contract approvals, and I'll get you as much of the $277 million as possible as soon as I can," Sevan promised before leaving.

I made a note to ask our ambassador to the UN, John Negroponte, to have his staff follow up. The UN was holding billions of dollars which belonged to the Iraqi people and I intended to get it for them.

Half an hour later, in the middle of a meeting with a congressional delegation led by Senator John McCain, Pat Kennedy passed me a note saying there had been a large explosion at the UN compound in eastern Baghdad. I immediately sent Pat to the site with instructions to offer all possible help to the UN.

Pat called in from the site a half an hour later. "The UN compound has been virtually destroyed. The scene is horrible. They've got nothing—no office space, no place to sleep or work."

"Tell them that we'll make available housing, medical care, and food in our compound for however long they need it." I told Scotty Norwood to have 250 cots moved into a large ceremonial hall in the palace for the UN and to mobilize our Health Ministry officials.

Sending word to the Governing Council that I planned to visit the bomb site at once, I suggested that they designate a delegation to accompany me. Then I placed a call to UN Secretary-General Kofi Annan. The State Department told me he was on vacation in Norway and I asked that they track him down ASAP. As I was preparing to leave, Scotty Norwood came back with word that the president, in Crawford, Texas, was planning to call me for an update about the bombing, which by now was leading the world news.

When neither call had come through fifteen minutes later, I left the palace with Ambassador David Richmond and swung by the Governing Council's building to pick up the three members chosen by the Council—Dr. Naseer Chaderchi, Sheik Abdul Karim al-Muhammadawi, and Ambassador Akila al-Hashimi.

As we drove in silence toward the UN compound, the State Department operations center called through on my cell phone with Kofi Annan in Norway. I voiced my own and the Coalition's deepest sympathy and outrage at the attack. I added that I had sent my chief of staff to the scene and we had offered beds, food, and all other necessary support to the UN employees. "We're ready to help in any way possible." Annan expressed his deep appreciation.

Five minutes later, the White House Situation Room put President Bush through to me.

"Mr. President," I said, "I can't give you an update yet because we're still en route to the site with members of the Governing Council."

"Tell them I admire their courage and emphasize that the United States will not be deterred from carrying on in Iraq," President Bush said. "And I hope that the UN will stay the course."

One side of what had been the UN's sprawling, three-story headquarters was now a jagged mound of smoking rubble. Hundreds of American and Iraqi Civil Defense soldiers were scrambling over the ruins, looking and listening for survivors.

Pat Kennedy, in dusty shirtsleeves, tense, hot, and bedraggled, met our car and took me aside.

"Truck bomb," he said, "a monster. They're still counting the dead. I've heard that Sergio survived the attack but is trapped in the debris."

Our troops were trying to free him and other UN employees. The explosion had been detonated just below de Mello's office, collapsing the entire corner of the building. Little was left of the truck but a rear axle at the bottom of a deep crater. The FBI office head, Tom Fuentes, came over to tell me that they had found a human hand near the crater, which led him to believe that this had been a suicide attack.

UN officials Benan Sevan, whom I had just met with, and Ramiro da Silva had sustained cuts and bruises and were in a daze. They, too, had heard that Sergio was trapped under the collapsing roof, but had survived to talk to rescuers. General Sanchez arrived to set up a command post.

Fifteen minutes later, Sanchez called me out of the crowd and took me over to a young American combat engineer, a "sapper," covered with dirt. The man's face was contorted by emotion.

"Sir," the young soldier said, "Mr. de Mello was trapped upside down in a very tight space under huge pieces of concrete. He couldn't move but was still conscious and could speak a little when we first found him."

The image was terrible.

"We worked real hard to get him out, Mr. Ambassador," he continued. "We just couldn't do it, sir. The slabs were too big."

Sergio must have realized he was doomed, because the soldier said his last words were, "Don't let them pull the UN out!"

I thanked the soldier for his brave efforts, patted him on the shoulder, and turned away in my own private grief. I felt sick. Sergio had been a good man and a good friend. He had proven to be a strong supporter of the Coalition's work here. His loss was certain to have a negative impact on the UN mission in Iraq. But I could tell no one at the site that Sergio was dead because there were reporters all over the place and the UN needed to notify his family first.

At the request of the White House, I did several stand-up television interviews at the bomb site during which I forced myself to say, "We don't know yet if Sergio de Mello has survived."

These were the most difficult interviews I've ever given, knowing that my friend lay dead, not thirty feet away, crushed under tons of concrete. My mind went to Francie and our children as I thought of how devastating the news was going to be for Sergio's family.

After I got back to my office, I had another talk with the president. I filled him in on the scene and Sergio's death. He asked me to reassure the Iraqis that we would not be driven out of Iraq by the terrorists. But he also wanted me to press the Governing Council to "get a move on" and start making tough decisions.

The next morning at CPA I called in all the senior intelligence and security advisers.

I reminded the group that we had talked about our intelligence problems many times and that in response to my demand for better coordination, they had recommended a "fusion cell" that would bring all of our government's intelligence resources against the terrorists together in one place.

"I want it done now, with no more delay," I said. "Forget about agency boundaries and reporting channels. Combine *all* your assets. We're in trouble here. The terrorists have arrived in a deadly serious way, and we've got to be just as serious."

I also said that we had to follow through on identifying the urgent staffing and technology needs about which Washington had been unresponsive. We had our own compound and several foreign missions to protect, not to mention the Iraqi Governing Council.

That was where I headed next. The Council members made statements of grief and outrage over the bombing.

Chaderchi spoke of "the heinous crimes of terrorists."

Abdul Aziz Hakim noted that "the attack was an effort to keep the Iraqi people from their destiny."

I let them carry on for an hour. "Look," I said, skipping the traditional politesse. "I spoke to the president yesterday and he asked me to convey two messages to you. The first is that America will not be scared off its responsibility here by terrorists, and secondly, that it's time for the Governing Council to act." I said that I was to speak to the president again in the afternoon and would report to him on what actions the Council had taken. They were facing a decisive twelve to twenty-four hours. "You have to show the Iraqi people that you're capable of governing and acting. The time for talk is over."

I suggested six steps they should take immediately: a strong statement condemning the bombing; a call to all Iraqis to join and support their own security forces, especially the newly formed Iraqi Civil Defense Corps (later renamed the Iraqi National Guard); an appeal to friendly countries, including Turkey, to join the military coalition; an aggressive press outreach strategy to show the Iraqi people that the Council was actively promoting the political path forward, governing *now*, not later.

I ended by suggesting that they approve a number of proposals they had had before them for weeks, including helping reintegrate the former soldiers into Iraqi society. Then I tabled a draft statement on the UN bombing and suggested they release it right after the meeting to the press waiting outside.

The members were shocked into silence. Gradually it dawned on them that the moment to act had arrived. They quietly sent a small group off to work on the draft statement.

The next day I forwarded my assessment to Washington on the Governing

Council's first month: ". . . the GC has so far been slow to take action on a host of serious issues before it without prodding and handholding by the CPA," I summarized.

Maybe, I thought, *the shock will finally provoke constructive action.*

That afternoon I joined an NSC meeting by video teleconference. We discussed strategy on the supplemental appropriation. Rumsfeld, Wolfowitz, and Rice had paved the way. The president said he had "no problem" with the CPA's new supplemental request of $20 billion. *Finally some good news.*

Then we turned to the UN bombing.

"I want to be very clear in this," President Bush said. "We have to be tough and consistent on combating terrorism here and now."

My turn came to talk about the situation on the ground in Iraq, and I was frank. "We need more and better counterterrorist intelligence in Iraq," I said. "We should put no less effort into counterterrorist intelligence than we do to the search for WMD."

Some in the SitRoom had heard me on this subject before, others had not.

"Mr. President," I concluded, "I recommend that you give a major speech to the nation after Labor Day setting out your vision for Iraq."

He nodded, but made no commitment.

Several hours later, Rice called to ask how she could help. "Colin and I are convinced that Iraq has become the decisive theater in the war on terrorism and that if we win in Iraq, Islamic terrorism can be defeated."

Vermont was cool, green, and quiet at the end of August. The day after arriving, Friday the 29th, I had calls to make to Baghdad, and there were plenty of e-mails to answer. But these were almost pleasant chores because there was no grit on the telephone mouthpiece, and no dust on the computer keyboard.

I had my family around me. Francie was feeling well, here in the country. Our dog, Minny, was running circles around our granddaughter, Sophia, who was talking now, just not in any recognizable language.

I hurried through some budget figures over breakfast and then Clay called from Baghdad. The news was awful.

"Another massive bomb, Jerry," he said. "This time in Najaf. At least one hundred dead."

As usual, first reports were vague and contradictory, but there was no doubt that a major attack had occurred. And it appeared that one of the dead was a leading ayatollah and member of the *marjaiya*, Muhammed Baqir al-Hakim, older brother of Abdul Aziz Hakim, an important member of the Governing Council. The country was deeply shocked by this terrorism in the Shia heart-land.

Within minutes, the phones in our farmhouse started ringing. For hours, I juggled calls from Baghdad, the Pentagon, and the White House. Soon it was clear.

"I've got to go back," I told Francie.

"When, Jer? You just got here. You've lost so much weight. You need to rest."

"Today . . ." I said, my voice cracking.

Francie had her arms around me. "Jer, honey . . . Maybe things will quiet down and you can come right back." We all tried to assure each other that that was possible. But none of us really believed it.

Then suddenly an Army car with security men in it was crunching up the driveway to take me to the Hartford airport, where an Air Force Gulfstream jet would pick me up for the long flight back to Baghdad.

As the car pulled away I looked back and saw everyone I loved, standing on the front porch, crying.

∎·TWO

Chapter 6
"DON'T BOTHER US WITH HISTORY"

■ BAGHDAD
AUGUST 31, 2003

The C-130 crewman swayed between the cargo pallets, clinging to an overhead cable like a gymnast. "Strap down real tight." With the engines throttled back, his voice seemed to boom.

The plane's nose tilted steeply, and I saw the propeller blades on the right wing flatten into a blurred gray disk. The lights of Baghdad International Airport's two runways spun with increasing speed as the pilot dived into a tight spiral, keeping the aircraft centered above the field.

We'd been briefed about what to expect on an "assault landing," the maneuver designed to minimize the threat of heat-seeking missiles. The principle was to avoid a long, low approach over villages where insurgents could shoot shoulder-fired missiles. The day before, a SAM-7 missile had been fired at an Air Force transport taking off. The missile had missed, but our pilot had explained before we'd taken off from Amman, "We don't want the bad guys to get lucky tonight."

Roger that, as the GIs said.

Steeper still, the noise of the slipstream whistling above the idled engines. The flight crew made a final corkscrew on the right wingtip, the engines roared again, and we leveled out only moments before the wheels squealed on the concrete.

Nineteen hours after leaving the States, I was back in Iraq.

On the long flight to Jordan, I'd read a stack of messages from the CPA staff on the security situation following the Najaf bomb that had killed Ayatollah Muhammed Baqir al-Hakim. Shiite leaders had organized a massive "march" (a combined trek and motorcade) from Baghdad to the holy cities of Karbala and Najaf. The demonstration blended mass grief and anger, and had the potential of exploding into more violence.

A new team of bodyguards, many of them tough former Navy SEALs from the contractor Blackwater USA, now handled my personal security because of the increased threat to me. Their presence in the Chevy Suburban—they clutched short black submachine guns as they quietly watched the deserted Airport Road—heightened the sense that Iraq had become even more dangerous. Our convoy now consisted of two armored Humvees, a lead armored Suburban with Blackwater "shooters," my armored car, another armored Suburban with more shooters, and two following Humvees. But I wasn't thinking of my safety as much as the vulnerability of over 300,000 Shiites traveling south for the funeral of the slain ayatollah. Successful insurgent attacks on the mourners could ignite open sectarian war. And we had neither enough Coalition troops nor Iraqi police to contain possible violence that could pit Shia against Sunni in several cities.

"The march went off without incident," Clay reported as my senior staff team briefed me at CPA headquarters. "They'll circle the Karbala shrine for a couple of hours tomorrow and then march to the funeral in Najaf on Tuesday."

"*That's* something, at least," I said. "How're things with the GC?" I asked, turning to Scott Carpenter.

"They're still in session," he said, glancing at his watch. "More or less. Looks like they've finally settled on a cabinet and are debating whether to announce the list tonight."

That the Council had been able to overcome their rivalries and animosities to agree on a list of ministers was a notable achievement. The problem was that Ibrahim al-Jaafari, the GC's rotating president for August, was reluctant to let the incoming September president, Ahmad Chalabi, gain political points by presenting the names of the new cabinet to the nation. So Jaafari wanted to rush the announcement out before his term expired.

Jaafari was the only senior Council member still there when my British colleague, David Richmond, and I reached the GC building at 9:00 P.M. After the usual exchange of niceties and our condolences over the martyred ayatollah, Jaafari launched himself into an excited and familiar discourse about "Iraqis doing more for their own security."

"We entirely agree. But what exactly do you propose?" I asked, a question I'd posed to the GC for weeks. "You already know that we are working day and night to double the size of Iraq's police and the civil defense forces."

"Well, I think it is tragic that such an incident could occur in our holy city," Jaafari insisted. "The Coalition should have done more for security there."

"Dr. Jaafari, I have explained several times to you and your colleagues that the senior clerics in Najaf asked Coalition troops to stay well clear of the shrines. And out of respect for those holy sites, we did exactly that." So the assassins had been able to plant the bomb that had killed Ayatollah Muhammed Baqir al-Hakim and his throng of worshippers with apparent ease.

The meeting ended with Jaafari promising that three Council members of a joint Council-Coalition security committee we had proposed a month earlier would finally come to a meeting with their counterparts at the CPA in the morning.

Despite my jet lag, I felt I had to take time before going to bed to review the Governing Council's list of proposed cabinet ministers. Looking over the names with Americans and Brits on our Governance Team in my office, I said, "Well, at least they did something. And considering how much time these guys have wasted over the past two months, that's good news."

"Yeah," Scott replied, "but the way in which they chose these folks is discouraging." He explained that they had selected the ministers in the same manner they had used for the constitutional Preparatory Committee (which we called the PrepComm). "Once again, they simply agreed that each of the twenty-five GC members could choose one minister. In effect, they've just replicated themselves again without making any real effort to broaden the Council's political base."

Meghan O'Sullivan said that this formula had posed a dilemma: There had been only twenty-one ministries in the prewar Cabinet, so the GC had created four new ministries to allow each member a piece of the pie. "Jobs for the boys," is how one GC member had put it.

"On the other hand," Clay observed, "they've at least stayed away from our red lines." He was referring to the warning I'd issued that we would not accept Islamists in the ministries of Interior or Education.

Among the thirteen Shiites who would run some key ministries there were religious and secular people but no sectarian extremists. As we had expected, the Kurds had divvied up their five cabinet positions between the two main Kurdish parties. Sunnis had landed five ministries, including the critical Electricity Ministry and the Justice Ministry, which would play a crucial role in establishing the rule of law. An Assyrian Christian was the new minister of Transport, and a Turkman, Rashad Mindan, who had a British doctorate in civil engineering, was the incoming minister of Science and Technology. Jules Chappell, the British diplomat who had worked hard to bring Iraqi women back into the country's life, expressed disappointment that there was only one woman among the ministers—Nasreen Bewari, a young Kurd who had served in the Kurdish cabinet with distinction.

To assemble this cabinet, the most influential members of the Council— Jaafari, Hakim, Talabani, and Chalabi—had thrown some pretty sharp elbows.

Our intelligence services had run the candidates' names through their databases and found no record that any of the ministers had been ranking Baathists, though once again we knew that our information on that matter was rather scant. "They look like a pretty capable bunch." I concluded, "I'm too tired to deal with this anymore tonight. Just let them go ahead and make the announcement as they wish. I'm going to have a shower and sleep."

As the others rose from the marble table to leave, Clay hung back, something clearly troubling him.

"Jerry," he said, "I'm really concerned about the mood in the Pentagon."

"What's up?"

"Well, I'm hearing from various contacts back there that the services, particularly the Army, are getting quite worried about the troop rotation next spring."

Most of the American troops now in Iraq would finish their year in Iraq in the February–April 2004 period. Unless our forces were to be substantially reduced, the Army and Marines would have to identify at least five division-strength replacement units. Clay dropped a draft memo from CENTCOM on my desk. In it General Abizaid proposed to send a brigadier general to Iraq to "synchronize, coordinate, and focus" all the Iraqi security forces, including the New Iraqi Army, police, and border patrol.

"Look," I told Clay. "We agree that all this training needs to be speeded up. But there is an underlying message here that somehow, in a short period, these Iraqi forces will be able to replace ours. It just can't happen that quickly if we're going to have professional police and Iraqi Army guys."

"But I'm telling you that's *exactly* what worries me," Clay said. "There appear to be folks in Washington and Tampa trying to convince themselves and maybe Rumsfeld, too, that by next spring one Iraqi policeman or border patrol guard will equal a trooper from the 4th ID or 3rd Armored Cavalry Regiment."

"Well," I said, "we do have to go as fast as possible getting Iraqis trained. But they've got to be professional, not the sort of incompetent criminals Saddam had in his police."

"Slocombe's already crashing to compress the army program to a year," Clay said.

During a brief visit to Iraq in August, Don Rumsfeld had pushed for an accelerated training plan that would "stand up" twenty-seven battalions of the NIA in one year instead of Slocombe's originally planned two. An expanded

Coalition training contingent under Major General Paul Eaton was now hard at work at their base in Kirkush, about one hundred miles northeast of Baghdad, and would soon graduate the first 500-man battalion.

"Slocombe thinks Eaton can pull it off," Clay added. "But it'll be a hell of a challenge. And what're we going to do about the police now that the Hungarian option has collapsed?"

Just before leaving the States, I'd received the news that the Hungarian parliament was stalling on our request to train the new Iraqi Police Service (IPS) there.

Wearily I replied, "Bring Bernie in first thing tomorrow. And I'll have to raise our concerns with Don when he's here next week. Now I'm going to go off and see my new digs."

"The house has got a lot going for it, sir," Frank Gallagher, chief of my Blackwater security contingent, commented. "Nice thick walls."

That was the main reason for my move from the trailers near the palace: security. At Rumsfeld's request, the U.S. Secret Service had done a survey of my security and had concluded that I was the most threatened American official anywhere in the world. Not only was the Green Zone, as the military had come to call the palace area, vulnerable to the increasingly frequent mortar and rocket attacks, intelligence reports revealed I was high on the insurgents' assassination list. And, among the hundreds of Iraqis working in the palace in jobs ranging from janitor to high-level liaisons with our ministry teams, there was lots of room for an assassin. One report Blackwater took seriously suggested that one of the Iraqi barbers in the palace had been hired to kill me when I got a haircut. Blackwater wanted me out of the trailer I had shared with Clay and into a building they could defend and which would offer more protection against both incoming fire and lurking insurgent killers.

I stood in front of the ugly villa in the fading light. It was vintage Saddam regime: overbuilt, gracelessly ostentatious. There were several similar houses down here among the untended palms three hundred yards southeast of the main palace. The whole palace area had been a sort of family compound for Saddam. He had built a number of these marble monstrosities for his sons and their in-laws. Word had it that this one had been the home of Qusay's mother-in-law.

I walked through the large, echoing unfurnished rooms, filled with marble arches and faux crystal chandeliers hanging from the high ceilings. The place had all the charm of a railway station waiting room. I already felt nostalgic for my Spartan little trailer.

"You can move in a couple days, sir," Gallagher added. "As soon as we get the shelter built." I knew and liked Frank, who by one of those coincidences of life had been the head of Henry Kissinger's security detail when I was managing director of Kissinger Associates in the 1990s. Frank had been a "special operator" in the Marines. I trusted him totally.

Mortar rounds and rockets had begun to fall around CPA headquarters in recent weeks. So my Blackwater security team had insisted on having a concrete and armored-glass command post and shelter on the northeast corner of the ground floor of the new house because most of the mortar and rockets were launched from the southwest, just across the Tigris River.

Walking back to my trailer in the relative cool, I felt ambivalent about the new quarters. The house was a trade-off between increased safety and comfort and further isolation from my staff, the life of the city, and the country itself. But I was determined to continue traveling widely from the headquarters compound—both around Baghdad and around Iraq—despite the danger.

Bernie Kerik looked physically exhausted, but still determined. For weeks he'd been working long hours, trying to rebuild the Iraqi police while helping modernize the Interior Ministry. Kerik obviously knew something was up because he said in the ironic tones of a New York street cop, "Why do I get the feeling this isn't gonna be a good-news session, Boss?"

"The police training deal in Hungary is dead, Bernie," I said, handing him the latest messages. "Their parliament has to 'study' and debate the issue. Meaning no decision before the end of the year at the earliest."

"We can't wait that long," he said.

"Right," I said. "So we're going to drop Hungary."

"Clay," I added, "since Bernie's going back to the States, you've got to pick this one up. Get over to Amman ASAP to see if we can finalize the proposal to train police in Jordan."

"Are we absolutely sure there's no way to do this training in Iraq?" Clay asked.

"Clay, we've been through this a dozen times. There's simply no way this can be done here in the time frame Ambassador Bremer has laid out," Kerik replied in exasperation. "The controlling factor is enough facility space . . . classrooms, firing ranges. You name it. Just doesn't exist in Iraq. We're talking about training thirty-five or forty thousand officers in two years."

Maybe less, I thought, but didn't say so.

"I ran the biggest force in the country and had America's largest training program, six thousand cadets a year," Bernie continued. "The program here would dwarf that."

"Well, Clay," I said, "get over to Jordan and come up with a plan. I need it yesterday. Draft a quick letter from me to the king saying I hope he'll ask his folks to help you."

Clay mentioned that he would need to take Doug Brand, Bernie's highly capable British number two, and I readily agreed.

Two days later I got an update call on the supplemental budget from Reuben Jeffery, head of the CPA office in the Pentagon. Reuben had served in Baghdad for several months in the summer before returning to Washington to watch out for our interests inside the Beltway. A former investment banker, Reuben had come to Iraq for the selfless purpose of helping Iraqis like so many volunteers. He had a good grasp on the complex problems we faced. And he knew that most Washington bureaucrats didn't understand. He was my eyes and ears on interagency activities inside the Executive Branch.

"I'm not clear about the current thinking on the supplemental," Reuben told me. The Pentagon, OMB, and the White House were still refining tactics on taking the supplemental to the Hill. "I think OMB has stopped screwing around with the numbers so it looks like the CPA's share of the supplemental request will be close to the full $20 billion you suggested."

That was a rare piece of good news during a time when virtually every call and e-mail brought details of some fresh problem or crisis. The proposal that David Oliver and his number crunchers had finished for me to present to Washington in August had identified rebuilding Iraq's security forces as our top priority—at a cost of $6 billion. We'd also emphasized expanding power generation and revamping the oil industry.

These were priorities worth every penny of the supplemental funds required to achieve them: Iraqi security forces who could protect their country; a dependable supply of electrical power, which would also help restore people's hope in a prosperous, stable future; and an oil industry that could begin to meet its immense potential as the patrimony of the Iraqi people.

But $20 billion was still a lot of money. Congress would want me to dance through a lot of hoops for that amount, I realized.

But I'm ready to be a congressional punching bag in front of the TV cameras if it means getting the money Iraq needs.

I didn't realize then how hard they could punch. Or how low.

As I considered this, there was a hollow thump off to the west. Probably another roadside bomb.

That Wednesday night I received a warning from the Governing Council that Muqtada al-Sadr was planning to issue a fatwa after Friday prayers in Najaf calling on his faithful to wage jihad against the Coalition. Technically al-Sadr—at best a young theology student—could not issue such a religious decree because he was not a full-fledged cleric. But his unemployed, increasingly desperate followers in Baghdad's Sadr City slum might not make this distinction.

My adviser for Baghdad City, Andy Morrison, told me that al-Sadr's people were trying to take over the Coalition's reconstruction projects in Sadr City by intimidating Iraqis working on them—seeking to get control of our money and to gain credit for the work accomplished. This was a strong-arm gangster tactic. We also had disturbing reports of his agents encouraging unrest in the northern city of Kirkuk, a tinderbox of ethnic tensions in the best of times.

I huddled with Clay and Hume. The Governing Council was sending a delegation to Najaf the next day to ask Ayatollah Sistani to intervene.

"If Sistani slaps Muqtada hard enough," Hume said, "the punk loses face."

"And that would help if and when the Iraqis manage to arrest him for murder," Clay added.

"Well, those are 'good things,' as Rumsfeld would say," I quipped. "But if Muqtada *does* unleash his gangs, there could be serious violence against our troops, especially in Sadr City."

The new Iraqi interior minister, Nouri Badran, came to visit me at my office later that week. A trim, secular Shiite in his early fifties, Badran was GC member Ayad Allawi's brother-in-law. Badran had survived repeated assassination and kidnapping attempts by Saddam's henchmen in the 1990s. I expected tough decisiveness from him as he organized the vital post-Saddam ministry. So I was not surprised as he laid out a concise plan to overhaul Interior, which was responsible for regular police, border guards, and the paramilitary units we then called the Iraqi Civil Defense Corps, but which would later be renamed the Iraqi National Guard.

"Ambassador," Badran said, "I hope you will agree with me. The key to crushing this violence lies in the police."

He spoke with suppressed energy, as if he had rehearsed this statement. I was reminded that exercising this kind of power for a long-repressed Shiite who had lived for decades under Saddam as a hunted man had to be both exhilarating and daunting. For him to open the meeting with the statement that agreed with my own conclusion about the solution to violence in Iraq suggested that Badran had been well coached by his powerful relative. Among the Governing Council leaders, Allawi had displayed the most tough-minded practicality.

Badran stated that he had already devised a number of "new policies" in his first week in office, but before proceeding, he wanted my approval.

His first priority would be to establish a "special police unit," drawn from former Republican Guard soldiers, a quick reaction force under police command that would intervene to disrupt insurgent attacks.

That sounded interesting; a small unit of these special police would bring to the anti-insurgent fight skills and experience far beyond those of Coalition forces — language, cultural awareness, basic street smarts, and networks of informers. *But can we trust them?* I wondered. Republican Guard troops were universally considered loyal Baathists. Moreover, I knew that his patron, Allawi, himself a former Baath Party member before joining the exile resistance, opposed a forceful application of the de-Baathification policy. Partly this was Allawi's way to get back at his archrival, Chalabi, the strongest proponent of broad de-Baathification.

"Can you vet them adequately?" I asked.

"It can be done, Ambassador," Badran replied.

"Okay," I said. "Go ahead on the condition that they are very thoroughly vetted." The graves at Al-Hillah passed through my mind. "And that these men receive some basic human and civil rights training before being deployed."

As Badran turned to leave, I reminded him of his responsibility toward the Coalition. "Be sure to work closely with our advisers on all aspects of police training, Minister."

"Of course, Ambassador," Badran said. "We will become close colleagues and friends."

Within days, I would have reason to remember those words.

Don Rumsfeld flew back to Baghdad on Thursday, September 4. If the roller-coaster assault landing had impressed him, he didn't show it.

I knew that the principal reason for his trip was to assess personally the options to reduce American forces. And I also knew that he was putting a lot of pressure on the military to find a rationale to make that happen.

It would be my job to make the case that we needed to keep enough troops in Iraq to stabilize the country.

That night after he'd conferred with his military commanders, Rumsfeld came to the palace for dinner with my senior colleagues and me. We were a small group sitting in the conference room over bland Army chow: Secretary Rumsfeld, Pat Kennedy, Bill the CIA station chief, British Ambassador David Richmond, Clay McManaway, and me.

Despite his draining travel schedule and nonstop meetings, Rumsfeld dominated the dinner discussion, which ranged freely. "You're all doing a lot of good work here," he said. "There are some remarkable accomplishments. But I just don't see a steady line of advance. Maybe we need better metrics . . . a more efficient way to measure how we're meeting our goals."

"That's why we developed the Strategic Plan you saw in July," I reminded him. But I didn't want my colleagues to get bogged down writing lots of reports. We needed to keep our focus on getting things done, fast.

"As you'll recall, Mr. Secretary, our plan has built-in goals and specific metrics. We're coming up on the first ninety-day mark and intend to sit down and figure out how we've done against our three-month targets."

October 1 was almost three weeks away. Rumsfeld didn't seem mollified.

A little later, he stunned us all by commenting, "I wonder if all of you working here have a sufficient sense of urgency."

The table went silent. We sat rigidly at our places. If I had not had a long diplomatic career, I might have unleashed the outrage that churned inside. I took a couple of breaths before answering, but my voice was brittle.

"Mr. Secretary," I said, pointing toward the echoing marble corridors of the palace, "you can stop any of the thousands of people working here . . . from a PFC stirring scrambled eggs in the kitchen to feed the midnight shift to old retread ambassadors like Clay and me and I doubt you'll find *any* of us that doesn't have a sense of great urgency." I added that all of these people were volunteers working eighteen to twenty hours a day, seven days a week, because they knew our job was both important and urgent.

Rumsfeld seemed a bit taken aback. The awkward moment stretched painfully. Finally, the secretary spoke again. "What I meant to say was that I know you're all working, but do you have the right priorities? You can't do everything, so you need to be clear about what is the most important."

That was simple. "It's security," I said. "Because without that we can't achieve our other goals—economic and political."

"I agree, Jerry. But that means moving as fast as possible on getting Iraq's security forces stood up."

Here we go again, I thought.

I briefly reviewed our accelerated plans for the army, which Rumsfeld himself had directed a month earlier. I added that Clay and Doug Brand were headed to Jordan to finalize plans for the world's largest police training program.

The discussion flowed naturally to the link between intelligence and improved effectiveness against the Baathist insurgency and foreign terrorism. Everybody agreed that we had to improve our intelligence collection.

"Actually," I said, "I have the feeling that with the establishment of the intel fusion cell here, we're better coordinated across agency lines on intelligence than folks are in Washington. George Tenet admitted to me last week that he'd like to duplicate our model back there."

That was not a point that Rumsfeld wanted to pursue in this setting. The rivalry between the Pentagon's various intelligence units and the CIA was becoming a sore subject in Washington.

Before going to bed, I e-mailed Francie that Rumsfeld's comment about lack of urgency among the CPA staff had really "frosted me." But now I was more concerned than angry. It was increasingly clear that the Pentagon's apparent preoccupation with the spring troop rotation was creating unhealthy pressures to wish a competent Iraqi security force into being faster than possible.

The president addressed the nation on Iraq, the wider war on terrorism, and the pending supplemental appropriation on the evening of Sunday, September 7. I'd had some input in drafting the speech, and felt it presented a persuasive case for supporting our work.

After reviewing the accomplishments in destroying the Al-Qaeda–Taliban terror alliance in Afghanistan, the president turned to Iraq. "We are helping the long-suffering people of that country to build a decent and democratic society at the center of the Middle East. Together, we are transforming a place of torture chambers and mass graves into a nation of laws and free institutions. The undertaking is difficult and costly—yet worthy of our country, and critical to our security."

President Bush stated that he'd authorized Colin Powell to introduce a UN Security Council resolution authorizing the "creation of a multinational force in Iraq, to be led by Americans."

I doubted that the Security Council, fractured by divisions between the Anglo-Americans and the continental Europeans, would agree to this. But it was worth making the effort—if only to expose the French, Germans, and Russians as spoilers.

The president spelled out how he intended to ask Congress for a total of $87 billion for Afghanistan, Iraq, and the overall war on terror. He stressed that Iraqis were increasingly shouldering the burden of their own security and that the training of more of them was accelerating. It was a point I was glad that his speechwriters had not hyped.

Overall, it was a confident, well-reasoned speech, which I thought would resonate with most Americans but raise the hackles of the president's opponents in Congress.

I convoked my first meeting with the new Iraqi ministers on September 16. They ranged themselves and their aides around the large square table in the Convention Center's conference room. I sat at the top of the table beside the newly arrived British ambassador, Sir Jeremy Greenstock. A career diplomat I had known for years, Jeremy's last post had been as U.K. ambassador to the UN. Prime Minister Tony Blair called him out of retirement to "heavy up" the British presence in Baghdad. Jeremy brought with him another able British official, Raad Alkadiri. Raad's father was Iraqi so he spoke fluent Arabic and had a deep understanding of Iraqi society. He immediately became a valued member of the U.S.-U.K. Governance Team.

Working another of his miracles, Pat Kennedy had repaired the room's simultaneous interpretation equipment (though the clocks were still inexplicably stopped at 12:32 P.M.). So ministers without English could hear our professional State Department interpreters put English words into Arabic—following my smiling "Sabah al-khair" ("Good morning"). In the summer I had begun taking a half-hour spoken Arabic lesson each morning at seven, after my run and the first read-through of the overnight cable traffic.

After congratulating them, I told the ministers that I admired their courage and dedication to rebuilding Iraq. "You are now charged with making the day-to-day decisions in your ministries, affecting the lives of all Iraqis. You have full authority to determine your budgets and choose personnel." But I cautioned that they should let CPA's senior advisers know in advance about any proposed major policy initiatives.

"Like it or not—and it's not pleasant being occupied, or being the occupier, I might add—the Coalition is still the sovereign power here."

Several of the ministers welcomed the meeting and thanked President Bush and Prime Minister Blair for liberating their country. Others were more interested in the huge supplemental budget the president had put before Congress.

"What's our role to be in allocating this money?" Finance Minister Kamel al-Keilani asked.

He was a Sunni Arab businessman in his mid-forties, from a prominent family and with a degree in management and economics, who had been appointed to the office by his relative, Ahmad Chalabi.

"We have worked closely with the acting ministers and Iraqi civil servants in each ministry to come up with the list of projects," I told them, adding that we would welcome their further suggestions. I emphasized that we had also developed Iraq's 2004 government budget with their colleagues, and while we expected it to be tight, each minister had latitude to shift money around within his ministry. "I have given my colleagues clear instructions that they are to help you in any way possible. Your success will be ours."

Finally, I told the ministers that that very morning the Governing Council had taken the momentous step of approving Peter McPherson's robust slate of economic reforms, the most important of which was repealing Saddam's prohibition against foreign investment.

I paid tribute to Ahmad Chalabi, who as chairman of the Governing Council's economic subcommittee had, at my request, shepherded the economic package through the GC in time to help the president make his case for the supplemental budget.

That had been Ahmad Chalabi at his best.

After the meeting, a group of advisers gathered around the table to discuss the session.

"I think we're off to a good start with the new cabinet," I said.

I made a point of meeting as many of the new Iraqi cabinet ministers as practical early in their tenure, asking my staff to schedule these meetings at the ministries. This made a useful contrast to Saddam's habit of summoning often-terrified ministers into his presence. And it helped me get out and around Baghdad as much as possible.

One of the more impressive members of the new cabinet was Hashim al-Shibli, the minister of justice. A quiet, well-spoken Sunni attorney in his mid-forties, he had worked for private firms around the region for over twenty years. He welcomed me into his nearly unfurnished office on the ground floor of the Justice Ministry over the obligatory glass of steaming tea.

"Ambassador, these are my priorities for your consideration," he said when we turned to business. He wanted my support in strengthening administrative courts, improving rights to legal counsel for defendants, and speeding reviews of pending Coalition detainees.

"We share the same goals, Minister."

But al-Shibli cautioned that Saddam had suborned the justice system and terrorized judges.

"The Coalition recognizes the problem," I responded, and reminded him that in June I had established a judicial review panel to vet Iraq's 860 judges. "We've been over the files of most of them now, and approved about 600 for service in the new courts."

"I've heard about that and welcome it. But we need to go further and separate the administration of the courts from the government, making the chief justice independent of this ministry."

I was delighted to hear this. For a senior Middle Eastern bureaucrat voluntarily to relinquish power was a refreshing change. I urged him to work with our lawyers to prepare a decree I could sign to formally establish an independent judiciary.

The minister closed the meeting by saying, "Please remember this, Ambassador Bremer: we are looking to the United States in building a New Iraq. If Iraq succeeds, Arab regimes across the region will topple."

To me, al-Shibli was proof that the Sunni community contained important leaders for Iraq's future, untainted by Baathism.

Two days later, I had the great joy of signing the CPA order establishing Iraq's first truly independent judiciary, a vital component of democratic checks and balances that had been first swept aside, and then crushed, when the Baathists had seized power.

I was sound asleep in the shuttered bedroom of my house when an explosion woke me, again. The blast was followed immediately by the newly installed Giant Voice loudspeaker system, which blared out, "Take cover! Take cover! Take cover!"

"Mortars, sir," one of the Blackwater security guards shouted. He shined a powerful flashlight to guide me down the cool marble stairs to the reinforced security command post, which doubled as the house's bomb shelter.

I'd just ducked inside the stuffy little room when another mortar round smacked down about two hundred meters to the north.

Five minutes later, a third struck the far side of the compound.

These were hasty, poorly aimed nuisance attacks rather than a coordinated barrage, most of them at night. But they did interrupt our sleep and remind us that the war continued.

When the Giant Voice commanded, all CPA employees, whether at work in the palace, or at rest in their trailers, were under orders to hurry into the basement of the palace. As the attacks became more routine, these evacuations took on a light, even festive, atmosphere. Groups would huddle in the basement corridors, continuing meetings begun upstairs, reading books, or just chatting with colleagues. Then, the "all clear" message would sound, and we'd all go back to work.

After it became apparent that most of the mortars were being fired from the southwest side of the Tigris, Blackwater moved my bedroom to one on the less exposed northeast corner of the house. I did sleep better there, but the roar of the Giant Voice would still wake me from the deepest dream.

"It's just not on, sir," complained Doug Brand, the very large and competent Yorkshire chief constable who became acting Senior Adviser to the Interior Ministry when Kerik left. "The gentleman is a proper bull in the china shop."

The object of his concern was the new Interior minister, Nouri Badran, who had sounded so focused only days earlier.

"What's he up to? I thought I had him calmed down the other day."

"Wish it were so, Boss. He's come loose and is crashing around the ministry. Been firing people, and pretty much thrown overboard the entire modern structure Bernie and I put together."

"We just don't have the luxury of screwing up police training. I'll look into it, Doug," I assured him. "Meanwhile, keep me closely informed."

Doug, who stood six foot seven in stocking feet, was unflappable. But my own temperature shot up when I verified the details of everything he had described. Minister Badran had arbitrarily changed the joint U.S.-Iraqi police patrols, against the advice of the colonel commanding our local MPs. Probably worse, Badran was standing up a special paramilitary force without informing our military. General Sanchez confirmed this a couple of days later and said that the step put both Coalition troops and Badran's people at risk. Then I learned that the minister had abruptly informed Susan Johnson, our Foreign Affairs Ministry adviser, that he intended to simply close down Iraq's borders for six months and expel "all unauthorized foreigners."

"It's a great idea in principle," I told my staff, "but how in the hell can it be enforced? We've got no visa policy, so there's no way even to define who is 'unauthorized.' And we simply don't yet have a trained border police." This had been one of the most corrupt of Saddam's security forces. They also collected customs duties.

"He's Ayad Allawi's brother-in-law," I reminded Doug. "I'll get onto Allawi to rein him in."

• • •

My concern about the Pentagon's fixation with the "metrics" of security forces training was confirmed on September 12 when I received a memo from Don Rumsfeld addressed to General Abizaid and me.

FROM: Donald Rumsfeld
SUBJECT: Reporting on Security Issues

It seems to me that reporting from now on about security issues ought to include U.S. forces, international forces and Iraqi forces. We need to array them all, because they are now what comprise the security forces for Iraq.

Our goal should be to ramp up the Iraqi numbers, try to get some additional international forces and find ways to put less stress on our forces, enabling us to reduce the U.S. role. The faster the Iraqi forces grow, the lower the percentage will be of U.S. forces out of the total forces.
Thanks

I read the memo twice and laid it on my desk. Two short paragraphs. A lot of potential problems. I asked Clay to come in.

"Just what I was worried about," he said, reading the memo and shaking his head. "They're getting worked up back there about the troop rotation. And they think by pumping up the Iraqi numbers they can justify a drawdown of our forces. This is becoming dangerous."

As he and I had often discussed, there was a world of difference between an American staff sergeant commanding a Bradley fighting vehicle and a new Iraqi police officer who might have fired his rusty Soviet-era Makarov 9 mm pistol a few times. There were almost 38,000 Iraqi police officers back on duty and we needed a minimum of 35,000 more. Clay reminded me that Bernie Kerik's estimate was that at least 40 percent of those on duty would probably have to be washed out for incompetence or human rights abuses or both. A professional Iraqi police force was a long way off.

Rumsfeld's memo made clear that real pressure was building in Washington to "ramp up the Iraqi numbers" so as to "put less stress on our forces, enabling us to reduce the U.S. role." Of course this was the correct goal. From the start we had recognized that in the long run, Iraqi security would have to depend on Iraqi forces. But they had to be professionally trained. And this, I had insisted, would take time, at least a year according to our experts.

The acceleration of building the New Iraqi Army was also moving forward.

In August, I had visited their training base at Kirkush, northeast of Baghdad, and seen the excellent job Major General Paul Eaton and his team were doing with the first NIA battalion. But recruiting and training a professional army was a labor-intensive and time-consuming job. Even if we received a generous supplemental, there was no guarantee that the Coalition could meet Walt Slocombe's revised goal of training twenty-seven battalions in one year. It would only further confuse the issue if we started including the lightly armed officers of the Iraqi Police Service and the slowly growing Iraqi National Guard paramilitaries into the reports on total security forces in Iraq.

"Jerry, you'd better stake out some clear warning flags on this one when you go back to Washington to fight for the supplemental," Clay said. "Otherwise this movie isn't going to have a happy ending."

Meanwhile, it appeared, we were headed for what the Governance Team called a "train wreck" over the process for writing Iraq's constitution.

The issue went to the heart of the Coalition's goals for the country. After almost four decades of tyranny, Iraq's stability would depend on developing robust political institutions and clear protection of individual and minority rights. By establishing the rule of law as well as checks and balances in government, a constitution would be vital to shape Iraq's institutions and protect citizens' rights.

Our plan, which I had laid out in detail in an op-ed piece in the *Washington Post* the day after the president's speech, foresaw a process which followed the pattern established in 1925 under the British. A Constitutional Convention, composed of a selected group of representative Iraqis, would draft a new constitution to be put to the people by referendum. Elections would be held for a sovereign Iraqi parliament based on the terms laid out in the constitution and the Coalition would give sovereignty over to that elected government.

I recognized that identifying a representative group of Iraqis to write a new constitution would be a challenge. My decades as a diplomat told me that compromises on the key issues involved in a constitution were not going to be easy to reach, especially in a society as brutalized and fractured as Iraq's. But the constitution was a vital building block.

Sistani had insisted in his June fatwa that the Constitutional Convention be elected, which, because Iraq had no electoral laws or mechanics, we knew would delay the process of turning over sovereignty to the Iraqis. We had suggested, and the GC had agreed, to name a constitutional Preparatory Committee (PrepComm) to find a way to move forward quickly.

But on September 10, the plans began going awry. Scott Carpenter, with Meghan, Lydia Khalil, and Roman Martinez in tow, came into my office late that afternoon. "The PrepComm has gone off the rails," Scott said. "They've apparently decided to recommend to the Governing Council that the Constitutional Convention be directly elected."

Yet another twist to untangle.

"Well it's a great and admirable idea, guys," I told the group huddled around my marble table. "But we know it can't be done quickly."

Election experts from the UN, NGOs, and Coalition governments had been very clear in their assessments: it would take at least nine to twelve months to prepare such elections. There hadn't been a census since 1987, there were no constituency boundaries, no national political parties, no political-party laws, no electoral rolls, and no electoral law. The only experience most Iraqis had with voting was the Baathists' sham elections.

"Here's the net effect of that," Roman summarized. "If a constitution is to be the first step, and if a Constitutional Convention has to be elected, we're looking at delaying the return of sovereignty to an Iraqi government for up to two years."

That would prolong the occupation. I doubted whether public opinion in either Iraq or America would tolerate that. But the PrepComm's recommendation for an elected convention conformed to Ayatollah Sistani's fatwa, so many of the GC's Shia members would likely agree with the process because they could not risk openly defying him.

I was determined not to relinquish sovereignty to a violent and divided nation until we had established a practical political process leading to the creation of a constitution.

Some Council members, Chalabi and Pachachi in particular, saw opportunity in the dilemma. Their solution, echoing French proposals at the UN, was to have the Coalition immediately hand sovereignty to the Governing Council without a constitution.

So when Secretary of State Powell visited in mid-September, at my urging he strongly endorsed our original political process in a meeting with the Governing Council. Powell added it was "absolutely essential" that governmental legitimacy rest on a constitutional basis leading to elections. In his meeting, Powell bluntly described the alternative approach of giving sovereignty to the GC as "entirely unacceptable."

Our problem was exacerbated by Ayatollah Sistani's enigmatic public position, which shifted between spiritual isolation and direct participation in the political process. With his black turban, dark clerical robes, and flowing gray-white beard, the ayatollah was figuratively and literally the *éminence grise* of Najaf's sacred precinct.

Ayatollah Ali Husseini Sistani was the most senior leader of the Najaf *marjaiya*, and the spiritual head of the Hawza, the revered center of Shia learning for centuries until the mullahs took over Iran in 1979 and moved the center of the Shia sect across the border to the Iranian city of Qom. Sistani played a role within Shiadom analogous to that of the pope among Catholics. Like the pope, Sistani did not directly operate on the daily hurly-burly of politics, but exerted his influence through private discussions with devout followers and the occasional public statement or decree.

But in his Spartan audience room off a narrow alleyway in Najaf, Sistani often thrashed out the fine points of political tactics with allies on the Governing Council. For example, on September 4, the ayatollah had told visiting Council members that Iraq needed tighter border controls and an effective internal intelligence service, measures that many of his Shia faithful might have seen as reminiscent of the Baathists, but which would be acceptable when it was made known Sistani blessed them. However, the ayatollah also told the Council members that he opposed foreign troops from Iraq's neighbors joining the Coalition in Iraq. Several of Sistani's allies on the Council embraced this position.

That was not welcome news in Washington. Although the Pentagon and the State Department continued to push to get Turks into Iraq, the option was effectively dead on arrival because of Sistani's position. Millions of Shiites considered him the *marja al-taqlid*, an infallible spiritual guide whose life and wisdom were to be "emulated." And now those Shia in the Governing Council would make common cause with the Kurds, who vehemently opposed the introduction of Turkish troops into Iraq through their territory.

Hume and the other regional experts on the Governance Team assured me that Ayatollah Sistani's ultimate goal for Iraq was not an Iranian-style mullah-ruled theocracy. But I'd realized since my June meeting in Qatar with the president, Colin Powell, and Condi Rice that anxiety over such a specter lingered in Washington.

Just after Liberation, the ayatollah had let it be known through private channels that he would not meet with anyone from the Coalition. And I had not pressed for a personal meeting. Hume, who understood Islam and the Arab world well, succinctly analyzed this situation. "He can't be *publicly* seen as cooperating with the occupying powers, Jerry," he had told me. "Shades of 1920 and all that. And he's got to protect his flanks from the hotheads like Muqtada. But the ayatollah *will* work with us. We share the same goals."

While both the Arab and the Western media lamented the supposed breach between Ayatollah Sistani and the Coalition, throughout the Coalition's time in Iraq he and I communicated regularly on vital issues through intermediaries.

And Hume was right. In the early summer, Sistani had sent word to me that his position had not been taken "out of hostility to the Coalition." Rather, the ayatollah believed that avoiding public contact with the Coalition allowed him to be more useful in "our joint pursuits," that he would forfeit some of his credibility among the faithful were he to cooperate openly with Coalition officials, as had many secular Shiites and Sunnis, as well as devout but lower-ranking Shia clergy.

When I had learned in early July that Sistani still thought the Coalition planned to write Iraq's constitution, and that he was adamant that Iraqis write it, I sent him a message through several channels stressing important points: we came as liberators not occupiers; we agreed that the constitution should be written by Iraqis; and the Governing Council would decide the appropriate process—which they were trying to do.

In subsequent exchanges I assured the ayatollah that I was well aware of the suffering of the Shia, noting that my first trip outside Baghdad had been to Al-Hillah's mass graves. And I pointed out that the Coalition was pumping lots of money into reconstruction projects in the Shia heartland.

Sistani and I also exchanged regular messages on the security situation in Najaf, particularly in August as Muqtada al-Sadr became a serious threat. I told the ayatollah that he and I "shared a responsibility to avoid unnecessary violence." Neither of us wanted Shia-on-Sunni violence, or vice versa. We both desired a stable, democratic Iraq at peace with its neighbors.

Between July and mid-September alone, I had more than a dozen exchanges with the ayatollah. Sistani repeatedly expressed his personal gratitude for all that the Coalition had done for the Shia and for Iraq. But he remained insistent that the Constitutional Convention "must be directly elected."

In an effort to work another indirect channel to Sistani, I had taken Secretary Powell to dinner at the house of Ayatollah Hussein al-Sadr, Baghdad's most senior Shia cleric. A courageous opponent of Saddam, Sayyid al-Sadr had been under house arrest for years, leaving him time to author over a hundred books on Islam, except when the police came and took him away for interrogation. He was then usually hung from a ceiling fan at the police station and beaten for hours on end. I visited the ayatollah regularly and was moved by his spirituality and courage.

I knew that Hussein al-Sadr saw Sistani weekly, so a couple of weeks before Powell's visit, I had suggested to him that perhaps the Constitutional Convention could be "selected" by some process from among various elements of society, rather than "elected." This evening at my suggestion, Powell said it was important that we grant sovereignty in an orderly manner after a representative body of Iraqis had written a constitution and the people had voted on it. Al-Sadr responded with a vague reference to the possibility of selecting the Constitutional Convention, which was progress.

However, Sistani remained unmoved. And his inflexible position would prove to be the undoing of our first plan for Iraq's political process.

Although the political situation was unsettled and the insurgency raged, factions were forming in Washington and at the United Nations that shared the goal of granting sovereignty prematurely to Iraq. In Washington, the "sovereignty now" campaign (an echo of the early-power-transfer policy of April) seemed to be centered on Deputy Secretary of Defense Paul Wolfowitz, Under Secretary for Policy Douglas Feith, and John Hannah in the vice president's office. They were close to Ahmad Chalabi, who had been directly lobbying for this policy during two extended visits to the States since May, and who was back in the U.S. as September's president of the GC.

At the United Nations, the Security Council was debating the resolution to expand UN military, development, and political "assistance" in Iraq following the August bombing. This gave an opening to the French to add their voice to the demand that we simply turn Iraq over to the Governing Council despite the fact that after its appointment, France had refused to recognize the Council.

A call on September 13 from Rumsfeld made me uneasy. He expressed enthusiasm for the concept of granting sovereignty as soon as possible to the Council or some other group of Iraqis. I told him bluntly that I disagreed, so he rather briskly replied, "Well then, send me a paper giving me your reasons."

The same day, I laid out my concerns in a memo to him. I said that we agreed that Iraqis should be given political and security responsibility quickly, in a manner that had a fair chance of success. I reviewed the main difference between us and the GC, which centered on whether a Constitutional Convention (CC) should be elected, noting that the PrepComm's recommendation for an elected CC "by our assessment and the UN's . . . effectively puts off any visible movement toward Iraqi sovereignty for almost two years." For this reason, the idea was supported by only a few on the GC.

Addressing the subject of turning sovereignty over to the GC, I stressed, "We must make clear that this alternate path to sovereignty is unacceptable to us. The Governing Council has no mandate to rule Iraq. Its members, however capable as individuals, have little support. They lack credibility in large sectors of the population. As yet, they have hesitated in making important policy decisions unless pushed and prodded by the CPA.

"The Council is a leaky vessel. To grant them sovereignty before a constitution and elections not only mocks our avowed commitment to a constitutional process, it risks failure of that process. Left to their own devices with only the 'guiding hand' of the UN, it is entirely possible that the GC would dissolve itself, or worse, be dominated by one or two individuals."

I'd stated my case as forcefully as I could. Very late the same night I received a short note from the secretary of defense: "I agree with your memo and will send it to POTUS [President Bush] and members of the NSC. You're on the mark."

If only things in Washington were always that simple . . .

In the third week of September John Abizaid and Rick Sanchez came to brief me on their efforts to combine their strategic plan with the CPA's. It seemed they were making progress. Security was much better in the Kurdish north and most of the Shiite south. Training of the NIA was accelerating. Clay had reached agreement with the Jordanians to train up to 1,500 Iraqi police a month, though construction work at the training base in Jordan meant we couldn't start until right after Ramadan at the end of November.

But in the Sunni Triangle, and several parts of Baghdad, the insurgency remained a serious threat, which was beginning to affect the Coalition's economic recovery projects. Some European contractors were intimidated by ambushes on their vehicles and attacks on their work sites.

But Abizaid assured me our Combined Joint Task Force 7 troops and "special operators" were rolling up more insurgent networks than the enemy could replace. "Jerry," Abizaid said, "I recommend that Rick's people take over police training from the CPA."

We'd been expecting something like this proposal and I didn't like it. It would mean U.S. forces training Iraqi police, while at the same time fighting insurgents. Although our soldiers were the best combat troops in the world, they had been trained and equipped for fast-moving operations where they killed the enemy, not for community policing and criminal investigations. And I wondered about the military's motives. Pushing tens of thousands of Iraqi police recruits through truncated training courses in order to replace American troops didn't appear to me to be a sensible long-term approach to the country's security.

"We've been around this track before, John," I said. "I am fully on board with moving as fast as we can to stand up Iraqi security forces. Hell, that's why I made it the biggest element in the supplemental. But I'm really not convinced that the Army knows how to train professional police, and now that we finally have the Jordanian option worked out, I don't want to switch tracks again."

When Abizaid and Sanchez left, the debate was unresolved.

The next afternoon, my suspicion that the military still hoped to replace U.S. troops with unprepared Iraqi police in the spring was verified during a video teleconference linking CENTCOM and the CPA with Rumsfeld, Wolfowitz, and Abizaid. The secretary said that Abizaid put forward a hypothetical possibility that sufficient Iraqi security forces would be in place by March to allow us to pull a U.S. division out of Iraq.

Rumsfeld noted that he felt it was still too early to know if this would work since it would depend on how quickly we could train the Iraqi forces.

"Mr. Secretary," I said, bending close to the microphone in the small teleconference room, "we have to be realistic." I reviewed the facts. We had about 40,000 Iraqi police on duty, but these were basically former street police, only some of whom had had even a three-week refresher course. Kerik had estimated that eventually almost half of them would have to be washed out.

I went through the plans to train police in Jordan, noting that the program would produce 25,000 professional officers in fifteen months. But not a day before. And, while we were moving more quickly on training the New Iraqi Army, their basic responsibility should be to protect the country from external enemies, not to provide internal security. Well-armed military forces with public order duties were the bane of many Third World countries.

I got the impression that nobody in the conference wanted to hear this assessment.

"Well," Rumsfeld said, "we should just accelerate these training programs."

"Mr. Secretary, we are moving ahead at maximum speed." The Jordan program would train four times as many police in one year as had ever been attempted anywhere in the world.

Paul Wolfowitz suggested that Iraqi police would be better than our troops because they were native Arabic speakers and could thus provide superior intelligence about the insurgency.

"That's true, Paul," I said. "I agree. And we sure could use better intel on the bad guys. But we're not going to succeed in Iraq in the long run unless we leave behind a professional police force."

The creeping air of desperation about the troop rotation concerned me. Our troops and their leaders were dedicated to selfless service and accomplishing their missions. But securing the peace in Iraq after the conventional military campaign had been won was going to be a drawn-out, chaotic business—as I had cautioned the president and his national security advisers in Qatar. I had the uneasy feeling that the challenges of the spring troop rotation were pushing the Pentagon's leaders to consider steps detrimental to long-term success in Iraq.

I was back at the Pentagon on September 20 preparing for the upcoming week of testimony on the Hill when Clay called from Baghdad.

"Akila al-Hashimi was shot this morning leaving her house. She's in Al-Yarmouk Hospital."

One of only three women on the Governing Council, Akila was a sophisticated secular Shiite and former career diplomat. She had been preparing to accompany the Iraqi delegation to the UN General Assembly in New York.

"How bad?"

"I don't think she's gonna make it, Jerry," Clay said. "She's hit in the stomach with AK-47 fire and lost a lot of blood."

"Have we done everything we possibly can?"

"Yes. We had her transferred to our hospital in the Green Zone and I've been over there. I held her hand but she didn't respond and I also spoke to her relatives. It doesn't look good, frankly."

First Sergio, then Hakim, now this. Where will it ever end?

While reviewing my strategy for Hill testimony with Don Rumsfeld on Sunday, September 21, I learned that Doug Feith's office had drafted a policy paper calling for "some form" of early sovereignty. Don hadn't read it yet, but promised to get me a copy to review overnight.

Somebody's got to finally drive a stake through that concept.

On the morning of Monday, September 22, Paul Wolfowitz and I met alone in his Pentagon office just down the E-Ring corridor from Rumsfeld's suite. The subject was Feith's paper suggesting that we simply give sovereignty to the Governing Council by naming it a "Provisional Government."

I'd read it Sunday: old fish in a new wrapper.

Paul and I sat at a round table just inside the door to his office. We'd known each other for more than twenty years, and I respected his brilliance and insight on complex matters. I shared his belief that a democratic Iraq could revolutionize the region. But I was certain this would take time and patience.

After we had settled at the table over coffee, Paul asked, "What do you think of the policy shop's paper?"

"Frankly, not much. Your guys don't seem to understand how ineffective the GC is turning out to be." I chose my words, did not mince them. "Those people couldn't organize a parade, let alone run the country."

Paul did not look pleased. "But, we've got to move quickly on the political front," he said. "What if we just expanded the GC to a group of 100 or 200 to make them more representative, and *then* gave them sovereignty?"

"I guess we could do that, at least in theory," I replied. "But it'd be enormously time-consuming . . . and a waste of the time we consumed." I reminded him that it had taken the U.S.-U.K. Governance Team, about fifty of them, working twenty hours a day for more than two months, to come up with the initial twenty-five Iraqis for the GC. "God knows how long it would take to expand them."

"Well, why not just let the GC expand itself, then?"

"Paul, these guys have shown no capacity to broaden their representativeness, neither back in May, nor when they appointed the PrepComm, nor two weeks ago when they named the ministers."

Wolfowitz did not seem persuaded and shifted the subject to the security situation. Couldn't we find ways to speed up the training of Iraqis so they could replace Americans?

Where have I heard that before?

I reminded him that we had accelerated the police training to four times the largest number ever trained anywhere in a year.

"We're also doubling the pace of training of the New Iraqi Army. Going to have twenty-seven battalions in a year, instead of in two. But it's unrealistic to think that either of these forces will have any substantial capabilities by the time of our spring rotation, Paul. And the military is misleading you if you're being told otherwise."

"Seems to me that we should be able to use the Iraqi army in a substantial way for some of the security issues by then," he replied.

"But Paul, if there's one clear lesson from the past forty years it's that we should not encourage a professional army to have internal security duties"— especially in Iraq, where the army was Saddam's chosen instrument of repression.

"Well, I don't agree, Jerry. And I think the security situation is such that we'll have to make use of whatever Iraqi forces we have at hand."

He snapped shut the manila folder that held Feith's policy paper.

I left uneasy about the trend of thinking in the Pentagon.

My concern with the overall situation deepened that week as I was escorted around the committee rooms of Congress. Over a period of twenty years I'd often testified to Congress, but I'd never encountered the animosity I now faced from some representatives and senators. This was September 2003. We were well into the 2004 election season.

Over the next four days I testified nine times before congressional committees. I felt in good hands as Tom Korologos escorted me from room to room, greeting Republican and Democrat congressmen with equal cheeriness. With the glare of the television lights, my recollections of that week's testimony became as blurry as my vision. But certain days stood out.

At the Senate Appropriations Committee, there was the expected negativity from the Democrats and support from the Republicans. Committee chairman Senator Ted Stevens of Alaska made it clear that he intended to push the supplemental request down for a floor vote as soon as possible. The Democrat side complained about the amount of money involved and that the administration had "no plan" for Iraq. When I reminded them that the CPA had sent our full fifty-seven-page Strategic Plan to every member of Congress on July 23, the Democrat members professed to have never seen it. Moreover I'd unveiled the plan at a National Press Club speech the same week. The DOD staffer who had hand delivered all 535 copies of the plan—one to each office on the Hill—in July was with me today.

"Most likely," he whispered to me, "the Democrats' staffs just threw it away."

On Tuesday, September 23, the Senate Republican Caucus invited me to address their weekly lunch meeting. The meeting went well. But there were still a number of senators who wanted to see the supplemental turned into a loan, or at least collateralized against future oil earnings. I spoke against this idea. Iraq was already almost crippled with Saddam's multibillion-dollar debt. We could not take the chance of burdening a fragile new Iraqi government with even more outstanding loans.

By tradition, any speaker invited to one party's caucus had to also be made available to the other's. I went around the corner to the Democrats' lunch caucus. From the moment I entered the room, I knew there was trouble. Most of the forty-nine Democrat senators were seated around lunch tables. Minority

Leader Tom Daschle was standing at the front of the room, but he didn't bother to introduce me. He just waved me to a lectern.

I started to explain why the supplemental appropriation was important by noting "the lessons of history," having in mind the failures following World War I and the success after World War II. Senator Jay Rockefeller of West Virginia rudely interrupted, "We all know our history, Mr. Ambassador. Don't bother us with history."

I paused and then continued to describe how after World War I, the Allies had withdrawn after saddling Germany with crushing debt.

"We don't want to hear about history!" Rockefeller shouted.

The hell with you, I thought. I plunged on. "What I have to say about the history of those two wars is relevant to the president's request. And presumably therefore relevant to senators making decisions about how to vote on that request." I explained the rationale for the supplemental for about seven minutes as the senators sat, arms crossed, glaring.

Senator Joe Biden of Delaware, who had supported war in Iraq, posed the first question, which was more of a lecture about the importance of an international rather than a unilateral effort in Iraq. I said that our effort was in fact already international. Dozens of other countries were contributing troops. I had citizens from twenty-five other countries on the CPA staff. More than sixty countries had already pledged to help with reconstruction. "Spare me that Coalition stuff," was his only response.

Later that week, I testified to the Senate Armed Services Committee, a session that followed the template of my Appropriations appearance. The Republicans were conciliatory, the Democrats querulous. Senator Ted Kennedy, perhaps reflecting Democrat embarrassment at having ignored our Strategic Plan when it was given to them two months earlier, waved a copy for the cameras and called our work "a joke." Left unsaid was what precisely he found amusing about the plan.

My last hearing was before the House Foreign Affairs Committee, which was generally supportive of the president in Iraq. Democrat Tom Lantos of California, who had been a staunch ally in the war against terrorism when I was Reagan's ambassador at large for counterterrorism, made a strong argument for the supplemental. But several Democrats launched into accusations against contractors for their "obscene profits." Other Democrats lectured me about the "tens of thousands" of innocent Iraqi civilians that our forces had allegedly killed.

Congresswoman Diane E. Watson from Los Angeles demanded to know exactly how many Iraqis had died since the war began and chastised me for not knowing. As I began my reply, she had cut me off, noting that her time had expired. So I asked the chairman for permission to answer. No, Representative Watson insisted. Her time was over, and so was the hearing.

But I persisted. Several Democrats urged the chairman to allow me to continue. I explained that the liberation of Iraq had produced fewer casualties, military or civilian, than any major military operation in history. But Watson was also not interested in history. She loudly exited stage right, accompanied by a glaring staff. I carried on: even after fifty years' study, historians did not know how many civilians had been killed in World War II. But we shouldn't lose our perspective. In Iraq, our troops had done a noble thing in liberating a country of 25 million people from one of the world's most vicious dictatorships.

There was one pleasant interlude during that stressful week: On Wednesday, September 24, President and Laura Bush invited Francie and me to join them for a private dinner at the White House. Once again, the president took care to ensure that the dinner was known in Washington circles. The *Washington Post* referred to this as our "double date."

Francie and I went up the elevator in the East Wing to the family's private quarters, and when the elevator door slid open, the Bushes were there with hands extended.

The president was informally dressed in slacks and a dark blue sport shirt; Mrs. Bush was a little more formal in a suit and high heels. They were relaxed and soon so were we. One immediate bond was the Bushes' pets, Spot the Brittany spaniel; Barney, the black Scottie; and the even blacker cat, India. The pets milled underfoot with charming ill discipline, which gave the residence the feel of a well-loved family home.

The president drew me over to a yellow couch at the end of the room and we talked intently about Iraq as Francie and Mrs. Bush discussed books. At least I supposed that's what they were talking about because both are passionate readers, and, it turns out, both read in bed. I learned that the president and I end our days with almost identical words: "Please! Put your book down and turn out the damn light." The president sipped a nonalcoholic beer, the rest of us had white wine.

The president asked about Iraq.

"I'm optimistic about the long term," I said. I repeated what I had told him in June in Doha, that the Iraqi people are resourceful and hardworking. "All we have to do is give them a chance."

The president wondered about the Iraqis' views on Islamic government. "Are the ayatollahs going to take over?"

I said the Coalition had just begun public-opinion polling in September. "From everything we can tell so far—though I wouldn't bet my bottom dollar on polls at this stage—it seems very few Shia want a theocratic government." It would be important to future stability to encourage Iraq to adopt a constitution protecting individual rights and embodying some kind of a federal system which would balance the historic power of Baghdad with authority for the provinces.

"How're your hearings on the supplemental going?"

"Grueling," I admitted. "Nine appearances in four days, but I get the impression that both parties will support the request in the end." My analysis was that despite the hostility I had encountered, most in Congress would recognize the need to help rebuild Iraq and continue the war on terrorism.

The president asked about the security situation.

"Frankly, I still think we don't have adequate intelligence about the insurgency," I said. "And my experience in counterterrorism has also convinced me that we're up against a growing and sophisticated threat. I've raised these concerns with George Tenet."

President Bush absorbed this but did not respond.

"How are the Iraqi forces doing?"

"So-so. We're going to graduate the first battalion of the army in a couple of weeks. But, frankly, Mr. President, I'm concerned with how the Pentagon is counting Iraqis in the police and Civil Defense Corps."

"What do you mean, 'counting'?"

"Well, they seem to be counting every Iraqi in uniform as part of the overall available force levels. That's misleading. It suggests that an Iraqi policeman is equal to a soldier in the 1st AD or the 101st Airborne. Just not so."

He asked what was driving this tendency, and I said I thought there was understandable concern in the Army about the troop rotation coming up in early 2004. "In the long run, Iraq's security has to depend on Iraqis and especially on a professional police force. And we've got a program to produce that force. But it'll take another sixteen to eighteen months. Before then, we shouldn't fool ourselves about Iraqi capabilities."

The conversation moved to Ahmad Chalabi, who was in New York with Iraq's UN General Assembly delegation.

"You know, Mr. President, he's playing along with the French, pushing us to just turn sovereignty over to the Governing Council now."

"But are those guys up to running Iraq?"

"No, they're not. I called Chalabi two days ago to ask him to knock it off. He promised me he would, and then yesterday, there he is again in the *New York Times*, attacking our plans. He's incorrigible."

"Yeah, Condi showed the article to me." The president said that Chalabi was telling American congressmen that Iraq could "easily" double or triple its oil production. "Unrealistic, and it undercuts my supplemental request, especially with some of the wavering Republicans. Really pisses me off. I had planned to lay into him when he came through the receiving line at the reception I hosted in New York yesterday. But he had his daughter with him and I didn't think it appropriate to chew him out in front of her. But he is being a real pain in the you-know-what."

"I entirely agree, Mr. President," I replied. "But Chalabi *is* something of a tragic figure. Clearly very bright; one of the few Iraqi leaders who understands a modern economy. He did yeoman's work getting that economic package through the Governing Council. Couldn't have done it without him. But in the end, his ambition and cleverness will do him in."

"Has Chalabi outrun his favor over at the Pentagon?" the president wondered.

"I don't think he's outrun it yet, but he's getting pretty close."

I didn't mention that earlier that afternoon I had called the vice president's chief of staff, Scooter Libby, about Chalabi's activities, and he had told me that "folks around here are pretty fed up with him, too."

"I had a very frank talk with Chirac the other day," the president said, referring to the French president. "Told him that some people in America were getting the impression that France wanted us to fail in Iraq. 'Non, Non,' says Jacques, 'that's wrong.' Well, I told him, every time you speak on the subject, many people get that impression."

We chuckled. I told the president that I had studied and lived in France, had a house and many friends there. But I found the French posturing on Iraq inexcusable.

After about forty-five minutes, Mrs. Bush suggested we go in for dinner. We ate in a small private dining room around a square table. Next to the president was a little console table holding a red telephone. Mrs. Bush said that they always said grace before meals as Francie and I did, so we held hands, bowed our heads, and prayed.

We chatted about subjects common to middle-aged couples, kids mostly, and in our case, our granddaughter, too. But inevitably the talk veered back to Iraq. I told the president that one of my favorite members of the Governing Council, Akila al-Hashimi, had died that morning.

"That's just awful," he said, obviously moved.

"I think we should pray for her family too," Francie said.

The president nodded and suggested Francie lead the prayer. So we held hands, bowed our heads again, and asked God to comfort and keep Akila and her family "in the palm of His hand."

Flying back to Iraq four nights later, I awakened somewhere over the Atlantic in the dark cool cabin of the Air Force G-5. I suddenly remembered the White House dinner, and pictured the four of us praying for the soul of a brave Muslim woman named Akila. Just after we'd prayed, I had tried to lighten the mood by telling the Bushes of my last conversation with her.

"You Americans are going too far with this democracy stuff, Mr. Ambassador," Akila had lightly scolded me one day on the margins of a GC meeting.

"What do you mean by that?"

"Well, last night I planned to take my kids out to dinner and chose a restaurant. They wanted to go to another place, and insisted that—being democrats now—we put it to a family vote. And I lost."

Chapter 7
CAN AMERICA
STAND THE HEAT?

■ BAGHDAD
OCTOBER 2, 2003

The newly refurbished district hall was crowded. Before liberation, this eastern Baghdad neighborhood was known as 7 Nisan ("April 7"), the date of the Iraqi Baath Party's founding in 1951. When the local council was chosen in the citywide elections organized by the CPA in June, its first act was to rename the neighborhood 9 Nisan to mark the collapse of Saddam Hussein's regime. Under Saddam, the building had been the headquarters of an attack helicopter squadron. *Maybe*, I thought, watching schoolchildren singing and dancing before us on the stage, *one of the Mi-28 gunship units that slaughtered thousands of Shiites in 1991 had been based here*.

The children swayed to the beat of drums and reed flutes, boys in checked kefiya headdresses of both Shiite and Sunni tribes, as well as Kurdish turbans, and the girls in embroidered shirts and silver bangles. They seemed tangible proof that our experiment in local self-government was bearing fruit. Under Saddam, the Baathist Party in Baghdad had controlled almost every aspect of people's lives, right down to routing water lines to a neighborhood mosque or market, and repaving streets. Now, in dozens of Iraqi cities, people had selected local representatives who were answerable to them to meet these responsibilities.

Seated beside me was the new chairman of the District Council, Dr. Ziyad Cattan, a Ph.D. economist who had spent twenty years in Germany and returned after Liberation. Having traded a comfortable life in Europe "to serve my country" for a minimal salary and the drudgery of rebuilding 9 Nisan, he embodied the dedication so many Iraqis felt for their nation.

To end the children's presentation, a full-throated boy of seven blasted out a poem, extolling the glory of a free Iraq and lamenting the horror of brutal tyranny with its mass graves. This had my seatmate, the district chairman, in tears.

I remarked that the building itself represented the change which had come to be since April 9. Before, Saddam's army, an instrument of his terror, had used the compound to repress his people. But today, the people's representatives worked here on their behalf, rebuilding schools, women's centers, and clinics, establishing parks and playgrounds, and finding jobs for over five thousand unemployed in the process. I concluded that the building's transformation symbolized Iraq's "Future of Hope."

Several Iraqi and a couple of Western reporters were covering the ceremony. *I wonder how much media we'll get*, I thought, returning to my armored Suburban. *Good news is no news.*

But there was plenty of good news around for those who wanted to see it.

Driving back to the CPA, I reviewed my daily reports on essential services. Electrical power generation the previous day had reached 4,217 MW, a post-Liberation record and basically at prewar levels. Within days, we would get generators from two large plants back onstream, and that would take us past the ninety-day goal set in our Strategic Plan. And the day before we had produced a record 1.96 million barrels of oil, meaning we would hit our 2 million–barrel daily target three months ahead of schedule. There had been another attack on the northern pipeline, so our exports still lagged. But we were gradually taking control of oil production, the heart of Iraq's economy.

I was convinced that in spite of setbacks, we could see the corner we needed to turn on essential services. At some point—we weren't there yet—we should have enough power capacity and oil in reserve that isolated attacks on electrical towers and pipelines would have less impact, and thus the incentive for such attacks should begin to decline. Once that happened, we would be over the tipping point in the infrastructure battle. Of course, our enemies could make the same calculation, and their strategy would no doubt be to step up sabotage. This meant we had to sustain a robust military presence to ensure security for these reconstruction projects.

But the Western and Arab press focused almost exclusively on insurgent attacks, and ignored optimistic stories such as the opening of the 9 Nisan District Council.

As my convoy crossed the Al-Jumhuriya Bridge toward the fortified Green Zone in the heavy afternoon traffic, I pictured those children in the District Council hall. They had worn the colorful dress of Shiite Marsh Arabs and

Sunni Bedouin, of Kurds and Turkmen, unselfconsciously. All the hard work and frustration of building a new Iraq was worth it when you thought of those kids' future.

"We almost had a real bad day, sir," my security chief, Frank Gallagher, said two hours later, closing my office door behind him.

Frank was clearly distressed, which was very unusual: an 82 mm mortar round could explode thirty yards away and Frank, an ex-Marine, wouldn't break a sweat. He flipped through the pages of his black notebook.

"Mr. Ambassador, the bad guys had a hit team out for you on the way back from the District Council ceremony this afternoon," he reported. "At *least* one hit team."

I sat back, feeling angry. "What's the deal?"

"Radio intercepts," Frank said. "All in what the intel guys are calling 'military-jargon Iraqi Arabic.' First message was as we were mounting up the convoy to leave the District Council compound. 'Target is in second Chevrolet,' that message said. 'In front of third machine gun truck.' That's what they call the Humvees."

I remembered climbing into the air-conditioned Suburban in the dusty lot of the District Council. Lots of people were milling around, as usual. *One of them was marking me for death.* "What else?"

"The second radio replies that they are proceeding in a van to intercept your convoy with five RPGs."

The rocket-propelled grenade was ubiquitous among terrorist bands. They were simple to fire and very accurate, with a shaped warhead that cut through armor, and they were killing our soldiers every week in Iraq's cities. If an RPG had hit my vehicle, everyone inside would have been incinerated.

"Why didn't they hit us, Frank?"

"The bastard got stuck in traffic, sir," Frank said. "He calls in for some other team to take over the ambush, but nobody answers. It was a real close call, boss."

For weeks, I'd accepted the possibility of an assassin infiltrating the marble corridors of the palace, as well as the dangers from regular rocket and mortar attacks. These radio intercepts indicated that the insurgents meant business. But I had a job to do and was damned if the insurgents were going to stop me from traveling around Baghdad and Iraq.

"Thanks, Frank," I said. "While you're here, let's go over my travel schedule to Kirkush on Saturday."

Meeting in the Oval Office, May 6, 2003, with President George W. Bush and Secretary of Defense Donald Rumsfeld

Bremer and his wife, Francie

Bremer at his desk in Baghdad

4

Welcoming Prime Minister Tony Blair to Basra

5

Meeting American troops

With Major General David Petraeus, commander of 101st Airborne. British Ambassador John
Sawers in background

6

Hume Horan, Senior Adviser with the
Coalition Provisional Authority in Baghdad

On the move around Iraq

7

8

A Kurdish welcome in Sulaymaniya

Kurdish leaders Jalal Talabani (*left*) and Massoud Barzani (*right*)

UN Special Representative Sergio de Mello introducing the Governing Council July 13, 2003, a month before he was killed by a car bomb at UN Headquarters in Baghdad

GoverningCouncil members *(left to right)*: Adnan Pachachi, Abdul Aziz Hakim, Jalal Talabani, Ibrahim al-Jaafari, Yonadam Kanna

12

13

Meeting with the Governing Council *(left to right)*: Lieutenant General Ricardo Sanchez, Bremer, General John Abizaid, Ahmad Chalabi, Akila Hashimi

Planning reconstruction with tribal leaders in central Iraq

14

Checking in from the field during a refueling stop at Balad airbase north of Baghdad

15

Talking to National Security Adviser Condoleezza Rice from Kurdistan

16

Dinner at Ayatollah Hussein al-Sadr's house *(left to right)*: Ayatollah al-Sadr, Iraqi National Security Adviser Mowaffak al-Rubaie, Dan Senor, Bremer

17

Farewell call by General Tommy Franks. At right, seated, Ambassador Clayton McManaway

In the Oval Office with the president, Andrew Card, Condi Rice and the vice president

Greeting Secretary of State Colin Powell at Baghdad Airport

21

Meeting with Deputy Secretary of Defense Paul Wolfowitz and General
Abizaid in Bremer's office

22

Under Secretary of Defense Douglas Feith

23

Greeting young Iraqi soccer players

24

With the chairman of Nisan 9 Council and a young singer October 2, 2003, minutes before an aborted assassination attempt on Bremer

Dr. Adel Mehdi, senior member of the SCIRI party and prominent deputy member of the Governing Council

25

26

President Bush greets General Sanchez during his surprise visit to Iraq for Thanksgiving, November 27, 2003

Sanchez and Bremer announce Saddam's capture, December 14, 2003

27

Saddam Hussein
as prisoner

28

29

Governing Council
member Ahmad
Chalabi confronts
Saddam in prison,
December 14, 2003

Opening Women's
Center in Baghdad,
on International
Women's Day,
March 8, 2004

30

4:00 A.M., March 8, 2004: The
Interim Constitution is agreed

Interim Constitution signed by
Sayyid Mohammad Bahr al-Uloum,
senior member of the
Governing Council

Congratulations to the Governance Team on helping with the constitution *(left to right)*: Lydia Khalil, Scott Carpenter, Roman Martinez, Irfan
Siddiq, Meghan O'Sullivan

34

Ambassador Dick Jones, CPA Deputy, addresses a town council in Baquba

Congratulating Iraqi National Guardsmen in training

35

(Left to right) David Richmond, Bob Blackwill, Lakhdar Brahimi, Bremer, Sheik Ghazi at funeral of assassinated Governing Council President Izzadin Salim, May 18, 2004

36

37

A daily meeting with Prime Minister Ayad Allawi, June 2004

Meeting Vice President Ibrahim al-Jaafari, June 2004

38

39

At the monument to Saddam's victims at Al-Hillah, with Sheik al-Qizwini and survivors, June 27, 2004

Sovereignty is passed to Iraqi Chief Justice Medhat al-Mahmoud and Prime Minister Allawi, 10:26 A.M., June 28, 2004

40

President Bush and Prime Minister Blair shake hands on receiving news of the transfer of sovereignty while at a NATO summit in Ankara, Turkey

41

42

Boarding a C-130, waving farewell to Deputy Prime Minister Barham Saleh, June 28, 2004

I wanted to make the point that irrespective of the threat, I was going to keep on the move. Frank got the message and on his way out of my office, I later learned, told Brian McCormack that he was deeply concerned by my plan for that trip. That night when I wrote my e-mail to Francie, I described the inspiring ceremony at the District Council hall. I did not mention Frank's report.

The ranks of troops marched flawlessly on the sandy parade ground at Kirkush. I stood beside the Governing Council's October president, Ayad Allawi, as the graduating battalion took their position before the reviewing stand.

"They look splendid," Allawi said proudly.

The sun glinted off the soldiers' new AK-47s. The troops wore the "chocolate chip" fatigues made familiar in Operation Desert Storm twelve years earlier, which reinforced the sense that these 500 men had been transformed into allies of the Coalition. Their eight weeks of training had been grueling. Beyond the skills of light infantry, their American trainers had taught them self-reliance and loyalty to their unit and country. This first battalion of the NIA would be attached to the U.S. 4th Infantry Division patrolling the Iranian border.

After a drumbeat flourish, the soldiers raised their right hands and took the oath of allegiance. "I am a patriot," they chanted. "I voluntarily serve in the cause of freedom for my country, Iraq."

Arrayed to the left of the parade ground were the ranks of incoming trainees. They would begin their training at dawn—after hours of scrubbing and polishing the barracks of the departing battalion—fulfilling a ritual common to all professional armies.

The hundreds of guests in the reviewing stand had to squint in the sunlight. But I saw that Allawi wasn't just narrowing his eyes. The emotions of the moment had brought him to tears.

I, too, felt pride. In many respects, this ceremony was one of the most important events since Liberation. Another of the ninety-day milestones established in our Strategic Plan, and we'd met that goal almost to the day. As we had expected, most of these young men were veterans of the old army. But now their mission was to defend, not to repress, their fellow citizens. As I had promised Abdul Aziz Hakim in May, the commander of this first battalion was a Shiite, a veteran of Saddam's army who at last had a chance to serve his country freed of the taint of Baathism.

But, as usual, this day was not free of dispute. At the landing zone before boarding our Black Hawk for the flight back to Baghdad, I took Allawi aside to note that the morning's New York Times had yet another story quoting Governing Council members Pachachi, Chalabi, and the GC's one Turkmen member, Songul Chapouk, criticizing the supplemental budget request.

"The president has made a substantial commitment to Iraqi reconstruction at no small political risk to himself," I reminded Allawi. "It's stupid for members of the GC to publicly criticize his plan while our Congress is debating it. That can only harm both the president and the Iraqi people."

"*I* understand," Allawi said. "But many of the others on the Council lack experience in such complicated matters."

Council members wanted lucrative hunks of the supplemental to be spent in Iraq, not on foreign contractors. I agreed with this objective. I reminded Allawi that I had ordered all contractors to allocate as much work to Iraqi subcontractors and to employ as many Iraqis as possible. Bechtel, our largest contractor, had a target of placing 70 percent of its contracts within Iraq and had already hired over 40,000 Iraqis.

Allawi agreed to speak to the GC members.

If the training of the New Iraqi Army was proceeding well, the dispute within our government over police training dragged on. The next day, I met with a congressional delegation headed by Senator Mitch McConnell, the influential Kentucky Republican. Lieutenant General Sanchez gave what I felt was an overly optimistic briefing on the progress that Iraqi Civil Defense Corps, police, and Coalition forces were making against the insurgency. He announced that the Coalition military were "recruiting and training" police across the country and now had almost 54,000 on duty.

Where the hell did that number come from? I wondered. Then I remembered that General Abizaid had told me a couple of days before of his plan to reduce American forces from fifteen to eleven brigades in January. He was counting on additional foreign troops and Iraqi security forces to make up the difference.

I didn't interrupt Rick's presentation to the senators. But I realized that I had to put down some markers when he'd finished. The error of equating Iraqi police and Coalition forces just wouldn't go away. Most of these police were not "trained." You couldn't take a former traffic cop and turn him into a professional police officer with the three-week refresher course now being offered by various Coalition military units in Iraq. Moreover, if the military continued to count these police toward the total number of security forces necessary to maintain order in Iraq, it might undercut the rationale for money in the supplemental to professionally train 40,000 police in Jordan.

When Sanchez finished, I spoke out.

"We've got to be careful not to rush the political transition so much that we leave behind a wobbly civil structure. Just as important, we've got to ensure that we create a fully professional, modern, and nonpolitical police and armed forces."

I looked from the senators to Rick Sanchez. There was a hot and mounting tension in the CPA conference room. I was glad that Pat Kennedy had got the air-conditioning going.

After that strained session, I asked Doug Brand, our lanky Yorkshire police officer who was now acting Senior Adviser to the Interior Ministry, to come in with Clay to discuss police training. "Let's review the situation, Doug. At the end of August, Bernie Kerik said that many of the 35,000 police then on the rolls would have to be dropped for incompetence, corruption, or previous human rights abuses. Now Sanchez reports that we've got 54,000 police officers on patrol a month later. How the hell could *that* happen?"

"Apparently General Sanchez is operating under an order from General Abizaid to recruit 30,000 police officers in thirty days," Doug said. "The Army is sweeping up half-educated men off the streets, running them through a three-week training course, arming them, and then calling them 'police.' It's a scandal, pure and simple."

"You know the military, Clay. Can you find me the order they're using to do this hiring?"

"I can get it," Clay said simply.

The military seemed to be proceeding with its plans to replace American combat units with ill-trained Iraqi police. But before I could raise this problem during that afternoon's secure call to Rumsfeld, he asked me to find some positive, newsworthy "interim steps" that we could take to "migrate" political authority to the Iraqis. "We've got to show some forward motion on the political front, Jerry."

That's Feith's Defense policy shop-talking.

Rumsfeld conceded that the economic area was in pretty good shape. I agreed, noting that we'd seen a burst of economic activity since Liberation, including the mixed blessing of hundreds of thousands of new cars jamming Iraq's streets. In a repeat of our conversations in September, the secretary again pressed for some way to demonstrate "motion" in the political field. Then he said that Abizaid was now factoring the "Iraqi role" in security into his reporting. This was important to show positive movement to the Iraqi people.

It was my turn to clear the decks. First, I told the secretary that I agreed we had to get the Governing Council moving or put some other mechanism in place. Then I turned to the security question. "Mr. Secretary, I have to be frank," I said. "You're seeing inflated numbers on police rosters. We shouldn't kid ourselves thinking that the Iraqis are better prepared than they are. We needed a professional police force here, one that's trained to a high standard. That's the whole point of the program in Jordan."

Rumsfeld did not seem convinced. He said that it was better to get the "process started quickly" by having our Army bring in these extra police.

I disagreed. I told him of Doug Brand's description of the Army pulling guys off the street and running them through a short "training" course.

At the end of the call, Rumsfeld seemed to understand, saying he would "push back" on the police in the total-force projection numbers when his office announced them the next week.

I thought that Rumsfeld had sounded tired, a bit more impatient than usual. The conflict in Iraq had come to a political boil in Washington—the presidential election was only a year off—and the secretary of defense was no doubt feeling the heat.

One of the problems facing the American government was that we had found no stockpiles of weapons of mass destruction, the principal *casus belli*.

Dr. David Kay and his large Iraq Survey Group had scoured the country for months. On October 2, Kay had delivered his initial report to a joint House and Senate committee. His bottom line was clear: at the war's outbreak, Saddam Hussein had almost certainly not possessed the thousands of tons of poison gas and their delivery warheads, the hundreds of kilos of deadly biological warfare agents, or the industrial system and fissile material needed to produce nuclear weapons that the intelligence services of all major Western countries judged he had.

Still the WMD picture remained ambiguous. In the 1990s, Saddam Hussein had obstructed the work of UN weapons inspectors. His biological weapons program, whose existence he repeatedly denied, had come to light only after a defector revealed it. In November 2002, the United Nations Security Council had found Iraq in violation of sixteen UN resolutions and demanded that it come clean about its WMD programs.

Kay stressed to Congress that his report was a "snapshot." He stated that his team had found disturbing evidence of compartmentalized biological warfare programs in secret laboratories, whose personnel might have fled abroad, "and may have taken evidence and even weapons-related materials with them." While the team had not found the materials yet, "we are not yet at the point where we can say definitely either that such weapons do not exist or that they existed before the war and our only task is to find where they had gone." Kay had told me before returning to Washington to testify that he was almost certain that the Mukhabarat had cloaked an experimental germ-warfare program and that he was going to report this to Congress.

Indeed, Kay described to Congress a secret "network of laboratories within the Iraqi Intelligence Service" dedicated to chemical and biological warfare, which United Nations WMD inspectors did not discover during their frenetic searching in early 2003. Kay also had uncovered "dual-use" facilities capable of producing both poison gas and fertilizer. He and his team were able to uncover this information only because the Baathist regime's wall of secrecy had been smashed.

For years I had condemned Saddam's support for terrorism. The bipartisan National Commission on Terrorism, which I had chaired, reported to President Clinton and the Congress, fifteen months before 9/11, that America faced the daunting prospect of Islamist extremists conducting mass casualty terrorism on our soil. American security would be gravely threatened if terrorists got their hands on WMD. So I had been fully behind the president's decision to invade Iraq and topple Saddam's dangerous regime. Like David Kay, I'd been surprised when his Iraq Survey Group hadn't unearthed stocks of WMD.

But having seen firsthand the graves in the hills of Iraqi Kurdistan and the gruesome photos of the Kurds of Halabja killed by Saddam's chemical weapons, I sleep easier knowing Saddam Hussein had been deposed and no longer had access to such weapons of terror. Whether he had an actual WMD arsenal or only the military-industrial base primed and ready to assemble one, I am convinced that we prevented the tyrant from massacring more innocent people.

When Kay gave his initial report to Congress, I wasn't surprised that most media accounts focused on his admission of not finding WMD stocks, and downplayed his uncertainty as to whether such weapons might have once existed, might still remain hidden, or have been spirited out of the country.

Kay's conclusions must have been bitter news on the Pentagon E-Ring. Some of the prewar American intelligence on Iraqi WMD stockpiles had been provided by Ahmad Chalabi's Iraqi National Congress exiles to the Office of the Secretary of Defense (OSD). Now there was no video showing stacks of Sarin gas warheads or vials of anthrax spores to counterbalance the ceaseless negativism in the world media. Rumsfeld needed the occupation to show progress quickly. And he wanted to reduce U.S. casualties.

We shared these goals. We didn't agree on the way to achieve them.

• • •

After my military briefing the next morning, I asked General Sanchez to stay behind. We needed to clear the air on training the Iraqi police. In four months of confronting difficult problems from different perspectives, Sanchez and I had enjoyed good relations. But our professional relationship was blurred. Military protocol gave ambassadors four-star rank, and Rick was a lieutenant general, a three-star. He reported directly to General Abizaid at CENTCOM. But I was the president's personal representative in Iraq, and the military were under orders to "coordinate" their actions with me.

"We're not on the same page on the police program, Rick."

He considered this in his quiet way. "All right, sir," he said cautiously.

"Look," I continued. "I've told the SecDef and Abizaid that there's an important role for the military in this project. And that's to help us find about 200,000 potential police recruits from whom we can select thirty-five or forty thousand cadets for training in Jordan. Now it seems that your command is pushing thousands of young Iraqis through three-week training and sending them out to augment your units.

"General," I said. "That's got to stop. This program is creating a bogus police force with little capability and less credibility in the eyes of the Iraqis. And the inflated numbers could mislead our national leadership into believing that Iraq is better prepared to defend itself than it is."

"All right, sir," Sanchez said formally. "I understand your instructions. We'll stop recruiting."

"Good," I said. "But we've still got the problem of what to do with these policemen already on the payroll. Maybe we can move some of them over to the Facilities Protection Service where training's less important." The FPS was an organization we were recruiting to provide static guards around key ministries and other buildings.

"I'll work it, sir," Rick said.

I was pulling on my running shoes just after dawn when the bedside phone rang. Strange. Too early for anyone in Iraq to call, and probably too late for some bureaucrat in Washington to twist the eight-thousand-mile screwdriver.

"Dad, I'm glad I got you."

It was my son, Paul. I fought the impulse to ask if his mother was all right.

"Have you seen the New York Times?"

"No, Paul," I joked. "Abdullah the paper boy hasn't arrived yet."

"Better check it out on the Web, Dad. It looks like the president has told the NSC to take over the CPA from the Pentagon."

I downloaded the online edition of that morning's *Times* and found Washington correspondent David Sanger's story.

Bush Overhauls Approach to Iraq

The White House has ordered a major reorganization of U.S. efforts to quell violence in Iraq and Afghanistan and to speed the reconstruction of both countries, according to senior administration officials.

The new structure, which includes the creation of an "Iraq Stabilization Group" that will be run by the national security adviser, Condoleezza Rice, appears to be part of an effort to assert more direct control over events.

Henceforth, the story asserted, Condi Rice, not Don Rumsfeld, would be the president's point person for Iraq. But I would still report to the Defense Department.

"This puts accountability right into the White House," a senior administration official said.

Toward the end of the article, the author stated:

State Department officials have complained bitterly that they have been shut out of decision-making about Iraq, even as attacks on American troops have increased, lights have gone out, and oil production remained stuck far below even prewar levels.

The reorganization was a surprise to me. I could not tell from the *Times* piece what had inspired it. There was an assertion that certain people felt we had been slow in restoring essential services. I e-mailed Reuben Jeffery, our CPA Washington representative, that this morning's figures showed almost 5,000 MW of electrical power generated and that oil production had reached 1,946,000 barrels at midnight and would top 2 million a day this week. I added that we were on track to introduce the new currency in a few days, that *all* the schools and clinics had been reopened, as well as most of the banks. And the CPA almost certainly had more junior, mid-grade, and senior Foreign Service officers and retired ambassadors working in Iraq than anywhere but the State Department itself.

"Find out what the hell's going on back there," I urged him.

• • •

Rice called that afternoon. She'd heard from Reuben about my concerns.

"That reporter got it all wrong, Jerry."

The reorganization had not been meant to reflect any unhappiness with the CPA: rather the intention of the new organization was to help us mobilize support from the bureaucracy.

"Good," I said. "But I'm still concerned about how the story'll be read in the Washington hothouse. Given the way it's worded, people might conclude that the CPA's relations with the Pentagon have been weakened, which would give me real trouble with the military here."

"Not so," she said. "We just wanted to help the CPA accelerate your work."

"Well," I said. "Inaccurate *Times* stories have a habit of never going away. They get something wrong, it enters the common wisdom, and you can never set the record straight."

"Tell me about it, Jerry.".

We discussed the Governing Council's paralysis on the constitutional process.

"What are we going to do if the GC continues to insist on electing the Constitutional Convention?" Rice asked. "I don't think the political situation in Washington will support another year of the current status. Can we put together some kind of a provisional government?"

I paused to reflect that now every senior member on the president's foreign policy team—Powell, Rumsfeld, and Rice—had pushed this idea at me over the past three weeks. It was getting mighty lonely out here.

"Condi, we're working our butts off on that problem. But what's important is to start a *coherent* political process, even if it takes a year to complete."

"Well, we've just got to get the Governing Council off the dime."

I reminded her that, given the upcoming month of Ramadan, at best the GC might be able to get a locally selected Constitutional Convention (CC) afloat in early 2004.

"What do you recommend?"

"Look, security is our main problem," I said. "Some of that's due to the 100,000 hardened criminals Saddam freed. Those guys don't give a fig for an Iraqi government, provisional or otherwise. The Baathists, whose goal is to shoot their way back into power, are paying them to plant IEDs. Neither they, the professional terrorists, nor the jihadis could care less about Iraqi self-government. So the proposition that rushing to a temporary government will fix our security problem strikes me as wrong. And if we draw down our military too soon, we'll just encourage more, not less, violence from these guys."

"Well, I'm becoming agnostic on the issue," Rice said. "And I recognize that you're the guy on the scene."

That last made me feel a little less lonely. But as I noted in my nightly message to Francie, "If America cannot stand the heat after less than six months, we are going to have a very untidy century."

It was clear that we were reaching a crisis point on the Governing Council's ineffectiveness. A few days later I met with Scott Carpenter and Tom Krajeski, another Foreign Service officer, Scott's deputy in Governance.

"Guys, realistically, does the GC have a future?"

I was seeking their judgment on whether the twenty-four members, still split along sectarian and ethnic lines, could cooperate long enough to organize a representative Constitutional Convention.

"They haven't changed their stripes much in three months," Tom said.

"Or their work habits," Scott added. "They want more authority, but they don't know how to use it."

"Look," I told them. "It's clear to me that folks in Washington are getting impatient. Lots of pressure just to turn over sovereignty ASAP. I'm sure that would be a mistake. So somehow we've got to get a constitutional process started, working around Sistani's fatwa. And we've either got to make the GC effective or make it go away."

"When we get the CC convened, we could take some Governing Council members, throw them together with the ministers, and call the resulting body the 'Provisional Government,' " Scott offered. "Meanwhile we put the remaining members of the Council into the CC to help write the constitution, and we do it all so as to expand the Sunnis' place at the table."

Scott was hitting on a key point. For months we had been seeking ways to get the Sunnis more engaged in the political process. Now that we finally had CPA officials in provincial capitals in the Sunni regions, our staff was broadening contacts with Sunni leaders. But as we'd found before (and as the UN and Iraqi politicians themselves would find later), identifying responsible Sunni leaders was difficult. Saddam had either co-opted or killed most of them.

Scott's idea for a provisional government might just work, I said. "But how do we convene the CC?"

"How about picking up on the PrepComm's second option, some kind of 'local election' process?" Scott asked.

"I floated that idea past Hakim the other day and he was still adamant on full general elections," I reminded them. "But maybe there's something we can work with there. Get back to me tomorrow with your thoughts."

•   •   •

I sat at the wide marble table a few minutes, thinking. Their concept was logical. But unfortunately developments in Iraq were not always logical. Certainly Ayatollah Sistani operated on a different rational plane than we Westerners. From his austere quarters in Najaf, Sistani viewed Iraq and the wider world through the perspective of Shia Islamic theology, as well as hard-nosed politics. He had issued thousands of fatwas on a bewildering range of issues, even on how and when the faithful should drink water. And, despite his cloistered image, the Grand Ayatollah was determined to influence the political process, albeit indirectly. I doubted he would backtrack on his decree that the delegates to the Constitutional Convention must be elected since this would guarantee the Shiites a majority at the convention.

Perhaps the folks in Governance could come up with a process that enabled the GC to convene a representative Constitutional Convention, with a Shiite majority, that bypassed the protracted national elections that Sistani demanded. If not, the CPA and the Iraqis would be stuck in an untenable state between occupation and sovereignty.

Something is going to have to give.

Late on the night of October 10, I was at my desk when I heard the crackling and thumps of a firefight across the river.

"Big shoot-out in Sadr City, sir," Colonel Norwood reported.

The noise was echoing in the distance as I entered my house closer to the river an hour later. We'd received more reports: Over 300 armed men had attacked a patrol of the 2nd Armored Cavalry Regiment, which was responsible for security in the sprawling Shiite slum where 2 million people lived in the squalor that Saddam had imposed on them. Two of our soldiers had been killed and several wounded.

The attack was the work of Muqtada al-Sadr's "Mahdi Army" militia. Muqtada's defiance of the Coalition, as well as distribution of largesse from Sadr City mosques, had attracted new members to his ranks. He had named the ragtag irregulars for the messianic figure of the Mahdi, the "hidden" imam who had entered the realm of spiritual occultation as the young son of the last surviving Shiite imam in the 9th century. To devout Shiites, the Mahdi would return to bring justice and guide humanity.

The previous week, Muqtada had begun virulent verbal attacks on the Coalition, which he'd named "terrorist occupiers." We'd tried to rein in Muqtada indirectly through moderate Shiite leaders. But the young radical did not listen to their appeals. He'd taken to wearing a white burial cloth instead of a dark imam's robe, a symbol that he welcomed martyrdom. Equally disturbing, Muqtada was collaborating with a radical Sunni cleric, Ahmed al-Kubaisi, and was busing Sunni extremists from the Sunni Triangle to the south to augment his small militia.

Early the next morning I met privately with Sanchez to discuss the attack.

"We've been too soft on Muqtada," I said. "And this is how he pays us back."

"I agree completely, sir," he said. "We're going to saturate Sadr City with patrols today and take down anyone with a weapon."

The next day, Bill, the station chief, brought me a report that Muqtada had just proclaimed the creation of an alternate Iraqi "government." Muqtada boldly equated himself and his rebellion with "our imam and leader, Imam al-Mahdi."

"He's going to swear in his 'ministers' tomorrow, Mr. Ambassador."

"The hell he is," I replied. "If we don't deal with this guy soon, it might be too late to stop him."

I soon heard from Mike Gfoeller, the CPA representative in Al-Hillah. Using the precise language of the professional diplomat, Mike wrote that Muqtada's statement was part of his overall strategy. He had set up illegal roadblocks in Najaf and Karbala. His followers were taking over mosques in Karbala for that weekend's celebration of the birthday of Imam al-Mahdi. This would allow Muqtada to control huge amounts of charitable donations by an expected million pilgrims. He was also attempting to infiltrate the sacred precinct in Najaf, an even more lucrative source of funds. He was storing weapons and ammunition in the holy mosques.

Mike's report warned that if Muqtada won another standoff with the Coalition, it would greatly enhance his still small following among the Shia. Then we would be faced with a second insurgency, a rebellion not by Baathists and jihadis, but by fanatical Shiites.

"Sadr's statement is essentially a declaration of political war on the Coalition," Mike reported, and urged, as he had in August, that the Iraqi police arrest him on the outstanding murder charges.

I called Clay, Doug Brand, and Rick Sanchez to a crisis-team meeting. We needed a combined political-police-military operation. "We can't afford to let him get away with it again. We've got to get the Iraqi police to arrest him and the others named on the August arrest warrants."

Our plan was to have Coalition forces back up the Iraqi police to prevent Muqtada from slipping back to Sadr City, where rooting him out would be bloody and destabilizing.

"I'm going to need twenty-four hours to issue warning orders to our units," Rick said. "Preferably forty-eight."

"Why?" I asked. "Don't you have quick reaction forces down there?"

Rick shook his head. The 1st Marine Expeditionary Force had rotated home and been replaced by foreign troops. "The Spanish commander in Najaf refuses to cooperate. Says going into a city on this kind of mission violates his ROE."

Rules of Engagement were crippling us.

After the others left, I turned to Clay. "I'm worried the DOD squirrel cage will tie us in knots for days on this unless I can get fast action from Rumsfeld." For the second time in a week, I sent the secretary an update on the crisis, this time warning, "The time for moving against Muqtada al-Sadr is upon us." I reminded him that Muqtada's arrest would be an Iraqi operation, but that we should expect trouble anyway and be prepared to move right after the Shia holidays, in three days.

Rumsfeld was taking a rare, well-deserved vacation, and I spent a tense afternoon as the Pentagon tracked him down.

Finally, I connected with Paul Wolfowitz. "I understand the gravity of the situation," he said, adding that whatever we did "will have to be your call." He said he would discuss the crisis immediately with Rumsfeld, who was still traveling. "Have you spoken to Abizaid?"

"I've got a call in to him."

When General Abizaid and I spoke several hours later, he told me he'd talked to Wolfowitz. From his discussion with the deputy secretary, Abizaid had the impression that Paul was "going soft" on the planned Iraqi Coalition operation to arrest Muqtada and dislodge his militia from the holy cities. Certainly, the risks were great. There could be riots not only in Sadr City, but also in other Shiite cities of the south where essential services were still slow in coming and unemployment remained high.

I had a growing concern that once more the great blunt instrument of the U.S. government would be too paralyzed by inertia to react effectively.

In my nightly e-mail to Francie I commented:

We have to stop Muqtada now or risk a much wider conflict in the Shia heartland as he continues to advance. But of course there will be the usual voices for delay, compromise, and attenuation. One is reminded of Churchill's comment on the period from Munich to the Polish invasion when the voices of moderation led directly to the "bull's-eye of disaster."

That day marked the beginning of one of the most frustrating periods of my tenure in Iraq. I believed that the Coalition's public failure to deal decisively with Muqtada and his militia would signal to the better-organized Baathist insurgency and the jihadis and international terrorists that our resolve could be challenged, perhaps even defeated.

As the Muqtada crisis developed, I met with Scott Carpenter and our Governance Team. They had arrived at a political strategy that we called the "Grand Bargain" to deal with two related problems: the GC's ineffectiveness and the need to produce a credible political path forward.

"The idea is to use the GC's craving for more authority as a lever to get them to reorganize themselves and to call an early Constitutional Convention," Scott explained. "It may be a bit of a long shot, but might just work."

Under the plan, we would show the GC a "menu" of authorities we would be prepared to transfer to them, including designating them as a "Provisional Government," provided the Council revamp their cumbersome operating procedures and provided that they convene the Constitutional Convention.

Roman Martinez questioned whether there was a logical connection between the two steps. "What does the Provisional Government have to do with the convening of the CC?"

"Nothing. It's a straight political bargain," I explained. "It's as if a senator from Nebraska promises to back a New York colleague's dam bill in return for the New Yorker agreeing to support a road in Nebraska. Many of the GC—especially the secular Shiites—want a Provisional Government. We want an appointed Constitutional Convention. It's a horse trade pure and simple. But we've got to get them moving," I said.

"Well," Scott said, "the UN resolution should help concentrate their minds."

At our suggestion, the U.S. government had added to Resolution 1511, which had just passed, a requirement that the Governing Council provide the Security Council a timetable for Iraq's political process by December 15.

"So the pressure will really be on them finally to get with the program," Scott said.

"Shape up or be shipped out," I said. "A good formula."

•   •   •

In mid-October, I attended my weekly meeting of the Governing Council, taking my customary seat beside the October president, Ayad Allawi. We had suggested using this session to review the GC's first three months. But it looked like most of the Council had better things to do. I counted only seven full members around the green baize table. The remainder of the seats were taken by substitutes, several of them junior associates whose faces were unknown to me.

Allawi opened the discussion by asking if "any of the brothers" had comments they wished to make about the GC's performance to date.

Samir Sumaidy asked for the floor. A descendant of the Prophet Muhammad, he was a Sunni sheik from the troubled western province of Anbar, heart of the Sunni Triangle. Samir's decades in exile as a successful businessman had changed him. His name evoked the restive tribes of Anbar, but his suits said Savile Row. An amateur poet, Samir was clean-shaven, with an open, pleasant face and a sharp, precise mind.

"There's good news and bad news, I think, Mr. Chairman," he began. "On the one hand, the Council has managed to take some positive steps, like appointing the ministers and getting a measure of international recognition for itself. But clearly our performance has not been what we should expect. We have been slow hiring the staff we need. And I must note with regret that there has been lots of absenteeism among our members, too. Even today."

The communist GC member, Hamid Majid Moussa, added, "The hopes we had for the Council three months ago have largely been unrealized." He explained that security in the country had deteriorated and that unemployment was still a problem. At least "some of this" was the fault of the GC, he concluded.

Mohammad Bahr al-Uloum, the feisty elderly Shia imam, said, with a note of despair, that the security problems had "drained the energy out of the Governing Council."

After several others spoke, Allawi asked if I would like to respond.

"It's true that the Council can be proud of some of its accomplishments. We have said for months that the Coalition has a big stake in your success. But much more must be done to succeed," I said.

I recommended three areas for improvement. First, as Samir had noted, the GC simply had to get itself properly staffed. "You have serious responsibilities to the Iraqi people, but cannot realistically expect to run a country of 25 million with a staff of a dozen. We have continually encouraged you to hire staff. I have more than three thousand people working day and night for me. If you were properly organized, these people could become your 'back office staff,' preparing proposals and papers for your consideration."

I added that the GC had to improve its internal procedures and rules. They were trying to do everything as a Committee of the Whole. (Or as I put it in my e-mails, a "Committee of the Black Hole," since nothing ever emerged from the Council.)

"And you are all simply going to have to work a lot harder. Members of the Council cannot expect to be taken seriously by Iraqis, or by the Coalition, if you are not acting. To rule is to decide." I suggested that they adopt quorum rules, and keep track of and publish attendance by members. This brought nervous shifting in seats and tight smiles all around.

At the end of the meeting, I drew their attention to the UN resolution. It called on the CPA to devolve more authorities on the GC, but also required the Governing Council to give the Security Council a timeline for the return of sovereignty.

"We're going to have to work together on both issues," I stressed. "I'm anxious to delegate more authorities to the Council, but you have to help me by cleaning up your organization and procedures."

In the car driving back to the palace, I asked Scott Carpenter what he made of the session.

"Pretty discouraging," he said. "These guys won't even show up to discuss their future. Hard to see how we can put across the 'Grand Bargain.' "

"Agree," I said. "Somehow, we've got to get them focused. Perhaps I should start weekly meetings with the ministers, essentially remind the GC that *some* Iraqis are working hard for their country right now."

Meanwhile a steady stream of reports from CPA offices in Karbala, Najaf, and Al-Hillah showed that Muqtada's rebellion was spreading. Karbala was the main focus of his current challenge—not just to the Coalition, but especially to the moderate Shiite leadership under Grand Ayatollah Sistani.

The Mahdi Army was trying to take over the city, attacking the governate building and TV station, and occupying a police station where they stole five patrol cars, weapons, and uniforms. A local sheik loyal to Muqtada, al-Kazemi, had taken over the important Al-Mukhayyam Mosque and was training youths on weapons and drilling them in military formations near the shrine. Muqtada had set up a "trial court" for offenses against Islam and announced that he did not recognize the authority of the CPA or the Coalition military.

Sistani clearly felt threatened by the young radical. We learned that he had sent 200 armed men to Karbala to confront Muqtada's forces. Some of Sistani's fighters were reportedly members of SCIRI's militia, the Badr Corps.

"That'll be a bad precedent," I told Clay, "because it'll convince SCIRI that the Coalition won't provide security, and so they shouldn't disband their militia, as we've been demanding."

Terrified citizens of Karbala thronged to the local CPA compound and demanded that we act against Muqtada's gangs. One of their leaders reportedly said, "What good is calling yourself the government if you are not prepared to take action?"

Precisely my sentiments.

The city was in the area of operations of a Bulgarian battalion under the Polish Division. The Army Joint Ops center in Baghdad was getting reports from them that there was nothing going on in the city, which was certainly untrue.

While we were laying out a course of action, General Sanchez arrived to admit that the Coalition military in Karbala was operating in the dark. He, too, was frustrated and did not know what was going on. He was choppering down to Babylon in the morning to meet with the Polish Division commander, Major General Andrzej Tyszkiewicz, who had "objected" to his order to intervene to separate the local combatants in Karbala.

"And then he refused my order to state his objections to action in writing," Rick added with disgust.

He promised to put some competent American military eyes on the situation in Karbala.

"Rick," I said, "at least let's throw a military cordon well north of Karbala and Najaf on the roads from Baghdad to keep Muqtada's followers away. Your troops should inspect each bus *very* carefully—like all day."

The American military managed to block the roads from the north. But there was fighting between Muqtada's Mahdi Army and SCIRI's Badr Corps in the ancient lanes of Karbala. Sanchez reported from Babylon that he doubted the Iraqi police alone would be able to arrest Muqtada, who was holed up in his old thick-walled apartment in the sister holy city of Najaf, surrounded by a company of bodyguards armed with automatic weapons and RPGs, dangerously close to the shrine of Imam Ali, and near the quarters of the Grand Ayatollah.

The gun battles in the two holy cities continued for several days as we tried to devise a Coalition plan to deal with Muqtada. Gfoeller reported that between fifty and sixty people had been killed and unknown numbers wounded. He added that the use of larger-caliber automatic weapons and RPGs threatened irreparable damage to Shia Islam's most sacred sites.

We needed to deal with this threat as cleanly and decisively as possible, but in a manner that would convince *every* group in Iraq that hoped to maintain a militia that the Coalition would not tolerate such defiance.

I sent a note to Rice saying "the situation with Muqtada is quickly unraveling." I reported that he had attacked the governate building and TV station in Karbala and had taken many hostages.

In an NSC teleconference later that evening, I briefed the president on the crisis. I was gratified that he counseled us to be very firm.

On October 16, there was more bad news. The night before, Muqtada's fighters had killed three more Americans in Karbala. He had sent a taped message to the local governor threatening his life, and Gfoeller had reports of spreading unrest by Muqtada's men in the southern cities of Basra, Amara, Diwaniya, and Nasiriya. The standoff at the Karbala mosque continued, where we understood al-Kazemi was holding fifteen hostages.

Meanwhile some of Muqtada's forces had occupied the District Council office in Sadr City. When the Iraqi police refused to expel them, I fired the police chief there and called for Sanchez and Gfoeller. "Rick," I said, "if the Iraqi police won't take back that District Council building, then one of your commanders has got to do it. It's essential that we restore law and order around here."

I sent Mike to Karbala to get me some solid "ground truth."

This was deeply troubling. I couldn't tell if the military was intentionally slow-walking the issue again, as they had in August, or if they just didn't have the capability or the orders necessary to get the job done. And I wasn't getting a good sense of the temperature in the Pentagon.

Later that day, Doug Brand returned from Karbala. The local cops who had cordoned off the mosque had allowed an "unknown number" of Muqtada's militiamen to walk away from the building with their weapons. This was the "water-into-the-sand" outcome that I had feared. And there were still an unknown number of armed men with hostages inside the mosque. The lesson was that you could defy both Iraqi authority and the Coalition without fear. By that night, Muqtada's militiamen responsible for the ambush death of our Armored Cavalry soldiers still occupied the Sadr City District Council in open defiance of the Iraqi police.

The same day, Mowaffak al-Rubaie, a Shia GC member who had accompanied a delegation to Najaf to discuss the Muqtada crisis with Sistani, asked to see me with an urgent message from the ayatollah.

"Ambassador," Mowaffak said. "I stayed behind yesterday to give the ayatollah your letter about the political process."

Rubaie, a British-educated physician and protégé of Baghdad's leading Shia ayatollah, Hussein al-Sadr, had been one of the channels for my message to Sistani about our joint responsibility for seeking a political path forward. I had asked Rubaie to take a message to Sistani about our mutual interest in finding a way for Iraqis to write their constitution as quickly as possible, but stressing again the technical problems involved in holding elections quickly.

Rubaie had found "the ayatollah transfixed by the threat of Muqtada." He described how, as Muqtada's uprising spread, Sistani had retreated even deeper into his warren of buildings near the Najaf shrine. Two nights earlier, Muqtada had arrived unannounced with a gang of followers, demanding to see the Grand Ayatollah. Sistani had refused and sent his son, Mohammed Ridha, to talk to the group. The meeting had turned into a shouting match, with Muqtada screaming at the clerics.

Sistani had told Rubaie that his preferred option was that Muqtada simply "was no longer around."

By that I assumed that he wanted the young man dead.

Rubaie said he had tried to engage Sistani in a discussion of the constitutional process. But the ayatollah was so preoccupied with Muqtada that he had waved his hands at the question, saying, "Elections? Who can talk of elections at a time like this?"

Rubaie stunned me with another piece of news. Sistani had told him that Syrian President Bashar Assad had recently sent him a confidential message suggesting that the ayatollah should "issue a fatwa calling for a jihad against the Coalition," as Shia leaders had done in 1920 against the British.

This was an act of extraordinary irresponsibility from Syria's president. We had good intelligence showing that many insurgents and terrorists were coming into Iraq through Syria. But this message from Assad essentially incited Shia rebellion. If he were to succeed, the Coalition would face an extremely bloody two-front uprising, costing thousands of lives, including Americans.

The persistence of the Muqtada crisis reinforced my conviction that we had to maintain a firm military presence in Iraq until we had enough professionally trained Iraqi security forces on the ground, and effective Iraqi political leadership in power, to assure stability.

I wrote about my frustrations in my e-mail to Francie that night:

> The crisis in Karbala could have been avoided if we had acted back in August when I recommended we encourage the Iraqi police to arrest Muqtada. I was completely isolated.

It is a perfect, and sad, illustration that the temptation to avoid hard decisions wins only temporary relief. And it only increases the pain once the decision can no longer be avoided.

On October 18, the Governing Council and Iraqi political parties at last issued a joint statement on law and order and delivered it to the imams in Karbala and Najaf. This gave the cachet of local authority to the pending operations against Muqtada.

The operation in Sadr City went well. Troops of the 1st Armored Division moved on the estimated 200 Mahdi Army irregulars occupying the Sadr City District Council. There was little resistance, no American casualties, and we didn't have to use helicopter gunships. Our troops captured more than forty suspects, twenty-seven of whom we had detained.

In Karbala, the plan was for the Iraqi police to take down the mosque, with Coalition forces providing perimeter security. It would be important for the police to be very visible, making arrests and managing crowd control.

The operation in Karbala on the night of Monday, October 20, was a qualified success. The Iraqi police gave the fugitives in the mosque an ultimatum to surrender, which they ignored. The police and members of the Iraqi Civil Defense Corps then went into the mosque and asked our forces to follow in behind. There was no resistance, although there were many improvised gun emplacements inside and on the roof of the mosque. The next morning, Interior Minister Nouri Badran did a good job of explaining to the nation that this had been an Iraqi operation and that they had requested Coalition assistance.

So, we've had two operations in three days, each without much difficulty, I reflected. No American casualties and so far no adverse political reaction. However, we had not captured either of the two main targets, Muqtada or his henchman, al-Kazemi. And we had stopped over 40,000 people trying to leave Sadr City to travel to Karbala, which showed that Muqtada had the capacity (and the money—possibly from the Iranians) to influence dangerously large numbers of fanatical followers.

The CPA adviser on the private sector, Tom Foley, offered me a welcome reprieve from Muqtada's depredations when he suggested I accompany him to one of his regular meetings with Iraqi businessmen. One cool evening in mid-October we traveled across the Tigris to the Al-Hambra Hotel, one of the seedier establishments in Baghdad's hotel district. In an ill-lighted, damp room, we met with about fifteen Iraqi businessmen. I knew several from earlier meetings, including our Monday night economic seminars. This was an opportunity to bring them up to date on our thinking on broad economic matters.

I opened the session by repeating the message I had delivered at the World Economic Forum—Iraq needed a vibrant private sector to succeed. "Our top priority now is finding ways to get credit and capital into your hands, the hands of responsible Iraqi businessmen."

But I reported that we had found the state banks unable to make commercial loans. "They were political instruments of the state and made loans for political, not commercial, purposes." The banking law we had encouraged the GC to pass would allow foreign banks into Iraq. And, I added, this was just part of a broader effort to create a body of modern commercial law.

Tom reviewed our analysis of Iraq's State Owned Enterprises (SOEs). "We've really gone at them hard, with their 'parent' ministries, and have concluded that at least some of them can survive in a private market." But he added there were others which just as clearly could not compete, and still others whose viability we couldn't assess.

During the long discussion that followed, one businessman was eager to hear more about our plans for the new currency. I said that we were confident that the exchange, which was to begin in days, would be a success despite the enormous logistical challenges. We would have to distribute some 2,200 tons of new currency, enough to fill twenty-seven 747 cargo jets—and recall an estimated 9,000 tons of old currency, in a country without a banking system, no telephones, lousy roads, and a war.

"It's impressive," the businessman agreed. "But will you keep the old multiple exchange rates we're accustomed to?"

I told him we would not, since that system had lent itself to corruption, with some favored firms allowed to buy foreign exchange at one one-thousandth the official rate. "So we've decided to let the New Iraqi Dinar float freely against all currencies," I explained. The reaction around the table suggested that not all of them were happy with this decision.

A cement plant owner asked about the Iraqi government budget. I told them that I had just approved the 2004 budget with revenues of $13.5 billion. "But we'll still run a deficit because of the huge subsidies built into the system." I mentioned our plans to phase out the distorting energy subsidies, and again the nervous smiles suggested that some of them benefited from that subsidy.

As our SUV pulled away from the hotel, Tom and I agreed that several of the businessmen were impressive and ready for a competitive marketplace. But, as

I had frequently lamented to my colleagues, "There's no Ludwig Erhard in Iraq—or at least we haven't found him yet."

I envied my predecessors in occupied Germany because in Erhard, a midgrade civil servant, they had an astute man who was able to become the architect of Germany's postwar economic recovery.

On October 21, I paid a call on Dr. Ibrahim al-Jaafari, who had been out of the country for more than a month. My Iraqi friends had promised summer would end "a few days before the Ramadan moon" and they'd been right, for today there were a few cool sprinkles of rain in the air.

"We simply have to improve the performance of the Council," I told him.

"With respect, Ambassador," he said. "If the Council is weak you have no one to blame but yourself, since you appointed it. And we cannot expect the Council to act responsibly if it doesn't have authority."

Jaafari was soft-spoken.

I reminded him of the authorities we had already granted. "I'm prepared to grant more," I added. "But for that to happen, the Council has to carry out its responsibility to get the Constitutional Convention going fast. And it has to undertake a thoroughgoing reorganization of its procedures."

I floated the idea that the GC might establish a sort of "Prime Ministry" of two or three GC members. He thought this might be possible, but said that such a body would still have to rotate, perhaps among the nine-member Council presidency, the P-9. Then the other Governing Council members could be divided into committees, each of which would have direct responsibility to oversee three or four ministries.

"It might work," I said, "if you could avoid the monthly rotation which would never allow Council members to master the portfolios." And they'd have to hire staff, be prepared to work hard, and adopt better voting procedures.

I reviewed our thinking on the constitution and in particular our concern about the delay which a direct election would entail. "So why not try out the idea of locally elected delegates," I asked, referring to the PrepComm's second option. As a Shia, Jaafari officially remained concerned about the views of the Hawza clerics in Najaf. But he looked at me with a shrewd expression. "I suggest that you talk to the Grand Ayatollah and the Hawza about your idea."

I told him I had sent just such a message to Sistani through three emissaries in the past ten days to assure the ayatollah that we wanted the constitutional process to be seen as legitimate in the Iraqis' eyes. "We agree that the constitution must be written by Iraqis for Iraqis," I emphasized. I said that we felt that a locally elected Constitutional Convention would meet the need for legitimacy, particularly since convention delegates would then embark on a broad public information campaign and that the draft constitution would be put to all Iraqis in a referendum.

"Dr. Jaafari, I told the ayatollah that I understood he could not reverse his fatwa on elections." I leaned closer to Jaafari and spoke slowly, for emphasis, "but I also said that he, like I, had a responsibility to work for the New Iraq."

I told Jaafari, as I had in his sweltering Karbala office in May, that the Shia must not repeat the disastrous mistake they had made in the 1920s, which had locked them out of power for eighty years.

Jaafari said he liked my message to Sistani. "I want to be helpful," he finally said.

"Well, Dr. Jaafari," I said. "In my view, the most helpful thing you and other leading Shia can do is to help us find a solution to the election issue and to explain that solution to the Hawza."

Jaafari asked about the current status of Muqtada.

"The time is drawing near for the Iraqi police to take action," I said.

"Why have you not acted sooner?" he asked. "If only you had dealt with him while he was still sitting in the corner . . . Now he is at the table and it is more difficult."

"I hope members of the Council like you publicly support the Iraqi police and Coalition when we take action to restore law and order."

"I want to be of help," he repeated.

The Governance Team came to my office to review the bidding.

"I sense some faint signs of hope among the Shia," Meghan O'Sullivan commented. "They may finally be realizing that they have to shape up."

"Perhaps . . ." I mused. "But look at the P-9, for God's sake. When I asked to meet them yesterday to discuss the path ahead, half of them didn't even show up. Pachachi hasn't been in Iraq since August, Chalabi's been gone a month, again. Barzani and Talabani haven't been to Baghdad in weeks. How are we going to persuade anyone to take this crowd seriously?"

I was about to leave for the international donors conference in Madrid called by the UN to encourage countries to contribute to Iraq's reconstruction. Then there would be an inevitably unpleasant head-knocking session of "consultations" in Washington. I wished that I had a better political framework to carry with me.

• • •

The Madrid Conference was another of those glitzy shindigs at which not much work actually is done because the countries' foreign and finance ministries work out their contributions in advance.

I gave my speech, dined with some old Spanish friends in my suite to avoid the ultratight security elsewhere in the hotel, and met with a couple of important colleagues.

Colin Powell was the most important. We had about an hour alone.

He started the conversation by asking about the status of more foreign troops for the Coalition.

"I doubt we'll ever get Turkish troops into Iraq," I said. I reminded him that the problem was not just the Kurds' opposition to their traditional enemies, the Turks. Sistani's position, too, had solidified most of the Shia against them.

"Abizaid continues to push for them," Powell said.

"Not really," I replied. "Abizaid's argument is that from a purely military point of view, he could use them. But he understands, and I know Sanchez does, too, that if we could somehow get the Turks in, it would actually worsen our security. The Kurds would slip away and the Shia would be under great pressure to resist, too."

Powell understood the dynamics.

"So rather than break our pick on a fight we can't win, I'm encouraging the GC to start a broad dialogue with the Turks," I said, "including ways in which the Turks can participate in Iraq's economy, which is what they really want. After that dialogue is under way, I'll suggest the Council invite some other countries to come in . . . maybe Pakistan, Bangladesh, and Morocco."

Powell agreed with this approach. He said the Turks were starting to back off a bit anyway.

"Frankly, Colin, I detect mounting concern at the Pentagon, fed by the Army, about the coming troop rotation."

Powell said the problem was that the president might have to mobilize more of the National Guard, including in key states in an election year.

"I realize we're entering a campaign year," I said. "But my job is to advise the president as best I can on what's right for Iraq. We have to be careful not to mislead him into thinking that the Iraqis are suddenly ready to look after their own security."

I said that the military had been playing jiggery-pokery with the numbers of police. And they were trying to get the New Iraqi Army more involved in internal security. "I've got three 'red lines' about Iraq," I said. "We must leave behind a professional, uncorrupt police force, attentive to human rights; we must not have an army involved in internal affairs, and no militia; and we should pass sovereignty to an Iraqi government elected on the basis of a constitution."

"A tall order, Jerry."

"Well," I answered, "we run a real risk if we compromise on these issues. In five to eight years the situation in Iraq could descend into chaos or civil war or tyranny—or all three." I recalled that Iraq's history was full of mistakes on each of these issues. We had to build a success story here that, like Germany and Japan, still looked good after fifty years. "The president can always decide that he doesn't support this approach. But that's the way I see it."

Powell listened impassively. His only reaction was, "Well, Jerry, you have to tell it like it is to the president, but . . ."

Then he asked what I was planning to do with the Governing Council. He reminded me that at his September visit, he'd had the impression that they "aren't ready for prime time."

"You got that right," I replied. I went over the concept of the "Grand Bargain."

He was skeptical that the GC could ever work. "You got a Plan B up your sleeve?"

I said that we had looked at various other ideas, one of which was to find a way to give the ministers more profile. "I shocked a few of the GC by saying I was considering having weekly 'cabinet' meetings with the ministers. Maybe that'll get them moving."

On Monday morning, October 27, Secretary Rumsfeld, General Dick Myers, General Abizaid, and I met at the White House with the president, Condi Rice, and Andy Card.

The president led off by asking me for an update on the political situation. I detailed the problems we were having with the GC, but noted that the Madrid Conference had been a success. "Most Iraqis support your vision of a peaceful, democratic Iraq," I told him.

Abizaid conceded that the recent attacks on our troops showed the insurgents' "newly sophisticated methods." He and I agreed that we had to find ways to get the Sunnis engaged in the political process. But I remarked that the problem was they had no political organizations or widely recognized leaders because Saddam had killed or co-opted them all. I detailed the problems of forging an Iraqi government.

We discussed ways of strengthening Iraqi security forces. Abizaid recommended bringing back qualified officers from Saddam's army.

"There are risks in that," I said. "We've got to proceed with great care so we don't give the impression that we're reconstituting the old regime."

"Well, one thing is clear," the president said firmly. "We stay the course in Iraq. We don't show any weakness in the wake of these new attacks. There'll be no loss of resolve now."

Hours later, I was deep into a third and seemingly endless meeting at the Pentagon on Iraq policy with Rumsfeld's senior uniformed officers and civilian staff. Once again the subject was the "Wolfowitz-Feith Option," which Paul and I had discussed at the Pentagon on September 22. Their suggestion was that the GC simply appoint an "interim legislature" and that we turn sovereignty over to the Iraqis by April 9, 2004, the first anniversary of the fall of Baghdad.

I thought of Clay's warning before I went to Washington to fight for the supplemental. *This is the same bad movie and it doesn't have a happy ending.*

"What's your opinion, Jerry," Rumsfeld asked.

"Mr. Secretary," I began, "I don't think it would be responsible to turn over sovereignty to a nonelected Iraqi body with no constitution in place. There'd be no checks and balances on the entity we'd handed power to. We'd risk Iraq falling into disorder or civil war, with no constitution to shape Iraq's political structure and to guarantee individual and minority rights. I can't support such an outcome."

I expressed skepticism that a body appointed by the Governing Council would somehow be more legitimate than the GC itself. "And I don't understand what the powers of the legislature would be." Nobody had an answer to this question.

So Rumsfeld said, "Whatever you say they should be."

"But since I think it's a lousy idea," I said, "I don't have an answer, either."

"Well," Rumsfeld said briskly, "that's your homework assignment."

During a meeting of the National Security Council Principals the next morning at the White House, we again reviewed two alternative political approaches.

The CPA option was to stick with the plan to turn sovereignty over to an Iraqi government elected on the basis of a constitution. We proposed an accelerated timetable allowing this to happen by the end of 2004. The Pentagon advocated the earliest possible divestment of power to an Iraqi government, arguing this would abolish the stigma of "occupier" from the Coalition forces.

Abizaid and I each said that no Iraqi, insurgent or not, would be fooled by such semantics. We would still have lots of forces in the country, which would certainly look to most Iraqis like an "occupying" army, whatever we called it.

Abizaid presented the military's plans to accelerate the recruitment of Iraqi security forces, which provoked Vice President Cheney to wonder how this acceleration would reduce attacks on our people and on the Iraqis. There was no good answer to this question because he had put his finger on the central assumption.

During the meeting, I got the impression that Secretary Rumsfeld had cast me as the odd man out, swimming against the stream. I suppose I was.

Andy Card caught my arm as we left the Situation Room. "Got a minute, Jerry? I'd like a quick chat." We went up one flight of stairs to the office of the chief of staff. Card closed the door behind us.

"I want to help you in any way I can," he said. "But you've got to be absolutely frank with the president about your views. I've got the impression that people in Washington are 'gaming' you."

I knew what he meant: when a policy failed, it was handy for the senior bureaucrats to find scapegoats.

Well, we're not going to fail, I thought.

"Don't worry. I'll be absolutely frank with the president. I always have been." I explained that I felt the military was deeply concerned about the spring troop rotation and that this was driving a lot of their thinking. "Frankly, this early sovereignty idea would make the president's vision of Iraq very difficult, if not impossible, to realize."

I confessed that the option might buy the president some leeway for 2004, though I added that my perspective, and hopefully his, went well beyond that. "We've got to do what's right for Iraq for five, ten, twenty years ahead. I also recognize that it's possible that doing the right thing might make the president's life next year more difficult. It might even cost him the election. But frankly, as far as I'm concerned, the only appropriate perspective is to do the right thing for history."

Card said he agreed and wondered if I should have a private meeting with the president. I replied that this would be awkward, given that my boss Rumsfeld disagreed with me.

Perhaps a phone call would be better, Card suggested.

Before leaving Andy's office, I told him I'd like to wrap up my tour in Iraq in May after a year in the country. "That'll be the longest year of my life."

Next, I stopped at Rice's office, at her request.

"Jerry," she said, "I share your concern about the military's nervousness. But we do have to move ahead on the political front, too." She told me that she was still agnostic between the options, and would recommend that the president not choose one the next day.

"Well," I protested, "I *am* going to need guidance."

We agreed that the NSC Iraq Stabilization Group would work with CPA Governance to see if we could devise something between the two options.

The president chaired the full NSC meeting the next day.

Abizaid first briefed on the military situation and our plans to accelerate the training of Iraqi security forces. He stressed the importance of getting the Sunnis involved more and said he thought we had a three-month window of opportunity to do this. The president bore in on this point, wondering if the Sunnis had a different vision than other Iraqis. "Aren't they interested in living in peace like the others?" What exactly would they do after those three months? Did the Sunnis have a different vision for Iraq at that point? Abizaid and Rumsfeld replied that they thought there was a risk then that the center of gravity in the Sunni community might slip away from us.

At Rumsfeld's request, I outlined the two options for going forward—the Pentagon's and mine. Powell noted that the real problem in Iraq was security and so, while it was useful to move on the political front, nothing we did there would matter if we didn't solve the security problems.

The president listened carefully to the political and military options before us in Iraq. He did not commit himself. However, he brought the meeting to a close with a resolute statement: "We are going to succeed in Iraq despite the difficult times we are going through. Nobody should be in any doubt. We will do the right thing irrespective of what the newspapers or political opponents say about it. Success in Iraq will change the world. The American people need to have no doubt that we're confident about the outcome. We may not succeed by the time of the election. So be it."

That was all the guidance I needed.

On the way out of the SitRoom the president pulled me aside and asked if we could get together. What was my schedule?

I was available at his convenience.

Looking at his pocket schedule he asked if we could meet at 1:00 P.M. I said sure.

"Hey," he said. "Why not come by at noon and we can work out together."

I didn't have the right clothes with me.

"We'll fix you up," he said. "Come by 'the Oval' at noon."

Instead of eating a salad together as we had in May, the president and I worked out in his private third-floor gym, me wearing shorts and running shoes borrowed from his closet.

I knew that when he was still running regularly, the president had inaugurated the "Crawford 100 Degree" club, giving a running shirt to anyone who ran with him in Crawford when the temperature was over 100. Brian McCormack, my creative special assistant, somehow had a couple of T-shirts made up, one of which I gave the president. It was marked "Baghdad 120 Degree Club."

This day the president decided to use the elliptical machine, so I took the treadmill. We shared lamentations about our knees—he too has had problems with a torn meniscus. Neither of us could really run anymore. Since we weren't working out hard, we could talk as we exercised and we covered the waterfront. After about a forty-five-minute session, we repaired to the second floor to cool down.

Andy Card had told President Bush about my hope to leave Iraq not later than May. He respected that and was only concerned to put in place a succession plan.

"What kind of guy do you think should replace you, Jerry?"

"I hadn't thought much about it. Been too busy I guess."

"Not necessarily someone like you," he said. "Could a businessman do it?"

"I don't think so," I replied. "What's needed is someone who has significant political skills and preferably, though not essential, area expertise. Perhaps you should look at someone from State."

Bush grimaced.

"Don't forget I was a State employee. You could look at retired people."

He spoke of his foreign policy team. "Tenet's under lots of pressure, but I am going to stick with him," the president said. "I like him. In fact the foreign policy team I have now I'll keep throughout my first term."

As we cooled down in the upstairs library and ate sandwiches, the president asked me about my relationship with Rumsfeld. "What kind of a person is he to work for? Does he really micromanage?"

"I like Don, Mr. President," I said. "I've known him thirty years, admire him, and consider him highly intelligent. But he *does* micromanage."

This seemed to surprise the president.

"Don terrifies his civilian subordinates, so that I can rarely get any decisions out of anyone but him. This works all right, but isn't ideal," I said.

While Bush considered this, I took the opportunity again to alert him about the numbers game.

"There's a tendency in DOD to equate an Iraqi policeman with an American soldier and to assume that what matters is the aggregate total number of people—Coalition and Iraqis—involved in security at any given moment. This is flat-out misleading."

I said that although the secretary of defense had insisted that the planned troop reductions would be "condition driven," this was not entirely correct. In fact the drawdown seemed more driven by the Army's concern over their planned spring troop rotation. I said I had been struck by Abizaid's assessment at the NSC meeting that we had to "defeat the insurgency in three months" which happened to coincide with that rotation. "I recommend that when the time comes to decide on that rotation and draw down, you look very closely at the actual security situation on the ground before deciding, Mr. President."

I said that I agreed with Powell's comment that we had to fix the security problem or none of the other areas—governance, reconstruction—could succeed. We simply were not finding and killing enough bad guys.

"Is our intelligence good enough?"

"No, sir. It's not. We have too many people looking for WMD and not enough looking for terrorists. I've been pushing, as has Abizaid, to get this rebalanced and the process is finally under way."

"What else you got for me?"

"Frankly, I'm concerned that a lot of the Pentagon's frenetic push on the political stuff is meant to set me up as a fall guy."

He looked surprised. "What do you mean by that?"

"Well, in effect the DOD position would be that they'd recommended a quick end to 'occupation,' but I had resisted, and so any problems from here on out were my fault."

"Don't worry about that," the president said as we got up from lunch. "I'll cover you here. And we are *not* going to fail in Iraq."

When we had showered and dressed, the president said, "Come on down with me to give the ladies a thrill." I hadn't the foggiest idea what he was talking about, but in the small dining room where Francie and I had dined a month earlier we found Mrs. Bush lunching with two other women. The president introduced me, and noted that we each had on bright red "power ties."

After some polite talk with Mrs. Bush's guests, he looked at his watch, saying, "We've got to go. Jerry's got a country to run. And so do I."

Chapter 8
ROAD MAP TO DEMOCRACY

■ BAGHDAD
OCTOBER 2003

On my return from Washington, Friday morning, October 31, I met with Clay and the Governance Team, who had been expanding our efforts to reach out to the Sunnis. The team had come up with several good ideas, including channeling more money through Sunni tribal sheiks into public works projects, just as we'd done with the irrigation renewal in the Shiite south. They had identified a number of potential Sunni leaders who were probably fence-sitting, waiting to see if the Coalition had staying power.

"The Sunni outreach is important," I said, explaining that I'd decided to ask my British colleague David Richmond, who had good Arabic and regional experience, to take full-time responsibility for this important project.

Turning to our problems with the GC, I told them that it was clear from my meetings in Washington that, like us, people there were running out of patience with the Iraqi leaders. The seven-step path that I had described in a *Washington Post* op-ed in September provided for the Governing Council to convene a Constitutional Convention. The problem was Sistani's fatwa requiring that the convention be elected. But elections would take a year to organize. Then the Iraqis would need time to write their constitution, which in turn would have to be submitted for approval by the public in a referendum. In all, following this process would mean delaying the transfer of sovereignty until late 2005. Again, I was sure that neither the Iraqis nor Coalition partners could wait this long.

Anticipating this problem back in July, we had suggested that the Governing Council ask its Preparatory Committee for alternatives on how to select the convention delegates. We'd hoped the committee could provide political cover for the GC to approve a mechanism other than direct elections. At the end of

September, the PrepComm came up with two options—electing the delegates in a national direct election, or choosing representatives using regional caucuses. Our soundings showed that 20 of the GC's 24 members preferred the caucuses, but for more than a month they had been unable to overcome the pressure from the Shia Islamists, and thus could not agree on how to proceed. Our path to a constitution and sovereignty was now in jeopardy.

"We may have only a couple of weeks to see if the GC can pull itself together," I told them. "There's a good chance they'll flunk the test, so we've got to find another approach."

The Governance Team had been looking at alternatives since early October, when we sensed that the GC would not be able to agree on a path forward. Our challenge was to identify a plan that salvaged our most important objectives. The team said it was now clear to the GC, and others in the Iraqi political class with whom we were in touch, that Sistani would not give way on elections. And it was unlikely the GC majority would go against the wishes of the Shia Islamists. Moreover, we realized that a "victory" that left those sectarian Shia— and Sistani—opposed to the way forward would be no victory. Hence the stalemate, within the Governing Council and between us and the GC.

"Ambassador Bremer," Roman said, "you keep saying the GC is not 'stepping up to the plate.' That's true. But they can't because to go against Sistani would be political suicide for the Shia Islamists."

I recognized that he was right. But as usual in Iraq, our problem was still more complicated. The Kurds and Sunnis didn't want the U.S. to give up authority unless they had confidence that they would not be at the mercy of the Shia Islamists. So they insisted on having written guarantees in place concerning federalism and minority rights *before* the U.S. government relinquished political control. To achieve this, they wanted a constitution.

And, finally, several members of the Governing Council, including Chalabi and Pachachi, and some people in the Pentagon continued to press for an immediate handover of sovereignty to the Iraqis, perhaps even to the GC itself, without either a constitution or elections.

"It's going to be a helluva job to square all these demands," I noted after we'd reviewed the situation.

We were interrupted by a smacking explosion nearby—so close that the heavy drapery on the window whooshed into the room with the shock wave, and then fell back. And then the Giant Voice sounded its mechanical warning: "Take Cover! Take Cover! Take Cover!"

Moving into the palace basement, we decided that instead of trying to force the seven-step process forward, we would rearrange the step sequence and allow the occupation to end before a permanent constitution was in place, in order to meet Iraqi demands and growing U.S. pressures. But we agreed that this should be done only if we could ensure that basic principles of democracy and national unity could be put in place in an interim constitution. And we still wanted national elections as soon as practicable.

One idea was to have the GC, with some qualified Iraqis, write an interim constitution and use that as the basis for elections to a Transitional National Assembly. That body would in turn select an interim Iraqi government to which we would turn over sovereignty.

"It just might work," Roman said.

I decided to give the GC's nine-member presidency council (P-9) one last chance to salvage the seven-step political process. To make this an informal meeting that encouraged a freer exchange, I invited them to my house on November 6, recognizing that the added pressure of hunger and thirst—the *iftar*, or Ramadan fast-breaking meal was looming—might curtail pontification.

Sitting in my sparsely furnished living room, I told the Iraqi leaders that the Coalition needed to work with an effective Iraqi authority, "an organization that can make reasoned decisions quickly . . . Each of those traits is important . . . reasoned . . . decisions . . . quickly. I'm anxious to give such a body much more authority. But the current Council is not capable of this. I would prefer to work with it, but if the GC cannot become better organized, I am prepared to work with some other group of Iraqis—perhaps the cabinet ministers . . ."

I had never tried to bluff the Council, so they appeared to realize my threat to cut them adrift was serious. They were all listening closely as I went to the heart of the matter—launching the constitutional process as quickly as possible. I repeated our position that holding direct nationwide elections for the Constitutional Convention as Sistani demanded would delay the return of sovereignty by up to two years. "Do you really want to be responsible for that delay?"

I said we understood that a majority of the Council favored picking up the PrepComm's recommendation for regional caucuses to choose the Constitutional Convention's delegates. "If you act now, we can convene the Convention by mid-January," I said. Our internal planning suggested that if it took six months to write the constitution, we would return sovereignty to Iraq by the end of 2004.

The P-9 members slipped into a long discussion among themselves, which my interpreter struggled to follow. But it was clear, as we had predicted, that they were not willing to convene the Constitutional Convention without a national vote.

The devout Shia, especially Abdul Aziz Hakim, were adamant about direct elections, Hakim remarking, in essence, "It has been decided" (by the ayatollah's Islamist allies on the Council). In his black sayyid's turban, dark robe, and tinted glasses, Hakim was clearly such an ally.

Chalabi and Pachachi focused their remarks on the establishment of a fully sovereign Iraqi government as the key political event in Iraq's immediate future, and not the constitutional process. And Talabani, the GC's president for November, in an attempt to smooth things over, emphasized the need to reach a "consensus."

The meeting was going nowhere.

"Democracy is truly great," I said. "But democracy is majority rule, with protection of minority rights. It is *not* indecisive rule by consensus, which can lead to paralysis."

With that thought, I closed the meeting, wishing them a pleasant *iftar*.

As I escorted the Council's P-9 leaders to their cars, I realized that our seven-step process was dead. But I was determined that the New Iraq *would* eventually have a representative constitutional government. We needed an alternative path forward. And we did not have time to waste.

We decided to float the idea of an interim constitution, which we hoped would get us past the Sistani fatwa and allow us to transfer sovereignty to an Iraqi government under a legal framework establishing Iraq's political institutions, structure, and democracy while protecting minority and human rights. But we would also agree to the condition set forth in Sistani's fatwa—that elections be held as soon as possible for a body to draft Iraq's permanent constitution.

We knew that most Iraqis would be suspicious of having yet another "interim" constitution. Saddam had written several interim documents over the past thirty-five years, and ignored any of the provisions he chose, particularly those dealing with human rights. To meet President Bush's vision for the New Iraq, the interim constitution would have to establish guarantees of fundamental individual rights, address the contentious issue of federalism, and establish checks and balances to protect against a slide back into tyranny. Of course, Iraq's democracy would not be like America's. The Iraqis would have to decide their own structure. But these basic principles would be essential, we judged, for long-term stability in a country riven by sectarian tensions. So our objective would be to try to embed these points so thoroughly in the interim document that they would stand a chance of surviving into any subsequent permanent constitution.

Over the next couple of days, the Governance Team identified several key Council members in favor of moving to an interim constitution. After getting Rice's agreement to the concept on November 7, I spoke with Dr. Adnan Pachachi, the elderly Sunni who'd been foreign minister in the 1960s, and was one of the most sensible and serious people on the Governing Council. I knew Pachachi placed special emphasis on individual rights and freedoms and had helped draft a Basic Law, similar to a constitution, for the United Arab Emirates, where he had lived in exile.

When I dropped the idea of an interim constitution on him Pachachi seized on it and agreed to present it to the full GC as his own.

The next evening at Talabani's house, the Kurdish leader told me that Pachachi had broached the concept of an interim constitution at the GC meeting that morning.

"What do you think of the idea, Mr. Ambassador? It would be useful to know the Coalition's position before we take it any further."

I had to suppress a smile. Pachachi had taken the CPA's plan as his own, and now Talabani was endorsing "Pachachi's idea."

"Frankly," I said, "we would have preferred a permanent constitution first. But Sistani has blocked that path. And we need a way out of the impasse. Maybe this is it. But the interim constitution has to be more than a simple agreement of principles."

I noted that such a document had to protect individual rights, including freedom of religion, describe the modalities for selecting a transitional government, and define its authorities. And, to ensure that the constitution really was "interim," it had to include a clear "sunset provision" to dissolve at a date certain.

Talabani waved his hands in a big circle, agreeing to all these points. "But," he raised a finger, "we Kurds will also want the document to address our concerns, especially our demand for a federal system—you know, to protect our autonomy."

"Mr. Talabani," I replied, "you are an old friend to the United States with many admirers in Washington. You and I need to get a decision on the path ahead while you're still Council president." Hakim, a Shia Islamist, would take over as president December 1.

Beaming, Talabani promised, "The Council will meet every day, Ambassador."

As we discussed concrete tactics, I formed a mental image of the obstacles we must overcome. One set of skeptics we would have to convince sat at desks in the Pentagon. The other group was hidden in the maze of medieval lanes in Najaf.

On November 10, with Talabani's assurance that the new path was under "intense discussion" at the Governing Council, I decided I'd talk to key Washington principals.

Given the often confusing, always intense political tugging and pushing under way in Iraq, I needed to be sure the Washington principals had a clear understanding of our strategy.

Robert Blackwill of the NSC's Iraq Stabilization Group had arrived in Baghdad a few days earlier to get a sense of how we were doing on the Sunni outreach initiative. The complex and frustrating task of building bridges to the Sunnis was one of our top priorities, and I was glad an NSC insider was here to see the progress we were making and to offer suggestions about improving it. When Rice had recommended his visit, I'd agreed, with the caveat that Bob, whom I had known for decades, coordinate his activities with me.

Bob would doubtless be reporting on his own back to Rice. So I wanted to be sure that our new approach was also well understood at the Pentagon and the State Department.

I asked Roman Martinez to draft a short message for me to send Rumsfeld, Powell, and Rice so that they had it before an NSC Principals Committee meeting scheduled later that day.

"I'll also try to call the SecDef and Powell before then," I told him.

As usual, his draft was concise, but complete, and it encapsulated my thinking:

Our new path would have the GC, working with Iraqi lawyers and in coordination with the CPA, draft an interim constitution. If we started the process immediately, we hoped to finish the constitution by mid-March and then to hold national elections for a Transitional National Assembly by the summer of 2004. That assembly would choose an Iraqi government to which the Coalition would cede sovereignty. Another set of elections would be held as soon as possible thereafter to choose a Constitutional Convention to write Iraq's permanent constitution.

My cable summarized: "Thus far, GC members have responded favorably to these ideas, though no plan has been presented formally. This alternative would meet many of the concerns about the political timetable raised by members of the GC over the past few months. It would give Kurds and Sunnis, worried about Shia domination, the ability to ensure that basic freedoms are protected and that federalism is established in Iraq for at least the period noted in the Constitution. It would meet the requirement of the religious Shia that Iraq's permanent Constitution be drafted by a directly elected body. Finally, it would satisfy Chalabi, Hakim, and Pachachi's desire to establish a fully sovereign Iraqi government as soon as possible."

The cable concluded that I considered this plan to be at the "outer edge" of what was acceptable for our interests in Iraq. Even if the interim constitution contained language binding the transitional government to a clear political process and fundamental rights, the odds of this process leading to a stable Iraq were still not high, probably no better than 60-40. And only that good, I noted, if we were "resolute and robust" in the prosecution of the war and showed the political will to see it through.

After signing off on the message, I discussed the insurgency with Bill, the chief of station, who showed me the CIA's latest security assessment. "The Agency will receive this in time for tomorrow's NSC Principals' meeting," he explained, handing over the four-page document.

The station's argument was persuasive, and disturbing: "The enemy believes American leadership is more focused on an exit strategy than with prosecuting the war." And the Coalition did not have a clear message to the Iraqi people.

As administrator, I was invited to comment on the station's report. I concurred with the overall assessment but said I disagreed that the problem was due to lack of a clear message. "We are giving many Iraqis the impression that the U.S. is determined to leave and to leave quickly." And I endorsed the need for a military strategy "to establish dependable and enduring security for the Iraqi people as the overriding requirement for ultimate success."

When Bill left, I reflected that we were nearing a critical junction in Iraq. If those who favored an immediate turnover of sovereignty prevailed, I could see no way that we would be able to assemble the vital components of representative government. The insurgents would eventually win. Equally, if the sectarian-ethnic factions in Iraq succeeded, the country would splinter irreparably. Bloody civil war would follow. The insurgents would win.

I remembered President Bush's words the last time we'd spoken. We were *not* going to fail in Iraq.

I agreed. Iraq had a future of hope and I was going to do my damnedest to help it get there.

I spent November 10 sounding out key Shia leaders about the new political plan. Both the SCIRI- and Dawa-affiliated Governing Council members were pleased with the approach and said they were confident Ayatollah Sistani would support it. I told them we were counting on them to ensure his support. Then I asked Meghan and Roman to talk to Chalabi, who was uncharacteristically flustered and clearly stated his opposition to early national elections. He was apparently aware of his very low support in the Iraqi population. So while he wanted a sovereign government soon, he probably believed he could wield more influence if it were selected by a simple expansion of the GC instead of by elections.

Then I began a series of telephone calls to the NSC Principals, starting with Rumsfeld. He hadn't had time to study our cable, so I walked him through the plan. He seemed mildly enthusiastic, but said that Rice, Powell, and Cheney had told him they felt the new path took "too long." Couldn't we get earlier "milestones": January 30, 2004, versus March 15 for finishing the interim constitution, for example?

I told him that even if we got an interim constitution in place earlier, elections for a transitional legislature would control the timing on passing sovereignty. And the timing of elections would be determined by how quickly we could establish a voters' list, an electoral law, and a political parties law. Our NGO contractor, the International Foundation for Election Systems (IFES), had told us it would take at least six to nine months to complete voter registration. But I agreed to bring forward the deadline for the interim constitution to March 1.

Rumsfeld suggested I explain this to Rice, Powell, and the vice president.

"How will they ever conduct elections in that security environment?" Rice asked after I described the process in a call a little after midnight in Baghdad.

"Well, perhaps the situation will improve," I said. "But even if there's violence during the elections, this path'll be better than the stalemate we've got now."

"Jerry," she said, "*some* people here are still leaning toward handing sovereignty to an appointed government in April with no constitution."

This sounded like the people in the Pentagon's policy office. I told her, "I strongly recommend against that route. It doesn't serve the president's or America's interests in Iraq. I'm not offering a perfect solution, Condi, but at least we've found a way to give Iraq's political life a structure through the interim constitution and to engage the Iraqi people in the political process in 2004."

"I'll support it, though earlier is better," she said. "What's your guess about transfer of sovereignty?"

"Well, if we take IFES's best case on voters' lists, and don't lose any time, we should be able to do it this side of August," I said.

Ten minutes later, Condi called back. "This new proposal is too important for you to explain on the secure video with the president at Wednesday's NSC meeting. You'd better find a plane and get back by tomorrow morning Washington time, brief the Principals, and then have a meeting with the president face to face." Since it was already past midnight in Baghdad, this meant I had to get moving right away to be at the NSC Principals' meeting later the same day.

While Pat Kennedy scrambled to find a plane that would take me and a small group of CPA staff back in time for the next day's meeting, I called the others on my list.

When I reached the vice president, he expressed concern about the timeline. "But on the other hand I'm concerned that early elections may favor the extremists and Islamists," he said. I agreed with that point, but noted that we had to move out of the box we were in.

In my next call, Colin Powell expressed concern that the timeline was still too long. (I was concerned that it was too compressed.) But in the end he said he was fine with any practical option. However, our No. 1 priority remained "fixing the security situation."

As if to underscore his words, automatic-weapons fire sounded from the direction of Airport Road.

My final call before getting into the convoy for the late-night drive to the airport was to Talabani. "Sorry to bother you so late, Mr. President," I began, "but my government will need a couple of days to work through the Talabani-Pachachi plan. Please do your best to keep the Governing Council quiet."

"Mr. Ambassador, of course I will."

"Another thing: You've got to get Sistani's blessing for this plan. Send someone down to Najaf or go there yourself if necessary. I can't ask my government to endorse a new course without some assurances that Najaf will be okay with it."

"I understand. Bon voyage and good luck, Ambassador."

It was cold in the open belly of the C-141 medical evacuation Starlifter parked on the tarmac. My party from the CPA sat in the cargo bay on hard seats forward of the casualties, waiting for the last ambulances to unload. Stretchers hung three high in a cat's cradle of nylon straps, the rows leading back toward the gaping tail ramp. I could hear moans and occasional cries of pain as the medics hoisted new litters into place. But most of the wounded were sedated. Or just stoically quiet.

Shivering in my sport coat, I hoped they were also bundled against the damp chill. The first big autumn storm had dumped snow in the mountains of Kurdistan and trailed a front south across Iraq's river valleys, kicking up a chilly sandstorm.

Dan Senor, Brian McCormack, Roman Martinez, Bob Blackwill, and I had rushed to leave the Green Zone after midnight for the drive to the airport. From here, there'd be a five-hour medevac flight to Ramstein, Germany, where we'd board another Air Force plane for Washington. As soon as I arrived in Washington early that morning, I would attend a crucial meeting of the National Security Council Principals in the White House. "Wheels up" from Baghdad had been scheduled for 2:00 A.M., but the bad weather had slowed the incoming medevac Black Hawks.

Behind us, the nurses and medics in gray flight suits and tan desert fatigues moved with quiet efficiency and compassion among the stacked litters, checking IV drips, monitoring vital signs, and adjusting the oxygen flow to one critical case on a respirator. A multiple-wrapped layer of gauze bandage completely covered the patient's head, with the respirator tube protruding like a diver's mouthpiece.

Burns, I thought, picturing a roadside IED engulfing a Humvee in a fireball. I closed my eyes and prayed for these brave young Americans. Traveling around Iraq, I encountered troops on patrol, manning checkpoints, or helping rebuild the country. Despite the harsh summer heat, the sandstorms, and now the chill rain, our soldiers remained ready to defeat the growing insurgency. They were always cheerful when I spoke to them, willing to accept the risks—and the sacrifices.

Flying choppers in darkness in this kind of weather was dangerous, but probably not as dangerous as in daylight. Nine days earlier, on the sunny morning of November 2, insurgents had launched shoulder-fired surface-to-air missiles at two big U.S. Army Chinook helicopters near Fallujah, the most rebellious city in the Sunni Triangle. The aircraft were carrying full loads of troops to Baghdad Airport for two-week R&R leaves. As the missiles' white smoke trails spiraled up, the aircrew popped magnesium flares to decoy the heat-seeking warheads. But one Chinook was hit and crashed, killing fifteen soldiers and wounding twenty, two of them mortally.

The Fallujah shootdown was the single deadliest day for Coalition troops since the heavy fighting of the invasion. The loss galvanized American and international media, dramatizing the obvious fact that resistance from a shadowy enemy remained the major obstacle the Coalition and most Iraqis faced. Since then, Black Hawk helicopters carrying me around the country had orders to fly low and fast to reduce the danger of ground attack.

I heard the whack of rotor blades as another medevac helicopter landed. A few minutes later, ambulance headlights swept through the open compartment. I looked back to see medics carrying a stretcher into the plane and two soldiers following on crutches.

An Air Force captain with a stethoscope around the collar of her flight suit approached our seats. "Sorry, sir," she said above the noise of the departing chopper. "But we're going to be a while longer. Another case inbound."

"Don't worry about us, Captain," I said.

Brian checked the luminous dial of his watch. It was 2:35 A.M. in Iraq, and we had at least fourteen hours of flying ahead of us.

"Going to be a long, long night," he said.

I started the old riff we'd perfected flying military aircraft over the previous five months.

"Well, we'll get there . . ."

". . . when we get there, sir," Brian finished.

But when will that *be?*

I tried to lean back in my seat, but it didn't move. Maybe I was tired enough to doze off, just sitting here. No luck. My thoughts were churning.

A final Black Hawk landed, and medics secured the stretchers in the webbing slings. The big clamshell doors in the tail whirred closed as the jet's four engines started, one after another. I inserted the yellow foam earplugs and tried to lean back in the unyielding seat. It was 3:15 A.M., November 11.

Whatever my discomfort, it was nothing compared to what those brave young men and women behind us faced.

At cruising altitude, the cabin temperature steadied to a nagging chill, making sleep difficult. But I did doze. When I'd wake, the proximity to the wounded soldiers brought home the grinding realities of the insurgency: ambushed patrols, snipers, and especially roadside IEDs. I had an uneasy feeling that the military was still struggling to find effective means to combat the enemy. When I would probe my military colleagues on this, I often got a sense that I had stepped out of my "lane." Our generals were certainly right to be concerned about the upcoming troop rotation. But I simply didn't agree that our problems could be solved by expanding untrained Iraqi security forces as quickly as possible—including reconstituting units under Baathist officers—or by simply handing over sovereignty to the Governing Council.

I thought back to the morning of November 3, the day after the Chinook loss. Clay had given me a paper summarizing our security challenges. His central thesis, with which I agreed, was that there was no overall strategy for defeating the enemy. He stressed the need for better intelligence about the insurgents and terrorists. We both knew that this was the hardest kind of intelligence to obtain. "But damn it, Jerry," he said, "unless we get better intel on these guys, get a real handle on the nature of the enemy, we're not going to win here."

His second point was that the Army seemed to have gone into a passive or reactive mode since late August, when the roadside IED and car bomb offensive got under way. Two months later, our military operations didn't seem to be running at the same tempo as in the summer. Units of the 82nd Airborne Division in Anbar Province—the Sunni insurgents' home turf—were no longer patrolling the cities as actively as they had following Liberation. This lowered the risk of casualties, but gave the impression that we'd ceded towns like Fallujah to the enemy. "Our offensive operations do not seem governed by a strategy beyond searching and routing members of the enemy's ranks." He pointed out that we had been in and out of Fallujah several times since Liberation. "We go in, move around a bit, capture some bad guys and then leave," Clay said. "As soon as we go, they take over again. We are not doing the most important thing in this kind of an insurgency: denying the enemy bases of cooperation or support.

"And we're simply not killing enough bad guys," was Clay's terse summary.

I told him that if it was any consolation, I had the impression from my meetings in Washington in late October that the vice president, Powell, and Rice shared the view that we had a serious security problem in Iraq, one that wouldn't be solved just by moving more quickly on the political front.

Clay's memo had led me to try to telephone Scooter Libby, Vice President Cheney's chief of staff, on November 6. He'd been out, and to my surprise the vice president had called back.

I told him of my growing unease about deteriorating security. Roadside bombs and ambushes were killing not only our troops, but also civilian contractors working on reconstruction. "Mr. Vice President," I said, "in my view, we do not have a military strategy for victory in Iraq. It seems to me that our policy is driven more by our troop rotation schedule than by a strategy to win." We appeared to have slipped into a "garrison" mentality. It was probably not a coincidence that attacks on Coalition military and civilian contractors had escalated over the past two months, during which time we had not run a single major military operation. Now, five days after the shootdown in Fallujah there had still been no Coalition reaction. The insurgency had the potential to reverse everything we'd accomplished and ultimately to ignite a civil war, with Sunni

Baathists fighting Shiite and Kurdish militias, and Iraq fragmenting along sectarian and geographical fault lines.

"The impression may well be growing among the insurgents that we won't stay the course, Mr. Vice President," I said, "what with all this talk of reducing American force levels, throwing Iraqis into the mix, and pushing for a quick end to the occupation."

"I've been asking the same question," he said. "What's our strategy to win? My impression is that the Pentagon's mind-set is that the war's over and they're now in the 'mopping-up' phase. They fail to see that we're in a major battle against terrorists in Iraq and elsewhere."

I repeated my concern about pushing untrained Iraqis to the security forces.

"I've got similar concerns, Jerry," Cheney said. "But I do believe it's important to get more Iraqis involved. This worked in Pakistan, clamping down on the Taliban and Al-Qaeda in Waziristan, and in Saudi, cutting off bin Laden's financial backing."

"I agree with the objective, Mr. Vice President," I replied. "We've said all along that defending Iraq must eventually be Iraq's responsibility. But adding unprofessional Iraqi security forces can't substitute for a military strategy."

He asked where the political process stood. I told him that I would move it along as fast as possible. "But we can't deceive ourselves that this is some kind of miracle cure for Iraq's problems. In fact, since the terrorists are thoroughly antidemocratic, to the degree that we produce a credible path toward democracy, they'll almost certainly increase their attacks."

"Do you want me to raise these issues with people here, citing your concerns, or do it on my own?"

"I'd prefer you did it on your own if you're comfortable," I said. "Frankly, I haven't been successful in getting my views accepted at the Pentagon. But I gather from my conversations with the president that he's rock solid on this."

"You bet," Cheney said.

He thanked me for calling and invited me to do so at any time. I said I appreciated his interest and promised not to abuse that offer.

The next day, November 7, had been a bad day. At the morning military briefing, Rick Sanchez announced that we'd had four more soldiers killed in attacks, including another helicopter shootdown, this one near Tikrit.

That afternoon, I had a long private meeting with John Abizaid, who'd been back in Iraq for two days, meeting with his senior officers and troops across the country.

"They're confident," he said, "but a bit too conservative on their interventions against the bad guys. I encouraged them to be more aggressive."

"I'm all for that, John."

He told me he was going back to visit the 82nd Airborne in Ramadi and wondered if I had any objection to his meeting tribal sheiks there. "My basic message will be, 'Come along with us or else.'"

This sounded right to me. It was another way to reach out to the Sunnis in the West. "But we need to be prepared to follow up and hit hard. Those guys don't bluff easily," I said.

"We will be."

I was pleased to hear John proposing a steady increase of military pressure in the Sunni Triangle, which I had favored for two months. But he had more on his mind. "I'm concerned that people in Washington might try to drive a wedge between us. Some of them are saying you believe all the problems in Iraq can be solved with better security."

I told Abizaid this was inaccurate and probably reflected an exchange I'd had with General Peter Pace at the NSC a few days before. "Pace said, 'The most important military strategy is to accelerate the governance track.' In other words, slap together an Iraqi government, grant it sovereignty, and end the occupation. I had to object to that." Of course we had to do these things. But central to all was better security.

Abizaid noted he was fed up that my Senior Adviser on National Security, Walt Slocombe, still opposed rehiring Sunni field-grade army officers. "We need experienced Iraqi commanders who can lead troops. And I'm sick of reading his opinion on the subject in newspapers."

Slocombe had been responding to reporters' questions and explaining our efforts to create the New Iraqi Army. A number of those questions had been sparked by the leaks of anonymous uniformed officers and Pentagon officials looking for someone to blame for the largely unpredicted insurgency we were now fighting.

I told Abizaid I agreed with Slocombe that we needed to be very careful. We could perhaps bring back selected colonels and brigadiers, but only if they were individually vetted. "We can't be reinstalling Baathist leaders or killers. And as long as unnamed 'senior military officers' and 'Pentagon officials' are trying to hang us in the press, we'll be forced to respond."

He was silent a moment.

"Listen," he said, "I've always told you that I opposed disbanding the army, but I've never gone to the press with my opinion."

Always? Disbanding?

Way back in May, Walt Slocombe had consulted CENTCOM while we prepared CPA Order No. 2, dissolving the old Iraqi Defense Ministry, Saddam's intelligence services, and security forces. The order recognized the reality that the Iraqi army had disbanded itself as Coalition forces swept into the country. We had coordinated the CPA decision—and had reviewed every word of the order—with Paul Wolfowitz and Doug Feith before issuing the decree on May 23. Lieutenant General David McKiernan, Abizaid's commander on the ground, had been fully consulted, too.

"Well, John," I said as the conversation ended, "I appreciate your position, but I disagree with it. All my conversations with Shia and Kurdish leaders since arriving convince me that bringing back Saddam's army would have set off a civil war here. If you think we've got problems now, imagine what they *would* have been."

Our plane arrived at Andrews Air Force Base at 8:00 A.M., which gave me time for a quick shower at the base before heading straight to the White House Situation Room. At Condi Rice's request, the meeting was "Principals only," no aides or assistants. She chaired the session, with the vice president seated to her right. Colin Powell, Don Rumsfeld, George Tenet, and Andy Card represented State, Defense, CIA, and the White House, respectively. Marine General Pete Pace sat in for Joint Chiefs chairman Dick Myers.

As we gathered around the long mahogany table, it was clear we had reached a watershed in our post-Liberation relations with Iraq. What was decided in Washington in the next few days would shape our overall military and political strategy and cast the mold for victory or defeat. So it was essential to overcome my fatigue and outline as clearly as possible the CPA's proposed new way forward. Rice had asked me to strip the plan to its basic structure so that everyone on the NSC would understand our intent.

First I reviewed how we had come to the current impasse. The Coalition's strategic goal was to lay the foundations for a durable democracy in Iraq. We believed that that required a constitution to define boundaries for Iraq's political life and institutions. Our original plan had foreseen convening a convention of representative Iraqis who would write the permanent constitution. This would be followed by the election of a government to which we would hand over sovereignty.

But Sistani was not budging from his insistence, formalized in his June fatwa, that a permanent constitution had to be written by Iraqis chosen in full, direct nationwide elections. And the Governing Council was unwilling or unable to confront him on this issue. Because Iraq lacked any electoral system, following Sistani's path would force a long delay in returning sovereignty to

Iraqis. The political climates in Iraq, America, and Britain argued against such a delay.

I described the new plan. The Governing Council, aided by Iraqi legal experts, would write an interim constitution by March 1. And in the summer there would be elections for a transitional government to which we would cede sovereignty—we hoped by July 1. A Constitutional Convention elected in early 2005 would write the permanent constitution.

Rice and Powell expressed concern about trying to hold elections as early as the summer of 2004. I agreed that this was risky. All the electoral experts we had consulted, and the UN, believed that a minimum of six to nine months would be needed to conduct them. Elections in June were "doable," but they would be "rough and ready" because there would not be time to conduct a census or establish electoral rolls. And there was no margin for delay. But I felt it important to transfer sovereignty to an elected government if possible.

I told the group that there was an alternative to elections for selecting a government—caucuses at the governorate level—a proposal that reflected the PrepComm's second option. This process would produce a less legitimate government, but would allow for local variations in how the transitional government was chosen. And security might be less of a concern.

In the animated discussion that ensued, Colin Powell repeated several times that the proposal's timeline was "very ambitious." He could only recommend this course to the president if we were certain to obtain the support of the Governing Council and of Sistani.

"Well," I said, "Hakim and Jaafari have assured me that Sistani will support the plan. To be sure, I've also asked Talabani to double-check with the ayatollah. Ideally, we'd like him to endorse the process publicly. But my experts think that very unlikely. At a minimum, we'd settle for his silent acquiescence." As for the concern about holding elections amid violence, we had to be realistic. "There *will* be violence," I admitted. "But we've got to accept the fact that elections in Iraq will be violent for years to come. There are weapons all over the place. It's a violent society, like Colombia."

The vice president suggested an alternative approach that I knew Chalabi and Pachachi had been shopping. "Maybe the Governing Council should just choose an executive body that we could recognize as the transitional government."

I responded that this was a risky strategy and repeated my view that we needed at least to get an interim constitution in place before handing sovereignty over to an elected or selected body. Such a document would help protect individual and minority rights and establish a governmental structure.

Rice weighed in strongly on the importance of a constitution to structure Iraq's political life and to protect the minority rights of Sunni Arabs and Kurds.

The discussion swirled around the pros and cons of the new path.

At one point Powell said simply and bluntly, "All this will be irrelevant until we deal with the security situation."

"You all know my position," I said. "There's no political fix to the security problem. We should move quickly with the process of getting elections and transferring sovereignty because it's what we and the Iraqis want. But we've got to recognize that by itself this won't defeat the terrorists."

Before we adjourned, it was agreed that my proposal for a political path forward would be discussed at the NSC meeting with the president the next day. He would have to decide the timeline to be put to the Iraqis, and whether we recommended that the interim government be chosen by elections or by caucuses.

Despite the tensions, we'd made progress.

Riding to the White House the next morning with Rumsfeld, we reviewed a paper that Meghan, back in Baghdad, had prepared overnight on what could go wrong with the new political process. The most serious risks were that the Iraqi people would reject the concept of an interim constitution, the Governing Council could not agree on a text, or we could not keep Sistani and the Shia aboard for the new process.

"From a political point of view, I prefer elections," I told Rumsfeld, as we reached the White House gate. "But I heard overnight that the International Foundation for Election Systems, our NGO contractor, is now waffling on being able to pull them off by the end of June."

"Not an unreasonable assumption," he replied.

"That could screw things up royally," I continued. "We'd lose control of the timing of the process. It would be a hell of a fix for us to discover in May that the Iraqi elections would have to be postponed to the autumn or later."

"But you're still going to support elections?"

"I'll make the case for them," I said. "But, frankly with IFES now waffling, I think it'd be safer to use the caucus system to choose the interim government."

In the White House SitRoom, with the president in the chair, I reviewed our proposal. I went through a paper titled "Transition to Sovereignty," which the Governance Team and I had worked on late the night before. It laid out the proposal for moving ahead and listed the pros and cons of elections versus caucuses. Elections would ensure maximum legitimacy of the transitional assembly, but they could favor the best-organized parties, including Islamists, and there was a real risk elections could not be conducted by summer. Caucuses were more manageable and it would be easier to stick to the timetable. On the other hand, they would be seen as less legitimate.

Colin Powell once more commented that the timetable was "exceptionally ambitious," and that we had to be assured of support from the Governing Council and Sistani. I briefed the president on our efforts to address this problem. Secretary Rumsfeld noted that it was important to move responsibility quickly to the Iraqis to show them that they could run their own country.

Bush agreed, but added, "We need to be patient while the Iraqi security forces are trained. And we should accept the reality that we can't get a permanent constitution right away."

Turning to me, the president asked, "Wouldn't the caucuses allow for better security? I mean you wouldn't have the spectacle of lines at polls getting bombed or shot at."

I told him that our experts were becoming doubtful about being able to hold elections by June 2004. But recalling the principles he and I had discussed in May, I added that using caucuses would mean denying Iraqis the right to elections before we transferred sovereignty.

"Well," he said, "we'd need to remind people that the caucuses are just a way station to full democratic elections to a permanent government."

He wondered if the caucus process might help with the Sunnis.

"Not necessarily," I admitted. "The basic problem for them is the prospect that the Shia might retaliate for what the Sunnis did to them for a thousand years. So building guarantees of minority rights into the interim constitution will be an important reassurance for the Sunnis."

Before we broke up, I said it would be important that the new political process be presented as the Iraqis' idea, not ours. "This'll call for some discipline in the days ahead," I added, thinking of leaks.

President Bush laughed warmly. "Hey, Bremer," he said. "I agree with that. And I suggest that maybe this can be the one meeting in history where everybody doesn't rush out to tell the press what we decided."

There were sage nods around the table.

We'd reached the end of the agenda and, as is his practice, the president did not announce his decision about elections or regional caucuses to the group. He concluded the meeting on a broader point. "I believe in the inherent goodness of the Iraqi people. They have a basic instinct to live in peace, guided by universal values which are beyond politics." As he stood up, he added, "It's important for everyone to know that we're going to stay the course and that I'm determined to succeed."

Once more I witnessed his unshakable confidence.

• • •

President Bush, Vice President Cheney, Card, Rice, Wolfowitz, and I went up to the Oval Office for a brief follow-up discussion. "I'm going to go with the caucus approach to the interim government," the president announced. "The elections are just too risky in the time left to July."

He asked the others to leave, so that he and I could meet alone. We sat side by side next to the fireplace.

"How you doing, Jerry?" he asked. "Holding up?"

"I'm fine, Mr. President, pleased with the outcome of these discussions. It's going to be a rough six or seven months, but we'll get through it."

"What's the real situation on the ground?"

He wanted and deserved an honest answer, and I wasn't in line for another star or another job.

"Mr. President, we have to deal more effectively with the security situation. The intelligence is just not good. And I'm personally not persuaded that the military has a strategy to win."

He nodded. Perhaps Cheney had raised this concern with him.

"You know, Mr. President," I said, "one of my favorite presidential moments was when McClellan was marching the Army of the Potomac up and down and refusing to give battle to the Confederates. Lincoln cabled him, 'If you're not going to use the army, could I borrow it?' "

Bush laughed, but made no comment.

He returned to my service in Iraq. "How's that timeline going to affect what you told me about not staying past May?"

"I'll stay on to get the interim government up," I said. "The only other option would be leaving as soon as the interim constitution is drafted."

"No," he said. "You should remain until the job is done—until we pass sovereignty back to the Iraqis. When are you planning to visit us again?"

"I'm hoping to come back for the December 9 Iraqi National Symphony concert at the Kennedy Center."

He remembered the event, buzzed his secretary, and asked that she be sure to block it on his calendar and to invite Francie and me as his guests. I thanked him.

"You're doing a great job," he said, walking me to the door. "Keep it up."

Back in Baghdad, we got the good news that a top SCIRI member, Dr. Adel Mahdi, had traveled to Najaf on November 13 at Talabani's request. Talabani told me that Adel had briefed Ayatollah Sistani on the new process and that Sistani had "approved" it. Talabani added that he himself had traveled to Karbala, the other Shia holy city, the day before. He had met with a number of lesser ayatollahs whom he characterized as "pleased" with the new plan. This confirmed what we had been told many times—that Sistani and the religious Shia would go along with any political process that led to a constitution drafted by an elected body.

On the other hand, our Governance Team was unhappy that we had dropped elections for the interim government. But as they knew, our election experts were no longer confident that elections could be prepared by summer. So I told them to "stop moping," reminding them that politics is the art of the possible. "If we've learned nothing here in the last six months, we've learned that maxim—every day."

On the evening of November 14, I again met with the Governing Council's nine-member presidency at my house. Dr. Adel represented SCIRI because the party's leader, Abdul Aziz Hakim, was out of the country.

I went through the new road map, and thanked them for their support and Talabani for his leadership. The GC leadership was thrilled. Adel reported that Sistani had approved of the new process. It was agreed that Talabani would convene the entire Governing Council the following morning to discuss—and, we hoped, to approve—the new path. They would then invite me and my British colleague, David Richmond, to meet the full GC at about noon, with a press announcement planned for 3:00 P.M.

Late that night, I reached Condi Rice, who was delighted to hear about our progress and intention to announce the plan the next day. I cautioned, more out of bitter experience than certain knowledge, that she should not bet everything on success yet.

"This is, after all, Iraq," I said.

The next day, November 15, Richmond and I were called to Talabani's house at about 12:30 P.M. Our Governance Team had reduced the plan to a proposed agreement between the CPA and the Governing Council and had sent the draft to Talabani the night before. The full GC had been in session for several hours and had conducted a rather disorganized discussion of the new plan. We found the members gathered around a long oval table in the dining room. As GC president, Talabani was at the head. Staff members crowded the walls.

We started reading through the three-page draft document and got along quite well until we hit the word *federal*.

This inspired several Kurds to give stirring speeches on the nature of federalism. They were not about to let go of their autonomous region.

Talabani, himself a principal Kurdish leader, had to remind them repeatedly that the substance of the federalism chapter in the interim constitution would be drafted between now and March 1, 2004. "So we should leave it alone for now," he urged.

No sooner had the Kurds receded than the Shia arose. The biggest problem came from the SCIRI representative, Dr. Adel Mahdi. Until now Adel had been helpful and the previous night he had been enthusiastic. But today he became agitated over the method by which the provincial caucuses would be chosen. In effect, he wanted the Governing Council to select each caucus itself, which would undercut the opportunity to broaden the political dialogue to reach more Sunnis. And it would give the GC, increasingly unpopular with the Iraqi public, too much say in the makeup of the interim government.

Most of the other GC members disagreed with Adel. A heated discussion dragged on for almost an hour.

"We cannot proceed until this important issue is resolved," Adel said ominously.

Finally, I suggested that the GC designate three people to go into the other room to find a compromise for the selection of the caucuses. Almost an hour later, the negotiators returned to report that they'd been unable to reach agreement. As it transpired, Adel and a few others on the Council remained opposed to the proposed formula for selecting the delegates. He suggested that the Council "indefinitely delay" the decision on this crucial issue.

"No," I said. "We have to reach agreement on the entire package. I'm prepared to stay all day."

Again, I was mindful that by now there were some stomachs grumbling around the table as the hour of *iftar* drew near.

But Adel was joined by several other Shia Islamists who expressed concern that the Council would be unable to control the process of selecting the caucuses. That of course was correct. That was our objective.

General confusion ensued about the overall process, with several members also objecting that under the plan the Governing Council would dissolve, like the CPA, upon assumption of a sovereign Iraqi government.

"But that's essential," I said. "Iraq can't have two governments at the same time, the Governing Council and the new interim government. So the GC has to dissolve then, just like us."

Talabani and Chalabi got that straightened out to the satisfaction of the others, but Adel was still grumbling.

The discussion continued for another half hour. It became clear that

Talabani's repeated assurances that "all was well with the GC and the new plan" had been, at a minimum, exaggerated. We had real problems here.

"Listen," I said, raising my right hand to bring silence. "Frankly, I'm disappointed in the Council's deliberations. The Coalition has come a very long way to meet your interests. If we don't reach agreement today, I will have to answer questions from the press because someone from the Council leaked the story to the American press last night." A wave of furtive expressions around the table. "So we don't have the luxury of silence. Moreover, Mr. Talabani has called a press conference for 3:00 P.M. If I speak to the press, I'll have to explain that we were unable to agree because the Governing Council is standing in the way of returning sovereignty to the Iraqi people and is trying to control the process by which the interim government will be chosen."

Now there were queasy expressions on the faces around the long dining room table.

But my words produced action. After another brief bout of squabbling, Talabani put the plan to a vote, which carried twenty in favor to accept the plan. Four Shiites, including Adel, voted against the deal.

As Talabani, Richmond, and I signed the agreement, I felt a wave of relief and optimism which I forced myself to quash as we left for the press conference at the Council center. Talabani and I announced the agreement to the press that afternoon.

We'd won a major skirmish, but there'd been a last-minute switch by some Shia, and we had some serious work to do with them. If Ayatollah Sistani chose to back them, we could still lose the Shia.

The next morning I called the senior staff into the conference room to review the impact of the November 15 Agreement on our work.

"We plan to be out of here by next July," I said.

Some beamed with relief; others looked troubled.

"And I know you've all got a lot of unfinished work," I continued.

Our Strategic Plan was now 153 pages long, and maybe a third of the priority tasks had been completed. I asked each Senior Adviser to identify the most urgent tasks their ministry had to finish before we handed over sovereignty. "After I've got your individual inputs, I'll sort them out for missionwide priorities and the planning staff will update the overall plan."

I reminded the advisers that the president had just signed the $18.6 billion supplemental budget for Iraqi reconstruction. And that we had to move fast if these projects were to have a useful impact in the short time left.

"All right," I said in closing, "remember, we don't want to leave these ministries orphans. Make sure your Iraqi counterparts can continue to function once we're withdrawn." I added that I intended to establish several Iraqi institutions to fight corruption, the bane of many developing countries and something that had flourished under Saddam. Each ministry would get an inspector general and we would set up an independent national Commission on Public Integrity.

The mood in the room was a mixture of pride that we'd reached a political settlement and concern that the fragile Iraqi institutions we'd worked with would not survive the battering that we all knew lay ahead.

After the meeting I asked my senior economic adviser, Marek Belka, to come to my office to discuss the issue of economic reforms. Marek, who had twice been Poland's deputy prime minister and minister of finance, had replaced Peter McPherson in September. He'd brought with him to the CPA job an unusual combination of intelligence, academic achievement, and practical experience. Based on his work in Poland as a hands-on economist who'd pushed basic reform, Marek had arrived in Baghdad determined to phase out Saddam's pervasive subsidies that were stymieing the free market.

"But this new sovereignty deadline means we'll have to slow down on that," I regretfully told him.

He nodded. "You're right. All we can do is prepare the Iraqis as best we can."

It had been hard for me to concentrate this cool Sunday morning. Late the previous night, Clay had come to my house for a private word.

"I went to the doctor about my cough, Jerry," he said. "They took a chest X-ray and found a shadow. It's probably cancer."

No! Not Clay!

He'd smoked heavily once, but not for years, and I'd assumed his cough had been due to the sandstorms and Baghdad's dust.

"I've got to get a biopsy," Clay added. "So I'm heading back to the States on Monday."

Naturally, I prayed the test would be negative. But I was also overcome considering the gap he'd leave behind. Clay was more than a strong deputy. We were completely in tune, yet Clay never hesitated to keep me honest and on track when he thought I needed it.

I stared at him a moment. "You'll be back, Clay."

"Sure," he said.

But we both knew that he wouldn't.

• • •

At sunset Sunday I attended the Governing Council's *iftar* meal. These were always relaxed, a pleasant and productive way to socialize with the members. This evening I was accompanied by Ambassador Dick Jones, my new chief policy officer and, with Clay's departure, effectively my new deputy. Dick was another of the many seasoned American diplomats who served selflessly in Iraq. He had been ambassador to Lebanon and Kazakhstan, spoke fluent Arabic, and was currently our ambassador in neighboring Kuwait. Even with all Dick's experience, I knew it would be important to have someone to help him navigate the CPA maze. So I assigned Matt Fuller, one of my most able special assistants, to be Dick's chief of staff. Matt had been with me since the day I arrived and I knew Dick would be in good hands.

During the meal, Dr. Mowaffak al-Rubaie, one of my prime conduits to the Shia leadership, including Ayatollah Sistani, took me aside.

"Dr. Adel is trying to reopen the November 15 Agreement," Rubaie said. "Very unwisely, he has called for the thirteen Shiite members on the Council to meet tomorrow to discuss this."

Damn, I thought. *The ink is hardly dry on the agreement and here we go again.* News media accounts of the "historic" breakthrough were zipping through cyberspace as we stood here nibbling our spicy chicken and lamb kabobs.

"There will be *no* reopening of the agreement," I said coldly. "The Council overwhelmingly approved it. The president and the British prime minister have both publicly welcomed it."

Rubaie, the honest messenger, looked stricken. *That was okay. Maybe he'd tell the crew in Najaf how angry I was.*

I added that I was particularly unhappy with Adel. "Three times last week Adel told me that he strongly approved of the agreement, including Friday night when he told us Sistani had approved the plan. Why's he suddenly become such a stubborn opponent?"

"He must have gotten new instructions," he said, shrugging.

But from whom? I wondered. Adel had assured me twice that his party's leader, Abdul Aziz Hakim, had approved the new plan.

"Look, Dr. Rubaie," I said. "Let me be very frank. If the Shia persist on this route, two consequences are likely. And both are bad. It'll split the Council and thus destroy it. And then we'll have to delay the return to sovereignty by two years while we find some other path forward. And if that happens, I'll be forced to tell the Iraqi people that this delay is due to the Shia."

Rubaie looked even grimmer.

"Remember," I said, "the Coalition has gone a very long way to accommodate Ayatollah Sistani. And every Shiite in Iraq should bear this in mind."

Later I asked Meghan to sound out Adel, to discover what had knocked him out of kilter. Adel was one of the most impressive Iraqi politicians I had met. Educated as an economist, he had spent his exile in France, where his family still lived. He and I shared a love of French cuisine and though he was a senior member of the Islamist SCIRI party, he was reasonable.

"Adel's angry because we forced a vote on the agreement. He says it was a violation of the principle of consensus, which the GC had agreed to use for all important decisions," Meghan reported after seeing him. "But he has substantive concerns as well."

Adel was worried that the Governing Council would cease to exist after it had finally achieved some international acceptability.

"Maybe we can finesse that by saying that while the GC as a body disappears, members can be grandfathered into the Transitional Assembly," I told Meghan.

She said that he also was worried about the makeup of the current provincial councils, which would play an important role in selecting the caucuses.

I met Adel later the same day and repeated that the Governing Council would have to go out of existence at the turnover of sovereignty, but added that we might find a way to give its members a role in the next government. I told him we agreed there were problems with some provincial councils. Many of these had been cobbled together by our military commanders in the immediate wake of Liberation, often with little appreciation of the local political situations. We knew there were Baathists out there, not just in the Sunni Triangle, but in some big cities.

I explained that already before the November 15 Agreement, we had developed a plan to review and "refresh" those councils, weeding out former Baathists with bad records, and that we wanted to work with the GC in that process. But, I emphasized, we needed to get a move on. Adel seemed somewhat mollified by my points, which I assumed would quickly make their way to Najaf.

By November 24, forty-six Coalition troops had been killed during the month—the bloodiest since Liberation—mainly by IEDs, hit-and-run RPG attacks, and snipers. In addition, a number of civilian contractor truck drivers had been wounded and a few killed during convoy ambushes. Conditions were getting worse.

That afternoon, John Abizaid, Rick Sanchez, and I joined the NSC meeting by secure video teleconference, most of which was taken up by John's somber assessment of the situation.

Abizaid said that his command now believed that "five thousand hardcore Baathists" were our most serious threat. He hoped to have good intelligence on the insurgency's regional and national structure in "a couple of weeks."

Then he said something that surprised me: we should keep Iraqi security forces visibly in the front, but we "shouldn't overestimate the capabilities" of these Iraqi forces. They were "nowhere near ready yet to go on their own."

"And," he added, "the police are weak."

Most of the hard military work would still have to be done by the Coalition. *Hallelujah. Finally I heard a realistic assessment of Iraqi security capabilities.*

But just as I began to think the old rosy scenario had disappeared, Abizaid resumed an upbeat tone. In the January-February time frame, he said, we could move to greater reliance on Iraqi forces. By April, "most of the close-in fighting" would be by Iraqis, with most insurgent areas under Iraqi control.

Looking at John Abizaid's tired eyes on the video screen, I sympathized with him. He was an honest soldier and patriotic American who'd been asked to defeat terrorists and a growing insurgency without enough troops, while sustaining minimum casualties.

It was going to be a long year ahead.

On the morning of November 26, I read on CNN.com that Rumsfeld had testified to the Senate the day before that we were considering "recalling" some units of the Iraqi army. According to the story, Rumsfeld told a Senate committee that it might be possible "to actually reach back in and see if units below some officer level" that hadn't been tainted by Baathism could be reactivated.

That was news to me. I shot Reuben an e-mail to find out what was going on.

Whatever was happening, the lingering itch to "stand up" parts of Saddam's army had obviously not disappeared at the Pentagon.

I remembered Andy Card's warning in late October that people in Washington were "gaming" me to take the fall because of the decision in May to "disband" the Iraqi army.

Eric Schmitt, a *New York Times* reporter, had e-mailed Dan Senor several weeks earlier that DOD Under Secretary Douglas Feith had not given me a "ringing endorsement" when asked on the record about who had been involved in drafting CPA Order No. 2 abolishing the old Iraqi military and security services. According to Schmitt, Feith told him, "What happened instead was that the Army didn't hang together the way it might have. And when the Army was dissolved, had dissolved itself, Bremer and Slocombe on their way over to Iraq, came up with a concept that basically said since the Army has dissolved itself we can take advantage of that situation by starting afresh."

Schmitt had asked if Feith had supported that plan. Feith would not discuss who played what role in the debate.

Which, of course, left the impression that Walt and I had acted independently. I asked Dan Senor to get our side of the story out and to alert the DOD spokesman, my old palace roomie Larry Di Rita.

It must have worked because in a November 20 *Washington Post* article, Feith alluded to the fact that he had in reality "played a role" in the demobilization decision. The *Post* also quoted a Rumsfeld statement on television in which he had said the Iraqi army "just disbanded and went home." And Walt Slocombe commented for the same article that the decision on Order No. 2 had not been "something that was dreamed up by somebody at the last minute and done at the insistence of the people in Baghdad. It was discussed." He cited with whom, and when: Wolfowitz early in May and "with Feith several times, including on May 22, the night before Bremer issued the formal order."

So the record was straighter, but we'd taken to elbowing each other, rather than serving the president and our country.

(Douglas Feith apparently changed course again on this subject when he spoke on the record to *New York Times* reporter Michael Gordon in October 2004. Discussing the pros and cons of trying to resurrect a viable force from the ashes of Saddam's army, Feith said, "When we saw that the army did not remain in units, that the people had disappeared, that looters had stripped all the infrastructure, all the various pros that weighed in favor of using the army had been negated by events. And we were left with the cons, a bad, corrupt, cruel, and undemocratic army.")

Trying to absorb all this was like grabbing fog. The instant history of the front page and seventy-second TV news segments had already etched into America's consciousness that Walt and I had made a grave error in demobilizing the Iraqi forces. Now apparently, the Pentagon was preparing the ground to "correct that mistake" by recalling units of Saddam's old army without regard for the violent political opposition such a move would spark among Iraqis long oppressed by that army. Since Liberation, Shiite leaders had encouraged their followers to cooperate with the Coalition. I knew that if we carelessly brought back units of the old army, we could put this cooperation at risk, possibly even driving the Shia to oppose the Coalition. That would cost lives and greatly complicate our task.

Earlier in November, Bob Blackwill had warned me that there was "stark naked panic" at the Pentagon about the upcoming troop rotation and that Rumsfeld seemed to have lost his self-confidence.

At the time, I'd thought he was exaggerating.

Right now, at least, I didn't have time to dwell on this. Since my Washington trip in late October, I'd been harboring a secret: President Bush was to have his Thanksgiving dinner in Iraq.

Within the CPA, only Brian McCormack and I had known. Working with Joe Hagin, the president's deputy chief of staff, Brian had devised a cover story that there'd be a gala USO show out at the big mess hall at Baghdad International and that I wanted to host Thanksgiving dinner for the troops. But Brian was getting alarmed at the lack of interest his liaison officer at the 1st Armored Division was showing in distributing tickets to the "show." I told him to relax. As soon as the military was cut in on the secret, they would snap to and fast.

And they did, for on Sunday, November 23, just four days before Thanksgiving, the White House told Abizaid about the president's trip. Sanchez was told Monday and things began to hum. Brian and the local commander huddled under wraps at the airport with Greg Jenkins, the chief White House advance man, and the Secret Service advance team to nail down the details.

Everybody was jumpy about security. On Saturday, November 22, insurgents had fired a SAM-7 missile at a DHL Airbus cargo jet that had just taken off from the airport. The heat-seeking warhead had exploded inside one of the jet's engines, but the pilots managed to make a safe emergency landing. Saddam's army had possessed thousands of these ground-to-air missiles, which is why I had vetoed reopening the Baghdad airport to commercial traffic in July. What would happen if scores of insurgents infiltrated the district around the airport and launched a massive "SAM trap" for Air Force One?

Troops weren't shanghaied to attend the "USO show," but word went down through the 1st AD that each unit was expected to contribute a representative group of men and women soldiers. After all, if USO performers were coming all this way, the Army should make them feel welcome.

I had to do some arm-twisting among the local press corps to get a handful of print and television reporters to agree to attend a USO show where I was scheduled to read the president's holiday greetings and deliver a pep talk to the troops. The journalists rightly considered this a puff piece unworthy of hardened war correspondents.

And then there was the Governing Council. Ten days earlier, I'd invited them all to "a special Thanksgiving dinner," hoping that traditional Muslim politesse would oblige them to reciprocate for all the Ramadan *iftars* I'd attended. We didn't want to push them for fear that they'd figure out something was afoot. But I insisted that Jalal Talabani, the GC's November president, attend. In the end, only five Council members accepted: Talabani, Chalabi, Rubaie, Dr. Raja Khuzai, and Barzani.

Toward sunset on Thanksgiving afternoon, I got word that the president's plane was inbound. The Council members had been asked to gather at the helicopter landing zone near the palace. Barzani arrived at the Green Zone with fifty unlicensed bodyguards, a number of whom were carrying illegal RPGs. After considerable shouting and pushing, the 1st AD troops guarding the checkpoint disarmed Barzani's men. The American commander wanted to arrest them all, but Pat Kennedy talked him out of it. Barzani sent me word that if he didn't get his weapons back, he would not come to dinner.

"Let him stay behind," I told the commander as the rest of us boarded the Black Hawks.

The dinner tables had been set up in the big Bob Hope Dining Facility, a sort of overgrown Quonset hut that seated six hundred soldiers. All soldiers had been ordered to check their weapons at the door.

I led the Council members to several tables at the front of the room, near a raised platform, backed by a huge drape of camouflage netting. The setup certainly looked plausible for a show by a USO troupe.

While awaiting dinner and the "entertainment," Rick Sanchez and I worked the room, shaking hands and having our pictures taken with the soldiers.

I hope they don't use up all their film on the junior varsity.

Brian whispered that Air Force One was on final approach. Rick Sanchez went out to greet the president planeside, and 1st AD Commander Brigadier General Marty Dempsey and I slipped behind the camouflage net. About five minutes later, President Bush walked in from the tarmac, looking well rested, and glanced around.

"Welcome to Free Iraq, Mr. President," I said.

He gave me a big hug.

Marty Dempsey presented the president a 1st AD jacket, which he immediately pulled on. Then I described the plan that had been Brian McCormack's brainstorm.

President Bush laughed and said, "That's great."

Sanchez and I walked around the net and went to the podium, where Rick said a few words of greeting to the troops, and then turned to me. "Mr. Ambassador," he said, "would you please read the president's Thanksgiving declaration."

I took the page from my jacket as if I were about to read Bush's words, but then paused before the microphone. "Thank you, General," I said. "But by tradition, the most senior U.S. government representative present should read it." I paused for effect. "Is there any representative more senior than me in the room?"

At that point, the president of the United States came around the side of the net, walked to the center of the stage, and the room exploded. The shouting, applause, and yelling created a palpable rush of air, a sound wave I could actually feel. The troops were on their feet, hooting and hollering, waving their arms. Camera strobes flashed in an unbroken glare that lasted several minutes.

The president spoke of his pride in the soldiers, gave his thanks, and our country's thanks, for their sacrifice, and assured them that the American people stood solidly behind them. Soldiers from grizzled sergeants-major to teenage privates were crying openly. Tears ran down the president's cheeks, too.

The president made his way among the tables, shaking hands, posing for pictures, and then took his place behind the chow line to serve up turkey and trimmings.

After about an hour, while the soldiers were eating, the president and I drove to another building at the airport to meet with the four Council members.

On the way over, I told him we had a new problem with Sistani. "Talabani was down in Najaf yesterday and reports that the ayatollah now insists that the transitional legislature that will assume sovereignty in June should be elected. This is a complete reversal of Sistani's earlier position and of the November 15 Agreement."

To confuse the issue further, also the day before, SCIRI's Hakim had held a press conference after conferring with Sistani, who, Hakim claimed, "expressed concern about the real gaps" in that agreement. But later that day, I'd received a private message from Sistani stating that *he* was displeased with Hakim's public remarks. "It's a first-class shmozzle, Mr. President. These GC guys have got to get it sorted out."

Bush nodded. "I'll make it clear to the Council members where we stand."

And he did, leaning on them firmly to follow the November 15 Agreement and proceed along the timeline to sovereignty that it had established. "You're all going to have to show leadership on this," President Bush said. "I want you to tell your fellow Council members my wishes." He also asked them to convey his high regards to Ayatollah Sistani.

The four promised they would do both.

I escorted the president to his armored Suburban for the ride across the tarmac to his plane.

"Stay on top of this, Jerry," he said. "We're making progress, and I know it's not easy."

"I'm not giving up," I told him.

After the dramatic visit, we turned our attention to figuring out what was up with Sistani and the Shia Islamists. It became apparent that Dr. Adel and SCIRI had carried clouded messages — we couldn't tell whether intentionally or not — to Sistani two weeks earlier about the proposed path forward. Our analysis suggested that the Shia Islamists and Sistani had separate concerns.

Those on the GC, at least at this point, fully accepted the idea of an unelected transitional legislature assuming sovereign authority on the basis of an interim constitution. Their concern, as reflected by Dr. Adel, was the extent to which the Council would be able to control the process of selecting this body. They wanted more control than we could comfortably give them.

Sistani, on the other hand, seemed to have added an entirely new demand that the interim government to which sovereignty was transferred be elected. Such a demand threatened the November 15 Agreement, which had been crafted to meet his earlier requirement that the Constitutional Convention be elected.

"He's moved the goalposts," I told the Governance Team. We were not the only ones caught out by Sistani's shift. Abdul Aziz Hakim, who saw Sistani regularly, was puzzled because he had been assured by the ayatollah that there was no need for elections for the interim government. My team canvassed the other Shia political leaders, who, too, were surprised that the ayatollah had added a brand-new demand.

To get a better read of the situation in Najaf, I employed my very private channel to Sistani: the Iraqi-American who headed the Iraqi Reconstruction and Development Council, Emad Dhia. A Detroit resident, Dhia had been born to a respected family in Najaf and had often proven useful as a discreet conduit to the Grand Ayatollah. I drafted a confidential letter to the ayatollah, using the vehicle of the traditional Eid message at the end of Ramadan. I could trust Dhia not to garble the message or twist it for partisan reasons.

After giving the Grand Ayatollah my warm greeting for Eid, I said,

I am writing to address your concerns and to express the great optimism I feel about the future of Iraq. For many months, I have listened carefully to your views about the importance of holding elections in Iraq for a body that will write Iraq's permanent constitution. The agreement of November 15 ensures that this will be the case. Free and direct elections will be held in Iraq as quickly as possible—by March 2005 at the very latest, but sooner if possible.

I continued that, while it would be ideal for the Iraqi people also to directly elect the interim government to which we would hand sovereignty, direct elections were not possible at this time. So the best alternative would be to pick up the Preparatory Committee's idea of "caucuses of citizens in every governate . . . Religious and tribal groups, political parties, civil society organizations, university faculties, and others will all be invited to nominate candidates to participate in these caucuses."

I added that the CPA recognized that there were problems with some provincial councils and said the Coalition would help the Governing Council remove the bad apples. "For far too long," I concluded,

the Shia of Iraq have suffered under unjust and tyrannical regimes. This horrible history must now come to an end. In my view, the November 15 agreement represents a great historical opportunity for the Shia, and for all the Iraqi people. This is the one chance the Iraqi people will have to build a political future for themselves based on the equal human dignity of each individual under God, on respect for the just teachings of Islam, and on peace.

I hope that you will share my optimism and will continue your important work in helping advance the future of this country.

That evening, Emad Dhia returned from Najaf with the ayatollah's answer. The news wasn't good.

"The Grand Ayatollah likes and respects you. He appreciates the chance to work with you on Iraq's future. But he wants to proceed with full direct elections for the transitional legislature," Emad said, reading his notes, "even if they are imperfect."

"What else?" I asked, thinking of all the hours of negotiations that had gone into the November 15 Agreement.

"The Grand Ayatollah does believe in democracy," Emad said optimistically. "And he's committed to working with the Coalition."

Despite Emad's confidence, we were again at loggerheads with Sistani. His message confirmed that Sistani had gone beyond his former insistence on elections to choose the convention for writing the permanent constitution. Now he rejected the idea of an unelected body assuming sovereignty. This was an explosive new demand.

Sitting at my laptop early the next morning, I listed six problems with the constitutional process that Sistani's stubborn insistence on elections could cause:

1. It will give the impression that the GC and CPA are being led around by the nose by the Shia.
2. This would have potentially grave consequences for the way the Sunni see the process—as CPA simply doing what they fear, giving in to the Shia majority.
3. It would encourage the Shia to keep pushing for still more changes. What happens when an emboldened Sistani next insists on Sharia in the interim constitution? Or that women cannot vote?
4. It would raise real doubts about GC managerial incompetence. If a decision by 20 of 24 members is not binding, what is? How can we delegate additional authority to a body which cannot make decisions, or make them stick? Do they propose to rule by consensus, in which case they are giving SCIRI a veto?
5. It is doubtful that we can conduct even reasonably credible elections by June.
6. If we can, there is an unknowable risk that they will be dominated by the best-organized groups—the Islamists (which may be why Sistani and SCIRI have now shifted their position)—or possibly by the Baathists.

I stared at blocks of words on my computer screen. Was this assessment too bleak? I didn't think so.

At the end of the month, our efforts to find a solution to these delicate political problems were undermined by a series of leaks. A *New York Times* story described Sistani's and SCIRI's opposition to the agreement and, citing unnamed "administration officials," added that the plan granting Iraq sovereignty by June 30, 2004, "would have to at least accommodate the ayatollah's insistence on a popular vote."

The next day, the *Washington Post* piled on, noting that "senior officials said the administration may be forced to organize elections to satisfy Grand Ayatollah Ali Sistani."

Reading the articles, I felt the anger rising. I was trying to preserve a constitution, even an interim one, as central to the path to democracy here. We could not get there if the Coalition was seen to cave in to the Shia or to Sistani. Moreover, that would severely undercut our efforts to reach out to the Sunnis. And the Kurds were deeply suspicious of the "black turbans" in Najaf and Karbala, as I had been repeatedly reminded for months.

I reached for my laptop and sent Condi Rice a private message:

I have been in Washington long enough to have little hope of instilling discipline into every corner of the bureaucracy. But the fact is that in the past week we have begun to lose the unity of policy and execution which has until now served us well. If it were just political score settling among the departments, it could be shrugged off. But this story poses a threat to our ability to implement the President's policies in a way best calculated to serve American interests here.

Later that night, physically exhausted and depressed, I sent Francie one of the most discouraged e-mails of my months in Iraq. The message concluded:

What a horrid day. This crisis may evolve into the end of my tour because I could imagine now that the administration will conclude they cannot get home with me, having been unable to deliver either of my two plans (though in both cases because of Sistani, and in the second case because he changed his mind). So it is the bottom of the eighth and time for a relief pitcher. He better be a long relief specialist.

Chapter 9
"WE GOT HIM!"

■ BAGHDAD
DECEMBER 2003

When I woke early the next morning, I realized that pessimism was not an option. I still had a job to do in Iraq.

During the first week in December, we worked to keep the political process alive, pursuing a double strategy: engaging possible allies on the Council, while trying to convince Ayatollah Sistani to be more flexible. The approach brought results.

On December 2, I sent Sistani another letter stressing "our overriding mutual objective that the permanent Constitution be written for, by Iraqis." I again emphasized that the interim constitution would respect "the Islamic identity of the majority of the Iraqi people." But I also stressed that the November 15 Agreement was the best way of achieving those goals. The next day, Emad Dhia reported that the ayatollah reacted favorably to my message.

On December 5, UN Secretary General Kofi Annan, in a report to the Security Council, endorsed the November 15 agreement and reported that it was unlikely elections could be held by the end of June. This helpful message was reinforced when Emad received a call from Sistani's son reporting on a meeting between the Grand Ayatollah and Abdul Aziz Hakim, who had conceded that an early nationwide election process was "unobtainable." To this news, the ayatollah told Hakim that the Shiite clerics might have to be flexible on "the election question." But apparently to save face, the Grand Ayatollah suggested that America ask for a UN team to come and evaluate the November 15 time schedule, "and declare the election is not attainable within the agreement's time frame." Then the UN could suggest a more practical solution to the problem, and the ayatollah and his subordinate clerics would accept it.

"We just might be able to pull these chestnuts out of the fire," I told Scott

Carpenter. But the ongoing political uncertainty now forced me to cancel my planned trip to America to accept the president's invitation to hear the Iraqi National Symphony. At least Francie and the kids would be able to attend.

The next day, Don Rumsfeld came on one of his quick trips through the region, conferring with his commanders. He was irritable with my staff and seemed oddly vague about substantive questions.

Rumsfeld agreed to my suggestion that he call on Hakim, the Governing Council's president for December. Over glasses of sweet tea at Hakim's house, he leaned hard on the SCIRI leader to stick with the November 15 Agreement, reminding him that a deal was a deal. Hakim squirmed, claiming that there were just a few "small details" to clarify.

As usual, I rode with Rumsfeld to the airport. It was a chilly winter night, and given the dangers on the route, the only vehicles on the road were Coalition.

At the airport, Rumsfeld pulled me aside.

"Look," he said, "it's clear to me that your reporting channel is now direct to the president and not through me."

Before I could reply, Rumsfeld continued.

"Condi has taken over political matters," he said. "I think that's a mistake. The last time the NSC got into operational issues, we had Iran-Contra. But she seems to have jumped into this with both feet."

"She certainly is on top of things, Don," I said, addressing him by his first name as usual in private.

"Well," he said with a tight smile, "I'm bowing out of the political process. Let Condi and the NSC handle things. It might make your life a little easier."

We shook hands, and he turned to leave. The conversation had been friendly, but Rumsfeld was clearly unhappy that Rice had stepped in and taken control of policy. I guessed he was also reacting to those saccharine press stories about my close relationship with the president. And probably Rumsfeld was just fed up with bureaucracy. So was I.

It was after 11:00 P.M. when Brian McCormack and I got into my armored SUV for the run back to the Green Zone. Our convoy, as usual, consisted of two "up-armored" Humvees sheathed in tan slabs of hardened steel, a lead-armored Suburban, our Suburban, another armored Suburban following, and two more Humvees. Overhead, we had a pair of buzzing Bell helicopters with two Blackwater snipers each.

Driving into town on Airport Road, Brian went through some scheduling questions. The World Economic Forum wanted me to come to Davos, Switzerland, in January for their annual meeting. As a businessman, I had attended previous sessions—and could now use some of the ski resort pampering—but was uncertain what purpose it would serve this year.

"What's the advantage to my going?"

He was looking at a note in his thick scheduling portfolio when an explosion—a combination hot glare and deafening blast—threw the rear of the heavy vehicle to the right. Even though my ears were ringing, I heard automatic gunfire.

"What was that?" I yelled to Frank Gallagher, who, as always, was riding shotgun in the front seat.

He had his M-4 automatic carbine raised and was scanning behind us.

"Bomb and AK fire, sir," he replied, pointing to a bullet hole in the window next to him. "Get down! They're hitting the rear window."

We'd been ambushed, a highly organized, skillfully executed assassination attempt.

I swung around and looked back. The Suburban's armored-glass rear window had been blown out by the IED. And now AK rounds were whipping through the open rectangle. I crouched down.

"Are you all right, sir?" Frank asked, as the car picked up speed.

I was breathing hard and had a dry taste in my mouth. If the bad guys had triggered the bomb a second sooner, we'd be dead.

"Fine," I managed to say. "Brian?"

"I'm okay."

Out ahead in the glaring street lamps, the two lead Humvees were now moving very fast, their gunners swinging the .50 caliber machine guns from side to side. Our driver pulled out in front of the lead Suburban, and we were pushing 80 mph. Behind us the follow car and Humvees were trying to keep up. But one of the Humvees had had its front tires blown out by the IED and was limping far back.

Turning to Brian, I picked up the conversation. "So why should I do Davos?"

He took a moment to compose himself, and then, looking back at his notes, said that several sessions were scheduled on Iraq. Adnan Pachachi, who would be GC president in January, was planning to attend and the organizers thought, as the top civilian, I should participate.

Speeding toward the palace with the stench of explosives lingering in the car, I considered. Davos, all those good meals . . . Francie could fly over and we could ski. That was about as far from Baghdad's Airport Road and IEDs as you could get.

"I'll need to get Dan Senor's views before deciding," I said.

•   •   •

I certainly felt in need of rest. The warping effect of "Baghdad time" was becoming even more pronounced. My days began at 5:00 A.M. After I'd read the overnight cables and e-mails, I had my Arabic lesson at 7:00, and my first meeting—usually the intel briefing—half an hour later.

If I wasn't scheduled to travel or consult the Governing Council, the appointments stacked up in my outer office like patients in a dentist's waiting room. They might include a British parliamentarian, a tribal sheik in a flowing robe, or the bright-eyed young representative of a humanitarian NGO. Sue Shea, my veteran executive assistant, would joke as she ushered in my next appointment, "Your three o'clock root canal is here."

Every afternoon, if in Baghdad, I had a call with Rice and there were almost daily secure video meetings with the NSC Principals or the president. And my day didn't end until I sent Francie an e-mail, usually well after midnight.

The phone beside my bed jolted me awake at 1:30 A.M., Sunday, December 14. I had barely gotten to sleep after another eighteen-hour day.

"Sorry to wake you, sir." It was my assistant military aide, Major Pat Carroll, an energetic Arabic-speaking Marine. "General Abizaid needs to talk to you right away, secure."

He was referring to the clunky red STU-III scrambler phone in my office at the house.

"Pat, the damn secure phone at the house is still out. Does it have to be secure?"

"I know, sir," Pat answered. "So I asked Abizaid's aide, and he insists that it's urgent and must be on a secure line."

"Okay. Call the command post and mobilize the Blackwater guys." I started throwing on my clothes.

Abizaid and I spoke almost daily, but it was very unusual for him to call in the middle of the night. And on a secure line.

This must be either very good or very bad news, I thought.

I suddenly pictured the wounded soldiers on the C-141 medevac plane. *Let's hope it's not more killed and wounded.*

Fifteen minutes later, I arrived in my dimly lit office in the palace.

My new deputy, Dick Jones, was there with a man from the CIA station. I asked Dick what was up.

Turning to the intel officer, Dick said, "I don't want to steal your thunder."

The Agency man said, "We think we've caught Saddam."

I picked up the red phone, and was put through to Abizaid at his headquarters in Qatar.

"John, what's this about Saddam?"

"We think we've got him," he replied. "Special Ops guys found a dirty, bearded man at the bottom of an unguarded spider hole just outside Tikrit."

"How do you know it's Saddam?" I asked.

"When our guys pulled him out of the hole, he said, 'I am Saddam Hussein, President of Iraq,' " John said. "They looked him over, and he has the scars and a tattoo we know Saddam has."

Abizaid and I also knew that for years Saddam had used doubles to confound his enemies. So I asked what more we could do to confirm we had really captured Saddam. "We've brought him down to Baghdad," John said. "We'll clean him up and show him to some of the other top regime leaders we've detained. We're also going to rush a DNA sample to Germany for verification. We've got a C-17 standing by."

"John, we've got to be 100 percent positive," I emphasized. "We'll be the laughingstock of the world if the news gets out and it's one of his damn doubles. How long will the DNA check take?"

"My guys tell me it'll be twenty-four to thirty-six hours."

"There's no way in hell this story will hold that long." I thought a moment. "We've got to make backup plans to announce it even before the DNA results come back. Let's talk again when the detainees have seen him."

I went back to bed but I couldn't sleep. My mind was flying from one image to the next, with thoughts careering. I saw those monumental bronze heads of the dictator at the palace entrance as the crane lowered them to the dusty grass. I saw the grandiose ramparts of Saddam's Babylon, rebuilt in his image. I also saw the rows of gaping grave pits at Al-Hillah. *Have we finally caught that son of a bitch?*

After about two hours' fitful sleep, I rose for a hectic day. While I was shoveling down some raisin bran at my desk, Pat Carroll brought me a cup of espresso.

"General Sanchez and General Fast are on their way to brief you on the latest," Pat said.

Jones joined me as we waited for the news.

Brigadier General Barbara Fast, the Coalition J-2 (senior intelligence officer), arrived with Rick—who looked even more sleep-deprived than I did.

Fast provided details of Saddam's capture that had been coming into her headquarters all night.

For many months after Liberation, we had been chasing every stray rumor or fragmentary report about Saddam's whereabouts. He was rumored to be hiding in this town or that, to have slipped into Syria, to be hiding in one of the many palaces he had built. At one point, we had a report from a "usually reliable source" that he was riding around Baghdad in the backseat of a taxi, wearing a long white beard and red hat. "Sort of like Santa Claus," as one skeptical analyst put it.

In the fall, we switched strategies because we had concluded that Saddam had separated from the high-level people soon after Liberation, knowing we'd be looking for them. Instead we started going after low-level "facilitators." Servants, gardeners, and chauffeurs who had worked for Saddam might provide a better path to the fugitive dictator. So Fast and the CIA had built a database of gofers and their contacts.

She told us that late Saturday morning, Coalition special operators had picked up one suspected "contact" outside Tikrit, the home of Saddam's clan. During his interrogation, the man said that he could lead them to someone "much more important" who was hiding near the farming village of Ad-Dwar, just west of the Tigris, fifteen kilometers southeast of the city. He stubbornly refused to divulge who this important subject might be, but based on our new search strategy, our soldiers took him seriously. The Special Operations forces planned a search-and-capture mission with the 4th Infantry Division, which controlled the area.

Around 8:00 Saturday night, the informant took a Special Ops team to two isolated farm compounds west of Ad-Dwar. The initial scan with night-vision equipment revealed several mud-brick houses and sheds, but no lights or other signs of people. The 4th ID threw a cordon of troops, armor, and helicopters around the area. Then the special operators went in for a closer look.

"The first hut was obviously abandoned," Fast said. "But at the second objective there were signs of recent occupation—bread and canned goods on the table in the hut, a stack of new T-shirts. It looked like somebody had been living there. Here's a picture. And there was a beat-up orange taxi parked next to a sheep pen outside the compound walls." General Fast laid another picture of a white-and-orange taxi normally seen in Iraq's cities on the marble table between us.

The soldiers had found no one hiding in the house or within the walled compound. They were about to leave, when one of the men looked down and saw an incongruous straight line in the thick dust. Mud bricks had been laid out in a rectangle. Scuffing with the toe of his boot, a soldier discovered a short length of rope.

"He pulled it," Fast said, "and a Styrofoam block—a hatch—popped open."

This was the entrance shaft of the "spider hole," about six feet deep. The soldiers yelled for whoever was down there to come out. But there was no reply. A sergeant shone a bright flashlight down the shaft and prepared to throw in a stun grenade.

But then a pair of dirty, empty hands and a head of unkempt graying hair appeared.

The bearded man spoke in accented English. "I am Saddam Hussein, President of Iraq," he said. "I want to negotiate."

Searching the narrow sleeping compartment dug out of the sandy dirt below, the troops found a pistol and a briefcase of "interesting" documents. Later that night, the team discovered two more of Saddam's facilitators, armed with AK-47s, who also had sacks containing $750,000 in hundred-dollar bills.

A Special Ops helicopter transported Saddam to a Military Intelligence detention center at Baghdad Airport, where he underwent a medical exam and initial questioning.

"The guards cleaned him up," Rick added. He had been at the airport when the chopper had arrived with the prisoner.

General Fast showed me the "before-and-after" photos of the prisoner.

The first pictures had been taken on arrival at the airport. Despite a shaggy, gray-streaked beard and tangled graying hair, the man was recognizable as Saddam by his intense dark eyes, wary but defiant.

"And this is him with a shave and a haircut," Rick Sanchez said.

The mustache was dark, the hair shorter. There could be no doubt: the face in this photo was Saddam Hussein.

Barbara explained that the intelligence team had next brought four "high-value prisoners" who had been close to Saddam to the facility to identify him: two vice presidents—including Tariq Aziz—another senior Baathist, and a personal secretary. Each prisoner had verified that the wizened man slouched on an army cot in that windowless room was in fact Saddam Hussein.

The intel people had recorded the prisoner's conversation with his fellow Baathists and were running the tape through digital "voice analysis" to compare speech patterns with archived recordings of Saddam. Just before dawn, the C-17 transport had taken off, the most critical cargo of the giant plane being a one-ounce handful of saliva swabs to be compared for DNA matches with Saddam family samples which the CIA had in Germany.

"The DOD's plan for Saddam's capture, Mr. Ambassador," Rick said, "calls for him to be transferred to an American Navy ship in the Gulf for safety's sake."

"We can't do that," I replied.

If Saddam Hussein were a Coalition prisoner of war, the Geneva Convention prevented us from showing him in captivity—either here or aboard a U.S. Navy ship in the Gulf. But if we spirited him out of the country and didn't release photos of the former dictator as our prisoner, many in Iraq—among the world's most conspiracy-minded nations—would refuse to believe that we'd captured the tyrant.

"The people are going to need proof that we have him," I told the two generals.

They understood. For months, the souks had been rife with rumors that we'd actually caught Saddam and had made a deal with him. The resettled Saddam now lived in comfort on "a farm in Florida," even though audio cassettes of a man claiming to be Saddam Hussein, exhorting "loyal Iraqis" to join the insurgency, had been aired by local and regional media.

We now had the chance to demonstrate, to all Iraqis and to the world, that Saddam Hussein had been captured, that there was no possibility of a resurgent Baathist regime in Baghdad.

Moreover, I reminded them that the Governing Council had only four days earlier finally approved establishing the Special Iraqi Tribunal to try Iraq's war criminals. They would certainly expect to take custody of the ex-president.

"Look," I said. "I understand it's important for the MI folks to exploit Saddam for whatever intel we can get. But it's vital that we find a way, Geneva Convention or not, to persuade Iraqis we finally have him."

I told the group that the best way to do this would be to get a small delegation from the Governing Council to visit Saddam. They could then confirm publicly they had seen the prisoner. I said I'd call Pachachi, who was acting GC president, and see what he could arrange.

After Sanchez and Fast left, Jones and I discussed our next steps.

"We've got to really run with this success," I told Dick. "It just might be the tipping point."

"It's great news," Dick agreed, and pointed out that with Saddam's entire family either dead or in custody, there was a real chance to put together an aggressive and well-designed Information Operation (IO). As American ambassador to Kuwait, Dick had overseen a multinational intelligence fusion cell and understood the importance of Information Operations. It could use personal contacts and the local and regional news media to introduce the idea to the insurgents that—with Saddam in Coalition custody—it was time for them to lay down their arms and for a process of reconciliation to begin.

I asked Dick to take the lead on the IO plan. "Let's avoid chest-beating by the U.S. and get the Iraqis out front as much as possible."

"I'll have my initial ideas to you later today," Dick said.

Then Sanchez called. "DOD's dropped the plan to take the subject out to a ship," he reported. We arranged to announce Saddam's capture jointly to the news media at the CPA convention center at 3:00 P.M. After that, we'd take a small delegation from the Governing Council to the airport to see the prisoner.

I found time to send a short note to Major General Ray Odierno, commander of the 4th Infantry Division. Ironically, I had been scheduled to visit him in Tikrit that same day. "You and your team are real heroes today. You have brought a great and wonderful day into the lives of all Iraqis and we are just plain proud of you all."

"This is going to be an interesting day," I told Sue Shea, who was cradling two phones beneath her chin, scrambling to rearrange my schedule.

"Aren't they all?" she asked.

Sanchez had told me that Rumsfeld had been keeping the president—who was at Camp David for the weekend—informed on the search-and-capture operation. Anticipating that the man we had in custody was in fact Saddam Hussein, President Bush planned to address the country on Sunday afternoon, once he had confirmation.

So just after 9:00 A.M. in Baghdad or 1:00 A.M. in Washington, I decided to wake up Condi Rice with the news. The White House SitRoom immediately put me through to her.

"There can be no doubt, Condi," I told her. "It's Saddam Hussein."

"I'll wake the president," she said. "He wants to know."

I spent several hours with my speechwriter Don Hamilton, honing my remarks announcing Saddam's capture. My press counselor, Dan Senor, happened to be at his mother's house in Toronto, where it was late at night. We read the draft text to him over the phone, and Dan made suggested edits. The words I spoke had to be clear and direct—easy for the simultaneous interpreter in the conference room to render into unambiguous Arabic.

And Dan stressed that we had to prove to the rumor-prone Iraqi people that the man we had in custody really was Saddam Hussein. This would require convincing both the Western and Arab news media that Saddam was our prisoner. When our troops had killed his two sons in July, it had been necessary to release gruesome photos of their corpses to end the souk rumors that they had escaped.

Now as we worked, reports came in that the exuberant new Iraqi news media were broadcasting breathless stories or hawking extra editions that we'd captured Saddam. Obviously the news had leaked among Sunni villagers around Tikrit, and almost immediately to the capital. Some accounts claimed that Saddam had escaped, or that he'd been killed. The media and the Iraqis were clamoring for confirmation from the Coalition.

Shortly before noon, I called Pachachi, and told him in confidence that the rumors were true: we had captured Saddam. He was speechless for a moment and then burst out, "What a great day for Iraq and for the Coalition. Congratulations, Mr. Ambassador!"

"General Sanchez and I plan to announce it this afternoon and I hope you might join us at the press conference," I said.

"I would be honored to, Mr. Ambassador." He agreed to pull together a small GC delegation to visit Saddam afterward.

Don Hamilton and I got back to work. My announcement had to be dramatic without seeming brazenly triumphant. Above all, the message had to focus on the meaning of this monumental event for the people of Iraq. I wanted to stress, yet again, Iraq's Future of Hope.

That afternoon the CPA conference center was packed to the walls. Western, Iraqi, and regional Arab reporters filled every seat. All the world's major networks were going to "go live" for the event.

Adnan Pachachi led the way onto the stage. I followed him with Rick Sanchez close behind me. They stood beside me as I took the microphone.

"Ladies and gentlemen," I said, indulging in a slight dramatic pause. "We got him!"

The three words had been suggested to me by my Arabic-speaking British press aide, Charles Heatley, just before I went onstage. They were easy to translate. "You need something short, a good sound bite," Charles had said. The effect was immediate and dramatic. Iraqi journalists were on their feet, cheering wildly, as were several Western reporters, but it was the expressions of undisguised joy among the Iraqis that were most moving. I realized that those of us born and raised in freedom could never appreciate the profound psychological impact of tyranny. As long as Saddam had been somewhere *out there*, Iraqis feared that he might return.

"Saddam Hussein was captured Saturday, December 13," I continued, "at about 8:30 P.M. local in a cellar in the town of Ad-Dwar, some fifteen kilometers south of Tikrit."

I wondered how the translator rendered the word "cellar." Dan and I had debated using "spider hole," but knew the translation of the GI slang would have been muddled. Whatever Arabic term was used, it would be a graphic demonstration that the dictator who'd squandered billions on palaces had literally fallen.

I explained that I wanted to say a few words to the people of Iraq before Dr. Pachachi and General Sanchez spoke.

"This is a great day in your history," I said. "For decades, hundreds of thousands of you suffered at the hands of this cruel man. For decades, Saddam Hussein divided you citizens against each other. For decades, he threatened and attacked your neighbors."

Some Iraqi reporters were taking notes. Others were sobbing in the audience to my left.

"Those days are over forever," I said. "Now it is time to look to the future, to your future of hope, to a future of reconciliation.

"Iraq's future, your future, has never been more full of hope.

"The tyrant is a prisoner.

"The economy is moving forward," I emphasized. "You have before you the prospect of sovereign government in a few months."

Beside me, Adnan Pachachi was barely controlling his emotions.

"With the arrest of Saddam Hussein," I continued, "there is a new opportunity for members of the former regime, whether military or civilian, to end their bitter opposition."

This was the heart of the message I wanted Iraqis, especially the Sunnis supporting the insurgency, to take from the press conference.

"Let them come forward now in a spirit of reconciliation and hope, lay down their arms and join you, their fellow citizens, in the task of building the New Iraq." I paused to make sure the interpreter had caught up. "Now is the time for all Iraqis—Arabs and Kurds, Sunnis, Shias, Christians, and Turkmen—to build a prosperous, democratic Iraq at peace with itself and with its neighbors."

Pachachi took the rostrum. He spoke in eloquently phrased Arabic of the joy he and all Iraqis now shared. Everyone in the country, he said, could "look forward to the future" with confidence that the "new Free Iraq" would be able to govern itself.

Then General Sanchez announced that "the long nightmare for Iraq is over" and gave a detailed briefing on the operation. He explained that the dictator had been discovered in a "remote farmhouse" near Tikrit. There had been no injuries, not a single shot fired. "Saddam Hussein, the *captive*," Rick said, emphasizing the word, "has been talkative and is being cooperative." He asked that the lights be dimmed and showed video of the capture site. The clip revealed the well-disguised spider hole with its vertical shaft, horizontal chamber, and camouflaged exhaust fan.

That footage was replaced by a close-up video of Saddam Hussein undergoing his initial medical exam in captivity. The instant Saddam's haggard face came up on the screen, there were again shouts, cries, and weeping from the Iraqis. Here at last, after thirty-five long, cruel years, was proof that this awful man—whose brutality had touched virtually every Iraqi household—was no longer free.

An Army medic with rubber gloves shone a flashlight into Saddam's mouth, his head starkly framed against a shabby background of chipped white institutional wall tiles. When several other pictures of the prisoner were flashed on the screen, emotions in the audience boiled up again. Several Iraqi reporters were back on their feet, shouting. "Death to Saddam!"

Pachachi, too, was now in tears.

For the next twenty minutes, Pachachi and Sanchez fielded questions. Pachachi stated that Saddam Hussein would face trial before the Special Tribunal, "the same as all the people who have committed crimes against humanity." He said he would ask the Governing Council to declare a national holiday in the coming week to celebrate Saddam's capture.

Again, Iraqi reporters jumped up. "*Allahu akbar!*" they shouted. "God is great!"

One Iraqi journalist asked the Council president if capturing Saddam would foster a "peaceful New Iraq."

Without being specific, Pachachi stated that the Council was working on institutions for a "transitional period" to a representative government voted into power by all the people of Iraq. That new nation would rest on a permanent constitution and a national parliament, he emphasized.

There was ringing applause as we left the stage.

After watching the press conference on television in Canada, Dan Senor called: "I bet even Al-Jazeera can't put a bad spin on *this* news."

Following the press conference, Council members Adnan Pachachi, Ahmad Chalabi, Mowaffak al-Rubaie, and Adel Mahdi traveled with Sanchez, Scott Carpenter, and me to meet Saddam at a secret location near the airport.

We were on the way to the palace helipad when my cell phone rang. It was Condi Rice.

"Well done, Jerry," she said warmly. "The press conference was really first-rate."

She added that there would be an NSC meeting in the morning on next steps needed to exploit Saddam's capture. "Can you send me a paper on this by the end of the day?"

"Sure." Baghdad was a place where no one rested on his laurels.

She also said that the president was coming into the office later that Sunday.

I turned to Adnan Pachachi. "Would you like to send a message to President Bush?"

Pachachi took the phone and asked Rice to pass his thanks, those of the Governing Council, and of the Iraqi people to the president and the American people. "It is a great, historic day for Iraq."

It was near sunset on the cool, clear afternoon when our Black Hawks landed near a nondescript masonry building, surrounded by concentric barbed-wire fences. Well-armed MPs guarded the only gate. Inside the entrance General Sanchez asked the Council members if they wanted to see Saddam on the TV monitor or in person.

They looked first toward the eldest, Adnan Pachachi, then to Adel Mahdi, and finally spoke almost in unison: they wanted to confront Saddam in person.

General Sanchez and a guard led us down a dim corridor about thirty feet long, painted in drab military yellow, and stopped at the end before a blank metal door on the left.

The door opened to reveal a brightly lit, oddly shaped room, about eight feet wide and probably twice that long. Two fluorescent lights hung from the ceiling, flickering slightly with the generator current.

The walls were the same chipped, dingy white tile shown in the press conference images, but now I saw that several tiles were missing, exposing dusty grout. Two military maps of Baghdad and vicinity were taped to the tiles on one wall. Just left of the entrance was the Coalition's "55 Most Wanted" poster with a number of faces crossed off. Saddam's ace of spades image was almost hidden beneath thick strokes of a red marker, so fresh I could smell the chemical bite of the ink.

The back half of the room was dominated by a low platform on which stood a table and several mismatched folding chairs. A tape recorder, several plastic water bottles, and some MRE ration packets were on the table.

The four Council members filed into the narrow room. The Americans stayed at the doorway. This was their show. To the right of the door, slouched on an army cot, wearing white Arab pajamas and a blue winter parka over his shoulders, sat Saddam Hussein. He had on cheap plastic sandals, and I noticed that his toenails were dirty and split, as if he'd been walking in the dust for weeks. Beside one foot stood a rectangular carton of orange juice with a pink straw sticking out.

Taped on the wall behind Saddam's head were the official Pentagon photos of Secretary Rumsfeld and President Bush. I liked that touch and silently congratulated the soldier who had thought it up.

Saddam was sitting quite still, watching us from beneath hooded eyelids. An Arabic-speaking American soldier stood protectively at Saddam's right shoulder, no doubt under orders to intervene if any of the Council members lunged for the prisoner.

"He just woke up, sir," the guard said to Sanchez. "I gave him some juice."

The four Council members arrayed themselves on the raised area. Chalabi grabbed one of the folding chairs and placed it at the very edge of the platform so that he could peer down on Saddam like a judge on a bench. Pachachi sat in front, but not near the edge. As if still in awe of the dictator, Dr. Adel moved a chair behind the table.

Mowaffak al-Rubaie declined to sit. He paced the platform, glowering at the prisoner. "Saddam Hussein," he shouted. "Saddam Hussein, you are cursed by God! You are cursed by God!"

I knew from my Arabic lessons that this was a serious insult, carrying the righteous emotional weight that "God damn you!" had evoked in Western Europe in previous centuries. The soldier now moved nearer to Sanchez and me and tried to keep up a running interpretation of the Iraqi's exchange with Saddam.

Saddam raised his face, glowering in the bright light. "Who are you to curse me, you traitor who has come with the Americans?"

He then turned to Adnan Pachachi, the foreign minister Saddam had sent into exile with a price on his head decades earlier. "My friend, Dr. Adnan," Saddam said, his tone softening, "why have you come with these traitors? You are not one of them. You are one of us." As if to emphasize "us," Saddam curved both hands inward and touched his fingertips to the center of his chest.

I exchanged a glance with Scott Carpenter. Saddam was trying to divide this Iraqi delegation almost from the moment he encountered them.

When Pachachi ignored the snare, Saddam made a show of scanning the other faces. "Who will introduce me to these great leaders of the New Iraq?" He asked contemptuously.

Speaking from behind the table like a prosecutor, Adel Mahdi pierced Saddam's sarcasm.

"How can you explain the Anfal operation and Halabja?" He referred to the brutal campaign of repression and use of chemical weapons against the Kurds. "Why did you give the orders?" Adel demanded.

"They were traitors and Iranians," Saddam muttered, waving his left hand, as if announcing the necessary extermination of rabid dogs.

Now all four Council members on the platform were shouting questions, well laced with insults, at Saddam. For a moment, he looked stunned. For decades no one had spoken to him in this way and lived to talk about it. Then Saddam pursed his lips and raised his chin in an expression of hauteur. He would listen to these inferiors, but reply only if he saw fit.

"Why didn't you have the courage to fight or at least die trying?" Rubaie shouted.

Saddam refused to answer him and instead turned to Sanchez, a general with three stars on his camouflage uniform.

"If you had been in my place," he asked the American commander, "would you have tried to resist?" He shrugged, but then turned back and answered scornfully. "And what do you know of combat, anyway?"

Mowaffak Rubaie was not intimidated. "At least your sons fought before they were killed."

I couldn't be sure, but it seemed that Saddam winced.

Now Adel Mahdi rose behind the table and leveled both arms, hands open — a rude gesture that got Saddam's attention. "What do you say now about the mass graves, about the tens of thousands you had executed and buried in them?"

Saddam lifted his chin disdainfully. "Executed?" He shook his head. "Did any of you ask their relatives who those criminals were? Thieves and traitors . . . Iranians."

Rubaie asked him about several prominent Baathists that Saddam had ordered killed in the early 1980s. "Why did you do it?"

"That's just street talk," he replied coldly. "And what business is that to you? They were Baathists." It was as if these men had been his property to dispose of as he pleased.

Now Adnan Pachachi leaned forward. "And why did you invade Kuwait? That began Iraq's slide into disaster."

Saddam almost smirked. "When I get something in my head, I act," he responded casually. "That's just the way I am."

"But to start a war . . ."

Saddam Hussein launched into a rambling discourse on his 1990 invasion. ". . . All fully justified," he said. "But it was tragic that the honest efforts of Mubarak and the French did not prevent hostilities."

Pachachi shook his head that the former dictator was so deluded. Then Saddam cocked his head to the right and gazed at him. "Dr. Adnan," he said sharply, "don't you also consider Kuwait the nineteenth province of Iraq?"

I remembered having heard of a Baathist Party book that Pachachi had officially "authored" while foreign minister, which had argued the regime's claim to Kuwait. "That was long, long ago," Pachachi said, and did not speak again.

A few minutes later, Rubaie stared at Saddam with undisguised hatred. "Why did you have Sayyid Muhammad al-Sadr murdered in 1999?"

Saddam pointed to his chest and made a dismissive play on words. The word "sadr" also meant "chest" in Arabic. ". . . Sadr? My foot!"

"And what of all the Hakim brothers?" Rubaie persisted.

Saddam did not answer.

Dr. Adel began to list other Shiite clerics whom the dictator had ordered murdered, but Saddam cut him off.

"That's street talk."

Pachachi now spoke in sorrow. "How could you have mistreated your country so badly?"

"I always held the people's interest first," Saddam said. "I was elected in fair elections. Even today," he continued, "I can go and sleep peacefully in any town in the country. Can you?"

His words were slurred and his hands shook.

I suddenly thought of Hitler in his bunker in April 1945, living in a dreamland, ordering nonexistent armies to destroy the Soviet juggernaut encircling Berlin.

Ahmad Chalabi rose and strode angrily from the room. The others followed.

As Rubaie passed Saddam's cot, he glared down. "Saddam Hussein, you are cursed by God," he repeated. "How will you meet your creator?"

If the words had emotional impact, Saddam hid it well. "I will meet him with a clear conscience and as a believer," he responded.

We were back in the dim corridor. Rubaie was still agitated. Pachachi was elated. Brian had brought him his cell phone, over which the White House Sit-Room had patched the president of the United States, who was personally offering his congratulations and best wishes to the people of Iraq. Ahmad Chalabi walked back inside from the outer compound. He was shaking his head, upset and disappointed in the meeting with Saddam. Any hope that the former dictator could be turned around and used to help persuade the insurgents to lay down their arms had been dashed. Almost panting in frustration, Chalabi repeated again and again, "He's learned nothing . . . nothing!"

As we went back to the Black Hawks, Scott looked at Sanchez and me. "None of us said a word," he said. "It was like we instinctively knew that this was an Iraqi deal."

Back at the office, by some miracle Brian McCormack produced a bottle of warm champagne. The Governance Team, Dick Jones, and I shared it out in tiny paper cups and drank to the success of our military.

I asked Dick and Scott to stay back to discuss ideas on the paper for the next day's NSC teleconference meeting.

"We'll have to figure out how to use Saddam's capture to promote reconciliation," I said. "Although he didn't seem too contrite, did he?"

"He was despicable," Scott said. "And also pathetic. But maybe we can exploit him."

"One way would be to play to Saddam's grandiose side and get him to sign a formal surrender for the good of the nation," I suggested.

"I'll note that in our NSC paper," Scott said.

"In any case," I said, "we want to use this to build momentum, both to pick apart the insurgency and to promote reconciliation."

There had always been doubt about Saddam's role in the insurgency. Some analysts believed that he might have given it some strategic direction. Most felt that if there were any center, it was directed by former regime vice president Izzat Ibrahim al-Douri, the zealous red-haired Baathist killer. The secret Mukhabarat document I'd seen back in July showed that Saddam had made plans for an insurgency. And the insurgency had forces to draw on from among the several thousand hardened Baathists in the two northern Republican Guard divisions that had joined forces with foreign jihadis. There were also the almost 100,000 convicted criminals Saddam had released from prison before the war. In any event, it was obvious that Saddam Hussein had not been exercising tactical control of the insurgents from that muddy hole near Ad-Dwar.

The news of Saddam's capture was sweeping Iraq, sparking frenzies of celebration among Kurds and Shia.

"Maybe now," I said, "the moderate Sunnis will realize Baathism is finally dead."

Scott said, "Maybe."

We also discussed using the capture as an opportunity to persuade the Governing Council to moderate the de-Baathification process. Since we had turned this process over to the Iraqis in early November, Chalabi assumed responsibility from the GC for the implementation of the de-Baathification decree and things were not going well. We had reports from our provincial offices and military commanders that many more people were being subjected to de-Baathification than foreseen in my initial order.

On the way back from visiting Saddam, I had pulled Pachachi and Dr. Adel aside and encouraged them to find a way to moderate the application of the policy as part of the effort to drain the insurgency of support. They had both made the point in their statements at the press conference. Now we would have to push Chalabi to follow through.

We wrapped up our preparations for the NSC paper by discussing what to do next with Saddam.

Scott emphasized that it would be important to turn Saddam and other senior Baathist detainees over to the Iraqi Special Tribunal as soon as possible. I'd asked the CPA general counsel, Brigadier General Scott Castle, about this matter earlier that morning. He'd reported that Saddam would be considered a POW. As a result, we would not be able to turn him over to the Iraqis until hostilities were over or until there was a sovereign Iraqi government. So I told the Governance Team that we needed to start by transferring to the Iraqis some other detainees who did not have POW status.

Nothing is ever simple in Iraq.

An hour later, the president called. "Bremer!" he said with obvious satisfaction. "How're you doing? Great work!"

"I was a bystander, Mr. President," I said. "It was our troops who did the job."

"Well," he said, "I watched the press conference. Your statement was great, and the message on reconciliation was perfect."

"Well, I'm glad, Mr. President, because some of my advisers thought it went too far. But I think we have to get the word on reconciliation out right away."

"I agree completely," the president said, and then returned to the press conference, noting the spontaneous outbursts of joy in the auditorium. "How'd you manage to maintain your composure?"

"I almost didn't. Pachachi was in tears, and the Iraqi journalists down in front were weeping and sobbing with joy."

"I'm going to speak to the nation at 1:00 P.M.," Bush said. "I'll warn the American people that the struggle is not over, and congratulate the Armed Forces and CIA for their terrific work. But I'll leave the reconciliation message to you and the Governing Council."

"They're issuing a statement in the morning," I said. "As you know, Rick Sanchez and I took four of them out to see Saddam this afternoon."

"What was it like being there?"

"Very strange. There were about eight of us in this small room. I could have reached over and touched him."

"What was his attitude?"

"He's a broken and defeated man, Mr. President," I said. "But defiant. His fingers jumped around nervously, and he mumbled several times. But then he'd summon up the strength to snap back at his accusers. The scene in that little room had real poignancy. After all, Saddam is still a man, even if he's a monster. Saddam has reached the end, the bottom, and you can see in his eyes that he knows it."

"How will the Iraqis' new Special Tribunal affect Saddam?" he asked.

Assuming Saddam was legally a POW, I said, we would not be able to transfer custody of him immediately. But we had a number of other detainees who were not POWs and I was working with the Governing Council to see if we could get them to do "perp walks" soon.

The president chuckled at the concept.

"Mr. President," I said, "we may have a real opportunity to pick apart the opposition now. But we'll need to match our reconciliation campaign with some very tough military measures against them."

"I agree completely," he said. And in his address, after congratulating our soldiers on their success, the president noted that "the capture of Saddam Hussein does not mean the end of violence in Iraq. We still face terrorists who would rather go on killing the innocent than accept the rise of liberty in the heart of the Middle East." But, he concluded, "The United States of America will not relent until this war is won."

On the morning of December 15, the Governing Council issued their statement on Saddam's capture to the Iraqi people. The message opened with a Koranic verse, damning "those who blaspheme in the homeland."

"At last, the myth of the despotic tyrant has collapsed," the text continued. "His disgraceful downfall has become the last act in the process of Iraq's liberation from the chains of oppression and fear. It is high time to turn a new page for building a unified and secure Iraq that provides hope for all its children."

The Council cited those who had suffered torture and carnage, all the victims of "Saddam's wars," and those uprooted from their homes, who now cried out "for justice to be restored."

Although the Council was working to restore "the spirit of tolerance to build National Unity on a sturdy foundation by the rejection of violence and vengeance . . . the Governing Council affirms that Saddam and Saddamists, terrorists and foreign infiltrators and those who participate in subversive acts and spread terrorism, will be tried as war criminals and as enemies of humanity by an Iraqi Special Tribunal, in Iraq, so that they will receive their just judgments."

The message concluded with a note of reconciliation. "We call upon those, be they military or civilian, who were duped and who have not committed crimes against the Iraqi people, to prove their loyalty to the nation as a step toward their return into the embrace of our generous people."

The epilogue was another Koranic verse: "We were not unjust to them even though they themselves were unjust."

Reading the text, I felt proud of them. *Maybe we can make some headway now.*

At that morning's senior staff meeting, everyone rose and gave Rick and me an ovation.

I held up my hands. "Thank General Sanchez," I said.

He also deferred. "Thank the troops. They're the ones who pulled it off."

As I moved around the palace corridors that morning, the Iraqi staff spontaneously burst into applause. They had danced in celebration for hours the previous afternoon to the slapping beat of flat drums in the crescent drive that had once been dominated by the heroic bronze sculptures of Saddam's head.

During the coming days and weeks, there were indications that the Coalition might be able to exploit Saddam Hussein's capture in a positive way.

Sharif Ali bin Hussein, the Pretender to the throne, came in to offer some advice about engaging with Sunni tribes, with which he retained regular contact and some influence. He also told me that he had been in touch indirectly with "people in the insurgency" and was willing to put out feelers about what it would take for them to stop their attacks.

I said we too felt that there was now a real opportunity to work with the opposition, many of whom had been fighting under the desperate belief that Saddam would return. Others, I added, had been sitting on the fence out of fear that Saddam would return. "He will not return. But we'd like a dialogue with both groups and would welcome your help."

Sharif Ali agreed to try to reach out to the insurgents.

I felt it was extremely important to try to capitalize on Saddam's capture by promoting reconciliation, a theme I had emphasized when I announced the dictator's capture. In meetings with Generals Abizaid and Sanchez, we agreed to increase rewards for men still on the Most Wanted deck, and also for lower-level players such as the "facilitator" who had led our troops to Saddam. I pressed the generals to further exploit the insurgents' setback by declaring an amnesty for enemy fighters who surrendered their arms and renounced violence.

Returning to a subject I had pressed for months, I encouraged the military to find a way to release as many of the thousands of detainees we held as possible, without endangering our security or intelligence collection. The military began work on a parole program for cooperative lower-level detainees we would be prepared to release if someone respectable gave a guarantee for their behavior. Some of these men, who had previously withheld information about insurgent networks, started talking now, knowing Saddam was in custody. This program gained momentum across Iraq by the end of December.

In that period, attacks on Coalition forces dropped by 22 percent.

I remember vividly the National Security Council meeting I attended via secure video teleconference on the afternoon of December 15.

The small VTC room was as stuffy as usual. On the screen, the NSC members sat around the White House SitRoom table.

John Abizaid briefed them and they discussed the implications of Saddam's capture for almost an hour.

The president looked up. "How'd Al-Jazeera play the story, Jerry?" he asked.

"Well, they tried very hard to find bad news, Mr. President," I said with a grin. "They sent a crew to the longest gas line in Baghdad, and the reporter asked the first driver he interviewed, 'You've been sitting in line for five hours for gas. What do you have to say about the Coalition?' The guy pumped his fist in the air and shouted, 'They got Saddam!' So the Al-Jazeera reporter tried a second driver who yelled, 'Al hamdulillah, God be praised! They captured Saddam!' The reporter asked the same question three or four more times — with the same result."

"Now *that* is a great story," the president said.

▪ THREE

Chapter 10
A BITTER
FIGHT BEGINS

■ BASRA, IRAQ
JANUARY 4, 2004

"Good afternoon, Jerry," Tony Blair said with his familiar smile. "Nice to see you again."

I'd flown to Basra that morning to confer with the British prime minister. Blair's handshake was firm, his manner relaxed. He'd mingled with soldiers and Royal Marines at the Basra airport before coming to the commander's quarters in the terminal.

Sir Jeremy Greenstock, the senior British civilian in the Coalition, had joined us.

Settling in over tea, the prime minister asked how things were going.

"Well, we've got three main problems: how to resolve the Shias' concerns about elections, how to reach out to the Sunni Arabs, and how to keep the Kurds on board."

Blair offered a sympathetic smile. "Quite a plateful."

"Let's start with the most difficult," I said. "The Shia and the elections."

I reviewed the efforts we'd made since the signing of the November 15 Agreement to persuade Sistani that it was not possible technically to hold elections by the June 30 deadline established in that agreement. But we couldn't be sure what his position was because he'd reversed himself—sometimes in response to the murky intrigues of his allies among Governing Council members.

In a December 15 message to me, Sistani had said that he wanted a UN panel to come to Iraq, study the matter for "thirty days," and then report to him that elections could not be conducted by June 30.

"Hopefully this means he's looking for a face-saving out," I told Blair.

We also hoped that, once persuaded that elections for the interim government were not possible, Sistani would support using the provincial caucus system set forth in the November 15 Agreement. This system would help meet our overall objective of engaging a broader group of Iraqis in selecting Iraq's Transitional National Assembly before the planned June 30 handover. "Prime Minister," I said, "I told the president last week that we may be up against traditional Persian negotiating techniques. Every time we make a concession, the other guy comes up with a new set of demands. That's certainly been our experience with Sistani the last six months."

Blair nodded. "They've been at this type of thing longer than we have."

"But if the ayatollah can simply throw out the agreed political process," I said, "it'll just confirm the Sunni Arabs' and Kurds' worst fear—that a single Shiite cleric is determining Iraq's future."

I told Blair that to our surprise, a few days earlier, Abdul Aziz Hakim, the GC's president for December, had sent a letter to Kofi Annan formally asking the UN if elections were possible and if not, to recommend an alternative way of bringing an Iraqi government into being before June 30. As the prime minister knew, the secretary-general had called for a meeting with the Governing Council and the Coalition in New York on January 19 which could be vital to keeping the political process moving.

I briefed the PM on our aggressive efforts to broaden the Coalition's outreach to Iraq's disgruntled Sunnis. This was a top priority but difficult to pull off. I'd earmarked several hundred million dollars for projects in the Sunni provinces.

"And the Kurds?" he asked, raising an eyebrow.

Like all astute British leaders, Blair was well versed in the history of empire and understood the inherent risk to a nation's stability that a long-repressed ethnic minority such as the Kurds posed.

"The Kurds are going to be a real problem," I admitted.

I had returned two days earlier from a visit to Kirkuk with members of the CPA Governance Team. We'd seen firsthand the tensions in that disputed city that controlled the wealth of the northern oil fields. On arrival, we'd found that a "peaceful" demonstration organized by Kurdish militiamen and politicians had erupted into violence, leaving four dead and several dozen injured. The Kurds claimed that Kirkuk was traditionally a Kurdish city, and that the population majority had shifted to the Arabs because of Saddam's policy of "Arabization" over the past thirty years.

Since Liberation, the Kurds had taken matters into their own hands. Kurdish Peshmerga militia had been forcing Arabs off farmland, out of houses and bazaar stalls. The Kurds were packing the police force and setting up a shadow government. Most ominously, they had kidnapped Arabs known to be cooperating with the Coalition.

I told Blair that I'd been blunt with the Kurdish leaders, warning them that the Coalition would not tolerate actions that provoked a breakup of Iraq. I'd stressed that we needed better cooperation from them on the Governing Council's drafting of the interim constitution, which was called the Transitional Administrative Law (TAL) in the November 15 Agreement.

"And how's that getting on?" the prime minister asked.

I responded that the TAL would be among the most important elements of the Coalition's legacy to the New Iraq. If done right, it would become Iraq's legal foundation and permit us to give sovereignty to a transitional government that had a reasonable chance of survival.

In December, the Governing Council had established a drafting committee to begin work on the TAL. The initial results had been mixed. We were concerned about Kurdish efforts to adopt inflexible positions, especially on the rights of the Kurdistan Regional Government and on the status of Kirkuk. Several Arabs on the GC had suggested that we play a role in moderating the Kurdish demands so I had assigned our Governance Team to work with the GC committee.

"We're going to follow two parallel tracks: the Governance Team will continue to work on details with the Arabs on the GC while I tackle the difficult issues directly with the Kurds." Then all the parties would come together to hammer out an interim constitution that would withstand the stresses of sovereignty beset by a stubborn insurgency. "And we need to do all this by March 1 to stay on the path outlined by the November 15 Agreement," I concluded.

"At the end of the day," Blair said, "I believe that the Iraqi people fundamentally want the same thing as we do for Iraq. That's a key point to retain through all these frustrating negotiations."

"The opinion polls, such as they are, convey a couple of clear messages: delight at Liberation, dismay at being occupied, balanced by an understanding that the Coalition is needed to ensure stability," I said.

"What's your opinion of the security situation?" Blair asked, working down a mental checklist of questions.

"Since the outset, our basic approach has been to make Iraqis increasingly responsible for their own security. We've had some important successes—and setbacks."

I added that the key would be the Iraqi police. In late November, the first Iraqi recruits had entered the largest police-training program in history in Jordan. It would take time for them to become fully professional, but the process was under way.

The prime minister asked about the former Iraqi army. I told him that Iraq's prewar army had been built around 400,000 ill-treated, ill-paid conscripts, most of them Shia suffering under brutal Sunni officers. I explained that those who weren't killed in the war simply fled and returned to civilian life. "Most of them are farmers, happy to be home alive with their families. We've encouraged them to join the New Army, the Civil Defense Corps, the Iraqi Police Service, or the Border Guards." I said that fully 60 percent of the recruits in the New Iraqi Army were former soldiers, as were 100 percent of the NCOs and officers. The percentage of ex-soldiers was even higher for the Civil Defense force. "And we've been paying the former army officers stipends since July. So unemployed former soldiers have plenty of options to wear the uniform of Iraq again if they want to. And if they're out shooting at us now, it's not for the money. It's because they want to return to power by force."

I told Blair that the June 30 date for turnover had required a reassessment of our economic plans. We would give priority to projects which created jobs and would not be able to undertake controversial programs to cut energy and food subsidies.

The prime minister agreed and brought the meeting to a close by relating that, during his trip through the region, Egypt's President Hosni Mubarak and Jordan's King Abdullah had told him that the Arab countries were beginning to recognize that we would succeed in Iraq. "They're starting to tailor their policies to the new realities. Our success here will have a major impact on the region."

As Blair rose to leave, we shook hands. "Well, failure is not an option," I said.

Once more he smiled warmly. "I agree completely."

Looking out the oval porthole of the C-130 as we flew north from Basra to Baghdad, I thought back on my talks with Jalal Talabani and Massoud Barzani in Kurdistan two days earlier. Irbil, where we'd met, was a pleasant town on a broad, well-shaded *tel*, the detritus of ancient civilizations. Nearby foothills were covered with pruned vineyards and neat rows of pistachio and apricot trees, and farther north, snowy ridges marked the border with Turkey.

Protected from Saddam by Coalition airpower since 1991, the Iraqi Kurds were accustomed to quasi-independence. After a de facto military alliance with the U.S.—and after internecine fighting—they'd formed their Kurdish Regional Government with its own parliament and cabinet. This privileged status encouraged them to demand a special position in a new, federal Iraqi state, which they had incorporated into their own draft of the TAL. We were willing to support the Kurdish demand for federalism—but only in the context of a unified Iraq, with a central government exercising authority over key national issues such as defense, foreign policy, and Iraq's natural resources.

I had told the Kurdish leaders that they had to be realistic. The TAL was an "interim" document, so sensitive issues like governorate boundaries and the final status of Kirkuk should be decided when Iraqis wrote their permanent constitution. I told them that we would not accept in the TAL a definition of federalism that was based on ethnicity, a central feature of the Kurd's draft.

Kirkuk was a major sore point. While the Kurds had legitimate grievances there, they should stop condoning the current violence and work with the Governing Council to approve our proposed Iraqi Property Claims Commission, designed to adjudicate competing claims. "We did not send our young men and women halfway around the world to free Iraqis from Saddam only to have the Iraqi nation disintegrate," I said.

Barzani remained silent. He was a hard case, a survivor used to stratagems and maneuver. During the brutal Anfal campaign that suppressed the Kurds in the 1980s, Saddam's army had murdered thousands of his tribesmen, including three of his brothers, many after ghastly torture. He was a man with a long memory.

For Barzani, reversing the Arabization of Kirkuk had become a sacred duty. He'd been giving speeches proclaiming that "Kirkuk is the Jerusalem of Kurdistan."

I told him that "the world already has one Jerusalem and it causes quite enough problems on its own," and suggested he drop the analogy.

Despite their offer to keep the dialogue open, I'd left Irbil with a sense of apprehension. It was early January, and we had only two months to agree to the interim constitution.

By Thursday, January 8, the Governing Council's TAL drafting committee was in Irbil, horse-trading with the Kurds. I was on my daily secure call with Condi Rice. I alerted her to a new Sistani problem stemming from a careless remark by Jeremy Greenstock. Following our meeting with Tony Blair, Greenstock had told the press, ". . . Sistani now understands what the secretary-general [Kofi Annan] has said, that the issue of holding elections on this time scale is impossible."

To make matters worse, Greenstock added, "There are signs that Sistani wants to draw back from the politics . . ."

The wire services were all over the story within hours.

We heard rumblings of unhappiness from Najaf almost at once. I told Rice that I'd just seen a report that Sistani felt it necessary to react to Greenstock's comments by publicly restating his insistence on direct national elections. So the advances made by our quiet, patient diplomacy in December had been reversed.

Sistani now moved beyond brooding to grumbling and to veiled threats to issue a fatwa condemning the entire November 15 Agreement while renewing his call for elections.

The week before I was scheduled to leave for America to prepare for the Governing Council's talks with Kofi Annan, Adnan Pachachi, January's Council president, undertook a political pilgrimage to Najaf to reinforce our message that securing Iraq's future stability would demand flexibility on *all* sides. Pachachi told me he was confident that he could persuade the ayatollah that elections would not be possible by June. "He's being misinformed by some people," he assured me. I replied that I was skeptical, but wished him luck.

A couple of days later, Pachachi returned from Najaf to report that his meeting with Sistani had been "entirely fruitless." The ayatollah had talked endlessly about how bad the November 15 Agreement was. Pachachi had reminded Sistani of Annan's December report to the Security Council endorsing the November 15 process and stating that elections were not possible by June. But the ayatollah had simply "waved off" any reference to the United Nations. According to a subdued Pachachi, "Sistani has in effect denied his previous interest in the United Nations sending a team out."

Instead of a fatwa, a blunt message was posted on Sistani's Web site. Sistani condemned the November 15 Agreement and mentioned that unidentified "experts" had confirmed that elections could be held within months.

"Here we go again," I told Scott Carpenter. "Is this more Persian carpet haggling, or has Sistani reached his final position?"

I decided to try my private channel to Sistani again and dispatched Emad Dhia to Najaf on January 13 to reiterate our commitment to full democracy. I told Ayatollah Sistani that as one of the oldest democracies in the world, America fully understood the importance of elections. But, I pointed out, UN and international experts had concluded elections were not possible by summer.

The next day Dhia returned to report he'd had a "good meeting" with Ayatollah Sistani, who'd been pleased to hear from me again. Contrary to what he'd told Pachachi just three days earlier—and had published on his Web site—the ayatollah said he would welcome a small United Nations delegation in Iraq. It should "speak to Iraqis" before issuing its judgment on elections.

"The Grand Ayatollah understands that direct national elections for the Transitional Assembly are not possible at this time," Emad said.

Sistani had told Emad that he did not want to "create problems."

He's said this repeatedly, I thought, *only to create them.* But new signs of flexibility were certainly welcome.

That afternoon, I called Rice to brief her on the Sistani message, which she greeted as "good news."

"Maybe," I said. "But don't forget Bremer's first Rule of Life in Iraq: If you get what appears to be good news, it usually means you're not fully informed."

There were some light moments during the difficult negotiations with the Iraqi politicians. At one Governing Council meeting, members discussed the Pentagon's announcement that we considered Saddam to be a prisoner of war. This had raised some concerns that the Iraqis would not get their hands on their former dictator. So I assured them that President Bush had said we would turn Saddam over to the Iraqi Special Tribunal at the earliest appropriate time.

Judge Wael Abdul Latif, a respected Shiite judge from Basra, took the floor. I expected a legal discourse. Indeed, he began by noting that the Geneva Convention required that a POW be treated according to the fashion to which he was accustomed. "As concerns Saddam," he said, smiling, "this will present a real challenge to the Coalition. Where will you find his cigars, especially since American law forbids you to buy Cuban cigars? How will you be able to find Saddam Hussein the chateaubriand beef and Jersey cream he is accustomed to? And the perfumes and tailored suits from France? And what about his baths in water buffalo milk?"

The Council chamber echoed with laughter.

That night I made a note: When a tyrant becomes the object of ridicule, he can no longer be feared.

In early January, on the recommendation of my Interior Ministry adviser, I faced the problem of salaries for the Iraqi Police Service. Their pay scale was clearly inadequate, and most had little incentive to risk their lives in the face of the mounting insurgency. So I raised police salaries and authorized hazard pay. But their salaries were still inadequate, and three weeks later when the police were threatening to strike, I increased their total take-home pay (salary and hazard pay) by another 65 percent. To do this we had to find another $275 million, and the raise in police pay also meant we faced pressure to increase soldiers' pay. But we couldn't expect Iraq's new security services to risk their lives without adequate compensation.

During this period, I discussed the complex problem of Iraqi militias with David Gompert, who had replaced Walt Slocombe as CPA Senior Adviser for defense and security affairs. Gompert was a former Navy officer and State Department official who had recently worked on security issues in Europe for the RAND Corporation.

It was clear that we had to do something about the militias that had evolved out of Kurdish and Shiite resistance to Saddam. We estimated that there were 60,000–100,000 fighters belonging to nine groups, each attached to a political party.

Gompert and I considered that we had three options. One was to do nothing.

"Ignoring them runs the risk of institutionalizing the political parties' forces in a fractured country," I told Gompert. We agreed that Iraq's long-term stability required that all military forces be under central government control. In theory, we could deal with the militias militarily. But he and I agreed that it was unrealistic to think that the Coalition was going to attack our recent Iraqi allies.

So we were left with only one realistic option, which was to come up with a program for the phased demobilization and reintegration into society of the militiamen. "And one size won't fit all," David said. In designing our "Transition and Reintegration" (T&R) program, we would have to take into account the situation of each militia group.

At least 50,000 of the militia belonged to the Kurdish Peshmerga who had fought alongside the Coalition to defeat Saddam. Because Kurdistan faced new security threats, especially from terrorists infiltrating from Iran and Syria, we did not expect and did not want to disband the Peshmerga completely. Rather, our aim was to bring a large number of them under the control of the national and Kurdistan regional governments, while retiring or retraining the rest.

The other militia were Shia attached to various political parties. The largest was SCIRI's Badr Corps, which had been supported by Iran for twenty years to fight Saddam. The Dawa, Iraqi National Congress, and Iraqi National Accord parties also had small militia. And finally there was Muqtada's undisciplined Mahdi Army. With these militias, our aims were more complex. We wanted to retire and retrain as many as possible from the Badr Corps and were willing to take large numbers of them as individuals into the new Iraqi security services. The Mahdi Army was more of a threat to the rule of law, however, so we wanted it dismantled, if necessary by force.

"But we shouldn't be naïve," I warned Gompert. "It's just not realistic to expect that political leaders will voluntarily disband their militias until the situation becomes clearer—both with the insurgency and with the political process." So Gompert proposed to negotiate with each political party a program to disband and reintegrate the party's militia. We calculated that since little would actually be done until the parties saw how a sovereign government performed, the entire process would take about eighteen months after the return of sovereignty in June.

"And Muqtada will probably never voluntarily disband his private army," Gompert said.

Gompert began intensive negotiations with the major political parties. Each party kept its eye on his talks with the others: SCIRI was suspicious that we might preserve the Peshmerga while dissolving the Badr Corps. It was soon obvious that the Badr Corps was not about to disband as long as the rival Mahdi Army was intimidating the Shiite heartland and while terrorists were killing Shia civilians and pilgrims.

Barzani and Talabani initially told Gompert that they would never agree to give up the Peshmerga, which they understandably considered the ultimate guarantor of the safety of the Kurdish people should the attempt to create a New Iraq fail.

After his initial round of talks with the parties, Gompert reported that this was by far the hardest, most frustrating negotiation he'd ever faced.

"Welcome to Iraq, David," I said with a smile.

On January 13, another congressional delegation came through Baghdad. Democratic Congressman John Murtha of Pennsylvania led the three-member group from the House Defense Appropriations Committee. They were supportive of our efforts and appreciated the difficult conditions we faced. It seemed to us that we were now getting more congressional visits than any post in the world, and almost always they were useful in broadening the congressmen's understanding of the challenges of building the New Iraq.

At this meeting, political officer Judy Van Rest briefed them on our democracy-building effort, including plans to create grassroots democracy centers nationwide. Many centers were already up and running and drawing Iraqi men and women eager to learn a citizen's rights and responsibilities in a free, democratic society.

"We're investing in Iraq's future," Judy said. "But I'm afraid you won't learn about *that* work in the news media. A car bombing is a lot more interesting than teaching women about voting . . ."

"And you won't read much about the schools, the hospitals, and the irrigation canals we've rebuilt," I added. "The networks devote a lot of air time to the destruction connected to the insurgency but precious little to 'good news' stories. It's really frustrating." The relentless litany of negative news stories was steadily undercutting public support for our efforts to stabilize and rebuild post-war Iraq.

John Murtha, a Marine combat veteran of Vietnam, understood the corrosive effect of unremitting pessimistic media coverage.

"Well, Ambassador," he said, "the people are still behind your work, at least in my district they are."

How long will that last if all they see and read in the media is so bleak?

When President Bush had signed into law an $18.6 billion supplemental appropriation for Iraqi reconstruction on November 4, we at the CPA were optimistic we would finally have adequate and flexible funding to begin the thousands of reconstruction projects needed to start the long process of rebuilding Iraq.

With the turnover of sovereignty now fixed for the summer, and faced with the insurgency, I saw a political imperative in getting these projects going as soon as possible so that Iraqis could see real progress on the ground before June 30. Our budget staff developed the project plans required for contracting federal moneys, and in a meeting on December 8, I instructed them to come up with a minimum of $500 million in "quick-dispersing" projects that we could have under way by spring.

However, the supplemental appropriation's funding stream was anything but quick. The bureaucracy in Washington imposed what I saw as overly rigid interpretations of the regulations on letting contracts, which already required long lead times. This was precisely the "business-as-usual" approach to reconstruction that John Hamre had warned about six months earlier. Since we'd already identified over five thousand projects large and small, this frustrating bureaucratic logjam could only slow things further. And it did.

On January 3, increasingly concerned over the slowness of Washington, I asked my staff to identify a half dozen large (more than $20 million each) projects for the Sunni area. "We'll just find the money somehow in the Iraqi budget," I told them.

On the morning of Thursday, January 15, General Sanchez and I met with Sharif Ali, the Pretender to the throne. After Saddam's capture in December,

Sharif Ali had offered to "reach out" to Sunni leaders who he said had influence over insurgents. We had encouraged this effort in the hopes that Saddam's capture might open a window of opportunity for reconciliation with some of the insurgents. Now, a month later, he asked to come report on his effort.

"I am making good progress," he said, "especially among the Sunni tribes in Al-Anbar Province. A cease-fire might be possible in some towns."

I thanked Sharif Ali for his efforts to get the message out that it was futile for the insurgency to continue. I added that the Coalition was working hard to strengthen Iraqi security forces, but that our troops would remain engaged until Iraqis could assume responsibility for their own defense. "Meanwhile," I said, "we're willing to pull Coalition forces out of selected cities if we have assurance that security there will be maintained. What we need now are mutual confidence-building measures."

I described our process of parole for detainees, noting that we had identified fifty-six from Al-Anbar Province who we were willing to release on receiving guarantees. But only eight guarantors had come forward for them.

"You could help us here," Sanchez said.

"We also need to know where your contacts in the province suggest that we have a trial cease-fire," I told him.

"Many Sunnis feel excluded from the political process. They are hardly represented on the Governing Council," he said. "They complain about your taking men into detention. I will try to help with the parole process but this is difficult because people do not want to have contact with the Americans."

I shook my head. "They can't have it both ways, complaining about detainees while not being willing to come forward as guarantors when we are prepared to release them."

Sharif Ali let this go and instead said he would discuss establishing a "period of calm" with his contacts, perhaps in the Fallujah-Ramadi region. "But this will not be easy," he said. "The Sunnis have felt so many injustices that you have to expect them to attack the Coalition. Most Sunnis feel that way."

His comment struck me as insupportable. First he said the Sunnis wanted a greater share of the political process, and two minutes later he asserted that "most" backed the insurgency. "If your view is correct," I said, "you'd better start praying for the Sunnis. It is a fundamental principle of democratic government that people do not shoot their way to power. General Sanchez and I have a responsibility for the safety of our men and women. If the Sunnis decide to use violence, there is no place for them in the New Iraq."

Sharif Ali quickly backed off. So I added that Sunnis needed to participate actively in building the New Iraq. "And there's no sense in complaining about the Governing Council. It's going to cease to exist in five months." They should focus on the future, not the past.

The Pretender left after assuring us he would use his influence to help.

As I left for the airport late on January 15 to prepare for Kofi Annan's January 19 meeting, there was good news and bad news. The good news was that our currency exchange program—which so many naysayers had predicted would fail—had been a great success. A single Iraqi currency, the New Iraqi Dinar, now circulated across the entire country. We had distributed several thousand tons of the new bills and collected and destroyed a staggering thirteen thousand tons of the old dinars—in a country without a modern banking system, unreliable telephone service, lousy roads, and an insurgency. The currency was floating freely against other currencies and had in fact strengthened 30 percent against the dollar since its introduction.

The project's success was due to the stupendous efforts of retired Brigadier General Hugh Tant and a "tiger team" of civilians and soldiers all over Iraq. Hugh's mission motto was "Teamwork that works." And it did.

On the other hand, there'd been street demonstrations in Basra, with tens of thousands of Shiites demanding elections within three months. The demonstrations had been organized by Shiite clerics and politicians loyal to Ayatollah Sistani. Ali al-Hakim al-Safi, a Shiite imam and Sistani disciple, told the chanting demonstrators, "We do not need to use violence to get our rights while there are still peaceful ways we can work together, but if we find peaceful means are no longer available to us we will have to seek other methods." This was ominous. If it represented Sistani's view, it contradicted the private message I'd received two days earlier.

The situation had begun to resemble one of those nightmares where you pull open a stuck door only to find another . . . and another . . .

On January 16, I took my usual seat in the White House Situation Room to attend a meeting of the NSC Principals. Sitting around the table were the vice president, Colin Powell, Don Rumsfeld, General Pete Pace, George Tenet, and Andy Card. Condi Rice chaired. I had arrived back in Washington aboard an Air Force cargo C-5 at 6:00 A.M. after an eighteen-hour flight from Baghdad.

Once more, we weighed the importance of establishing a constitutional structure that would unite the splintered country and allow us in good faith to divest sovereignty by June 30. The immediate problem was how to choose the new Iraqi government. America's position was that provincial caucuses were the most practical method of selecting the Transitional Assembly. This system had already proven successful and popular, in selecting several provincial councils in the south. But that morning's press had been filled with images of huge crowds of Shiites in Basra and now in Baghdad, waving banners of Ayatollah Sistani, chanting for elections. Dan Senor pointed out we'd have a real image problem if it looked as if America were against elections.

Rice asked me to give an overview of our strategy for the next six months.

"We face several interlocking political challenges," I said. Despite recent improvement in the security situation, there were unresolved problems with Sistani. I thought the UN could help select the interim government, "but only if the UN agrees to work within the framework of the November 15 Agreement."

The discussion shifted to the proposed United Nations special representative to Iraq, Lakhdar Brahimi, a former Algerian foreign minister and currently the UN special representative to Afghanistan. Rumsfeld and Cheney expressed concern about using him—Brahimi had strongly opposed the war. Rice countered that he had proven "very useful" in Afghanistan and could help in Iraq, particularly if the UN would clearly state that elections were not possible by June 30 and offer alternatives for selecting the new government. We should be flexible assessing those alternatives.

"Well, yeah," I said. "But we've got to be prepared to confront Sistani if the UN comes up with a credible alternative consistent with our objectives and timeline and Sistani still rejects it." If, on the other hand, we simply "caved" to Sistani, as some unnamed Washington officials were recently suggesting to the press, we risked pushing the Kurds toward secession, and the breakup of Iraq, civil war, and escalating regional instability.

The consensus was to give the United Nations a chance to help defuse the political impasse.

I made my way across the alley from the West Wing to the third floor of the Executive Office Building, where Vice President Cheney had provided me an office. Dan Senor greeted me with the news that he'd just learned that a "terrible story" was about to break in Baghdad.

"Apparently some MPs guarding detainees forced them to engage in homosexual acts," he said somberly. "They made one of them crawl around on the ground with a dog's leash around his neck. There may also have been women involved, whether our women MPs or women detainees isn't clear." One MP had reported this despicable activity to his commander.

"We've got to get out in front of this story ASAP by authorizing Kimmitt to announce that we've ordered an urgent investigation," Dan said.

Army Brigadier General Mark Kimmitt and Dan shared the daily Coalition press briefing duties in Baghdad. It was far better that Kimmitt carry this story to the press rather than the other way around.

"Do it," I said. "Right away. And make sure our statement condemns all inappropriate behavior and says people will be investigated and punished."

General Kimmitt later called a press conference, announcing that Lieutenant General Sanchez had ordered an investigation into "reported incidents of detainee abuse." Kimmitt added, "The investigation will be conducted in a thorough and professional manner."

That afternoon in an Oval Office meeting on Iraq, the issue of the MPs' alleged mistreatment of detainees came up.

The president leaned forward in his chair, his face solemn.

General Pete Pace gave a brief description of the story, stating that we did not have all the details.

Bush shook his head in anger. "I hope they find every last guilty person," he said, looking at the group. "We've got to punish them as soon as possible. I want them out of Iraq and in jail, ASAP." Again, he shook his head. "I want everybody to take a very hard press line on this."

When the meeting ended, the president held me back briefly, alone.

"How you doin', Bremer? You look tired. You going to make it?"

"I *am* exhausted. But I'm going to make it."

The president told me he had enjoyed seeing Francie and my family at the Iraqi Symphony performance. "You missed a great evening."

"Pace yourself, Jerry," he said, clapping his hand on my shoulder as we walked to the door.

I remembered those same words, six months before in Qatar. It seemed like a hundred years ago.

The meetings in New York between senior United Nations officials, the Iraqi delegation, and the Coalition representatives on Monday, January 19, 2004, went well.

January Council president Pachachi headed the Iraqi group, which included December's GC president, Abdul Aziz Hakim; Dr. Mohsen Hamid—the upcoming president for February and head of the Sunni Iraqi Islamic Party; Ahmad Chalabi; and Iraq's Kurdish foreign minister, Hoshyar Zebari.

Our purpose was to ask Secretary-General Annan to send a team to Iraq to answer the two questions put to him by the Governing Council: Are national elections possible before June 30? If not, could the UN suggest other means, such as caucuses, to put a new Iraqi government in place by then?

First the Coalition had a private meeting with the secretary-general. Annan announced that he did not want the UN to "snipe" at us from the sidelines and sought no separate political role for the organization. "But I need a frank assessment," he said. "Does Ayatollah Sistani want the UN brought in just to provide a face-saving way to change his position on elections?"

And Annan was also concerned about security. The bombing of the UN headquarters in Baghdad was on his mind, of course.

I told him that the Coalition welcomed the opportunity to reestablish a long-term partnership with the UN. We would do everything possible to give the organization's representatives in Iraq appropriate security. "There's broad agreement on implementing the November 15 Agreement, Mr. Secretary-General," I said, "although there's no consensus about choosing the Transitional National Assembly." I added that, based on my communications with the ayatollah, I thought Sistani wanted a democratic Iraq.

While the Iraqi delegation met with the secretary-general, I went across First Avenue to the U.S. mission to the UN and had a private talk in Ambassador Negroponte's office with Lakhdar Brahimi, the candidate to become the UN special representative for Iraq.

Brahimi was almost gaunt and looked older than seventy. But he had lively, intelligent eyes and responded with a smile when I greeted him formally in Arabic. We quickly switched to French and exchanged some pleasantries about Paris, where his wife lived.

Then, speaking English, Brahimi told me, "My responsibilities in Afghanistan have been very tiring, Ambassador Bremer. Frankly, I'd like to take a long leave in France, so I'm reluctant to accept the Iraq portfolio. How important is your June 30 deadline for the sovereignty transfer?"

"It's firm," I said. "We need to demonstrate that we'll carry out our agreement. The Iraqi people want sovereignty back. And we have to show that we're not going to be pushed around by Ayatollah Sistani." Brahimi said that he didn't think Iraq's interim government should be run by "people with black turbans." I told him I thought Sistani's basic concern was to ensure a Shia majority in the new government.

As Rice had suggested, Brahimi was an insightful thinker. I liked him, and was confident we would work together effectively.

The next morning back in Washington, before the Iraqi delegation arrived, Meghan and I briefed the president on the UN talks. The president was standing behind his desk in the Oval Office, munching on some cheese. Rice, Rumsfeld, and Powell were already there and when the president offered around a plate of cheese, grapes, and carrot sticks they all declined. I took a cracker and a piece of cheddar. As we talked, the president good-naturedly pointed out that I was scattering crumbs all over the rug. This provoked hearty condemnation of my eating habits from Rice and Powell. I said that I had forgotten where I was and was just following Baghdad rules. The president had a good laugh when I added, "You can dress him up, but you can't take him out . . ."

Drawing on a memo Meghan and I had sent the president the night before, I said it would be helpful to congratulate the Iraqis on the robust defense of individual liberties in the current TAL draft. "It's especially important for Hakim to hear about the importance we attach to freedom of religion," I stressed.

After our briefing, George Bush welcomed the Iraqis graciously. He pointed to the portraits of Washington and Lincoln, noting that this was a historic room, and that the American presidency was a democratic institution far more important than the men who held the office. "And what's exciting about Iraq today," he said, "is that you're building your own institutions of democracy."

The president invited Adnan Pachachi to sit in the "daddy chair," as the White House staff referred to the chair to the president's right. Pachachi thanked the president for receiving the delegation and thanked America for "liberating the Iraqi people." And he added, "After June, Iraq will continue to depend on our partnership. I am optimistic about the future of Iraq."

Pachachi told the president that he had been in the Oval Office once before, when he'd met President Lyndon Johnson, another Texan. "You are certainly different from him," he added.

"I'll take that as a compliment," the president responded with a chuckle. President Bush said that Iraqis should know that "we're going to stay until the job is done." We were determined to carry out the November 15 Agreement, and the June 30 deadline for sovereignty was "etched in stone."

Turning to Hakim, the president expressed sympathy for the loss of his brother in the August bombing in Najaf and added, "I know this must hurt your heart."

Hakim seemed moved, thanked the president, and said that sixty-three of his relatives, including eight of his brothers, had been killed by Saddam. Then he quickly shifted subjects. "We are entering a critical period. This must be guided by credibility and transparency. As Ayatollah Ali al-Sistani has noted, the best path to achieve this is elections." He looked placidly at his colleagues through his tinted glasses. "And this is also the view of the entire Governing Council . . ."

The other Iraqis were frowning in perplexity.

". . . therefore the transfer of sovereignty should be to an elected body," Hakim continued. "We note that demonstrations are being held concerning this matter in Iraq even today. They will continue until the demonstrators' objectives are achieved."

The silence in the room was painful.

President Bush did not respond. Finally, Hakim noted the importance of protecting the "Islamic identity of the Iraqi people."

President Bush responded that he, too, was a man of God. "I'd like to be sure that if I came to Iraq as a Christian, I'd be free to practice my religion."

This took Hakim aback and he replied that Iraqis respected the rights of all religious groups. "There will be no discrimination against anyone," he said.

President Bush spoke of his great respect for Ayatollah Sistani and asked Hakim to pass him his high regards. And then he reinforced his emphasis on the established November 15 Agreement timeline. "It's your choice how to choose the government," he said, "working with Ambassador Bremer."

The president also reminded the Iraqis that America's democracy had not been achieved overnight, but had evolved over many decades. There would be a solution to the June 30 questions, he said, "but once you solve that problem there'll be another in six months and another after that. That's why it's important for all of us to stick to our principles." He told the group that nobody should have any doubt whatsoever about the American commitment to a free, democratic Iraq. "We're going to stay until the job is done."

Later, the Iraqis and the CPA team met Colin Powell at the State Department.

Ahmad Chalabi offered unbidden praise for Sistani, "one of our country's greatest leaders." Chalabi smiled at Hakim while the interpreter translated.

That's a bit over the top, considering Chalabi's a secularist, I thought.

Secretary Powell gazed coolly at Hakim. "Earlier at the White House," Powell said, "you mentioned that the demonstrations would continue. I wonder if this is the best atmosphere to create."

Powell's stony expression and tone unnerved Hakim, who lamely protested that the demonstrations were actually a "show of support for the transfer of power, for the Governing Council, for democracy and against terrorism."

I hoped that Hakim would report to Sistani that America's leaders were not easily intimidated.

While in Washington, I got word from Dick Jones in Baghdad that Muqtada al-Sadr's men had marched on the mosque of the Imam Ali in Najaf. The local police had chased them off, but the mob returned in larger numbers and announced their intention to establish a "Sharia court" in the Sacred Precinct to "try" four Iraqi policemen they had kidnapped several days before. The Spanish troops responsible for Najaf were getting nervous and talking about a "dialogue."

At my request, Dick sent in a cable recommending that we support the Iraqi police in arresting Muqtada. His message confirmed that the mob had left the shrine, but were still holding one of the kidnapped policemen. They had set up their "court" elsewhere in Najaf and were sentencing people who were then thrown into a secret "prison." The cable provoked CIA headquarters—without coordination with the Baghdad station—to send the president a paper warning that Muqtada's arrest would spark major unrest among the Shia.

Muqtada al-Sadr is not going away. We couldn't just stand by, letting him defy Iraq's fledgling justice system.

After I got back to Baghdad, the situation became even more exasperating. The insurgency intensified, with car bombings and IEDs targeting Coalition troops and the new Iraqi security forces.

Until mid-January, the insurgents' strategy was unclear to Coalition intelligence. We knew that we faced disgruntled Baathists and criminals. The key unknown was the role of international terrorists. Then we captured a Pakistani Al-Qaeda courier carrying a computer disc with a manifesto–cum–operational report. The author of this letter was the Jordanian-born Al-Qaeda ally, Abu Musab Zarqawi, who had fought in Afghanistan, been wounded in 2001, and had received medical treatment and sanctuary in Iraq before Liberation. The message was addressed to "the hawks of glory," code for Osama bin Laden and his lieutenants. It was a rambling screed against Americans, Jews and Israelis, and the Iraqi Shia.

Zarqawi's report acknowledged the increasingly difficult operational situation for the Islamist insurgents. As Iraqi security forces replaced Coalition troops, the insurgents had to fight this new enemy, "the real danger that we face, for it is made up of our fellow countrymen, who know us inside and out."

Another danger was the "masses" of Sunni Arabs who looked forward to a "sunny tomorrow, a prosperous future." It was up to the insurgent *mujahidin* to radicalize the Sunni and to galvanize resistance by increasing "martyrdom operations," of which Zarqawi claimed responsibility for twenty-five, "including among the Shia and their symbolic figures." Zarqawi admitted the Kurds were a "thorn" in the side of the insurgency. He identified the Iraqi security forces as another major target of the terrorists.

The insurgents' ultimate goal was to use suicide attacks to provoke the Shia into an open civil war with the Sunni masses. But Zarqawi was worried: "Democracy is coming, and there will be no excuse [for the insurgency] thereafter."

"What do you think of it?" I asked "Pete," the new Baghdad station chief. "The way I read it, they can see Iraq's moving toward democracy and they don't like it."

Pete, a short, stocky professional whose high complexion suggested an excitable temperament, frowned at the printout on my desk. "It all checks out, Mr. Ambassador."

"That means they're going to hit us hard in the next five months."

"Not just us," he said. "The Shia, the Kurds, the Sunni who've been vetted and are serving in the security forces . . ."

Within days of capturing the Zarqawi message, two suicide bombers struck the headquarters of the leading Kurdish political parties in Irbil during Eid al-Adha, a major Muslim festival. Almost seventy people were killed, including Barzani's deputy prime minister in the Kurdistan Regional Government.

I thought back to Rice's phone call on that terrible afternoon in August when—I now recognized—it had been Zarqawi's suicide bomber that had destroyed the United Nations building and killed my friend Sergio de Mello: "Colin and I are convinced that Iraq has become the decisive theater in the war on terrorism and that if we win in Iraq, international terrorism can be defeated."

But none of us knew just how bitter the fight would be.

Chapter 11
WRITING THE
CONSTITUTION

■ BAGHDAD
FEBRUARY 2003

"Baghdad time" gripped our lives. Few of us got more than three or four hours of sleep a night—what with mortar and rocket attacks and phones ringing at 3:00 A.M. when some bureaucrat inside the Beltway forgot about the time difference. Many of us staggered around like zombies with hangovers from sheer exhaustion.

The United Nations team, due to arrive soon, would, we hoped, finally quash the concept of nationwide elections before June 30. But we'd heard that Brahimi was skeptical about using caucuses to choose the new government. And in Washington anonymous "government officials" were whispering to the press that the June 30 sovereignty deadline might be "flexible." I suspected we were headed toward an outcome in which we would divest sovereignty to an appointed body. This prospect made it all the more vital to frame Iraq's political life through a good interim constitution.

The democratic process was spreading in every governorate. Dozens of trade, professional, and women's groups were meeting, electing officers, and discussing democracy. Even in Al-Anbar Province, where Zarqawi's terrorists and former Baathist insurgents attacked Coalition troops and Iraqi security forces almost daily, groups were exploring the merits of democratic values.

And in a project dear to my heart, with the guidance of Senior Adviser for sports, Mounzer Fatfat, we had conducted over five hundred separate elections at municipal and provincial levels to reconstitute Iraq's Olympic Committee—a prerequisite if Iraq was to be accepted back into the Olympics movement after being expelled a decade earlier.

• • •

On Saturday, February 7, we received a message from Sharif Ali that his contacts among Sunni insurgents in the Tigris River city of Baquba north of Baghdad had declared a unilateral cease-fire at dawn. It was scheduled to last until 6:00 A.M. on Tuesday.

I called a meeting with Sanchez's chief of staff, Marine Major General Jon Gallinetti, political officer Scott Carpenter, and Ron Schlicher, who worked with David Richmond and a team of Arabic speakers to broaden our outreach to the Sunnis. Ron was another senior American diplomat with fluent Arabic and long experience in the region. I told the group we needed to find the best means to exploit this opportunity. "If it's credible we have to come up with some reciprocal gestures," I told them.

General Gallinetti recommended testing the cease-fire by pulling forces back from parts of the city and reducing our overall military presence around Baquba. I concurred, and Scott and Ron said they'd sound out their own contacts in the province.

This was the first nibble we had had in our efforts to establish contact with the insurgents. The UN had also received some approaches, according to Dr. Rice, and I encouraged her to push the UN to follow up, too. "Our goal," I told my team, "is to establish a practical communications channel with the insurgents. Maybe we can get them to extend the cease-fire past Tuesday, and Sharif Ali can arrange cease-fires elsewhere."

On Monday, February 9, Sharif Ali returned for another meeting. The cease-fire appeared to have held for fifty hours.

I thanked him for his efforts and said we would like to work with him to calm the city. "We propose that you ask your contacts to extend the cease-fire for another week while we develop programs that would interest both sides." I had asked my colleagues to come up with a list of infrastructure projects that would pump jobs and money into the town, thus demonstrating tangible advantages of cooperation over insurrection. "What can you tell us about your contacts in Baquba? Are they similar to those you mentioned in the west of Al-Anbar? What do they want?"

"Those in Baquba are not tribal people. They are former intelligence, special security, and military officers. But I'm not in *direct* contact with them. I must pass through several levels of intermediaries, and that takes time."

"Will you propose a cease-fire extension?"

"Of course. As for their interests, they want to help establish a national command structure for the security services. They do not oppose the Coalition or the Americans, but they feel left out of the political life of Iraq and want to be included."

Some of the military and intelligence officers he had described would almost certainly never pass a thorough vetting. But some of them might. We had to keep this channel open, especially since Zarqawi himself had admitted that large segments of the Sunni community were souring on the insurgency.

"The Coalition has no principled objection to former army personnel," I said. "About 80 percent of the New Iraqi Army and Civil Defense Corps are former soldiers. All the officers and NCOs are."

I suggested that he press his contacts for a list of four or five issues specifically related to Baquba that they would like to discuss with us. This Sharif Ali agreed to do.

Just after sunset, Scotty Norwood entered my office. "The cease-fire in Baquba is over. An IED hit a convoy. One soldier killed. They found another IED and defused it."

That night I asked Ron Schlicher to call Sharif Ali to express our regret that the cease-fire did not hold. If his contacts knew who attacked our convoy, they should tell us. We heard nothing back. The insurgency continued. But I went on pressing the military to release detainees as soon as we found guarantors for them.

The drafting of the Transitional Administrative Law was making considerable progress. Almost daily, representatives of the GC drafting committee had met with a small group from our CPA Governance Team. Raad Alkadiri and Irfan Siddiq, with their fluent Arabic and area expertise, were especially helpful in this process. The drafting committee had refined the TAL's section on individual rights, defined the structures and mechanisms of the new government, and agreed to key principles such as the independence of the judiciary and civilian control of the military.

Meanwhile, I continued private discussions with the Kurds. We had developed a compromise that would allow the Kurdistan region to retain many elements of its recent autonomy, while at the same time preserving the preeminence of the federal government on issues of national policy. Still, a host of issues remained unresolved. How would the Arabs respond to the emerging compromise on federalism? Would the document recognize Kurdish as an official language, as the Kurds demanded? What would the constitution say about the role of Islam? And what about the role of women in Iraq's political structure? We needed answers to all these questions—and more—in order for the TAL to be approved by the March 1 deadline called for in the November 15 Agreement.

We also had a continuing Sistani problem. After Annan announced that Brahimi would visit, I wrote the ayatollah that I had "confidence that the UN can help us find an acceptable, transparent, and conclusive mechanism to create the Transitional National Assembly by June 30."

Ayatollah Sistani's verbal reply through Emad Dhia grudgingly conceded that he was "beginning to see" that elections might not be possible by summer. But he demanded assurances that they would take place within nine months of June 30.

I responded by assuring Sistani that the current draft of the TAL specified that elections would be held not later than March 2005, "and sooner if possible." I pledged that the Coalition would support implementation of that provision.

Lakhdar Brahimi came to Iraq and traveled to Najaf on February 12 to meet Ayatollah Sistani. Later that day, Brahimi privately informed me that he had persuaded the ayatollah that elections could not be held by the end of June. But as I'd feared, Sistani had told Brahimi he favored simply anointing the Governing Council as the interim government, probably because this would guarantee a continued Shia majority. Fortunately, Brahimi shared my view that, instead, we needed to broaden the political process, though he wasn't in favor of using the caucuses. He was inclined just to appoint what he called "a caretaker government." But he agreed that we would have to discuss this further when he returned to Iraq in early April.

Just when Brahimi finally convinced Sistani to abandon his demand for immediate elections, some of the major Washington players went wobbly on our "etched in stone" deadlines. During an NSC meeting on February 13, Don Rumsfeld suggested that since we now had so much leverage in Iraq, we might wish to divest sovereignty "in pieces," adding that we'd "always been willing to slide the date."

Always?

Colin Powell added that it wouldn't be a failure if we transferred sovereignty on August 1 instead of June 30 in order to be sure the Iraqi provisional government was ready to exercise power. The president said that it would be a defeat if the date slipped, but perhaps we could "calibrate sovereignty" in some way.

I could see a real threat to the complex political structure we were struggling to build. How could I hold the Iraqis to carry out the November 15 Agreement if Washington wasn't firm?

That night I sent a letter to President Bush through Condi Rice, and copied it to Rumsfeld and Powell, reviewing the situation in Iraq. "Brahimi says Sistani also agreed that sovereignty must be transferred on schedule in June. This is good news. Already the bazaars are alive with rumors that we are not serious about the June 30 handover. It is vital that our public statements not undercut this objective. Delay would ignite doubts about our ultimate intentions in Iraq and could well cost American lives."

I argued that it was just as important to stick to the deadline of the end of February for completing the TAL to discourage doubts about our commitment to carry out the other provisions of the November 15 Agreement. And I added that anointing the Governing Council as a caretaker government would be a mistake. We needed to use the new government to broaden participation in Iraq's political life, particularly by Sunnis. Moreover, the GC had shown itself unable to perform as an executive body.

Concerning the security situation, I asserted that the steady buildup of well-trained Iraqi forces coupled with "patience and a prudent mixture of sticks and the occasional carrot" would bring victory in time. The bad news was that we still had to confront a growing wave of international terrorists, led by fanatics like Zarqawi, whose "conclusion is that the terrorists must step up their attacks now," I wrote. "Thus we should expect more spectacular terrorist attacks in the run-up to July and perhaps beyond."

The silver lining, if any, was that we now knew from his letter that Zarqawi was resigned to the fact "that America is not going to abandon Iraq."

As often in Iraq, however, just when you thought things were bad, they got worse.

On February 14, Rick Sanchez brought word of a "highly professional" attack on the Fallujah police station in which three squads attacked simultaneously from different directions, overrunning the station, massacring the defenders, and releasing dozens of prisoners. Fallujah was in the area of responsibility of the 82nd Airborne Division, which Sanchez said had not responded vigorously. Perhaps there were good military reasons for that, I said, but what message did this convey to the people of Fallujah, remembering that we had also not responded strongly to the November shootdown of our Chinook on the outskirts of the city?

Another aggravating incident occurred a few days later when Ahmad Chalabi gave an interview to the British *Sunday Telegraph*. He casually dismissed the charge that his Iraqi National Congress had provided the American government with bogus intelligence on weapons of mass destruction. "We are heroes in error," he told the reporter. "As far as we're concerned, we've been entirely successful. That tyrant Saddam is gone and the Americans are in Baghdad. What was said before is not important. The Bush administration is looking for a scapegoat. We're ready to fall on our swords if he wants."

The next time I spoke to Rice, she said the *Telegraph* story had "really frosted" President Bush. He instructed American officials to "distance themselves" from Chalabi.

The insurgency flared, and then sputtered, only to blaze up again. But I was determined not to become a prisoner in the Green Zone. Now when we flew, the Black Hawks stayed low and clattered across the rooftops and grain fields at maximum speed. Wherever the choppers landed, our local military unit always provided a security detachment that usually included up-armored Humvees and more heavily armored Bradley fighting vehicles.

Visiting a provincial governor or cutting the ribbon at a renovated school or hospital or sharing a meal with the soldiers in their mess hall gave me the chance to rub shoulders with our enlisted-rank men and women who faced the enemy every day and every night. Many of them had lost a friend, killed or wounded, to IEDs planted along roadsides or to suicide car bombers. Yet the troops continued to perform their duty, walking dangerous night patrols through neighborhoods or villages known to be controlled by the "Ali Baba," slang for the insurgents. Despite this harsh environment, the troops, many still in their teens, somehow had the strength of character to befriend Iraqi civilians, especially children.

And our troops managed to keep their sense of humor. At one Jersey barrier checkpoint near Tikrit, a mud-spattered corporal waved my convoy through, then, recognizing me, raised his hand for the driver to stop.

"Hi, sir," he said cheerfully, "got any cold beer in there?"

It was a nasty winter afternoon with a damp "mudstorm" starting.

"Sorry, I don't," I smiled back at him.

The young man shivered as a rivulet of liquid sand dripped off the brim of his helmet and down the collar of his flak jacket.

"Well," he said. "Got any *warm* beer then?"

It would take a lot to weaken the morale of a soldier like that.

•   •   •

By the third week of February, we had moved into a new phase in the TAL negotiations. We had come to satisfactory resolutions in our talks with the Kurds, and also in the informal discussions with key members of the GC drafting committee. But the full Council had not seriously begun to focus on a unified draft. And with only ten days to the deadline established by the November 15 Agreement, many issues remained unresolved.

First among them was the role of religion. The Shia Islamist parties, SCIRI and Dawa, had proposed that the TAL assert that Islam is *"the"* basis of all law. The issue was a political hot button to all sides. In December, SCIRI's Hakim had taken advantage of his tenure as GC president to force through Resolution 137, which called for the imposition of Sharia across Iraq. This was anathema to the Kurds and Arab Sunnis, but also to secular Shiites, especially women. At the time, I had publicly refused to sign their resolution into law.

To underscore the importance we attached to the TAL's guarantees of individual rights, particularly those of women, on February 16, I opened a women's rights center we had funded in the holy city of Karbala. Throughout the country we were establishing these centers. I believed strongly that democracy was more likely to take root in Iraq if we could create constituencies that supported it. And after decades of war, women were certainly a majority of Iraq's population.

On this day, more than two hundred *abaya*-clad women crowded into the center, formerly the city's Baath Party headquarters, to hear me announce, "Anyone seeing all this talent and ability would recognize that barriers placed in the way of women are barriers to the development, growth, and prosperity of Iraq—indeed of the Arab world . . . No husband is better off because his wife is bound by chains of ignorance. No son is better off if his mother and sisters cannot read." I assured them that the Coalition would continue its robust activities to promote women's rights in Iraq and that "Iraq's future is not confined by the chains of dictatorship; Iraq's future is full of hope." I confirmed to the press afterward that I would not sign the GC's Resolution 137 purporting to establish Sharia law.

The TAL still had to address a number of issues relating to the protection of minority rights. In addition to broad autonomy in their northern region, the Kurds wanted assurances that they could veto a draft constitution if its provisions on federalism were insufficiently generous. Together with the Sunnis and secular Shia, the Kurds also pushed for institutional guarantees that would require a broad-based consensus for selecting a prime minister and taking major policy decisions. This would ensure that the Shia majority would not be able to impose its will on the rest of the country, but would need to forge compromises across groups. This meant the TAL would have to include significant checks and balances.

An important area agreed was the timetable for Iraq to move to democracy. The draft TAL explicitly endorsed the path described by the November 15 Agreement, providing for a return to sovereignty on June 30 and national elections not later than January 31, 2005. But it also laid out three additional steps. Iraqis would write their permanent constitution by August 15, 2005. That document would be submitted for ratification by October 15, and if approved, elections based on its provisions would be held by December 15, 2005. We knew we were locking them into a fast-paced schedule, but hoped that it would structure and concentrate political activity after we had left.

On Wednesday, February 25, after several late night sessions with Dick Jones and CPA lawyers to carefully review his text, Pachachi circulated to the broader GC committee a "Chairman's Draft" TAL that incorporated many of the changes agreed on in committee discussions. The draft's most remarkable feature was its second chapter, which guaranteed all Iraqis basic freedoms—of speech and religion, to join political parties and unions, and to strike. Citizens were all equal before the law, regardless of gender, sect, or ethnicity. The accused had a right to legal counsel and to a quick and public trial. It was a remarkable document, rare in the region. I congratulated Pachachi on an enormous achievement.

But the next day, instead of attending a Council meeting to work on the draft, the Shiite Islamists went to Najaf to consult Ayatollah Sistani about what the text said concerning Islam. This was unsettling, especially to the Kurds who'd always worried about the influence of the *marjaiya* in the new Iraq.

On February 27, the Islamists returned to the Council with the role of Islam still unsettled. In a surprise move, Pachachi opened the meeting by calling on one of the GC's female members, Dr. Raja Khuzai, a secular Shia doctor. She had brought a crowd of women and press into the council chamber, and proposed repealing Resolution 137. Caught off guard, the Council voted to repeal the resolution, which provoked loud ululations from the crowd and an angry walkout by the Islamist Shia members.

Pachachi kept the remaining members working on the draft constitution until after midnight, but recognized that without a quorum they couldn't reach final conclusions. A little after 1:00 A.M. on February 28, Pachachi ended the long session still not knowing if or when the Shia Islamists would return to the table.

Emotions were getting pretty raw and we had only thirty-six hours to our deadline. Later that night, Rubaie came in to tell me that the Shia were still divided on what the TAL should say about Islam.

Despite their youth and energy, even Scott, Meghan, Roman, Irfan, and Lydia Khalil looked tired and dejected. "Hey," I said, reading the latest TAL draft, "cheer up. Nobody ever said this would be easy." But as I spoke, my own voice sounded tinny in my ear, and the electric lights were ringed with annoying halos—the effects of extended sleep deprivation.

I now tried to reassure Sistani that the best hope for all the Iraqis—including the Shia—lay in completing a just Transitional Administrative Law. I wrote him noting that, thanks to Liberation, this year on March 2 for the first time in decades Iraqis would be allowed publicly to celebrate Ashura—the holiest day for the Shia, commemorating the martyrdom of the Prophet's grandson, Hussein ibn-Ali.

The Coalition would honor our promise to give sovereignty to an Iraqi government on June 30, I emphasized. I added that the Iraqi government elected in 2005 would be fully sovereign and would write a new constitution. "By the end of 2005, elections for a parliament will be held under that constitution." I reminded him that "the draft TAL respects Islam and makes it the religion of the state. The TAL respects the Islamic identity of the majority of Iraqi people. It also specifies that governments in the transitional period cannot make any changes to the TAL that infringe the rights of the Iraqi people or in any way affect the role of Islam."

I added that the TAL respected the rights of *every* citizen—a not-too-subtle reminder that Sharia law might infringe the rights of non-Muslims, as well as secular Muslims, and of emancipated women.

I heard back from Sistani in separate reports from Rubaie and Dhia. The ayatollah was "softening" on the role of Islam. Although Sistani expressed his "great appreciation" for what the Coalition had done for Iraqis, he wanted the TAL to be ratified by the Transitional National Assembly sometime after June 30, not by the current Governing Council. That was yet another new demand from the ayatollah. I had consistently held that the Coalition would fail in its obligations to the Iraqi people if we gave sovereignty to a body that lacked even an interim constitution to provide a legal framework for Iraq's move down the path to democracy. The goalposts seemed to move every week now.

Finally, on the evening of February 28, after a hectic day of lobbying, we managed to rope all the Council players into the Green Zone, the Shia in the GC building and the Kurds in nearby homes and offices. The TAL discussions were back on, with only a day to go.

Talabani had assured me that in "very frank" talks late the previous night he'd reached agreement with the Shia on Islam, on the establishment of two official languages (Arabic and Kurdish) with provisos that not everybody had to learn both, and on the ability of governorates outside the Kurdish region to merge, something the Shia sought to allow them to follow the Kurdish example of consolidation.

Knowing that Talabani had an appealing, but dangerous, tendency to sweep aside disagreements with an airy wave of the hand, I decided we should confirm the Shias' positions before the full Governing Council met for the "final" negotiating session. So our team spent three hours with Shiite leaders, including Bahr al-Uloum, Chalabi, Rubaie, and Adel. We were agreed on a number of issues, but, despite Talabani's optimism, the Shia clung to an unacceptable formula on the role of Islam.

After hours of negotiation, Bahr al-Uloum asked us to postpone any further discussion of the TAL until the next day at 10:00 A.M. We refused and I said we had to continue today and go through the night if necessary since the next day was February 29, our deadline. "We'll lock the doors, if we have to," I said.

We didn't lock the doors. But we also did not get much sleep.

Since it was clear that a number of sensitive issues remained, Dick Jones and I agreed to "divide and conquer." He and Barzani took some GC members into the large Council room to go through the latest TAL draft, article by article. I rounded up a representative working group of thirteen other members, and we repaired to a conference room on the second floor to try to agree on the most difficult subjects.

Perhaps recognizing the sensitivities of the major issues, the Council members asked me to chair this working group meeting. The biggest battles included whether governorates would be allowed to combine as the Shia wanted, and over the constitutional role of women, where the Islamist Shia tentatively agreed to a target of 25 percent female representation in the Transitional National Assembly.

But as before, the major issue was the role of Islam. The current draft said, "Islam is the official religion of the State, and is to be considered a principal source amongst other sources of legislation. This Law shall respect the Islamic identity of the majority of the people of Iraq, but guarantees the complete freedom of all religions and their religious practices."

The Islamist Shia insisted on changing "*a* principal source" to "*the* principal source." This was anathema to the non-Islamist members of the Council, who argued the point vigorously with their Islamist colleagues. We, too, resisted and after three exhausting hours the Shia retreated, accepting that Islam would be "a source" of legislation, but adding that no law contradicting the "basic tenets of Islam" could be enacted. The group agreed with Pachachi's proposal that neither could any law infringe the rights established in Chapter 2 of the TAL.

Rubaie called Najaf and happily reported that Sistani approved this formulation. Next, I called Rice at Camp David and got her green light, after noting that this text on the role of Islam was actually better than what the U.S. had accepted in the recently approved Afghan constitution.

At 2:00 A.M. on February 29, I concluded that we'd gone as far as we could that night, and went downstairs to find that Barzani and Dick Jones had managed to settle their group's lesser issues, which would help us when the full Council reconvened in the afternoon. But as I was about to return to my office, the Kurds suddenly presented a two-page list of demands to be included in the TAL. These were issues they had raised three weeks earlier and on which we believed we had agreement. Now, they'd changed their minds.

Here they are, hitting us with this in the middle of the night on the last day.

I convened the Kurds in a small, dark work room and made it clear that their last-minute demands were not only unreasonable, but also threatened the Kurds' "special" relationship with the United States. This quieted them, at least for what was left of the night.

In a final call to Rice, after briefing her on the state of play, I noted that all the sectarian and other tensions playing themselves out underlined the point that for now, at least, "We are the custodians of Iraqi unity."

Sunday, February 29, was an exhausting repeat of the day before. After fewer than three hours of sleep, I convened the Governance Team to discuss tactics. The GC's president for February, Mohsen Hamid, had scheduled a follow-up "working group" meeting for 11:00 A.M. and a GC plenary session at 2:00 P.M., "hopefully to finish the job." Before those meetings, I would sit down with the Kurds to try to get agreement on the demands they had sprung the night before. Then the "working group" would try to resolve the role of Islam before the plenary Council session.

With the Kurds, we were able quickly to clarify a couple of points they had raised late the previous night. But three issues remained: their request for "block grant" funds from the central treasury; the status of their militia, the Peshmerga; and the right to veto the ratification of the constitution.

We gave the Kurds some face-saving options on block grants. Concerning the Peshmerga, we'd agreed three weeks earlier that militia and armed forces not under central command would be prohibited "except as provided by federal law." This they now refused to accept and we put the issue aside for the time being.

Constitutional ratification remained the most difficult issue. The Kurds repeated their fundamental concern about the kind of permanent constitution the "black turbans" might write.

Talabani pointedly stated, "Mr. Ambassador, you are asking us to join an Iraq in which we'll have less freedom than we had while Saddam was in power." They proposed that ratification of the constitution would fail if a two-thirds majority in any three provinces voted against it. Since the Kurdish Regional Government comprised three provinces, this gave them a veto. I told them I'd have to check with Washington on this issue, and repeated that agreement on any one issue depended on agreement on all of them.

Barzani went into his seasoned tribal-leader crouch. His face and mouth, which at the best of times were tight and closed, became even more clenched. Lips pressed together, eyes narrowed, he almost seemed to draw into himself.

Everyone was exhausted, edgy.

While I was dealing with the Kurds, Dick Jones and Scott Carpenter grappled with Ahmad Chalabi, who had suddenly proposed Draconian anti-Baathist language for the TAL. Our de-Baathification policy had targeted only the top 1 percent of the party's members, but under Chalabi's direction, the Iraqi De-Baathification Council had broadened the policy, for example, depriving thousands of teachers of their jobs. This was contrary to our policy since we recognized that under Saddam teachers were effectively forced to join the party or lose their jobs. Clearly I had been wrong to give a political body like the Governing Council responsibility for overseeing the de-Baathification policy.

Now Chalabi wanted to add to the TAL an even broader disenfranchisement for former Baathists, which we believed would make hundreds of thousands more Iraqis ineligible for public office. Such a provision was certain to cause us major problems with the Sunnis. I sent word to the Kurds that in return for my supporting their positions, I expected them to help beat back this idea.

Meanwhile, Barzani went home to sulk. So now we'd had a walkout by the Shia on Friday and by the Kurds on Sunday. *Who could be next?*

There was no organized Sunni walkout, but I learned that Sheik Ghazi al-Yawar, the tribal Sunni from Mosul, had become so annoyed by the recent

Shia behavior that he was staying at home in a funk. I asked Samir Sumaidy, the dapper Sunni sheik from Anbar Province, to call Ghazi and try to get him back. Ghazi eventually pitched up, and I reconvened the small GC working group, which began reading through the texts of various disputed paragraphs.

Again, I served as chairman. Whenever we found a text on which there were significant differences, we sent a small team of Iraqis out of the room with Dick Jones or Scott Carpenter to try to find compromises. Sometimes this worked; sometimes not. Gradually across the hours we got a better sense of where the problems lay. I worked to keep the atmosphere light and it rarely became tense. It became clear we wouldn't finish by 2:00 P.M., so I suggested to Mohsen he postpone the plenary to 6:00 P.M.

At about 3:00 P.M. I sent out for food on the theory that we needed a breather and food would allow social talk.

During the break, I called Condi Rice and brought her up to date. She agreed we could accept the Kurdish proposal on ratification and, evidently hearing my fatigue, said, "Don't give up, Jerry."

"Don't worry," I told her.

Around 5:15 P.M., I reconvened with the Kurds, who agreed to alternative language on their militia, but started quibbling over the interpretation. I finally said, "Let's just go all the way back to the text you accepted three weeks ago." This broke the logjam. I told them we could accept their language on ratification, but reminded them that I expected their support for opposing the wide disenfranchisement Chalabi was proposing for former Baathists.

When I entered the plenary room, Council president Mohsen asked me to sit beside him as he chaired the meeting. Around 6:45 P.M. we launched into what promised to be a very long session to work through the remaining issues.

The procedure was simple, and grueling, moving through the preamble and all sixty-four articles of the TAL, one by one. Much of the text had been agreed the day before. But there were still problems, especially with Article 7 on the role of Islam. I persuaded Mohsen that we should skip over this article in the first round, in the hopes that agreement on subsequent articles would build momentum for compromise on this most sensitive issue.

The GC plugged away at the text and finally turned to Islam at 9:30 P.M. For the next two hours this was the only subject on the table. It was clear that there was still no consensus on the language that we had negotiated the night before with the working group—and which Rubaie had "cleared" with Sistani at 2:00 A.M. The Sunnis were still unhappy and said so. Dara Nor al-Din, the respected

Kurdish judge, arguing against the language prohibiting laws against Islam's tenets, gave an eloquent recital of the non-Islamic roots of Iraqi jurisprudence. But clearly this was not going to move the Shia.

Meanwhile, to keep us on our toes, the Kurds were telling our staff that they wanted to reopen the question of restrictions on the internal deployment of the army, which we had resolved weeks before. I sent them word that our entire deal was off if they did. They receded. And so it went.

By 11:15 P.M., it was apparent that the Kurds were going to support the latest Shia language on Islam, leaving the Sunnis isolated. Rubaie was telling people that he "would not change a word in the text" since it had been cleared with Sistani, a point certainly not calculated to make it easier for the Sunnis to come aboard. It also revived Kurdish concerns.

I felt that the debate had run its course. Everyone had had his say. It was time for action. I sensed an opportunity for a deal when one of the Sunnis recommended that a reference to "democratic values" be added into Article 7.

I suggested to Mohsen that he call a break and then took Rubaie aside to recommend that he propose adding into the article on Islam language referring to democratic principles. I persuaded him that he didn't have to check such an obvious point with Sistani. He agreed. So when the GC reconvened a little before midnight, I whispered to Mohsen to call on Rubaie.

Dr. Rubaie made an eloquent speech, regretting if his outspoken position on Islam had offended anyone. He had heard his "brothers" speak about Article 7 and in particular had noted their desire to balance the reference to the tenets of Islam with a reference to democratic principles. He suggested an amendment to the text, which would read that no law could be enacted that "contradicts the universally agreed tenets of Islam, the principles of democracy or the rights cited in Chapter 2 of the law."

Now for the first time in the marathon session, I asked for the floor, and after congratulating the Council on the seriousness of the discussion of this sensitive issue, said that we urged the adoption of Rubaie's amendment.

We were over the hump.

Between midnight and 3:00 A.M., the mood was alternately light and very grave. Having Article 7 behind us helped build psychological momentum for success. It was beginning to dawn on the Council that they were actually going to make it. Compromises became easier and we moved ahead quickly. Mohsen, exhausted, asked Pachachi to take the chair from him at about 1:30 while he rested.

At 2:15 A.M., Mahmoud Othman, a voluble Kurd, proposed to end the session, complaining that he was tired and hungry and wanted to go home and come back the next day. I whispered to Pachachi to resist, noting that Monday and Tuesday were major Shia holidays and we had to finish tonight.

Meanwhile on the margins of the conference room, Chalabi's nephew, Sam Chalabi, who had been very helpful in drafting the TAL, was raising questions with our staff about Article 58, which for us was the brightest of red lines. This article was in effect our "security agreement" providing the legal rationale for our post-sovereignty troop presence. Over the past month, we had painstakingly worked through this text with individual Council members, including Ahmad Chalabi, and the blood of nameless bureaucratic martyrs was written into every word of these three paragraphs. We did not want to reopen the text. So I had my team, led by Dick and Scott, go off with our lawyers and Chalabi's nephew to see if we could solve his problem without provoking a big floor debate.

This didn't seem to work.

At 3:00 A.M. I took Ahmad Chalabi aside and asked what he was trying to accomplish.

He said he wanted to make clear that after June 30, Iraq would be sovereign and that although our forces would stay, the occupation was indeed over. He wanted to add a sentence that nothing after June 30 should give the impression that the CPA continued to exercise sovereignty. I told him that was fine by me if it helped, though I noted that elsewhere in the TAL we explicitly said the CPA and GC would be dissolved on that date. That worked and we got past this article with no further discussion.

By 3:45 A.M., the excitement in the room was palpable as we moved through the final articles. Governing Council deputies, staff, and translators began spontaneously to gather behind the Council members seated at the large oval table, one, then two, then three deep, and cameras came out of people's pockets. We were around the last bend and the finish line was in sight. History was about to be made.

When the last article was done, Mohsen, now rested and back in the chair, gave a sincere, mercifully short speech thanking the Coalition.

I thanked the Governing Council for the opportunity to have been invited to sit at the table with them. They had made history today and would all look back on the day with pride. Their efforts had put Iraq again at the forefront of the region. This was a victory not just for the Council but for 25 million Iraqis. On November 15, we had together put Iraq on the path to a peaceful democratic state, and we had just taken a huge step along that path. Iraq had a future of hope, and I thanked them for their extraordinary work and understanding. "Ladies and gentlemen," I concluded, "we got it!"

Ahmad Chalabi rose to propose that the entire text be adopted unanimously and that was the only vote taken in the entire process. Pachachi closed the historic meeting by suggesting that the Governing Council and invited guests reconvene on March 3, after the Shiite holiday of Ashura, to sign the historic Transitional Administrative Law.

It was 4:20 A.M., March 1, 2004.

When we got back to the palace, I found two long-forgotten beers in the fridge, and Dick and I toasted our success. I called Rice. She was delighted and said she'd brief the president.

Later, he called, full of joy and praise for the work.

"I haven't pulled three consecutive all-nighters since Yale," I said. "And then it was usually for the wrong reason."

He laughed. "You probably got C's back then, Bremer, but this one's an A."

Unfortunately, the good feelings didn't last long. Later that day, Pete the station chief brought in what he called "credible evidence" that Zarqawi was planning to assassinate Sistani.

"This sounds like a page out of Zarqawi's book," I said. "He told bin Laden that he planned to attack the Shia leadership, and killing Sistani during Ashura has got to be a top priority."

"They don't come any higher," Pete said.

I worried what would happen to the country if one of Zarqawi's suicide bombers penetrated the concentric rings of troops and security guards around Najaf. The report called for immediate action. So I sent Sistani a warning message and dispatched aides to meet his security chief in Najaf to offer to help protect him during the Ashura holiday, when the city would be jammed with two million pilgrims.

How valid is this threat? I wondered.

I didn't have long to wait.

On Tuesday, March 2, the first day of Ashura, at least six rockets and bombs exploded in Karbala near the mosque of the Imam Hussein ibn-Ali, killing 112 pilgrims and maiming hundreds more. There were similar, less destructive, attacks at the main Shiite mosque in Baghdad, where my friend Ayatollah Hussein al-Sadr led the congregation.

I immediately sent a message to Ayatollah Sistani: "The terrorists are trying to knock Iraq off its path to a safe and democratic future. They will not succeed . . . with patience and faith in God, Iraq has a bright future."

That evening, Dhia brought the ayatollah's reply. He was outraged and worried and asked, "Why can't the Coalition stop these attacks?" Sistani said he was trying to cool things down, but there were limits to what he could do.

In my statement to the Iraqi people that day, I said that Zarqawi and his terrorists knew that when democracy came to Iraq, there would be no pretext for attacks. "Zarqawi has admitted that the terrorists are in a race against time. It is a race they will lose. They will lose because the Iraqi people want and will have democracy, freedom, and a sovereign Iraqi government."

Meanwhile, Muqtada continued his depredations in the south. One of the policemen he had kidnapped was released and told an Iraqi magistrate that the Mahdi Army had tortured him in Muqtada's "prison," where he also heard women screaming in the night. I encouraged General Sanchez to be ready to support Muqtada's arrest after the holidays were over, but Greenstock said that this would be a difficult time to go after him.

"There will never be a good time, Jeremy," I replied, noting that Muqtada's "army" had grown from 200 last August when I first urged his arrest to over 6,000 today.

Because of the Ashura attacks, the Governing Council's March president, Bahr al-Uloum, declared a three-day mourning period and delayed the TAL signing ceremony to Friday, March 5.

Don Hamilton, my speechwriter, who also kept track of polls, brought some light, if bitter relief to the week. "Look at this, Jerry," he said, dropping the latest poll on my desk. It showed that all across Iraq, people considered caucuses to be the best way to choose the interim government. But now it was too late because it was clear that Brahimi was moving toward simply appointing the interim government. I couldn't help reflecting later with the Governance Team, however, that our much-ridiculed caucus system would have produced a broader Iraqi participation in choosing the interim government.

On March 4, I received another letter from Ayatollah Sistani. It was a bombshell. He was unhappy about the TAL "draft"—the very document which Rubaie said he'd approved five days earlier. The law, he said, was "not democratic" because it allowed a two-thirds majority in any three provinces to veto the permanent constitution. He could not accept any "Kurdish veto" of the constitution and said that if this provision stayed in the TAL, he would have to speak out against it.

For more than ten months, the ayatollah and I had conducted a wide-ranging and friendly dialogue. Now everything was on the line. I knew that undoing the TAL's many compromises—which had been approved unanimously by the Governing Council—would be disastrous.

Following decades' experience as a diplomat, I tried to hide an iron fist inside my velvet glove. The TAL, I wrote Sistani, "reflects a careful balance of competing interests, hopes, and fears among Iraqis. We cannot withdraw the article on ratification. This would collapse the consensus, which would signal to the terrorists that they can derail our efforts to build a democratic and free Iraq . . . If you insist, your worst nightmare will occur at a time when your country can least afford it." Bravely, Emad Dhia once again boarded a Black Hawk for the trip to Najaf.

I discovered just how serious our problems were when Dr. Rubaie asked to see me at 10:00 P.M. on March 4. Now, less than twenty-four hours before the scheduled signing of the TAL, he came with a list of eight changes Sistani wanted in the agreed text, including the language on ratification. I told Rubaie I didn't see how we could operate this way. The entire Governing Council had adopted the text by consensus three days before.

"You Shia are playing with fire now," I fumed, "and risking the collapse of the entire process." I told him of the letter I had just sent Sistani about the dangers of fiddling with the agreed text. Chagrined, Rubaie agreed and said he would try to get Sistani to understand.

But the day was not yet done, for we now learned that the Shia had been caucusing for hours in Bahr al-Uloum's house, trying to persuade the Kurds to drop their demand for the clause on ratification. So I asked to see Bahr al-Uloum, and the diminutive, energetic fellow showed up a little after midnight. He begged me to "resolve" the issue between the Shia and Kurds. I declined and said that the Shia had agreed to the TAL three days earlier, had now created the problem, and would have to resolve it. He was disappointed, and as he left said he still hoped to go ahead with the signing ceremony the next day. I told him we could accept any phrasing on ratification they and the Kurds agreed to and wished him luck.

At a little after 2:00 A.M., I called Rice to brief her on the latest. I stressed that we wanted to keep the pressure on the Shia to solve this crisis and that we still hoped, somehow, to have the signing ceremony at 4:00 P.M. As I fell into an exhausted sleep, I was not confident we'd make it.

March 5 was a sad and poignant day, even by Iraqi standards. As dawn broke, we knew there was a good chance that many Shia, acting on Sistani's instructions, would refuse to sign the TAL. First, I received Sistani's reply. It didn't bode well.

"We appreciate the Ambassador's hard work. We are committed to the success of this process." But he could not accept the veto. "Can the blacks of America veto the vote of the American people? Can the Spanish people of America veto the entire will of the American people?"

This phrase caused Roman Martinez to joke that now *he* was offended since the ayatollah "has insulted my people."

Before the wheels had come off the process, I had agreed to go on the American morning TV shows to trumpet this "great day for Iraqi democracy." Given developments, this was going to be a hard act because I had to assert with a smile that all was well, knowing that we might be headed to disaster. I told Francie on the phone that I felt like a deckhand on the *Titanic*, saying, "Scraping sound? What scraping sound? It's just some guys moving the furniture around belowdecks."

Blissfully unaware of the brewing crisis, many Council members arrived at the GC building at 2:00 P.M. in their best clothes, with extended families in tow to witness history. For about an hour, they milled around, happily taking pictures and congratulating each other.

My staff reported that the Shia were still in caucus and that there had been a shouting match over the phone between some of them and Sistani's son about whether they could sign the TAL. At about 3:00 P.M., Talabani entered the room and had a whispered conversation with Barzani, who apparently was hearing for the first time about the Shia intransigence. He became visibly agitated.

Pachachi told me that five of the GC's thirteen Shia were in the room so we had a quorum and could get started. I disagreed and instructed our staff to stay out of the fight and "let the pressure build on the Shia."

At about 3:30 P.M., Chalabi and Rubaie arrived and called Barzani out for a private meeting. We now learned that the Shia were split, with several wanting to sign the TAL. Chalabi, apparently, was threatening to resign if the GC wouldn't sign. Jaafari and Rubaie allegedly were in favor, too. I told the staff that the split might prove useful to us.

Over the next two hours, there was much motion but little progress. I briefed Rice or her deputy Steve Hadley about once every half hour, as we watched the time for the 4:00 P.M. signing ceremony come and go. Chalabi reentered, pulled Pachachi and Rubaie aside in the back room, and sent word he would like me to join them. We sat at a dining table. Chalabi said that the Shia "want to find a solution."

"What do you have to offer to help find one?" I asked.

They had nothing to offer. So I suggested Chalabi might consider asking

Talabani what the Kurds wanted and perhaps a way forward could be found. But Dick Jones learned that the Kurdish price for dropping their ratification article was the immediate turnover to them of Kirkuk. This clearly was unacceptable.

Now several of the Sunnis came to me and said, "Look, we've got a quorum here in the room. Let's just call the meeting to order and you can sign the law yourself as administrator."

"No," I said. "You Iraqis have to do it. In four months we'll be gone and you'll have to learn to sort things out yourselves."

Word reached the room that one of Hakim's associates had told the press that the Shia refused to sign the TAL because it "gives the Kurds a veto."

In response, the Kurds unleashed Othman, who immediately denounced the Shiite spokesman to the press. Neither remark helped matters, so I had a Governance member call Dr. Adel, huddled with Hakim at his house, to get them to "correct the record," which they did. I asked Talabani to muzzle Othman, which he did.

It was now 5:30 P.M., and we were an hour and a half late for the signing ceremony. Rice told me the situation looked "really bad" on TV. Dan Senor confirmed that the huge press corps assembled for the ceremony was getting antsy.

"There are hundreds of reporters over there, staring at a table with twenty-five pens on it, a children's choir waiting to sing. It's a disaster. I should go background them."

I agreed. "Emphasize that democracy is a messy process."

Off he went to the most difficult press briefing he'd ever held.

At 7:37 P.M., the Governing Council was finally called to order after the Shia arrived from their caucus. March Council president Bahr al-Uloum was in the chair. Twenty-one principals were present.

Bahr al-Uloum apologized for the delay convening (almost six hours) and added that Article 61 on ratifying the permanent constitution had led to "changes in positions. The principle of consensus must be retained." We find ourselves in a "tragic situation," he said, acknowledging that there were several points of view and adding that he respected their proponents. The Shia did not want to abandon the process; they wanted to resolve the problem. "So," he asked, "should we delay the subject for another time?"

This question sparked a firestorm of protest. Several members pointedly noted that the entire text had been approved only four days before. It wasn't they who were changing their positions.

At this, Bahr al-Uloum became agitated. "This session is over. If I am not suitable to manage the meeting and am subjected to severe criticism, then I will decline to chair it." He suddenly rose from his chair and shuffled angrily toward the door amid considerable shouts and confusion from the others at the table.

His son and Chalabi jumped up and whispered to him. He returned, still gesticulating and muttering, to his seat.

The bickering continued. For the next several hours, I watched in silence as the Iraqis learned hard lessons about the need for flexibility and compromise in a democratic system.

Several times as the evening wore on, Condi Rice suggested that we put pressure on the Kurds to recede from their position on ratification. I disagreed. My concern was the serious strategic consequences of pressuring the Kurds to drop an agreed text to placate Sistani. This might give us a short-term win for the TV cameras. But if we forced the Kurds to cave while the U.S. was still robustly present in Iraq, there was little hope for a secular, united Iraq once we left. Far better, I argued, to let the Shia "stew" and see if they could face down Sistani.

To accelerate this process, I sent Dick to visit the Shia during one of their caucuses. He was blunt with them, saying they were jeopardizing a historic compromise and asking them to think hard about how they would "pay" the Kurds for going back on their Article 61 deal. On his return he gleefully reported he'd never seen a gloomier lot in his life. The pressure was starting to work.

Nonetheless, by 10:30 P.M. all attempts to find compromises among the Council members had failed. An agitated Bahr al-Uloum whispered to me that he needed time to visit Najaf to consult Sistani and other ayatollahs. I suggested a break to take stock of matters.

During the break, Talabani told me he was not budging on the ratification article. Next I spoke to Barzani and reminded him that we were the Kurds' allies, and saw the situation the same way they did. "But clearly the Shia have backed themselves into a corner and need time to work with Sistani." I asked if he could give them one day to go to Najaf. After complaining that he had already delayed returning to his mountaintop so he could be present at the planned signing ceremony, and protesting again about "the turbans," Barzani reluctantly agreed.

When I reported this to Bahr al-Uloum, he insisted he needed *two* days in Najaf. Fed up by now, I said, "You go see if you can persuade Barzani. I've done all I can." They held a whispered conversation in which Barzani agreed to give the Islamist Shia the weekend to try to resolve the problems with Sistani. But he added that he would go home the next morning, leaving his able deputy, Dr. Rowsch Shaways, to represent him. Back in the chair, Bahr al-Uloum announced that the Shia would need two days "to get final results." Then there would be a final decision session. "I hope you will all stand with us and be patient."

In my last call to Rice I admitted that our strategy of letting the Shia feel all the pressure was very high-risk. "There's a significant chance that they won't be able to bring Sistani around, and we'll never get the damn thing signed."

At the end of another long day, I gathered my weary Governance Team and told them to work on yet another "worst-case scenario" paper analyzing our options should the Shia return from Najaf empty-handed. We all agreed it was not a pretty prospect.

Over the next two days, as the Shia made their trek to Najaf, I tended to ongoing matters. On Saturday, I chaired one of my regular meetings with the Iraqi cabinet and emphasized that as part of our anticorruption plan I wanted each of them to nominate an inspector general for his ministry. I also told them I expected each minister to nominate at least one woman for deputy minister. Sunday morning, I went to work out with the Iraqi soccer team in Baghdad's Olympic Stadium and to share their joy in Iraq having just been accepted back into the Olympic movement on February 29.

Late Sunday afternoon Dr. Rubaie arrived back from Najaf and came straight to my office with a broad smile.

"It was a forceps delivery," he said with medical humor, "but we got what we wanted." After endless palaver, Ayatollah Sistani had agreed to allow his followers on the Governing Council to sign the Transitional Administrative Law.

"Al hamdulillah," thank God, I said. The GC members had in effect gotten Sistani to understand that if he wanted them to be credible political leaders, he couldn't micromanage them in politics. Our risky bet had paid off with a significant round won in favor of a secular Iraq.

Monday, March 8, was International Women's Day. I opened the first of nine Women's Centers we planned for Baghdad, a chance to emphasize the importance we attached to helping Iraq's women. As we sat on the floor and ate sweets and dates, I told the women at the center that the TAL required Iraq's electoral law to guarantee that 25 percent of Iraq's parliament be women, one of the highest percentages in the world.

"We are delighted with the results," their spokesman replied. "And Iraqi women are ready to participate, again after so many years, in the country's life."

The day's big event was the signing of the TAL. In our private meeting before the ceremony, the GC members spoke at length about the importance of this interim constitution. Chalabi thanked the others for giving the Shia time to consult in Najaf. Talabani said this was the best constitution anywhere in the region, and the group's sole Christian, Yonadam Kanna, said poetically that "today civilization begins anew in the cradle of civilization." At 1:00 P.M. we trooped from the Council building to the nearby convention center, greeted by a huge gaggle of press assembled for the signing.

Council President Bahr al-Uloum spoke with the simple eloquence of a respected spiritual leader. "We gather today for a great historical meeting in the spirit of brotherhood and true love that unites all Iraqi people. All the brothers, when they spoke, put the interests of the nation above all other interests. Let it be known that we came to this place and we are all one person today and one opinion."

Pachachi, who had worked so hard to shape the TAL's revolutionary chapter on individual rights, delivered a short, eloquent speech. Barzani spoke movingly. "For the first time in my life I feel like an Iraqi." Each member moved to a table at the front of the room to sign the most remarkable document in Iraq's long history.

The little boy who had chanted his poem at the 9 Nisan ceremonies back in October gave a rousing repeat performance to close the ceremonies.

Thank God and Amen.

Chapter 12
HITTING THE WALL

■ BAGHDAD
APRIL 2004

The television lights were bright and my eyes were tired. For three weeks my life had been even more stressful and my days longer than usual, and it showed. It was Friday, April 23, and we were in the midst of the Coalition's gravest crisis.

The technicians made final checks for camera angles and volume and signaled me to start. The red camera light blinked on.

> Good evening.
> Iraq faces a choice.
> You could take the path which leads to a new Iraq, a peaceful, democratic Iraq, an Iraq of political freedom and economic opportunity, an Iraq where the majority is not Sunni, Shia, Arab, Kurd or Turkmen, but Iraqi. This is the path to a bright and hopeful future.
> Or you could take the path which leads to the dark Iraq of the past where violence and fear rule, where power comes from a gun, and where only the powerful and ruthless are secure . . .

For the next twenty-one minutes I laid out the brutal facts for the Iraqi people. They and we were under assault by antidemocratic forces, forces which did not share our common vision for a peaceful and democratic Iraq.

> . . . Thousands of conversations with you over the past year have made me certain that the vast majority of Iraqis reject the brutality and darkness of the old days. You have told me you want a new Iraq that honors the best of your past, but provides freedom, equality, and opportunity for all.
> The Coalition shares your vision of Iraq's future, a future of hope. Working together we can create the future you want.

But we have much to do as we walk this path.

The enemies, domestic and foreign, of your bright future are trying to force you to take the path that leads backwards to brute force, division, and hatred. These antidemocratic forces will not disappear by themselves, but working together we can defeat them. We in the Coalition will do our part to restore security. But you must do your part, too.

If you do not defend your beloved country it will not be saved . . .

Three simultaneous crises since the signing of the TAL had driven us to this critical point.

The first crisis concerned the political process—yet again. We needed to convince Ayatollah Sistani and his followers on the Governing Council to support the return of Lakhdar Brahimi.

Sistani and the Shia were deeply disappointed with the report Brahimi had issued after his initial fact-finding trip in February. Brahimi had confirmed that elections for a national assembly were not possible before the end of 2004. But he had not proposed an alternative to the caucuses. So we needed Brahimi back in Iraq to build a consensus among the Iraqis, and with Sistani, on a mechanism for choosing the interim government to which we would give sovereignty.

Many Shiites were angry that Brahimi's report had not been sufficiently critical of Saddam's brutality. And they were suspicious of him as a Sunni Arab nationalist. Shiite members of the Governing Council had circulated a picture of Brahimi smoking a cigar with Saddam years earlier.

On his Web site on March 9, Sistani had again voiced "reservations about the November 15 Agreement" and added that "any law drafted for the transition period will not gain legitimacy unless approved by the elected national assembly."

In the following days, Sistani's colleagues, including those on the Governing Council, broadened their attacks on the TAL. Pamphlets were circulated at mosques in the south denouncing the interim constitution, creating an atmosphere of uncertainty about the political process.

Once more, on March 9, I dispatched Emad Dhia to Najaf to tell the ayatollah that no single group would be completely satisfied with the document because it represented compromises. I repeated that the U.S. would do all it could to ensure elections were held according to the TAL timetable. I argued that it was in Iraq's interest, and *his*, to bring the UN back.

Dhia had returned that evening with Sistani's reply. He was still "disappointed in the TAL," and noncommittal on Brahimi: "If he comes, will he listen?"

Meanwhile, the Governing Council was stalling, unwilling to invite Brahimi back, and it looked as if the political crisis would deepen. I dispatched Governance staff to lobby Council members and took advantage of a trip to Al-Kut, the capital of the eastern province of Wasit, to meet with Sistani's representative there. I told him that the TAL provided the only agreed path to Iraqi democracy. Bob Blackwill and I also made the rounds with the GC heavyweights.

Condi Rice was increasingly exasperated by the GC's inaction. "You simply have got to get them to invite Brahimi back. There is no Plan B." The stage was set for another dramatic meeting with the full Council, and on Wednesday, March 17, I warned them that they were risking a confrontation not just with the UN, but also with the United States. "And if the UN cannot help form an interim government," I said, "the Iraqi people will know who to blame."

This provoked chagrin around the oval table. In one of his usual complex discourses, Jaafari noted that Iraq could benefit from UN "participation and assistance," and conceded that it had actually been the GC that had first invited the UN to return to Iraq in January. So the Council reluctantly drafted a letter of invitation to the UN to bring Brahimi back.

But when I spoke with Rice that night, I balanced this welcome news by observing that Sistani's opposition to the TAL still presented a major obstacle. And "as the political process goes forward, there's bound to be more violence."

For much of March, renewed violence by Muqtada al-Sadr and his Mahdi Army was our second crisis. The radical Shiite preacher became more brazen. With a heavily armed cohort of bodyguards, he took over the main mosque in Kufa, sister city of Najaf, where the Prophet Muhammad's son-in-law had led worshippers in the 7th century.

This sacrilegious act symbolized Muqtada's determination to gain power by force. He was again wearing a white burial shroud over his dark cloak when he preached on Fridays at Kufa. Ostensibly, this symbolized his own thirst for martyrdom, but was more likely a crude charade meant to impress gullible followers, and to disguise the fact that, unlike his father, he had limited theological training.

Like many rabble-rousers, Muqtada al-Sadr was a charismatic orator. His Friday sermons had become unofficial pilgrimages for a still small but growing number of rootless and dispossessed Shia. And his oratory became more extreme as he called for resistance not just to the Coalition but to the Governing Council.

Then on March 12, members of his Mahdi Army attacked a gypsy town in Qadisiya Province near Najaf. They knocked down houses, burned the ruins, and dragged off eighteen "apostate" men who were later savagely tortured in Muqtada's "prison" in Najaf. Several dozen women and children from the town were missing.

On March 14, frustrated by Washington's inaction, I asked General Sanchez if he couldn't round up some of Muqtada's cronies. "The Iraqis have warrants for the arrest of about a dozen of them implicated in the al-Khoei murder."

"We'll work it, sir," he promised.

One of his problems was that Najaf, Kufa, and vicinity were the area of operations (AO) of a hodgepodge of Coalition forces under Polish command—Spanish, Bulgarian, Ukrainian, and Central American units, each with its own Rules of Engagement—and each reporting back to their own nervous capitals.

On March 23, I decided to get a firsthand assessment of the situation and flew down to Najaf to consult the regional CPA officers there.

Phil Kosnett, another able State Department professional, now the CPA rep in Najaf, told me that Muqtada had stationed at least sixty well-armed Mahdi militiamen inside the main Kufa mosque.

"We've got to get them out of there," I said.

Mike Gfoeller, who knew the conditions well, was troubled. "It's a lose-lose situation," he said. "If Coalition troops go in there and kill Mahdi fighters and shoot up the shrine, the militiamen become instant martyrs, and Muqtada's got his proof that we're Crusader devils."

"Yeah, but we can't just let him run loose," I said. "If the Kufa mosque is the head of the snake, let's at least try to chop up the body."

"It's not so easy, sir," Mike said. He pointed out that the Spanish troops, responsible for Najaf, were refusing to take any steps. Their lack of resolve emboldened Muqtada.

The next day I was jolted awake at 4:10 A.M. by another rocket attack on the Green Zone. The day went steadily downhill from there.

We received reports that Muqtada's Mahdi Army was broadly engaged across the south, setting up roadblocks, kidnapping, and torturing Iraqi policemen. And we now had firsthand testimony from a woman who said she had been repeatedly raped after being imprisoned by Muqtada's thugs. I said to Dick Jones, "These guys are starting to remind me of the Taliban."

I called General Abizaid and expressed my concern. "We're at risk of losing control of the whole damn region to Muqtada's militia," I said. "The Spanish refuse to act."

"We'll get on it, Jerry," he promised.

On March 26, Mike Gfoeller reported that Muqtada had attacked CPA-sponsored democracy centers in several southern cities. And the same day Coalition troops were drawn into a firefight with combined Mahdi Army and Badr Corps militiamen in the region. "Things aren't looking good down there," Sanchez told me.

After Friday prayers that day, Muqtada al-Sadr climbed the pulpit in the Kufa mosque and unleashed his most vicious diatribe to date. "No! No! to Jews!" he screamed. "No! No! to Israel! No! No! to America!" After damning the Coalition as a Zionist-American conspiracy, Muqtada praised the 9/11 terrorist attacks as "a miracle and a blessing from God."

CPA General Counsel Scott Castle informed me that Muqtada's statements were a clear violation of the law against incitement to violence because they could provoke civil disorder, including attacks on Coalition civilians and troops. "We have abundant grounds for issuing our own arrest warrant for him," he said.

I doubted Washington would support such a dramatic action.

Muqtada's newspaper mouthpiece had been encouraging violence since the summer when it printed the names of Iraqis who should be killed for working with the Coalition. Several had been assassinated. Now the paper printed the full text of Muqtada's latest inflammatory sermon calling for civil disorder, including his praise of the 9/11 attacks. I ordered the paper closed for sixty days for violating the law against inciting violence.

The Iraqi police, backed by Coalition forces, had little difficulty closing the paper's Sadr City offices. But by the time the police had sealed the doors and were leaving, an angry crowd of Shiites were shouting insults and threats outside the building.

I asked Rick Sanchez to come up with a plan to control Muqtada's militia in the south.

"Maybe we can begin to squeeze him in a serious way," I told Dick Jones.

"Maybe, Jerry," Dick said. "But we've been down this road before."

Meanwhile a third crisis was brewing in the west: security in Fallujah was steadily going to hell. Fallujah had a well-earned reputation as a tough town. A city of 300,000, Fallujah sprawled across a bend in the Euphrates, the crossroads of several traditional caravan trails west through the desert to Syria, which became useful smugglers' routes after the Gulf War when Saddam bypassed UN sanctions. When the British had taken over Mesopotamia from the Ottomans after World War I, the city was the center of a bloody rebellion. In an effort to control the town, Saddam Hussein had recruited loyal members of his elite military units and intelligence service from local tribes.

In April 2003, the 82nd Airborne Division had assumed responsibility for all of Al-Anbar Province west of Baghdad. But even when augmented by the 3rd Armored Cavalry Regiment and hundreds of military police, the 82nd Airborne had been unable to establish adequate security in the province, especially in cities like Fallujah and Ramadi, farther west on the Euphrates. By March 2004, there was a de facto standoff in Fallujah: the 82nd ringed the city but effectively ceded control of its streets to the townsmen. Insurgents continued to use the urban sanctuary to ambush American troops, plant IEDs, and stockpile weapons. We had done little after the November shootdown of our Chinook helicopter or after the professional attack on the Fallujah police station in February that killed fourteen officers. By now, the 82nd—due to rotate home—was conducting a few spot patrols in the city.

I raised my concerns with Generals Abizaid and Sanchez. "The 82nd isn't realistic about Anbar," I said. "The situation is *not* going to improve until we clean out Fallujah."

Abizaid agreed with this assessment. Sanchez did not.

The job of occupying Anbar Province and destroying the insurgents' safe havens would pass to the 1st Marine Expeditionary Force under Lieutenant General Jim Conway. I remembered that it had been the 1 MEF that had balked at arresting Muqtada the previous August. But that was in the past. On March 22, I met with General Conway to discuss the future. His troops were beginning to flow into Iraq from bases in Kuwait and to take over the 82nd's area of operations (AO).

Conway was a quintessential Marine officer, lean, intelligent, and aggressive. When I asked about his overall intentions, he said he planned to show the Iraqis "both the palm frond and the hammer," Marine jargon for the carrot-and-stick approach I had long favored for the Sunni Triangle. "People out there are about to learn the meaning of the Marine Corps watchword," he said, " 'no better friend, no worse enemy.' "

Conway explained that he didn't like the 82nd Airborne's current approach. They were limiting patrols in the city to forty-five minutes. "I want my Marines to be able to go anywhere, anytime in our AO. I intend to demonstrate that ability as soon as we're set up." Conway then went through some of the operational plans he hoped to put in place.

This was what I'd hoped to hear. "In the next ninety days, it's vital to show that we mean business and that we'll back up Iraqi forces," I responded.

I felt more optimistic about Anbar Province than I had for months.

Meanwhile, the Oil for Food scandal, which had been brewing for months, again burst into the public eye. By March, it was clear that there were going to be a number of investigations into allegations of wrongdoing. The UN had appointed a special investigating team under former Federal Reserve Chairman Paul Volcker, and the British parliament was taking steps to look into the matter. The American Congress, too, would no doubt soon do the same.

We learned that Ahmad Chalabi was trying to persuade the Governing Council to take control of any Iraqi investigation. I certainly wanted to get all the facts out quickly. But I was concerned about letting a political body, the GC, conduct the investigation. My concerns were increased when we heard that Chalabi wanted to have the Governing Council issue a no-bid contract to an accounting firm to conduct the investigation.

So I decided that instead the Iraqi Board of Supreme Audit, a once-more independent and respected Iraqi government body dating from the 1920s, should be put in charge of the investigation. To ensure a coordinated effort, I issued an order on March 15 instructing all Iraqi ministries to identify, inventory, and safeguard all OFF records in their files. I provided a budget to the Board of Supreme Audit to oversee the investigation and designated the Board as the single point of contact for UN, British, and any other legitimate groups looking into the matter.

Chalabi made it clear he was not happy with this decision and tried to paint me as opposed to getting to the bottom of the scandal. This was not the case at all. I shared his desire to see the malfeasance of Iraqis and others brought to light. But I thought this should be done in a way untainted by Iraqi politics.

A few days later I wrote President Bush and laid out the CPA's objectives for the next ninety days. I predicted that as Iraq moved toward democracy, terrorist attacks would likely increase. I said that Iraq's security forces were still largely "under-trained and unreliable . . . We should not mislead ourselves or the Iraqis into thinking that they will be capable of handling security here in July. That will take many months, perhaps years."

I told the president that I saw an opportunity to use the next three months to broaden the representation in Iraq's infant political structures. "We need to get more Sunni and more moderate Shia representation into the interim government. Inclusiveness should trump simplicity in the process of setting up the government."

This last point was directed at the ever-anonymous "Washington officials" still telling the press that we should simply turn sovereignty over to the Governing Council. I told the president that to "provide a measure of continuity" in the new government, I intended to work with the Governing Council to ensure that a capable set of deputy ministers was chosen soon.

But this was another area where the GC failed in its duty. The Council nominated eighty-two people as deputy ministers, but after several weeks, could not even provide résumés for a third of them. It looked like this was "jobs for the boys" all over again.

Meanwhile, I pressed ahead with my campaign to establish institutions to fight corruption. In a meeting with the elected Baghdad City Council the third week of March, I acknowledged that many Iraqis were concerned about corruption. So was I. Corruption had flourished under Saddam. For the past twelve years, it had been official policy to circumvent UN sanctions, so corruption was institutionalized in many ministries. The rule of law had been destroyed.

I described for the City Council the three independent agencies the CPA had created to protect the public interest: The Commission on Public Integrity was the main element of Iraq's anticorruption laws. It would work alongside a revitalized Board of Supreme Audit and the newly established inspectors general assigned to every ministry.

"The three entities—the auditors, the inspectors general, and the commission—form an integrated approach intended to combat corruption at every level of government across the country," I told them.

I realized that there was bound to be corruption at many levels of Iraqi society in the months and years to come. But I also hoped that the independent anticorruption institutions we had created would eventually prevail.

I closed on an optimistic note. "The Coalition and its member states will stand with the Iraqi people as they build a future of hope for their children and for their children's children.

"And they will have that future of hope."

The Fallujah crisis broke into the open on the morning of Wednesday, March 31. A small convoy of SUVs carrying Blackwater USA security guards was ambushed in the center of Fallujah. The gunmen raked the Americans' car with AK-47s. Then the vehicle was set alight. Dancing in frenzy, a mob of townsmen dragged the smoldering corpses from the wreckage and ripped at the charred flesh with shovels. Then two blackened, dismembered bodies were strung from the girders of the city's main bridge across the river.

Television crews taped this grisly scene, and by afternoon the horrible images appeared on Arab satellite television. An edited tape was shown later that day on American networks. The images immediately became icons of the brutal reality of the insurgency, and underscored the fact that the Coalition military did not control Fallujah.

The next morning, Rick Sanchez reported that he had "landed hard" on General Conway for not having sent troops into the city as soon as the Marines had learned that the Blackwater men had been ambushed.

"What the hell was his answer?" I asked.

Conway had been waiting for the Iraqi police to call for help.

"What's your next move?" I demanded of Sanchez. "We've got to react to this outrage or the enemy will conclude we're irresolute."

"We're dusting off the operation we planned last fall," Rick answered, "the one to clean out Fallujah that was postponed when the minister of interior got cold feet about sending police to help sort out the town."

The political pot continued to boil. By early April, it was clear that many mainstream religious Shia were following Sistani's lead in criticizing the TAL. On April 2, Rice told me that Chalabi was increasingly seen as acting against American interests by sliding toward the Shia rejectionists. She said that the "prevailing sentiment" in Washington was to kick him off the Governing Council. I recommended caution. There were also risks in simply excluding him.

Dick Jones and I called on Ayatollah Hussein al-Sadr on April 4 to warn him of the dangers of attacking the TAL. I knew he was in close contact with the *marjaiya* in Najaf. I hoped he'd reason with Sistani.

Seated in his book-lined library, I asked, "If Ayatollah Sistani does manage to discredit the interim constitution, where does that leave the Shia and Iraq?"

The learned old cleric gazed at me over the rims of his glasses but did not immediately answer.

"Please remember the lessons of 1920," I said. "This interim constitution is the only way for Iraq to get an elected, constitutional government. Your people have waited over eighty years for this opportunity."

I thought of the torture this spiritually and physically resilient imam had endured under Saddam.

"We've waited for centuries, Ambassador," he finally said.

From his tone, I got the impression he would counsel the path of compromise to Ayatollah Sistani.

Maybe. Just maybe.

Back in my office later that morning, I read a brief report on the successful operation in Najaf late the previous night to arrest Mustafa al-Yacoubi, one of Muqtada's top lieutenants and an accused accomplice of Muqtada's in the 2003 murder of Ayatollah al-Khoei.

Finally, we're taking action.

The digital clock on my desk said 1202 Hours 4 April 2004 as I sat down to a hasty sandwich. Sue Shea buzzed me.

"General Sanchez on the line. Urgent."

"All hell is breaking loose with Muqtada, sir," he said. "We're getting reports from a lot of different sectors, Sadr City, Najaf . . . Al-Kut. Demonstrators flooding the streets. A lot of them carrying AKs and RPGs . . ."

Muqtada's people had been holding loud but nonviolent demonstrations since we'd shut down his newspaper. Now the mobs were armed, chanting, "No to Israel! No to America! Free Mustafa al-Yacoubi!" as they surged around Iraqi police stations and CPA offices. While the Mahdi Army had not yet fired on Iraqi authorities or Coalition forces, the demonstrators were being whipped into a fury.

"What's happening in Fallujah, Rick?"

I didn't want any spillover between the Marines' offensive in Anbar and a potentially explosive upheaval with Muqtada's gangs.

He told me that before sunrise a combined force of 1,300 Marines, Iraqi Civil Defense Corps, and New Iraqi Army troops had set up roadblocks around the city, establishing an armed cordon. Loudspeaker Humvees supported by armored vehicles entered Fallujah, announcing a dusk-to-dawn curfew and threatening to overwhelm insurgents who refused to turn in their arms and surrender. The situation there was just as complex and dangerous as the crisis we faced in Sadr City and the south.

Shortly, Sanchez called again. "Muqtada's people are really swarming around our bases . . . especially in Sadr City and down in Najaf. They seem to think they can get the Spanish to cave in."

Between Muqtada and Fallujah, the next hours were going to be decisive. I opened my laptop and began to tap out a record of these events.

1227 HOURS: Brig. Gen. Fulgencio Coll, the Spanish commander in Najaf, has been trying to "negotiate" with Muqtada's gangs after they started demanding Yacoubi's release. Phil Kosnett was there to stiffen various spines. This morning, the Spanish put out an idiotic statement about the Yacoubi arrest, saying that the Spanish did not conduct the operation, that it was done by "the Coalition from Baghdad," and that it was for Yacoubi's part in the killing of an American soldier. I've instructed Dan Senor to have the Ministry of Interior put out a statement that Yacoubi was arrested on an Iraqi arrest warrant for the murder of Ayatollah Khoei. The Spanish statement should be disavowed root and branch.

1241: Just got word that our CPA compound in Najaf is being attacked by several hundred Muqtada guys. Kosnett is calling for gunships and reinforcements. He says that the Salvadorans' Special Forces are fighting and the Spanish are refusing to fight. I got Sanchez's deputy Maj. Gen. Joe Weber down here and asked what they are doing to reinforce the CPA in Najaf. I said I thought CJTF should relieve the Spanish commander forthwith. I called the Spanish ambassador and gave him unshirted hell. He said he was uninformed but would contact Madrid.

1400: Sanchez is in the ops center now trying to get air support on scene. He called to report, "We have at least one U.S. soldier killed and several wounded inside our compound." They were running out of ammunition and need help fast. A hell of a situation.

1510: Ana Palacio, the Spanish foreign minister, called from Madrid to say she knew nothing of the problems in Najaf, had spoken to the prime minister who didn't believe the report of the Spanish behavior. I got Weber back down. He says the Spanish are still "sitting on their asses." They are taking the position that unless they are specifically fired upon themselves, they will not engage, this despite the fact that Americans and Iraqis are dying under their very eyes. They are sitting in tanks around the compound and doing nothing. It is a perfect outrage—I call it the "Coalition of the not-at-all-willing."

1600: I briefed Condi about the day's events. Said it appeared to be a "straightforward power grab" by Muqtada. We need to react vigorously. We must not let him get away with this.

•   •   •

As the crises developed, Dan Senor and I discussed the importance of my continuing to follow my schedule if at all possible. The Iraqi people and the international community were watching to see if the insurgents could disrupt the Coalition's activities and throw Iraq off its path to sovereignty. So despite the pressures today and as soon as I finished the call to Rice, I went to the Green Zone convention center for the announcement of the new Iraqi security institutions that would be among the most crucial elements of the interim government.

Since abolishing the Baathist Defense Ministry and the Mukhabarat intelligence service the previous May, we had labored to lay the foundation for responsible institutions to replace them. David Gompert, Senior Adviser for national security, had worked for months with Ayad Allawi, chairman of the GC's Security Committee, to delineate the powers and the responsibilities of the new Defense Ministry, the Iraqi National Intelligence Service (INIS), and the Ministerial Committee for National Security. Finding the right new defense minister and INIS director had been difficult. Many candidates with the requisite skills that David vetted turned out to be Sunni Baathists with blood on their hands. But eventually he had identified solid men for the jobs.

This afternoon April's Council President Barzani announced that the interim minister of defense was Ali Allawi—a kinsman of both Governing Council members Ayad Allawi and Ahmad Chalabi—and the former interim minister of trade. He was a moderate and religious Shiite, a financier with degrees in engineering, planning, and management and a strong record working against Saddam.

Mohammed Abdullah Mohammed al-Shehwani became interim director general of INIS. A Sunni, he'd joined the Iraqi Army in 1955 and risen to major general before being forced into exile by Saddam in 1984. Three of his sons had been killed by Saddam in the 1990s.

GC member and Sistani associate Dr. Mowaffak al-Rubaie was the new national security adviser.

Gompert had also come up with a plan to establish a mechanism to coordinate Iraq's security policy, the Ministerial Committee for National Security, effectively an Iraqi version of our National Security Council. Until the interim government selected a prime minister, I would chair meetings of this committee.

We followed two principles in establishing these institutions, both designed to avoid the return to one-man tyranny. The first was civilian control of the military and intelligence service, a basic element of the TAL. Our system distributed power among the officials responsible for national security, which made interministerial cooperation vital. The concept of collaborative crisis management would be quickly tested in the April emergencies.

We had established these procedures not a minute too soon; the crises grew more threatening hourly.

1725: On returning to my office, I learned that Muqtada's activities were spreading in the south. Phil Kosnett was on the phone from Najaf. I told him how much I admired his bravery and prayed for his safety and that of his colleagues. He said they were doing "OK" but were concerned about tonight. They do not have sufficient effective force on the ground to deal with a likely attack with RPGs and mortars after dark. They have requested CJTF-7 to send in "fast movers" as military jets are called. But the planes haven't arrived on station and the situation is deteriorating. He said the Spanish are still, unbelievably, not engaged and show no signs of becoming so. Frank Gallagher, the head of my Blackwater Personal Security Detail, reports that he is hearing from his guys in Najaf that they cannot hold the compound tonight.

1730: I got Gen. Weber and Brig. Gen. Barbara Fast to my office to tell them that Kosnett, who is not a military guy, and the Blackwater man, who is, both say they cannot hold out tonight. They report that the Apache gunships are on station but not firing and they have only two more hours of daylight. They are going to contact Sanchez who is now on the ground in Najaf to get his assessment. The F-16s are on their way. I also asked them to seal off the city so Sadr's reinforcements cannot get in.

1735: Mike Gfoeller reports that the Sadr forces took over a Najaf police station, stripped it of all weapons and have now moved to the mosque in Kufa in response to a call by Muqtada for his forces to regroup.

1740: Now we have a report that shots have been fired at our office in Amara and that large crowds are gathering in Karbala. Gfoeller reports hearing from his tribal contacts that an attack similar to that in Najaf is planned against the CPA office in Karbala tonight. Gen. Weber came back to report that we have a Special Forces company arriving "soon" in Najaf and available for employment there. They better hurry.

1755: This just in from Nasariyah: the Mahdi Army apparently took control of several bridges there yesterday (why didn't the Italians react then?). Today a large crowd of them marched on the CPA headquarters and got into a fight with the Italians. Results not known at this point.

Now a report that Muqtada's people are moving on our offices in Kirkuk. This is the one that has the greatest potential to set off a real explosion because the situation in the city is already so tense. We are working up our security in all the cities.

1800: As we await the next word on the attacks, the Station Chief has presented me with an overall assessment of the situation in Iraq, which was apparently requested a week ago by the DCI in Langley. It is over-the-top pessimistic. "Catastrophic" failure awaits us as a "progressive collapse of Iraq" is under way. Four pages of this, which begins to smell of a classic "cover your ass." The Agency has become so totally shell-shocked by the beating they've taken in recent years, that virtually everything they write only emphasizes the negative.

2200: Sanchez came back in to say that the situation in Sadr City was bad: An ambush of a Humvee in that sector this afternoon in which three Americans were killed. Sanchez ordered elements of the 1st AD to go into the area in force. They are to take back the police stations, which Sadr people had seized. Even now I can hear the distant tap of automatic fire from across the river.

2310: Just briefed Condi on the situation and she briefed the president. We will have a secure videoconference tomorrow morning because we simply don't have enough information right now to recommend a course to the president.

0025: (5 April) The situation in Al-Hillah is deteriorating. Several thousand Mahdi fighters are reportedly assembling near the CPA compound. Gfoeller asked the Polish Commander for a quick reaction force three hours ago and nothing has happened. I am pushing CJTF to get a move on. Muqtada has just issued a "fatwa" which calls on the Coalition to release all our prisoners and on the Iraqis to force the Coalition to leave Iraq. So the lines are drawn and even the people in Washington can now see them.

0035: I briefed Rich Armitage [Powell's deputy], Steve Hadley, George Tenet and Pete Pace on the situation and suggested that State instruct our embassies in Coalition partner countries to approach their governments early Monday European time saying that this is "a massive and direct challenge to the Coalition." We must respond forcefully to Muqtada. There are lots of people sitting on various fences to see how we react (other militia, tribes, etc.)—and all those pleasant folks in Fallujah. If we show weakness now we will be pushing Iraq to civil war. We expect our partners to support us, publicly and on the ground. Armitage asked us to send this in ASAP by cable so they can instruct posts. Armitage also had the good grace to note that I had been calling for action against Muqtada for months and now it was "being forced upon us" (at a time when it is much harder than it would have been, I might add).

0100: The Chief of Police of Baghdad has heard that Muqtada is going to call a general strike in Baghdad this morning. He will put women and children in front of his demonstrations with the shooters behind. Lovely group.

0130: Dick and I have decided that getting some sleep is probably the best use of our time for the next few hours. They can always find us if they need us.

But before crawling into bed, I managed to complete an e-mail to Francie. For several months, I'd been planning to make a quick trip home for Easter. We'd also planned to celebrate her mother's ninetieth birthday with a large family re-union at our house in Vermont. I hadn't been out of Iraq since January. Easter was only six days away, but by now it was clear I couldn't leave Iraq. "We are faced with a full-fledged coup and we must react forcefully or lose the game," I wrote to her with regret. "I have to stay here."

As sleep gradually came over me, I remembered splintered details of the Marines' Fallujah operational plan. Early today, the 1 MEF would tighten the cordon around the city, probing toward the center. Troops would now be drag-ging themselves out of their sleeping bags, heating their MREs for breakfast, checking ammunition and grenades. In Sadr City, Al-Hillah, Najaf, and across the south, thousands of Mahdi Army zealots were also waking in the predawn cool, boiling water for tea, preparing for martyrdom.

The crises are converging.

The first reports on the morning of April 5 were that the Mahdi Army had made no further attacks on CPA posts in the southern cities. But Muqtada's militia were still swarming over Al-Hillah, Karbala, and Najaf, defying Coalition orders to disperse. The Salvadorans and Hondurans had engaged the enemy, but the heavier Spanish mechanized infantry forces had stayed out of the fight. In Baghdad, the 1st Armored Division had recaptured the four police stations overrun in Sadr City, at the cost of eight more American lives. We also had re-ports that Muqtada was now in contact with Sunni insurgents in Anbar Province.

Phil Kosnett e-mailed from Najaf that Spanish General Coll was seeking a "political" solution to the Muqtada crisis by offering the local governorship to a

Badr Corps militia commander, whom our intelligence identified as a possible Iranian agent (although Coll may not have been aware of this information). Coll seemed concerned that the Coalition would try to dislodge Muqtada's gunmen during the major Shiite holiday of Arbaeen, which fell on April 11 this year. Arbaeen, marking the fortieth day of mourning after Ashura, would likely draw millions of Shia pilgrims to Karbala and Najaf.

I sent Kosnett a clear message: tell General Coll to stop messing in politics and to start obeying orders. Only I had authority to appoint governors, and weeks earlier I had barred the Badr Corps man from office. Under *no* circumstances was he to negotiate with Muqtada. Coll was way "out of his lane." We would let justice run its course with respect to all of Muqtada's followers accused by the Iraqis of murder. If General Coll needed reinforcements to regain control of the cities in his area of operations, he should request them from CJTF. Phil delivered this message forcefully to the Spanish general and concluded his report to me by stating there could be "no political solution to the takeover of Najaf."

Rick Sanchez and I then discussed options to stop Muqtada's militia and eventually to regain control of Najaf. We recognized the latter was risky at the best of times and impossible during the week of Arbaeen. Still, Rick could reposition reliable Coalition forces, stiffened by American units, to prevent Muqtada from sending Mahdi Army reinforcements in the long caravans of battered white Kia minibuses carrying legitimate pilgrims to the holy city for the holiday.

And after Arbaeen, and *if* Washington concurred, we could crack down on Muqtada once and for all.

After Rick left, I did three American morning TV shows. The interviewers all had the same question: in view of the sudden explosion of violence, and calls by several senators, did the Coalition still plan to return Iraqi sovereignty on June 30? My answer had to be unequivocal: wavering now would cost lives on all sides.

"The president, who is the guy calling the shots, has been pretty clear that June 30 is the date we are going to stick to," I said.

The hosts unsuccessfully tried to budge me.

Sanchez sent word that the Marines were pushing through Fallujah's outlying districts and beginning to encounter resistance. "Nothing major yet," he said.

But Al-Jazeera Television was showing footage of what they claimed were unarmed civilian dead in Fallujah. That afternoon, the network broadcast an audiotape from the terrorist Abu Musab Zarqawi, threatening to "harvest" the heads of Islam's enemies in Iraq.

I realized Zarqawi was the mirror image of Muqtada, a *Sunni* Muslim fascist. *Somebody has to stop them both before the poison spreads.*

Later that day, I chaired a meeting of the newly established Iraqi Ministerial Committee for National Security. Muqtada was our main topic, and the Iraqi ministers were wobbly. The minister of justice thought we should find a way to make "a gesture" to Muqtada—in effect, offer concessions. Ali Allawi, the minister of defense, thought we should just let Muqtada "rot." The Sunni insurgency, he argued, was the overriding strategic threat.

I stressed the unfortunate consequences to Iraq's future stability if we began making concessions now.

Several ministers argued that Muqtada simply wanted to be "included in the government" and did not pose a "strategic threat to Iraq's stability." I countered that taking over several cities on the eve of Arbaeen posed as much a threat to Iraq as the attacks in Fallujah. This was a serious challenge now and would be an even greater challenge to a sovereign Iraqi government after June 30.

"If Muqtada al-Sadr is given some role in government now," I said, "he will be subverting the very foundation of democratic rule." It was a fundamental precept of democracy that you did not shoot your way to power.

Gompert, Rubaie, and I had hoped the committee would agree to a press statement condemning Muqtada and calling for firm action. But only the minister of finance, Kamel al-Keilani, and the new chief of the intelligence service, General al-Shehwani, both Sunnis, were inclined to move firmly against Muqtada. Rather than have the statement disapproved, I whispered to David and Rubaie not to propose the statement at all.

The latest intelligence reports from the south indicated Muqtada had gone to ground in the Kufa mosque and he was quite likely prepared to stay there until June 30. So we faced a real dilemma. Meanwhile, his troops swarmed on Najaf. Recapturing Najaf and Kufa during Arbaeen was unappealing in the extreme. But letting him run the cities for the holy week was not much better.

Late that night, Sanchez and I attended an NSC Principals' teleconference meeting with the vice president, Rice, Armitage, Rumsfeld, Pace, and Card. Abizaid was on from Tampa. "We're faced with a fundamental challenge to our authority and to all central authority in Iraq," I told the group. The issue would be as important after June 30 as before, perhaps more important. Lots of people were fence-sitting, waiting to see what we did about Muqtada and his "army"—

tribes and especially other militias. If we didn't react, they would conclude that they, too, had to take up arms to defend their interests. In such a case, the entire political process would be put at risk—the June 30 date, the elections next year, all of it. "Lack of a vigorous response to Muqtada will increase the chances of civil war." We were trying to get public statements of support from key Iraqis, particularly Shia. We'd also warned the political parties with their own militia (SCIRI and Dawa) to stay out of the way. We were giving tribes the same message.

I recommended that the Coalition pursue what I dubbed the "Anaconda Strategy," a term borrowed from the Civil War plan of General Winfield Scott to strangle the Confederacy by pushing in from its periphery. Since we could not retake the holy city by force, I proposed we hit other Muqtada targets—safe houses, training camps, Mahdi Army units, his colleagues—wherever and whenever we found them, except in Najaf.

There was a welcome unanimity backing the concept.

In the predawn darkness of April 6, I woke to the solid thumps and weird chainsaw buzz of an AC-130 Spectre gunship firing its cannons as it orbited unseen above Sadr City. Small bands of Muqtada's militiamen were holed up in government buildings they had seized, refusing to surrender. The gunship was blasting them out so that American troops wouldn't have to risk making ground assaults.

My bedroom windows rattled with the distant explosions. *I'm glad I'm not on the receiving end of that.*

But we hadn't started this fight. Muqtada had.

The next morning, Bob Blackwill, who was meeting daily with Brahimi, told me that he sensed Brahimi was close to abandoning his mission. The level of violence was frustrating his efforts to meet with Iraqis and he disagreed strongly with our approach to Fallujah. I immediately called him to urge him to stay on. Later, I called Secretary Powell to suggest he pass Kofi Annan the same message. Powell agreed, and added that he'd been "kicking himself" for not heeding my warnings about Muqtada over the past six months.

That afternoon, Blackwill brought Brahimi in for a briefing on the latest crisis in the south. I detailed Muqtada's illegal acts over the previous year and said, "Muqtada is fundamentally opposed to the kind of Iraq that we, the UN, and the Iraqis want."

The Algerian diplomat was more concerned about possible bloodshed in Fallujah, and threatened to quit Iraq. I stressed that his presence was essential and that continued UN engagement provided a powerful contrast to Muqtada's plan for Iraq. It was also essential to keeping the political process grinding forward, however slowly.

Brahimi said he appreciated the briefing, but that he was finding Iraqis very distracted by the Muqtada crisis and cited several who opposed arresting him.

"I've heard these arguments," I said. "And I don't find them persuasive. Muqtada is a menace to order in Iraq."

In the end Brahimi agreed to remain, "for now."

The news was bad again the next morning.

The Marines had lost eleven men in coordinated professional attacks at the provincial capital of Ramadi. Clearly, the assaults were meant to relieve pressure at nearby Fallujah. Then I got a detailed radio report from the CPA staff in Al-Kut, the capital of Wasit Province, where I'd recently discussed the TAL with Sistani's representative. The Mahdi Army had occupied the town the previous day and attacked the CPA compound with small arms and RPGs. Ukrainian Coalition forces had withdrawn from the city, leaving our CPA compound at the mercy of Muqtada's fighters. After frantic prodding all night by my British colleague David Richmond, the Ukrainians had finally agreed to go into the compound at 6:00 A.M. to rescue our people and guard the buildings.

But soon there were messages from Al-Kut, and Mike Gfoeller in Al-Hillah, that the Ukrainian commander said he planned to abandon the compound after extracting our people. I called Sanchez at 6:30 A.M. to say that this would be a terrible mistake. It was too late because at 7:15 we learned that the Ukrainians had gone in, recovered our staff, and abandoned the compound, which was immediately seized by Muqtada's men.

Moreover, five British employees of a security firm working for our CPA office were trapped on the roof of another building two hundred meters away, with Muqtada's gunmen on the ground floor. The Ukrainians had left without them. Four somehow escaped. The fifth was killed. I found myself pacing my office, speechless with rage at the Ukrainians.

The 1 MEF pressed ahead in Fallujah, with the Marines encountering in-depth defensive positions, with machine guns and mortar pits protected by riflemen and snipers. The enemy were fighting out of schools, hospitals, apartment buildings, and mosques, just as Saddam's forces had done. As the fighting increased, casualties mounted and Al-Jazeera documented each one. A Marine Cobra gunship fired a missile at a sniper in the minaret of a mosque, killing more than ten Iraqis, most likely all insurgents. But the edited television images provoked a sharp emotional response from Iraqis across the country.

As the Marines pushed deeper into the city, the Iraqi police and Civil Defense Corps forces backstopping them either abandoned their posts or went over to the other side. The local police commissioner was caught working with the insurgents. Iraqi Civil Defense soldiers had proven to be "useless" according to a senior Marine officer. Almost half of the first battalion of the New Iraqi Army deserted on their way to Fallujah.

Of the five battalions of the Civil Defense force in Baghdad, almost a third did not report for duty Tuesday, April 6. The battalions recruited from Sadr City had 80 percent absenteeism. All over the south, Iraqi policemen were absent or passive. "So much for the Iraqis taking over their own security," I told Dick.

But security was not our only worry. We had to keep the political process moving forward, despite the crises, which meant hammering out a workable plan for the interim government. I met with Brahimi and the UN's election expert, Carina Pirelli. We encouraged Pirelli to work quickly to establish the needed electoral system. She agreed to continue her consultations with the Governing Council and to set a May 15 deadline for making a decision on the electoral system.

But Brahimi was still wavering about his mission. He'd been unable to leave the Green Zone because of security, so his consultations had been restricted. After Blackwill and I urged him again, he finally agreed to stay until April 15, when he would announce the plan for choosing the interim government, and promised to return in early May to help select the interim government.

On April 7, Rick Sanchez and I attended the regular weekly Governing Council meeting. The mood was somber, with Muqtada's uprising and the fighting in Al-Anbar Province dominating the agenda. As soon as Rick finished his operational briefing, Hachem al-Hassani, the Sunni Islamist, laid into the Coalition for its "ruthless attacks" in Fallujah. Then Salama al-Khufaji, a Shiite Islamist dentist, spoke out vigorously. "All Iraq is in revolt," she said. "It was a terrible mistake to arrest Yacoubi and try to arrest Muqtada. There should be a negotiation." She also proposed that the Coalition announce a date for the withdrawal of all its forces.

Next, Songul Chapouk, the sole representative of the Turkmen community, spoke and became emotional. She ended up, face in her hands, sobbing.

But at this point Allawi's deputy, Rassim al-Awadi, raised his voice and called for "decisive action" against Muqtada. Then Samir Sumaidy, a prominent anti-Saddam Sunni from Anbar Province, spoke in favor of strong action. "These are terrible times," he admitted. "But what we do now will show our mettle. We need to be firm. The choice is clear: we cannot allow armed groups to determine events."

Several Shia followed with statements almost as strong as this, most also stressing the need to minimize civilian casualties. When they had finished, I asked for the floor.

"We all regret the loss of innocent life," I said. Without giving credence to Al-Jazeera, I noted that in every war civilian casualties occurred. Our military took extraordinary care to avoid them. I reminded the Iraqis that our young men and women had come halfway around the world to die for Iraq's freedom. "We must understand what's at stake today. We face a fundamental challenge to the future of Iraq. Is Iraq to be governed by law? This is the issue raised by the arrest of Yacoubi and the warrant for Muqtada. These warrants were issued by an Iraqi court pursuant to an investigation by an Iraqi magistrate."

No one in the Council could argue this fact.

But there was more, much more, about Muqtada. He was suspected of at least one other murder. He was operating illegal Sharia "courts and prisons" in Najaf. "And we have eyewitness accounts of men being tortured and women being raped and tortured in those prisons," I said.

Muqtada's men had seized a Palestinian who worked in our Najaf CPA office, broken his legs, and dragged him off to prison where we understood he was being tortured. "We all know where Muqtada learned these tactics . . . from Saddam. Is this the kind of Iraq you want?" I asked. "Is this the kind of Iraq for which Americans and Iraqis have died?

"The more fundamental question is how will the New Iraq be governed? Muqtada has given his answer. He has answered by attacking and killing Iraqi security forces and Coalition troops. He has answered by seizing Iraqi government buildings in Basra, Al-Kut, Baghdad, and Najaf. He has answered by robbing a bank in Baghdad, and by sending carloads of his gangs to the schools in Baghdad this morning threatening to shoot the children if the schools did not shut their doors.

"It's easy to see the kind of Iraq Muqtada wants. It's not democratic, it has no respect for rights or the law. Such an Iraq has nothing in common with the Iraq we've discussed around this table for the past ten months. It has nothing in common with the country the vast majority of Iraqis want, and for which we all pray."

The Council remained silent.

I reviewed the similar threat posed by the terrorists and insurgents in Fallu-jah. "Like Muqtada, they are against a democratic Iraq. The basic question we face is simple. In the new Iraq, does the power to rule come from the barrel of a gun or from a ballot box?"

Looking directly at al-Khufaji, I said it would be a terrible mistake to set a date for the departure of Coalition forces. It was obvious that Iraqi security forces were not ready to defend the country on their own. A fixed departure date would only encourage the insurgents and terrorists to outwait us and then renew their attacks.

Now members were nodding agreement.

"Many of you have asked if there was a peaceful solution to the crisis," I said. "The answer is yes: Muqtada can stop the bloodshed today by disbanding his army. And he has to face Iraqi justice. He will be treated with dignity. He will be considered innocent until proven guilty. He'll have the right to counsel and to remain silent. He will have an open and speedy trial. In short, he will enjoy all the rights guaranteed to him and every Iraqi in the TAL which he so vigorously denounces."

I studied the faces of the Islamist Shia. Muqtada represented even more of a threat to them than he did to the Coalition. Many of them were simply afraid to confront him. "Every member of the Council faces the choice of what kind of Iraq they want. Do you want an Iraq ruled by force, with a return to illegal courts, prisons where people are tortured and raped, where entire villages are razed? That isn't the Iraq we came to help you build. That isn't the Iraq you or most Iraqis want. *Now* is the time for you to choose your future. There is no middle ground."

The Council seemed dazed. Nobody spoke. Then the April president, Massoud Barzani, found his voice and gave an eloquent statement. "While thousands may demonstrate for Muqtada, there are millions who don't support him. The New Iraq cannot accept Muqtada. We did not liberate Iraq to turn it over to a new dictator. We need to be firm."

Adnan Pachachi quietly proposed that Barzani's statement be turned into a Council press release. This was put to a vote and won with twenty votes. Two Shia Islamists abstained but did not voice their opposition.

Maybe we're turning a corner.

Back at my office, I had the first of several secure calls with Rice.

I noted that despite our agreement to squeeze Muqtada, there was no sign the Anaconda strategy was being applied. "As far as I can tell, there've been no offensive operations against his outfit for more than thirty-six hours, since we had the Great Ukrainian Skedaddle in Al-Kut."

"Rumsfeld and Dick Myers briefed me on this," she said. "And I'm worried, too. Make the point with the president at today's NSC. You're the guy on the ground and he'll want to hear your assessment."

An hour later, I was staring at the video image of the White House SitRoom as General Abizaid ran through a series of slides. He listed various cities:

"Baghdad. Situation calm.

"Nasariya: Situation calm.

"Najaf: Situation calm."

Making sure our microphone was off, I turned to Bob Blackwill. "It's as if a British general were to brief London in July 1940: 'Paris: Situation calm.' Right. Just happens to be in enemy hands."

When Abizaid concluded, President Bush asked for my views.

"The question of whether a city is calm isn't the point," I began.

I explained that in Baghdad that morning carloads of Muqtada's men had driven up to schools and forced them to close at gunpoint. They had robbed a bank yesterday and attacked the Central Bank today. The political impact of our having left Al-Kut was very serious, for now Muqtada controlled two provincial capitals. "I wouldn't be surprised if he made a run at Karbala next," I added. He might then declare that the "liberation" of Iraq was under way. "We have to defeat Muqtada and all he stands for." Our strategic imperative was to keep the moderate Shia with us. But our strategic dilemma was that we couldn't move against Muqtada himself while he was holed up in the Kufa mosque. I said we should move aggressively against all his other "works" outside Najaf. "Every day that goes by without decisive action is going to persuade the moderates that we're not serious."

Colin Powell supported my argument for serious military action forcefully. "We need to retake Al-Kut immediately," he said.

The president agreed. "If he gets away with this, the situation will become immeasurably worse. He must *not* be allowed to gain the upper hand. It's better to do it now than later. When people are on the road to democracy, the U.S. will help them decisively against their enemies."

At this point Powell looked into the video camera, erasing the eight thousand miles between Baghdad and Washington. "Jerry's been pressing for action against Muqtada for months," he said. "We haven't acted on his advice. It's not just a question of his militia. At the end of the operation, Muqtada's got to be gone."

Cheney suggested that this was the time to remove the various bureaucratic obstacles to spending reconstruction funds I had been complaining about. I heartily agreed. (But for the next weeks, bureaucrats in DOD would continue to hold up spending on crucial politically sensitive projects in Al-Anbar Province and Sadr City.)

At the end of the meeting, the president said, "We need to be tougher than hell now. The American people want to know we're going after the bad guys. We need to get on the offensive and stay on the offensive."

So we all had our marching orders.

But this long day wasn't over. News came in that the Marines were encountering stiff opposition in Fallujah, and that Muqtada's militia was continuing to spread across the south. So Rice called for a second NSC meeting.

She telephoned before, and we agreed that the Abizaid briefing had been disappointing. I suggested that the president ask for a daily paper showing him precisely which offensive operations had been conducted against Muqtada in the past twenty-four hours. She liked the idea.

The second NSC meeting was disorganized.

Abizaid again briefed, starting his comments by noting that "contrary to what some may think, we are on the offensive," though his presentation demonstrated the opposite. Coalition forces might be able to go for Al-Kut by Tuesday next week, he said. And after April 11—Arbaeen—we'd go hard at Muqtada's offices and seek complete dismantlement of his "army."

Yet according to reports in Baghdad, the Mahdi Army had only about fifty fighters guarding Al-Kut. *Why wait another week to kick them out or kill them?*

Abizaid was clearly angry at what he saw as civilian interference and said he'd be in Baghdad in the morning.

I reviewed the total failure of the Iraqi security forces. The police had largely skedaddled, half the Civil Defense Corps was AWOL, and the new battalion of the army had refused to fight. Powell followed my comments by noting that we kept saying that half the forces in Iraq were Iraqis, and that that was the reason we could draw down our troop levels.

Encouragingly, the president said he wanted a daily report on military operations. And Abizaid said he would delay the planned departure of almost all the 1st Armored Division, giving Sanchez 20,000 additional troops for the crises.

On the morning of April 8, the twin military crises provoked a full-scale political crisis. First, Interior Minister Nouri Badran, who commanded the flagging

Iraqi Police Service, submitted his resignation. Even though he cloaked the move in the standard "personal reasons," it was unsettling that he abandoned the government during the ongoing crises. Next, Abu Hatem, the legenday Shiite warrior from the south—the "Lord of the Marshes" who held sway over vital tribes along the border with Iran—"suspended" his membership in the Governing Council. I had visited his tribal homelands in the marshes in September and had seen how popular Abu Hatem was down there.

I reached him on his cell phone in his tribal home in the southern city of Amara and asked him to reconsider. "Let me think," he said. "This is a difficult period." We agreed to meet the next day.

Within minutes, Minister of Human Rights Abdel Basit Turki announced his resignation. He was a moderate Sunni with family and clan ties in Al-Anbar Province. Next we heard that Pachachi, the senior GC member, was outraged by the Fallujah operation, which he publicly labeled "collective punishment." He too was on the verge of resigning.

Less than an hour later, Hachem al-Hassani, who represented the Sunni Iraqi Islamic Party, came in to tell me that his party's politburo had voted to "leave the Governing Council" in protest over the Marine offensive in Fallujah. Hachem added that Ghazi al-Yawar, one of the most prominent Sunnis on the Governing Council, also planned to quit the Council that afternoon.

"You must call for an immediate cease-fire in Fallujah," Hachem insisted. He wanted to lead a GC delegation to Fallujah to talk to the city's leaders about resolving the crisis.

We were at the most critical crisis of the occupation. The stakes couldn't be higher. The Governing Council—which for better or worse had to help lead the country over the next crucial months—was on the verge of disintegrating due to Sunni resignations over Fallujah. Moreover, there was a real possibility that Brahimi, outraged by the Fallujah situation, would withdraw his mission. This chain of events would leave us with a rump Governing Council, and with no way to persuade any respectable Sunnis to rejoin it. The CPA, by itself, without the UN, would have to cobble together an interim government. But if we did this quickly, in order to preserve the June 30 deadline, the resulting government would have minimal credibility in the eyes of the Iraqi public. Moreover, it was very unlikely such a government could adequately prosecute the war and prepare for elections. Therefore to lose both the Governing Council and the UN would mean losing the June 30 date, with no clear way to get a credible political process revived and no idea of how long that would require.

Failing to stick to the June 30 date would call into question the entire November 15 Agreement and the interim constitution, in particular the provisions for elections. If we missed the June 30 date, it would be impossible to hold elections as scheduled in January 2005. This would almost certainly provoke a major crisis with Sistani, who had reluctantly agreed to the UN's reengagement, and had only eventually come to understand that despite his problems with parts of the TAL, the document provided the only path forward. And he was adamant about holding elections as soon as possible, and not later than early 2005. So a major Shia outburst could also be expected if the current crises forced us off the June 30 date.

It was evident that continuing military operations in Fallujah would result in the collapse of the entire political process and force the postponement of Iraqi sovereignty. I was sure this would cause an upsurge in the insurgency and the deaths of more Americans. At the same time, I felt we needed to continue vigorous military operations against Muqtada.

Around 1:00 A.M. on Good Friday I'd managed to track down Sheik Ghazi and urged him not to leave the Governing Council. "I understand your concerns about Fallujah," I'd said. "But we need your common sense and wisdom on the Council. We're reviewing military options."

"I can wait until tomorrow, Ambassador," he said. "But I'm under tremendous pressure from my people."

I immediately sent Rick Sanchez a message telling him that the Sunnis on the Governing Council had requested a suspension of hostilities to send in more humanitarian supplies and to talk to the city's leadership. I asked him what conditions the military would need in order to agree to suspend offensive operations. Perhaps we could put such a proposal to the Sunni GC members to keep the Council from falling apart.

General Sanchez called from his office near the airport. He'd read my message and we agreed that he, Abizaid, and I would meet at the palace before noon.

"We can't wait long," I said. "The GC is cracking at the seams."

Still, there was some good news on the political front. Blackwill reported that Brahimi was a bit more optimistic, having had a few productive meetings with Iraqis the day before. Bob was urging Brahimi to announce details of the format and scope of the interim government he foresaw before leaving next week. This was essential to show Iraqis that despite the current crises, the path to sovereignty was still open.

And the morning intel reports showed that Coalition forces had attacked a number of Muqtada targets in the south. We appeared on the verge of retaking Al-Kut. We'd also smashed a couple of Muqtada's offices in Baghdad. Finally the Anaconda squeeze was on.

Over morning coffee, Dick Jones and I noted that as the strategy took effect, we were getting communications from various intermediaries purporting to put forward conditions for a "political resolution" of the Muqtada crisis. One idea that had come from Sistani late the night before was that the family of the murdered Ayatollah al-Khoei ask the Iraqi courts to delay any judicial action against Muqtada until after June 30. This had possibilities, only if Muqtada could be made to honor the agreement.

Abizaid and Sanchez came to the palace in late morning to discuss a temporary cessation of offensive action in Fallujah. I recognized that the idea of stopping offensive operations would be rough on the military, whom only days before I had encouraged to hit the insurgents hard. But the steady drumbeat in the Arab press had effectively changed conditions on the ground in Iraq and we had to take the political consequences into account. "The GC is fracturing over operations in Fallujah," I told them. But I also stressed that we needed to maintain a high tempo of operations against Muqtada wherever we found his forces outside the holy cities.

Both generals said they understood the repercussions of continuing in Fallujah.

General Abizaid seemed to have cooled off after the difficult NSC meeting the day before.

They outlined conditions under which our military would agree to suspend offensive operations. We would give these terms to the Governing Council's delegation to put to Fallujah's leaders: The city's sheiks must hand over the killers of our men. We also wanted the names of the foreign fighters there. The insurgents had to lay down arms. If they fired on us, we would react. I called Hachem with this proposal. It was 10:45 A.M.

"I suggest we announce it immediately," I said, "because Friday prayers start at noon."

Hachem said he'd try to reach his contacts in Fallujah immediately. With the approval of Abizaid and Sanchez, our joint public affairs teams quickly issued a press statement that at noon Coalition forces would initiate a unilateral "suspension of offensive operations." But we retained our right of self-defense.

As we'd agreed late the night before, "the Lord of the Marshes" came to see me in his flowing tribal robes. Abu Hatem was distraught. After his lengthy complaints about the problems of the south, I was able to persuade him to withdraw his resignation. Since he was the only member of the Council alleged to be in direct contact with Muqtada, I gave him the message that we wanted Muqtada to face the law and disband his militia. He would be treated with dignity and given all rights guaranteed by the TAL.

"I will be in Najaf tomorrow, Ambassador," Abu Hatem said. "I will pass Muqtada your message."

Before another NSC meeting late that Friday, I called Rice to prepare the president for bad news. "The situation in Fallujah isn't good, and we're trying a unilateral move," I said. "But it might not work. The Sunnis are very restive, and we still might have a wave of resignations from the Council. The Shia situation is also bad."

But we could continue to squeeze Muqtada as hard as possible in the hopes that he'd agree to terms. We had several channels going in Muqtada's direction but no idea who was on the other end of the line.

The NSC meeting was long and painful.

General Abizaid was frank about the difficult military situation, and I was candid about the tremendous political pressure being generated by the twin military crises. "Right now," I said, "it's mostly on the Sunnis. But if the Muqtada standoff continues, there's a risk of a Shia uprising at some point."

The president, Rice, and Powell pressed in on the issue of the political fragility. What would happen if a bunch of Governing Council members resigned? Could we find replacements?

"The short answer is 'not easily,' " I said.

When we'd hashed through various possible outcomes, none of them good, I said, "I've tasked my Governance Team to draft a paper that we're calling 'Thinking the Unthinkable.' "

The president offered that if the political situation were to fall apart, we'd have nobody to transfer sovereignty to in June. He ended the meeting with a firm statement that we would stick to the June 30 date.

Abizaid, Sanchez, Blackwill, and I talked for another half hour. John said he understood that the political situation would not permit continuation of the Fallujah offensive at this moment. We discussed whether the GC delegation would be able to calm things enough to get the story off Al-Jazeera.

"And I want to be sure that you and Rick understand that we're not going to attack Muqtada in Najaf," I said. "Let's not get crossways on *that* point. But we do need to be especially robust going after his outlying posts, his training camps, and safe houses."

Both senior commanders concurred.

Rice and Powell called me back to express their concerns about the political situation. Without the Governing Council or a similar institution, the entire political process was "gone," along with the June 30 sovereignty transfer.

"That's the main reason we're going to have to lay back a bit in Fallujah," I said. But I added that we needed to recognize that we were simply postponing an inevitable showdown with the insurgents and terrorists there. It was far better, I believed, that this occur after we had been seen to have publicly exhausted all efforts at a peaceful solution.

Colin Powell turned again to Muqtada. "I wish we'd acted six months ago when Jerry was urging action. Now we have to keep the GC and the whole country from breaking up."

"The president recognizes that we can't let either the Council or Iraq fall apart," Rice said.

It was Good Friday night and I needed to talk to Francie. I was worn down physically, psychologically, and spiritually by the long days and nights. Violence and failure seemed to loom everywhere I looked. I hadn't realized how much I'd wanted that time home for Easter. I was going to miss a reunion with my family. I felt nothing but darkness around me in Iraq.

"I've just about had it, Sweetie," I told her.

"Jer," she said calmly but firmly, "remember what you said when you left last May? 'I'm going to approach this like a marathon, and I know how to do marathons.' Sounds like you've just hit the wall."

"Feels like it, too," I wearily agreed.

"You've hit the wall before in marathons," she continued. "You know that the only thing to do is to pull yourself together and keep moving ahead one step at a time."

"Okay," I agreed weakly.

"Try. Remember everybody's looking to you to lead now."

"Okay. I'll try. And pray that God gives me the strength."

"He will, Jer. Now go to bed. I love you."

"I love you, too."

• • •

The next morning, Sistani's son sent a message that the ayatollah was concerned that we might storm Najaf as we had Fallujah. Couldn't a trial of Muqtada's deputy, Yacoubi, await a sovereign government?

In my reply to Sistani I noted that we, too, wanted to avoid bloodshed. Yacoubi was in the custody of the Iraqi police. As for Muqtada, I mentioned that we had sent the message through several channels that if he were to surrender to Iraqi authorities, we would ensure that he would be treated with dignity befitting an al-Sadr. "Our objective is not to kill or humiliate him, but to see that justice is done for the sake of his victims and the new democratic Iraq we all seek to build."

Perhaps Sistani and his colleagues would find a way to defuse the explosive situation in the holy cities, but I doubted it.

That Saturday afternoon, I called to brief Rice, who was spending Easter weekend with the Bushes in Texas. After we talked, the president came on the line. "How you doin', Bremer?"

"Okay, Mr. President."

"Well," he said, "I told you last year that I wanted a tough guy for a tough job and now I know I've got the right man. We knew there would be hard moments, and I appreciate your showing some calcium in your spine during this crisis."

"Thank you, Mr. President," I said. "Francie uses the analogy of a sick country with lots of poison in it. We're getting the poison to the surface, which has to be done to get the patient well. We're going to succeed here."

"Couldn't agree more, Jerry. Happy Easter!"

In his radio broadcast that day, President Bush condemned "a small faction attempting to derail Iraqi democracy and seize power." He emphasized that we would hand over sovereignty June 30.

At a subsequent NSC meeting that afternoon, Abizaid said the situation in Sunni areas was worse than expected. "We need to bring back more old army officers."

Powell jumped on that. "You don't need lots of full colonels and generals, just some lieutenant colonels with troop command experience."

"If we bring any back, they've got to be very carefully vetted," I insisted.

"We've got to remember that the Kurds and especially the Shia will be watching anything we do very closely."

Abizaid admitted that there was a risk that the Shia would see such moves as attempting to reestablish Saddam's army.

The president said, "As Jerry and I discussed this morning, there's a lot of poison in the system and it's now working its way out. We shouldn't be surprised that the Iraqis are hesitant to step up. They're still afraid we won't stay the course. Failure is not an option. We must and will succeed and after this period, we'll have a more peaceful Iraq."

After a discussion of Fallujah, he concluded, "We're being tested and so are the Iraqis. They want to be free. We all just need to be tough and smart."

When I reached my office, there was a printout of a news service story on my desk: Muqtada had just issued a call for a popular uprising that would include all ethnic groups.

Over the coming days, the situation remained very dicey. The Marines stayed away from central Fallujah, but shot any insurgents trying to fight their way out. All across the Shia heartland—except in the holy cities—Coalition forces were squeezing Muqtada's Mahdi Army.

Ironically the twin crises produced a modest breakthrough in the militia negotiations David Gompert had been so patiently pursuing for months. Gompert reported that the Anaconda strategy had two effects: it sent a clear message to SCIRI that we were prepared to use force against militias operating outside the law; and it helped show that SCIRI would not be defenseless against Muqtada's militia if it agreed to transition and reintegrate the Badr Corps. In turn, SCIRI's leader, Abdul Aziz Hakim, realized that we would work with them against the common threat.

At the same time, the Kurds became convinced that we did not want the Peshmerga to disappear but wanted them transitioned in large numbers into government forces to help provide security in Iraqi Kurdistan and elsewhere. When Gompert proposed that some 35,000 Peshmerga should be used as counterterrorist and other quick-reaction forces under the control of the Kurdish Regional Government (as provided for in the Transitional Administrative Law), the Kurds agreed.

Once the Kurds agreed, SCIRI did as well. But Gompert and I agreed that getting the groups to sign onto the reintegration process was no guarantee that they would actually comply. "There are simply too many unknowns for them to give up their forces until they see which way things are going," I told him.

• • •

One night during a rocket attack on the Green Zone, Blackwill and I were down in the shelter. I told him I thought that we were on the path to "resolving" both the Fallujah and Muqtada crises, but in ways that would simply freeze the problems for later resolution. "We'll have to fight again in Fallujah," I said. "And Muqtada won't see justice under our watch."

Bob replied that postponement was better than a full-scale revolt against occupation.

We talked daily with Brahimi about the shape of the interim government. At the CPA we were beginning to pencil in our preferences for the leaders of that government. For some months, I had felt that Ayad Allawi was probably the best choice for prime minister. Bob and I both felt that Allawi was tougher than any of his colleagues. And a newly sovereign Iraq would need a tough leader. But I didn't want to spoil Allawi's chances by pushing his candidacy. I hoped Brahimi would eventually see the logic of this choice, though Blackwill and I agreed that he would probably choke at the prospect of appointing a man known to have had connections with the CIA. This would be a difficult issue when Brahimi returned to Iraq in May. Another key unknown was whether Allawi's secularism would make him unacceptable to Sistani.

At his departure press conference on April 15, Brahimi announced his plan. He called for the establishment by the end of May of a "caretaker" government with a president, two deputy presidents, a prime minister, and cabinet. This would give that government a month "to prepare to assume responsibility for governing the country." He also advocated convening a national conference in the summer to elect a "consultative assembly."

Brahimi was purposely vague about how the new government could emerge. But it was clear this would not be selected by caucuses or chosen by the Governing Council. The government would emerge, as the GC had, from broad consultations among Iraqis with the UN and the CPA.

Brahimi drew attention to a comment I had made that "Iraqi unity requires a constitution that all Iraqi communities can support. It is a fundamental principle of democracy that the constitution should provide for majority rule but also protect minority rights."

• • •

Over the next few days, Abizaid and Pace of the Joint Chiefs of Staff continued to press for resumption of offensive operations in Fallujah, which Abizaid wanted the GC to endorse.

"That's a good way to break up the Governing Council once and for all," I told them.

The U.S. military also kept floating the idea of "bringing back" some members of Saddam's army. At a mid-April meeting of the Iraqi Ministerial Committee on National Security, Abizaid noted the need for an Iraqi chain of command and proposed using some former senior officers. Ali Allawi, the defense minister, was adamant that any officers brought back would have to be well vetted and that it would "not be appropriate to simply call some brigade back overnight."

In a subsequent meeting with the Governing Council, when Sanchez mentioned his intention to recall "several" Iraqi generals, many members, including Talabani, were firm that such a move had to be subjected to "strict vetting." This was still a very sensitive issue.

Rumsfeld and Rice were increasingly insistent that we had to announce urgent steps to deal with the crises. The idea was that I'd make the announcements in a major address to the nation. But there was a weeklong haggle over what I should say. Should we call back members of the army? Should we revoke our de-Baathification policy, as some in Washington now seemed to want?

I wearily reminded the others that Iraq was a zero-sum game. We needed to keep the Shia and Kurds in mind too. Calling back former senior army officers would not solve our problems. Neither would blasting our way into Fallujah—until we had strong Iraqi leadership in place to support these moves. I also reminded them that the problem with de-Baathification was not the policy but the way in which the Council's De-Baathification Committee had implemented that policy. In particular, tens of thousands of teachers, who had been forced to join the party to be eligible to teach, were now being denied their posts. This went well beyond the intent of our initial policy. Iraqi children were paying the price. But to say anything about de-Baathification would be to provoke a strong reaction from the Shia.

The crushing summer heat returned to the desert. On the asphalt roads around Fallujah and on the streets of Najaf, the thermal ripples rose in shimmering curtains from the pavement as our Marines and soldiers waited. The 1 MEF sent a few tentative patrols into Fallujah. Firing was sporadic. Overall, the unofficial cease-fire held. For ten days, we lost no Marines there. But Fallujah was not calm. Homegrown insurgents supported by foreign jihadis continued to fire at Marines and their Iraqi allies. The much-touted 36th Iraqi Civil Defense Corps Battalion refused to go back into the line after two days' refitting.

The cease-fire in Fallujah gradually took hold. On April 16 Abizaid called. "I think we've got some breathing space in Fallujah. I've spoken to Conway, and he's satisfied with his situation," he said.

But the broader security situation continued to deteriorate. Insurgents mounted attacks on the oil pipelines, denying the government petroleum revenues. Our military convoys were being struck so regularly that on April 17 it looked as if I would have to order food rationing at the CPA. There was a big jump in attacks in the Sunni-dominated western Baghdad suburb of Abu Ghraib, and intelligence reports suggested plans for major uprisings in other Sunni cities such as Baiji, Tikrit, and Mosul.

On April 21, before an NSC meeting scheduled later in the day, Condi Rice called to ask my opinion about Fallujah. "What if the president orders a full-scale assault?"

"I'm conflicted," I said. "Sooner or later, we've got to go back in there and get those guys. But frankly, the president must assume that if he orders an assault now, it will lead to the collapse of the entire political process." I told her this was the view of all of us at the CPA, including Blackwill, although we needed to be aware that we were merely postponing action there. But far better that action should occur after there was an Iraqi government in place and, one hoped, with better-trained Iraqi security forces to help with the operation. "There are no good options," I said.

"What about Muqtada al-Sadr?"

"On Muqtada, I think we're about right. The pressure from the Anaconda strategy seems to be working. We keep getting messages that he wants us to call it off. And the Najaf crowd is scared to death we'll assault the holy cities." I told her I could not imagine circumstances in which the president would order such an assault, but added, "I don't want to make a public commitment not to invade the holy cities because that'd relieve pressure on the Shia to deal with Muqtada."

At the subsequent NSC teleconference, General Abizaid briefed on the situation in Fallujah and noted they had plans to move decisively against the insurgents there in days. The president asked why it was necessary to move now. Why shouldn't we wait to let the political situation there develop? Abizaid said the operation could wait, though a show of strength was important at some point. The president was also concerned with the risk that we might create a larger backlash against us elsewhere in Iraq as we dealt with Fallujah.

President Bush clearly understood the risk the crisis in Fallujah posed to the entire political process and especially to the June 30 transfer of sovereignty. "Jerry can't stay out there for ten years."

"The longer I'm out here, the more I'm attracted to the idea of returning sovereignty to them as quickly as possible," I told him.

That got a good laugh. Then the president added with a deadpan look, "If things do go south, you'll probably have to stay another year or two."

"Well, in that case you'll have to tell that to Francie, Mr. President, because I won't."

"I'm not going to tell Francie!"

"You'll have to because I wouldn't dare," I answered.

On Friday, April 23, I addressed the Iraqi nation. The speech, entitled "Turning the Page," would be my most important. My intention was to help Iraqis see beyond the violence and uncertainty of the present, to a better future.

After laying out the need for each Iraqi to choose the path ahead, I noted that the Iraqi minister of defense had recently appointed carefully vetted senior military officers to fill out an Iraqi chain of command in the security forces. I called on the people of Fallujah to "support the legitimate Iraqi authorities" in bringing that crisis to an end. I announced a robust program to make public more information about Iraqi detainees we held.

And I commented on the sensitive problem of de-Baathification, noting that the policy we had announced in May was still valid and had been directed at only the top 1 percent of the party. But the policy had been poorly administered by the Governing Council's committee. So after consulting the minister of education, he and I had decided to reinstate as quickly as possible some ten thousand teachers who had lost their jobs purely because they were members of the party. Anyone later found to have committed crimes could then be fired. Although some press reports subsequently said we had changed our policy on de-Baathification, this was not the case.

I concluded with words of encouragement:

> Much is going to happen in the ten weeks before Iraqi sovereignty.
> In the days and months ahead the Coalition will work with you to provide security, justice and prosperity for all Iraqis.
> Such an Iraq will honor Iraq's history, a proud and ancient history stretching back to the beginnings of civilization.
> Such an Iraq will honor the generations who came before you.
> Such an Iraq will serve the generations who will come after you.

Such an Iraq will place Iraqis securely on the path to a future of hope for all.

Reactions to the speech were mixed. Sunnis welcomed the emphasis on broadening the political base and establishing an Iraqi military chain of command. Shia complained vigorously that we had "betrayed" our de-Baathification principles. I pointed out that I had explicitly said the policy was the right one for Iraq, but it needed to be better implemented. Chalabi said my proposal about the teachers was as if we had allowed the Nazis back into government in Germany.

The next day, I decided to fly out to Fallujah with Abizaid and Sanchez to get a firsthand feel for the situation on the ground. Dick Jones and the State Department's Ron Schlicher had worked for ten days with the local tribal and town leaders and the GC delegation to find a way out of the crisis.

Meeting with General Conway, we agreed to give local sheiks a few days to try to accomplish something with the insurgents holed up in the city. Then, if Conway could pull together some Iraqi police, the Marines might start joint American-Iraqi patrols into the city.

But the local sheiks proved hopeless. I told Sanchez and Jones that they wanted us to "just turn Fallujah over to them."

On the morning of April 30, Dan Senor rushed into my office.

"Better take a look, Ambassador," Dan said, clicking my satellite TV to CNN International.

Here was an Iraqi major general wearing the dark green field-dress uniform and beret of Saddam Hussein's Republican Guard surrounded by a chanting, ecstatic crowd of young men in a sun-blasted square.

"Fallujah," Dan said. "*Today.* The guy's name is General Jassim Mohammed Saleh. He's the guy the Marines chose to command what they're calling the 'Fallujah Brigade.' "

"What the *hell* is going on?" I demanded.

Almost immediately, the secure phone rang. It was General Abizaid calling from his forward headquarters at Doha. "Jerry, have you seen the news? I can't tell if we're winning or losing," he laughed.

I was not happy and told him so.

As we now learned, the Marines, apparently at the urging of the director of Iraqi intelligence, General Mohammed al-Shehwani, had decided to deal with Fallujah by recalling a former army general and letting him bring back some of his former colleagues, to constitute "a brigade." According to the Marines' plan, this group would "police the city," provided the Marines agreed to withdraw. The key assumption was that this Iraqi brigade of about 3,000 would accomplish our objectives for the city by capturing or killing the insurgents and the foreign fighters.

Abizaid said he, too, was concerned about this step by the Marines. He said he would call Sanchez and remind him that all command positions were subject to confirmation by the CJTF commander, and that he had not yet confirmed Saleh in his command.

Sanchez was chagrined. I got the impression that he too had been blindsided by the Marine commander in Fallujah.

At our daily meeting of the Ministerial Committee for National Security, Minister of Defense Ali Allawi expressed outrage at the appointment, noting that as minister he could have expected to be consulted. He asked Shehwani if Saleh had been a Republican Guard officer. Shehwani sheepishly admitted that was so. Allawi insisted that this could not be "a model" for handling security in Iraq or it would roil the entire country.

Immediately a highly perturbed Bahr al-Uloum called me. Sputtering, he told me Saleh was an ex–Republican Guard and had been involved in Saddam's bloody repression of the Shia in Karbala in 1991. He practically shouted. "How could you do such a thing?"

Later, speaking to Rice, I found that she had also been caught unaware by the appointment. "It looks awful on TV," she said. "The guy looks just like Saddam!"

I told her that obviously the Marines had not vetted him and that I was working to get Saleh moved aside ASAP. For comic relief, I told her the results of the latest public opinion poll. Iraqis had been asked to identify the country "most friendly to Iraq." The winner: "No country."

Two days later, General Saleh had been replaced by General Mohammed Latif. But the damage had been done when Saleh's image flashed across the television screens in teahouses in the Shia south and Kurdistan. And many Iraqis were profoundly upset by the continued existence of the "Fallujah Brigade" itself. At an Iraqi NSC meeting May 2, Defense Minister Allawi said it risked a "severe backlash among the Shia." He noted sarcastically that the unit would help stabilize the city only because the "enemy is inside the brigade."

At a stormy GC meeting the next day, many others unloaded on us. Judge Wael of Basra said, "The mafia has won and taken over there." Dr. Adel, the normally calm Shia member, added that the brigade was "a move to Iraqi disunity and civil war."

The violent reaction to the Fallujah Brigade was dramatic proof of the danger the Coalition would have courted by trying to recall Saddam's army, as some had proposed.

Although the potential violence in Fallujah, with all its possible repercussions, simmered near the surface, the other two crises were quieter. Muqtada al-Sadr was still holed up in the shrine in Kufa. The Coalition had killed several hundred of his militiamen and had effectively blocked reinforcements from reaching Muqtada. We had not resolved this challenge, but we would continue the military and political pressure on him and see whether this produced an acceptable nonviolent outcome.

On the political front, Brahimi and his UN team returned to Iraq the first week of May to begin to work with us on selecting the interim government. The Shia still grumbled about a secular Sunni Algerian having such authority, but there were no choreographed walkouts from the Governing Council, or protest resignations from the government over his role.

By early May, it had become clear that we had to tread lightly in Fallujah.

While Brahimi met with the Iraqis, Generals Conway and Sanchez came to discuss Anbar with Jones, Blackwill, and me. Conway put forward a pretty good plan. He would gradually test the Fallujah Brigade under General Latif's command to see if they were willing to take some serious responsibility for security. "In other words," he said, "will they fight?"

He was more optimistic than I, but he was the guy on the ground. He would begin some limited patrols sometime the following week. If those went well, he would gradually expand the scope of the missions—leading up to occupation of the city principally by Iraqi troops and police by June.

"These next three weeks are extremely delicate," I emphasized. "We're trying to assemble a government. Brahimi is neuralgic about Fallujah and could take up stakes if we're not careful. The period in June with a new government finding its sea legs may also be dicey. Then there is the post–July 1 situation. None of this is simple."

"We shouldn't do anything out there until July One," Rick Sanchez said. "Not worth the risk."

"Not necessarily true, Rick," I said. "It might be better to take the hard decision when the new government is formed than to wait until July. In any case, this will be a decision for the president."

"Well, he's the boss," Rick Sanchez said.

Chapter 13
CLIFFHANGER

■ BAGHDAD
MAY 2004

The Governance Team had just spread their notes on my conference table Thursday, May 6, when the whole office shook from a nearby blast. We flinched as the windows rattled, and dust drifted down.

"*That* sure didn't sound like a mortar," I said.

Frank Gallagher came in. "Big car bomb at the Fourteenth of July Bridge checkpoint, sir. Several people killed. Lots of wounded. Yeah, and it blew out some windows in your house." Gallagher added that Osama bin Laden had just posted a notice on an Al-Qaeda Web site announcing a reward of 10,000 grams of gold to anyone killing me.

"Well, that's pretty cheap of him, considering we have a $25 million reward for him! Keep me informed, Frank."

I pushed aside worries about where and when the next blast would come and turned back to the team.

"What's on the agenda, Scott?"

"We're still fine-tuning our political objectives for the rest of May, Mr. Ambassador," Carpenter said, passing around the team's talking points.

I'd asked him to have the team outline our political strategy to meet the timelines of the Transitional Administrative Law, which called for the installation of a new Iraqi interim government by the end of May, the body to which we were to divest sovereignty by July 1.

I studied the points: The Coalition's "main objective" was to use the appointment of the new government to broaden its base, especially by including more Sunnis and more people from the provinces. As always, the process involved complex "Iraqi math"—seeking qualified candidates, men and women, with appropriate regional representation, and a balance between party and nonparty, exile and nonexile candidates, while bearing in mind the necessity for a Shia majority.

We were nearing the end of an evolution that had begun twelve months earlier when the small group of exiles demanded that the Coalition simply hand their unrepresentative group the power to govern Iraq. Then, we had, instead, worked hard for two months to create a broader-based Governing Council. That Council had hammered out the November 15 Agreement and had written the interim constitution, the TAL. Now we were in the final presovereignty phase. The Coalition and the UN's Lakhdar Brahimi would consult with a broad range of Iraqi leaders to select an interim government that would include a president, prime minister, and council of ministers.

There were serious challenges. The security problems with Muqtada al-Sadr and Fallujah were unresolved. We'd simply postponed inevitable showdowns in order to preserve the fragile political process. The Islamist Shia had never accepted Brahimi, the secular Sunni Arab nationalist, and they were still uneasy about the UN, Saddam's longtime unofficial "ally" in their eyes. Some Shia worried that the CPA might not respect their majority status in Iraq and deny them a plurality in the interim government. Yet the Sunnis clearly needed broader representation in the new government. And the Kurds, well, they were sure to be demanding.

"It's a good thing my son just sent over plenty of espresso," I joked, laying down the memo. "It looks like more all-nighters in the next three weeks."

The coffee proved invaluable as Bob Blackwill and I worked with Brahimi to shape the new government. We were also coordinating with UN election expert Carina Pirelli in her effort to design an electoral system for Iraq. Both of them, I knew, loved good coffee. So Sue Shea had standing instructions to put espresso before them as soon as they sat down and to keep the coffee coming as needed.

Brahimi and the CPA started with different views on the composition of the new government. The crux was what Roman called the "technocrats versus politicians" debate. Brahimi didn't want politicians in the new government, preferring nonpolitical engineers, industrial and financial experts, and former state enterprise managers to run a caretaker cabinet. He envisioned replacing almost all the ministers in the existing Iraqi government, and excluding members of the Governing Council from the new cabinet, even making them ineligible to run for election in January.

The Coalition agreed that the new ministers must be competent and honest, though the British on our team, as Raad Alkadiri pointed out, were also skeptical about having too many politicians in the new government. But, like Brahimi, we recognized that political parties were not popular in Iraq—how could they be when Iraqis had only known the Baath Party? But we also knew that the interim government would need political support to make the tough decisions ahead. And despite the general unpopularity of political parties, some leaders had a measure of public support. I cautioned Brahimi that it would be risky to start with "a clean slate," ignoring the Governing Council and choosing a cabinet lacking in political experience. We had information that the Shiite politicians in the Governing Council were aware of Brahimi's distaste for them and that, encouraged by Chalabi, they were planning to "precook" a government with Ayatollah Sistani and present it to Brahimi and to us as fait accompli.

"If we don't consult the Council seriously on the postsovereignty government," I told the Algerian diplomat, "they're likely to upset the entire process." I stressed that it was better to have the main political parties inside the new government and responsible for its actions, than outside carping during the run-up to elections. This was especially important with regard to the more established parties—the Kurdish groups and, among the Shia, SCIRI and Dawa—which had demonstrated their ability to greatly complicate the political process at a number of key junctures. "Iraq is going to need real political leaders to help rally the people against the insurgency," I argued.

After many meetings, and lots of espresso, Brahimi agreed to "seriously consider" members of the Governing Council and political party notables for cabinet positions. On the Coalition side, we agreed that some ministries would be better led by nonpolitical technocrats.

We told Brahimi that our main interest was the top seven positions: the prime minister, and the ministers of defense, interior, finance, foreign affairs, oil, and trade. Much of the work identifying candidates fell to the CPA and especially to our provincial offices: the UN team admitted that because they had left Iraq the previous summer, they simply didn't have many contacts. The U.S.-U.K. Governance Team and Brahimi's colleagues worked to develop a joint list of candidate ministers, while Blackwill and I concentrated with Brahimi on interviewing candidates for the top jobs. We agreed that after the transfer of sovereignty, the new government should convene a "National Consultative Conference" of up to one thousand Iraqis from all over the country to broaden public discussion of Iraq's future.

The Governing Council remained restive. On May 3, Blackwill and I met with that month's president, Izzadin Salim, a scholarly, soft-spoken Shiite leader from Basra. As a founder of the anti-Baathist Islamic Dawa Party, Izzadin had survived several assassination attempts both in Iraq and while in exile in Iran.

Izzadin reviewed the political situation and let slip that he intended to call a joint Council-cabinet meeting the next day to vote on several alternative ways to choose the new government, including simply extending the GC. This confirmed our information and looked like a take-it-or-leave-it proposition—and one which would alienate Brahimi and probably send him back to New York. Bob and I argued to Izzadin that this was a bad idea, contrary to the spirit of "partnership and consultations," which we had all pledged to support. In the end, Izzadin agreed to drop the vote.

Meanwhile, we plugged away on building the new government with the UN, one name at a time.

In mid-May, I discussed the Abu Ghraib Prison abuse scandal with the Governing Council. I intended to face the issue squarely—before the members were overwhelmed by the groundswell of rumor and anti-Coalition propaganda sweeping the Middle East.

I'd been in Washington in January when the story broke. The Coalition had been open with the media about the scandal. The Army had immediately begun the first of many investigations. It was reported that enlisted-rank American Military Police prison guards, from a single night shift at Abu Ghraib, had been identified as suspects and were facing court-martial charges that included cruelty, assault, and indecent acts. Since the incidents had been made public in January, they had been subject to confidential Army investigations, and I had received no additional information about them other than what was in the press.

Then on April 28, 60 Minutes II had shown the abuse photos. Within hours, pictures of naked Iraqi prisoners, taunted and sexually humiliated by the MPs—including two smirking women soldiers—appeared on front pages and satellite television networks worldwide.

I was as outraged and repulsed by the photos as any American. So when Rick Sanchez and I met with the Governing Council on May 12, I began with a candid apology to all Iraqis for the behavior. Sanchez then gave a concise briefing. He apologized for the "inhumane treatment" and noted that the first court-martial would start in Baghdad the next week.

I added that many Iraqis had asked me for an explanation. "I've told my Iraqi friends, and I'm telling you now," I said, "that this behavior was outrageous. It does not represent America. President Bush has apologized, General Sanchez has apologized, and I apologize. Those found guilty will be punished under the law." I reminded them that this was a marked contrast to what happened under Saddam when far more savage torture was a matter of policy.

"In the year I've been in Iraq," I said, "I've traveled the country and seen thousands of American soldiers working alongside Iraqis to rebuild this country. Risking their lives, they have rebuilt schools, refurbished hospitals and municipal centers, and cleaned up sports fields so they can play soccer with Iraqi kids. That's the true face of America."

When I finished, Dr. Raja Khuzai said she'd recently led a delegation at our suggestion to Abu Ghraib Prison and had found that the medical care there was "much better" than in Iraqi hospitals.

Other Council members contributed their comments. They all regretted the Abu Ghraib misconduct, but most went on to criticize the Arab and international news media for having ignored Saddam's repression for years. "Where was Al-Jazeera when Saddam was having people jammed feet-first into wood shredders?" one asked.

"The BBC was silent when the police dragged off our wives and daughters to be raped," another said.

Adnan Pachachi asked if his assistant, Hata Abdul Wahab, could address the Council. Hata, a diminutive elderly Sunni career diplomat who had incurred Saddam's wrath in the 1970s, moved to the table. The Council room was completely silent as he told his story.

Iraqi intelligence officers had kidnapped and drugged him in Kuwait and driven him back to Baghdad, hidden in the car of the Iraqi ambassador. He was tortured every day for the next eight months: beatings, electric shock, water torture. He spent thirteen years in prison, five and a half in solitary confinement where he never saw daylight. "We must talk about what happened in Abu Ghraib Prison over the past thirty-five years," Hata said. "The world must know."

As he quietly told his story, I saw several GC members wiping tears from their eyes. It was a very powerful moment.

The next day, I discussed the situation with Don Rumsfeld, who had arrived with the chairman of the Joint Chiefs of Staff, General Dick Myers, to confer with Coalition military leaders. We met at their headquarters in Saddam's former Al-Faw Palace near Baghdad International Airport. Rumsfeld had just been through a tough congressional hearing over the scandal. "It's nice to be in Baghdad where there aren't so many people gunning for me," Rumsfeld quipped.

In preparation for his visit I'd asked my military aide, Colonel Norwood, to develop ideas to improve the handling of the thousands of Iraqis we had detained. For months I had been pressing the military to come up with better pro-

cedures. I was particularly frustrated that we couldn't seem to separate criminals who would be turned over to Iraqi courts from men who posed a security
threat or might provide good intelligence on the insurgency.

"We could set up an Iraqi detainees' ombudsman, for example," I told the
secretary. "After all, Iraqis will be responsible for prisoners in the future."

"I like that," Rumsfeld said. "What else?"

I suggested that we determine exactly who had been abused in our custody
and offer to pay compensation through a joint Iraqi-Coalition commission.

"Those who were abused should be compensated," he agreed. "What else?"

I worked through my list: putting Iraqi police observers into brigade-level detention centers and pushing our subordinate commanders to triage prisoners
early on, rather than just sending suspects into detention in Baghdad. I noted
that based on current trends, we would likely be holding 10,000 Iraqi detainees
when we turned over authority to a sovereign government. The political consequences were not hard to imagine. "The best way to reduce the political impact
of detention," I said, "is to reduce the number of detainees."

But to accomplish that, we had to dramatically reduce the authority of Military Intelligence to put an indefinite "hold" on a prisoner. "From my experience over the last year," I added, "this is the single most important roadblock to
releases." I suggested that we review each detainee's record every fifteen days instead of every sixty days and that a detainee could be held for a total of only
thirty days unless there was an explicit statement from authorities why he
should continue to be held. General Sanchez told the secretary that they were
working to accelerate the review process.

Rumsfeld and I also discussed the security crises that had exploded in April:
the Marines' operations in Fallujah and the Anaconda operations against
Muqtada's Mahdi Army.

Sanchez gave a brief presentation on where Coalition forces had hit con-
centrations of Muqtada's militia. He said that the Coalition and Iraqi police
had taken back the shrine in Karbala, capturing a very large weapons cache
there, which included mortars, machine guns, and explosives.

"Dr. Adel of SCIRI, a respected conservative Muslim, praised that operation," I said. "He told me we should 'keep up the pressure' on Muqtada."

"Well," Myers said, "I think we should just finish the job. It's time for us to
take our medicine and get it over with."

It was not clear exactly what the general had in mind by "finish the job." But
we had entered the most sensitive political period since my arrival in Iraq. We

could not simply move ahead militarily without weighing the political consequences.

"I don't think that's a good idea," I told them. "Our strategy of squeezing
Muqtada is working. My people tell me that his support base is fading. And
Rick's troops are regularly killing a lot of his militia." Islamist Shia political leaders had promised to organize public protests against what they considered
Muqtada's sacrilegious actions in the holy cities. We needed to avoid being provoked into a military confrontation in the holy cities and igniting a broader Shia
uprising.

"That's okay," Myers said, "as long as Muqtada's support is going down.
What if it starts to spike up?"

"Then we'll have to reexamine the situation." But we had to recognize the
fact that Muqtada's eventual fate would be messy. In the best of cases, he would
make a vague promise to submit to Iraqi justice; we would disarm his militia,
and eventually perhaps, Muqtada would submit to oversight by the Shia tribes
or the *marjaiya*.

Sanchez said that in about ten days he would run out of Mahdi Army targets
to go after. I replied that in that case, assuming we had freedom of movement,
we would switch to an economic strategy to win support in the Shia south with
more reconstruction programs. If we didn't have freedom of movement, then
by definition we'd still have military targets.

"What's your opinion of the Fallujah situation?" Rumsfeld asked me.

"Mr. Secretary, I'm not as optimistic as some of the military."

I explained that in the past two weeks, the new commander of the Fallujah
Brigade, General Mohammed Latif, had proven difficult, repeatedly refusing
to commit his Fallujah Brigade to combat. The city was one more muddled
problem, which would have to be postponed until a sovereign Iraqi government
was ready to tackle it.

That afternoon in the echoing marble conference room we also discussed the
best means of giving the Iraqi government a voice in overall security decision-
making. I said that once the interim government was in place, we should begin
talks with them about how decisions on combat tactics and the use of air support would be handled after June 30. "But we shouldn't expect that the interim
government will be a pushover," I cautioned. "In fact, the government will want
to show distance from us. And they *will* make mistakes."

"I'm all for making the Iraqis step up to responsibility as soon as possible,"
Rumsfeld said.

"And I'm convinced that the interim government will want to have successful elections in January," I said. "They know this will require security and that the Iraqi forces currently aren't up to the job. So they'll have to find a way to cooperate with Coalition forces to achieve their political goal. But they won't be patsies."

The meeting had reestablished in everybody's mind the link between politics and strategy. But I saw on the strained faces of the commanders around the conference table that they were uneasy about the complex and open-ended mission ahead.

The generals' concern reflected a broader disquiet: Coalition forces were spread too thin on the ground. During my morning intelligence briefings, I would sometimes picture an under-strength fire crew racing from one blaze to another. Even though more than thirty countries had already contributed troops to the Iraqi operation, the Pentagon was hoping allies might contribute still more forces. For months I'd been talking myself hoarse about the risk of overestimating the capabilities of Iraqi security forces. The collapse of those forces in the April crises had proved this point. But now attacks on our convoys were increasing. Insurgents were shutting down the export pipelines with depressing regularity. Work on reconstruction projects which Washington's red tape had slowed for months was now being complicated further by insurgent attacks. On May 2, I had e-mailed Francie to sum up my frustration. The April crises, I'd written, had shown Iraqi forces to be "ineffective, or worse." Many Coalition units had overly restrictive Rules of Engagement that rendered them useless. "They cannot fight, yet we have to provide them logistical support, hence more convoys to be protected." I told her I was concerned that we didn't have enough Coalition troops to cover all the bases.

While our Anaconda strategy was gradually working, we were paying the price for having waited so long to move against Muqtada. General Marty Dempsey, commander of the 1st Armored Division which was conducting operations against the upstart cleric, admitted to the New York Times on May 12 that our delay had allowed Muqtada to recruit and train troops. "We probably gave him six months more than we should have," Dempsey said.

As if to demonstrate our military quandary, on May 14—the day after the Coalition commanders' meeting—Muqtada renewed his attacks on Coalition and Iraqi forces in the south. His militia set up mortar positions near the

Karbala mosque and dug heavy weapons into the cemetery near the shrine of Imam Ali in Najaf. From these positions, they opened fire on our forces. The action was intended to show his strength despite the Coalition seizure of the Karbala arms cache and probably to provoke us into attacking the holy site itself.

This tactic was effectively blackmail. Muqtada made public his demands: establishing a "Najaf Brigade," apparently modeled on the Fallujah Brigade, for security, releasing all "political prisoners," and closing "the file on recent events." This was a reference to the murder charges and arrest warrant an Iraqi judge had filed against him. Muqtada claimed to be prepared to have his own case heard, but only by "a legitimate constitutional government elected in free national elections"—"in other words," I noted to Dick Jones, "not before February or March next year."

CPA offices in the south heard from tribal leaders that Muqtada was seeking direct negotiations with the Coalition. Several GC members also claimed to have reliable communications with him. We followed up each of these approaches, but received back confusing and contradictory messages. It wasn't clear that any of these alleged channels in fact reached Muqtada, or that he himself had settled on a true goal for a peaceful resolution of the crisis.

By firing on Coalition troops in Karbala and Najaf, Muqtada succeeded in luring our forces close to the shrines. Sanchez told me that he wanted to declare a unilateral cease-fire to avoid having our forces "cross any red lines."

"Let's hold off on that, Rick," I said, explaining that we'd had a flurry of contacts from people claiming they spoke for Muqtada. "I don't think we should declare a cease-fire without getting something in return."

Through intermediaries, I asked Ayatollah Sistani his opinion on conducting direct talks with Muqtada. His reply was swift and unambiguous.

"We do not know the reason for, or utility of, negotiating with Muqtada," Sistani said.

We continued efforts to build a new government that could survive until the January elections.

Brahimi came to see the usefulness of consulting the Governing Council on finding people for senior positions in the new government. Aware of how difficult it would be to coordinate on such a delicate matter with the full twenty-five member GC, Brahimi suggested that instead he, Blackwill, and I meet with a "troika" of the Council made up of the Council's immediate past, present, and future presidents. They were the Kurd, Massoud Barzani; Izzadin Salim, a

Shiite; and Sunni Ghazi al-Yawar, each of whom had solid support in his community. Izzadin and Ghazi had been added to the P-9 presidency of the Council in April when the monthly rotation among the original nine men had run its course.

Barzani hosted the first of these meetings at his mountaintop retreat in Salahuddin on Sunday, May 16. I stressed that time was running short if we were to have the government in place by the end of May.

Izzadin spoke insightfully: "It's important in establishing the interim government to reduce the opposition that the Governing Council faces in many regions. We need to include all elements of Iraqi society."

Brahimi had already agreed with our recommendation that several ministers from the current interim government be carried over to the postsovereignty IIG. These included Hoshyar Zebari, the minister of foreign affairs; Ayham al-Sammarae, minister of electricity; Nasreen Bewari, the female minister of municipalities; and several others who were doing a good job, and who also fulfilled Brahimi's desire to use as many technocrats as possible. He also shared our objective of getting more Sunnis involved but admitted that he was having difficulty identifying valid candidates.

But the Gordian knot in the political process would be identifying a president and a prime minister acceptable to the schismatic country. This would require balancing among the major groups, though Brahimi agreed with us that we must avoid establishing an inflexible Lebanon-style structure in which important positions were legally reserved for members of one ethnic or religious group.

Our immediate problem was, again, the Kurds. Jalal Talabani and his prime minister, Barham Saleh, came to call on me after spending several weeks in Washington, where Talabani had been pushing his candidacy as president in the new government. It fell to me to tell him that Brahimi and the Coalition had agreed that the post should go to an Arab Sunni. "For too long they have felt underrepresented in the New Iraq, Mr. Talabani," I told him. "We have to use this government as an opportunity to broaden Iraq's political base." Talabani, visibly distressed to hear this news, went back to his hometown of Sulaymaniya.

The security situation in several areas of Iraq was becoming graver. On May 17, I had a private meeting with General Sanchez to discuss the war.

"What would you do if you had two more divisions, Rick?" I asked him.

He was a practical soldier who didn't normally speculate about the hypothetical when there were so many concrete problems to address each day.

But he answered immediately. "I'd control Baghdad."

He hated the fact that the insurgents seemed able to operate openly in the capital.

I could see other uses for 35,000 or 40,000 additional troops. "But we also need to secure our LOCs," I said, referring to lines of communication, the vital road links and pipelines within Iraq and to neighboring countries. "And we need to do a better job protecting critical infrastructure, too." Without such heightened safeguarding, Iraq's oil revenues were being crimped and our reconstruction projects were slowing. "And actually we've never really controlled the borders," I added.

Rick smiled. "Got those spare troops handy, sir?"

I had fewer than sixty days left in my tenure as CPA administrator. So I had to do all in my power to leave behind the strongest possible political and security situation. The political foundation was coming along, but as always, I was worried about security. The April crisis had made clear that it would be a long time before Iraqi forces would be able to secure the country on their own. Could we get more Coalition soldiers to fill the gap?

On May 18, I gave Rice a heads-up that I intended to send Secretary Rumsfeld a very private message suggesting that the Coalition needed more troops. A courier would carry my note, I added, so there wouldn't be copies bouncing around.

That afternoon I sent my message to Rumsfeld. I noted that the deterioration of the security situation since April had made it clear, to me at least, that we were trying to cover too many fronts with too few resources. We were attempting to control borders, defend LOCs, and protect infrastructure. Iraqi oil exports had fallen because of lack of security. Even a year after Liberation, the military still could not provide adequate protection for movements to and from Baghdad International Airport. Most CPA posts in the south were under nightly attack by Muqtada's militia. "Friday night," I told him, "our Nasiriyah office was nearly overrun while the Italian Quick Reaction Force took seven hours to travel a few miles. We lowered the Coalition flag there yesterday." The CPA headquarters was basically "locked down."

I stressed that while I did not think our mission was on the brink, I felt we were in a dangerous situation. I recommended that he consider whether the Coalition could deploy one or two additional divisions for up to a year.

I verified that the secretary received my message. I did not hear back from him.

A few days later, Rice suggested that she, her deputy, Steve Hadley, Bob Blackwill, and I have a frank telephone discussion about security.

"The erosion of support for the Coalition has accelerated over the past three months," I said in that meeting, "despite progress on the political process, the TAL, and glimmerings of reconstruction activity—at last." The reason was quite simply the increase in insurgent attacks. I warned that we were sure to face more such attacks in the coming weeks as the enemy tried to derail progress along the path to democracy. "So the message to most Iraqis is that the Coalition can't provide them the most basic government service: security," I concluded. "We've become the worst of all things—an ineffective occupier."

Rice and Hadley listened but made few comments. Blackwill and I were not sure if our analysis would have any effect in Washington.

Meanwhile, we were still grappling with the problem of finding a president and a prime minister who would be both decisive in dealing with the insurgency and acceptable to the major elements of Iraqi society.

The clear front-runner for president was Adnan Pachachi, the elderly Sunni statesman who had played such a critical role in the development of the TAL. He was widely respected, had established a productive working relationship with the Coalition, and was a friend of Brahimi's. Though the Shia and Kurds had never embraced him, it was expected that he would be acceptable as the preeminent Sunni politician of the Governing Council.

The prime ministerial question was thornier. Brahimi's initial candidate was Hussein al-Shahristani, a Shiite nuclear scientist who had headed the Iraqi Atomic Energy Commission until 1979. Saddam had had him imprisoned for eleven years for refusing to cooperate in the Baathists' secret nuclear weapons program. Shahristani, educated in the U.K. and Canada, had spent much of his captivity in Abu Ghraib Prison either in solitary confinement or jammed into a dark, stifling pen with other prisoners who were forced to take turns lying down. He escaped in 1991 in the first Gulf War when Coalition bombs landed nearby. He had fled into exile where he rallied international support against Saddam, and returned to Karbala with his family in 2003. He set up private charitable organizations whose activities in the Shia south put him in contact with Ayatollah Sistani.

Apparently following Sistani's example, Shahristani had refused to meet with any Coalition officials, so he was relatively unknown to us. At Brahimi's urging, he agreed to meet Blackwill and me and we were impressed with his intelligence and sophistication. We still knew little about how he would be as prime minister.

I mentioned his name at a telephonic NSC meeting the next day. The president went straight to the heart of the matter as he saw it: "It's important to have someone who's willing to stand up and thank the American people for their sacrifice in liberating Iraq. I don't expect us to pick a yes man. But at least I want someone who will be grateful. Does Shahristani want the job? Will he support us? Is he courageous enough?"

I responded that Bob and I were having dinner with him the next night and would push hard on all these points.

At that dinner, Shahristani proved thoughtful, articulate, and wide-ranging in his interests, one of the more impressive Iraqi leaders I'd met. But as the long evening unfolded, my impression of him became mixed. He was grateful for the Liberation. "The new government must be hard on the insurgency. But I would want to use Coalition forces only where necessary." This was a logical point, but as we talked it became clear that he would be hesitant to find reasons to use those troops, even if Iraqi forces were not adequate to the challenge, which we knew would be the case for some time to come. The more we talked, the clearer became his ambivalence about Coalition forces.

Moreover, it became apparent that Shahristani was very much a Shiite. He had had little contact with Iraq north of Baghdad. And then he shocked us by saying that he and Ayatollah Sistani were of the opinion that a Sunni should become prime minister. "The job will be too difficult for anyone," he said. "Whoever takes it is likely to fail, so let a Sunni fail."

"That's shortsighted," I said bluntly, "and risks repeating the tragic mistake the Shia made in the 1920s when they opted out of the political process and bought themselves eighty years in internal exile."

At a minimum, his comments suggested he didn't want to be prime minister at all.

"Let's keep Shahristani in reserve," I told Bob. "But my impression is that he's too soft." Bob agreed. Still, Shahristani remained Brahimi's early choice for the post.

On the hot morning of Monday, May 17, the Governing Council president, Izzadin Salim, three members of his security squad, and three Iraqi passersby were killed when a suicide car bomb exploded at a checkpoint just outside the Green Zone.

Abu Musab Zarqawi had almost certainly organized the murder. But his intention to disrupt Iraq's progress toward sovereignty failed, and in an unforeseen way might have actually helped it. One unanticipated result of Izzadin's murder was that Sheik Ghazi al-Yawar, the Council's designated June rotating president, now assumed the May presidency. Following protocol, it was therefore to Ghazi that President Bush offered his telephoned condolences. Ghazi was American-educated, with a background in both private enterprise and politics. The president sent word to me that he'd been favorably impressed by Ghazi's open thanks to the Coalition for overthrowing Saddam and by his determination to continue the process to sovereignty and eventual democracy.

Blackwill and I began to see Ghazi as a possible candidate for the presidency.

At an NSC meeting on May 19, Blackwill and I reported on the pros and cons of Shahristani. I could see on the video screen that President Bush wasn't comfortable with him.

"Look," Bush said, "whoever it is, I want to be sure that he won't start playing to the gallery by attacking the Coalition right after taking office."

"Well," I answered, "there'll certainly be some politicians, especially those left out of the government, who'll do that."

Rumsfeld said, "We've got to have a prime minister who's solid as a rock."

"Absolutely," the president replied. "We've got to be certain the new PM won't ask us to leave the day after sovereignty."

I had to be frank on this vital question. "We can't be 100 percent sure of any Iraqi prime minister we choose," I said.

Powell noted that irrespective of what the new government said, it might be forced to ask for our departure if something went badly wrong. I reminded them how deeply unpopular the Coalition had become under the incessant barrage of Arab propaganda and mounting security concerns. Perhaps the end of the formal occupation would help bring greater acceptance of the need for Coalition troops. "But we can't seek full guarantees and expect them to hold up," I said.

The president also said that it was a risk to bet on someone he'd never met. "I trust Bremer and Blackwill on this but frankly I'd be a lot more comfortable knowing that the man has courage and wasn't weak. Whoever it is, he's got to be a leader. What do you suggest we do if we decide not to go with Shahristani?" Bush asked.

"We'd probably turn to Ayad Allawi," I answered, "although there are serious doubts that he'd be acceptable to Sistani."

I'd always respected Allawi's toughness; once he'd committed himself to a policy, he didn't let go.

"Okay," the president said. "Look, we just have to remind people that only one year has passed since Liberation. The transition to democracy will take time, and we have to be patient—all of us, the Coalition and the Iraqis. That's why I'm concerned about getting some solid statements of support of the Coalition from the new Iraqi government."

It was agreed that we should ask Brahimi to float Ghazi as a presidential candidate and Shahristani's name as possible prime minister. We needed to know if he could command broad support, and not just among Shia. And Blackwill and I would meet him again to probe further on his attitude toward Coalition forces remaining in Iraq after June 30.

But, given President Bush's firm criteria for the new Iraqi prime minister, I felt that Shahristani was just not the right man for the job. The challenge would be getting Brahimi to agree.

The next day, Blackwill and I turned our attention to the key position of defense minister. Ayad Allawi, chairman of the GC's Security Committee, was the U.S. government's first choice. While we were concerned that Sistani might not accept him as prime minister, Allawi's toughness was undisputed and so we thought he might be more acceptable as defense minister. That morning, Allawi came to talk politics with Bob and me.

"You know that President Bush and my government admire your long and courageous record of opposing Saddam and helping topple his regime," I began.

Allawi accepted this praise graciously. He was a tall, heavy-set man, who looked more like a retired linebacker than a neurologist, political leader, and survivor of decades of shadowy conflicts. When it was humid, Allawi still walked with great difficulty because of the pain from his knee where Saddam's killers had axed him in bed in London more than twenty years before.

"All patriotic Iraqis must now step forward to serve their country," I said. "We want you to become minister of defense."

"Naturally," he replied, "I've got questions about how you see the position. But before we begin, I have to tell you that I won't serve under Shahristani."

"Why?"

"He's too close to the Iranians."

Indeed, memories lasted centuries if not millennia in Mesopotamia. Dick Jones had warned me that Iraqis would never accept someone with an Iranian name. Confirming Dick's analysis, when I'd discussed the ideal qualities for the new premier with my friend Ayatollah Hussein al-Sadr, he'd said that he'd heard of one candidate who had "an Iranian name," Shahristani.

"But his family has lived in Iraq for three hundred years," I'd said.

"It's an Iranian name," the cleric replied.

On other issues related to the defense portfolio, Ayad Allawi listened carefully to our description of the minister's authority—and was clearly dissatisfied when we confirmed that the prime minister could fire anyone in his cabinet. Allawi reiterated that he would not serve under Shahristani.

We didn't have time to dwell on this latest twist.

Sheik Ghazi came in to bemoan the fact that I asked him not to lead the Iraqi delegation to the Arab League summit in Tunis that weekend.

"Look, Sheik Ghazi," I said. "This next week is crucial. We need you here for your wise counsel and the respect you've earned on the Governing Council."

I didn't add that because he'd favorably impressed President Bush, we were actively considering suggesting him for the position of president in the interim government. Pachachi had told our Governance Team that Ghazi—a Georgetown University graduate—was hoping to become Iraq's ambassador in Washington. But he would be more valuable to his country as the visible symbol of ethnic and sectarian reconciliation. The only problem there was that Pachachi was Brahimi's candidate for the presidency. For our part, Blackwill and I had been concerned by Pachachi's overly emotional reaction to the crisis in Fallujah. Ghazi reluctantly agreed to stay in Iraq for the next crucial weeks.

Almost immediately, we got word that the Kurds had called an urgent political confab in Irbil at which the two Kurdish parties would pass a resolution demanding either the presidency or premiership as their price for staying as part of Iraq. I contacted Dr. Rowsch, Barzani's deputy, who confirmed this was their intention.

I expressed my regret at this breach of the spirit of open consultations and said I'd send Blackwill up north that afternoon to discuss the matter with Barzani and Talabani.

Before Blackwill left, we met with Brahimi. I explained that we needed a broad representative reaction to Shahristani's possible candidacy because he was still unknown in Washington. Brahimi said he planned to "trail" Shahristani's name and several other names with leading Shia. I stressed that he needed to get reactions from Sunnis, too. I said we were picking up rumblings about his "Iranian" name.

"What do you think of Pachachi?" I asked.

"Frankly," Brahimi said, "I've become a bit ambivalent about him. He's eighty-four, and even if the job is mainly symbolic, he'd have to represent Iraq internationally at some important meetings."

All three of us had been senior diplomats long enough to recognize the truth in that.

"Why don't you float Ghazi's name as a candidate for president to see what you get?" Blackwill suggested. Brahimi agreed, I thought somewhat reluctantly, to try this out.

In the midst of these machinations, we had yet another crisis involving Chalabi's Iraqi National Congress. The first problem had begun in March, when a Finance Ministry employee told the Justice Ministry that Ibrahim Nouri Sabah, personal secretary to the minister of finance, had illegally recycled millions of dollars' worth of old currency turned in for destruction. Sabah had allegedly also solicited kickbacks from other employees. At the request of the minister of justice, I had referred the matter to the Central Criminal Court on March 16 for investigation by the Iraqis. Sabah was arrested March 24 on the basis of an Iraqi judge's warrant.

During the judge's subsequent investigation, Sabah provided evidence that officials of the Iraqi National Congress were involved in a scheme to obtain state property from the Finance Ministry and dispose of it for their own profit illegally. The investigation also found evidence of assaults and kidnapping of INC opponents. The deeper the Iraqi investigators dug, the more culpable the INC seemed to be, although its leaders appeared confident they could ride out the inquiry "until the Americans [the CPA] left" as one report had it.

Again responding to a request from the Iraqi minister of justice, on April 5, I had signed a second order authorizing the Central Criminal Court to investigate charges against INC officials.

"Let the chips fall where they will," I told Ed Schmults, the CPA's Justice Ministry adviser.

After collecting further evidence, Iraqi Judge Hussein Muathin subsequently issued arrest warrants for several senior INC officials, including its head of security, and search warrants for some INC buildings. Ahmad Chalabi was not named in the warrants.

Now an even more explosive matter involving Chalabi added to tensions. On May 3, *Newsweek* had reported that Chalabi told an Iranian operative that America had broken Iranian intelligence codes and was reading their secret messages. (Chalabi denied that he had done so, claiming the charges were a CIA smear.) Then on May 10, the Iraqi judge received a letter from the minister of finance, "directing" him to stop the investigation at his ministry. I canceled that order as being beyond the authority of the minister of finance.

Because the INC sites in the elite Mansour district, including Chalabi's villa, were heavily guarded and the Iraqi police did not believe they could conduct the searches safely alone, Judge Muathin sought Coalition assistance in executing the warrants. I alerted Rice's deputy, Steve Hadley, that we'd reached a crisis with the INC. I urged General Sanchez to authorize the use of Coalition forces, but only to provide perimeter security for the Iraqi police executing the warrants on the INC.

Early on Thursday, May 20, Iraqi police went to Chalabi's house and the nearby INC headquarters named in the Iraqi judge's search warrants. They searched for, but did not find, several fugitives, but removed office files, computers, and a number of unregistered weapons. Because of the company of American troops cordoning off the street, rumors quickly flashed that this had been a "Coalition" operation.

The Governing Council's "Shia House," a collection of Shiite political groups, was in an uproar for several hours. In meetings with Bahr al-Uloum and Jaafari, and in a message I sent to Sistani, I explained that the action was conducted by Iraqi police on the basis of an Iraqi court–issued search warrant. If Iraq was to establish the rule of law, no man could be above the law. And the independent Iraqi courts had to be allowed to operate free from political influence. This appeared to calm most of the Shia down.

Ahmad Chalabi erupted in outraged vituperation. He told reporters that the true impetus for the raid had been his opposition to former Baathists and his zeal in investigating the growing kickback scandal in the UN's Oil for Food program.

"Let my people go!" Chalabi shouted dramatically. "Let my people be free! It is time for the Iraqi people to run their own affairs."

The next day, Brahimi told me that the Shahristani candidacy was collapsing. Brahimi himself saw that Iraq would need an interim premier with both political skill and deep resolve. It was not an easy task to find such a person. "Shahristani just doesn't have the recognition in the country the prime minister will need," he concluded. Blackwill and I were relieved he had come to the same conclusion as we about Shahristani.

Brahimi also reported that Chalabi was actively organizing the Shia House against Brahimi's mission, still pushing to expand the Governing Council into the new cabinet and to secure one of the vice president positions for himself. To gather support among the Shia, Chalabi had reportedly told Dr. Adel Mahdi, SCIRI's deputy member of the GC, that he would support Adel's candidacy for the prime ministry in return for Mahdi's support for his plan.

The CPA and UN agreed that we did not want an Islamist prime minister. "Could you please speak to Dr. Adel and tell him we're not going to put him into that post?" Brahimi asked me. He wanted me to give the same message to Jaafari, who was also very actively campaigning for the prime ministry. I agreed, but not before getting Brahimi's agreement that we would offer Adel Mahdi, a trained economist, the Finance Ministry and Jaafari one of the vice presidencies as a way to keep both their parties involved in the interim government.

Within an hour, Adel Mahdi came to my office for a one-on-one meeting. Over the past year, I had come to respect him as one of the most sensible GC deputies. At my request, Meghan O'Sullivan had previewed our message to Adel. We had a general talk about the political process. I mentioned to him that there were several Sunnis being mentioned for president. The vice presidents were assumed to be a Shiite and a Kurd. "The prime minister," I added, "will be Shia, but probably a nonparty man," not the nationally recognized leader of a sectarian party.

"Ambassador, I must disagree," he replied with some heat. "The Shia House has met and chosen two candidates for premier, myself and Ibrahim Jaafari. If they choose Jaafari, that's fine with me and I will support him. On the other hand, I have support from many people—Talabani, Chalabi, Pachachi, and Ghazi."

"Well, Dr. Adel, I think it's important that SCIRI be represented in the cabinet," I said. "I had in mind to suggest you for minister of finance, which would fit well with your training as an economist."

Adel's pride was bruised, but he recovered by discussing the proper ethnic and sectarian balance in the new government. "And, of course," he added, "I think that SCIRI should have one of the top posts. I, myself, might be a vice president."

Later that afternoon, I met with Ibrahim Jaafari. Our meeting had been scheduled to take place in his house in a Baghdad suburb, but my advance security men came under attack on their way there and Frank Gallagher insisted we meet instead at Jaafari's office in the GC building.

I arrived to find Jaafari talking with his colleagues over steaming tea. I repeated what I'd told Adel: we thought the prime minister should not be the leader of a national party.

"This is a mistake," he said gruffly. "The street will *never* understand or accept that a Shia party man is not premier." The parties, he added, will want to choose that person "themselves." And "the other one," he said, meaning Shahristani, was not really an Iraqi.

"Would you be interested in one of the vice presidencies?" I asked.

"It depends who the president is," he said. "And on the overall position of the Shia in the government."

A vague answer. Obviously, Jaafari still hoped for the prime minister job.

On the presidency, Jaafari was dismissive of Pachachi. "Too emotional, picks too many fights with other Council members. And he used rough language with us." Then Jaafari added, "Ghazi is much better. He's less confrontational, and he *looks* like an Arab."

Despite all the difficulties, we made slow progress putting the new government together. Blackwill returned from Kurdistan with "firm" commitments from Talabani and Barzani not to upset progress by insisting on the presidency or premiership, though it was not clear what price, with regard to other cabinet posts, they would try to extract from this concession.

On May 24, Brahimi and the CPA met again with the Governing Council troika to discuss the prime ministership. The Iraqis mentioned several names — Adel, Shahristani, and, for the first time, Ayad Allawi. Ghazi made a strong pitch for the PM being a tough-minded party man who could rally public support for the new government. All three Iraqis were dismissive of Shahristani. Brahimi floated a couple of more nonparty names, but the response to each was unwelcoming. A renewed search — more of a chaotic scramble among the Iraqi politicians — ensued.

Let the dust settle. But don't wait too long.

The first sign of a breakthrough came the next day when Brahimi, Blackwill, and I again met the GC troika. Brahimi recounted his multiple interviews with candidates great and small, and we turned to the prime ministry.

Ghazi led off. "Iraq needs a tough prime minister. So my candidate is Ayad Allawi."

The other two troika members also supported Allawi. "He can do the job," Barzani said, no doubt thinking of killing insurgents and terrorists. Hamid Moussa, the communist who'd taken Izzadin's seat on the troika, added his support of Allawi. "A good man, an honest man."

My British colleague David Richmond wondered aloud whether Allawi would be acceptable to Sistani. We had assumed his secularism would strike him from Sistani's list.

Brahimi said, "Well, he probably wouldn't be the ayatollah's first choice." But he added that he'd just had a letter from Sistani's son, Mohammed Ridha, which said there "might be" worthy candidates from among the Shia House and listed Jaafari, Adel, and Ayad Allawi. Adel and Jaafari were out of the running — but Sistani accepting Allawi, *that* was unexpected progress.

But I kept Bremer's Rules of Life in Iraq firmly in mind. The Iraqis agreed to canvas their GC colleagues on the candidates for prime minister.

The next day we discussed an acceptable electoral system for the January elections with the UN's election expert, Carina Pirelli, and Brahimi. We agreed that one objective was to find the system least likely to provide an unfair advantage to highly organized groups like the Baathists and Shia Islamists. Since sticking to the TAL timetable was essential to keep the support of Sistani and the Shia, it was critical to find a process that could be implemented by the end of January.

Pirelli's elections experts and our NGO, the International Foundation for Election Systems, agreed that the only way to conduct credible elections in such a short period was to have votes counted in a single national constituency. There was no time to draw separate district boundaries. And there was no time to conduct a full census or produce a national electoral roll. The experts were satisfied that this system would not advantage these former Baathists or the Shia Islamists. Some in our Coalition governance group strongly disagreed. After much talk, I recommended, and the U.S. government agreed, that we endorse the experts' advice. "Whatever choice we make," I told the Governance Team, "it'll be known as 'proportionate disappointment.' "

I now had the job of persuading the Governing Council to disband itself once the new government was named. Although I was prepared to order its dissolution if necessary, it would be much better if they could be persuaded to do it.

During a long meeting with the Governing Council on May 26, I told them that Iraq was once again at "an historic moment. . . . Looking back at our many discussions around this table, day and night, over the past ten months, the Council can feel great pride in its contribution to Iraq's future. You have taken many risks. And two of your members have died serving their country.

"We're almost at the end of the journey we began together last July. But we must complete the last kilometer together and effect a smooth transition. We intend to announce the new government within a week. And that new government must have every chance to establish itself in the eyes of the Iraqi people." I was about to drop the hammer. "Therefore, the Governing Council should dissolve itself the day before the new government takes office. Such a peaceful transfer of power will be a lasting demonstration of the Council's respect for democratic principles."

To sweeten the proposition, I quickly added that Iraq should be able to continue to benefit from the expertise of GC members. We therefore proposed that any members not joining the new government would automatically become members of the National Consultative Council that would be convened in July. We would also continue their salaries, housing, cars, and personal security detachments until the elections in January. "Not everyone will be completely satisfied," I said. "But I sincerely hope all of you will support this process for the sake of your beloved Iraq."

The Council broke up with some grumbling, but most agreed to accept their fates.

Later that day, at another troika meeting, Ghazi, Barzani, and the cheerful communist Moussa all reported that their soundings revealed "strong support" for Ayad Allawi across the Governing Council. Apparently he'd been doing some astute backroom politicking and had lined up a majority of backers.

But we were far from out of the woods. The Shia House was again meeting to select its own slate for the new government in order to present it as a done deal. We understood that Chalabi was working with Bahr al-Uloum to persuade the Shia to boycott the interim government if this effort did not succeed.

"They're motivated by Iran," Barzani said scornfully, showing again his distrust of the Shia clergy.

Moussa, a secular Shia, added, "They'll never agree on a slate anyway."

But David Richmond noted that it was important the new PM have "broad support" in the Governing Council and not be elected by a narrow margin.

Ghazi added that there were really only four or five Council members who would likely vote against Allawi. One participant suggested to general laughter buying off Jaafari by offering him "a good university."

"Let's be careful how we treat Jaafari," I said. "He comes out on the top of all the polls and so does his party."

"Yes, but political parties all together have only about 10 percent support," Brahimi replied.

"If the Shia insist on an Islamic candidate," Barzani said adamantly, "then the Kurds will have to reassess their position."

At least we had consensus among this group on Allawi. *What would the full GC do the next day?*

Still later on May 26, Blackwill and I dined at Allawi's house. He suggested that much of his candidacy's snowballing support came from the tribes of central Iraq. As expected, the Shia House had been unable to agree on their own slate but had rejected the idea of boycotting the new government. We were quietly grateful for this news.

We probed Allawi on his thoughts about the new government. He was insistent that security and restoring the economy would be top priorities. We asked about elections.

Allawi's reply was ambivalent: "Yes, of course, but security is the most important matter. Elections should be held, if not in January, then February or March or anyway by summer."

That sounded a bit like a slippery slope. "Dr. Allawi," I said, "as you've agreed, Iraq can't be secure without American help. Americans are idealistic people. Most Americans will support our continued involvement if they're convinced that Iraq is moving toward democracy. Elections are an important element of that move. So I'm *certain* the president and American people will assume elections will happen as planned."

Allawi shrugged. I'd left him no way out. "But . . ." he began, and then took a deep breath. "Of course, you're right. We will work for the elections in January."

After dinner, I told Bob that it looked like we'd gotten the right answer on elections out of Allawi, but it had been just about as hard as getting the right answer on security out of Shahristani.

The security situation was improving in the south. The transfer of three brigades of the 1st Armored Division to the area south of Baghdad had kept the pressure on Muqtada al-Sadr and his Mahdi Army.

Muqtada was now having conversations with Sistani's son and planning to send his militia out of the holy cities—at least temporarily. Some of Muqtada's band had already left the holy shrines and filtered out of the city. When I met Sayyid Mohammad Bahr al-Uloum, he was brimming with good cheer over the "resolution" of the situation in Najaf. "There are people in the streets for the first time in months," he exclaimed.

There was only one big problem with this ostensible victory: the 1st AD would complete its planned departure from Iraq that summer, and when they did, Muqtada's men might just reoccupy the holy cities.

"Sooner or later," I told Dick Jones late one night, "the new Iraqi government will have to deal with this guy."

The last few days of May—which coincided with some nasty, enervating *shamal* sandstorms—were a nervy period of frayed tempers and tender egos.

On Thursday the 27th, Adnan Pachachi exploded, furious at his "son" the

Sunni Sheik Ghazi for supposedly maneuvering behind his back to gain the presidency. Then Brahimi came in to say he didn't think Ghazi would make a good choice for president "because it's not clear that he'd really bring much support from the Sunni world, or even Sunni tribes." Brahimi also admitted that there were questions about Pachachi's support among the nonurban Sunnis. On the other hand, he had no alternative candidates.

Brahimi then raised his concern about Allawi, saying that the problem was that the American media would report his appointment as a victory for the State Department and CIA over the Pentagon, given Chalabi's fall from its grace. This would play back into Iraq as the victory of one American "tribe" over another. "And we don't have enough 'new faces' in the government," he added.

Blackwill patiently indicated that twenty of the thirty-one people we proposed for the new government were new faces. But he admitted that if you looked only at the top posts, there were more old than new faces. On balance, the slate had as its backbone people and parties we had come to know and could work with, a group that could withstand popular pressure, but which was not simply the Governing Council in another form.

To broaden the government, we agreed to add a few more "ministers of state," a useful face-saving position customary in the Arab world.

And I finally persuaded Talabani to come back to the horse-trading in Baghdad.

Meanwhile insurgents killed several Russian technicians working on the Daura power plant, prompting their government to pressure Russian companies to withdraw all their employees everywhere in Iraq. Since this potentially involved several hundred skilled people, it threatened to deal a big blow to our efforts to get more electricity on the grid.

On the evening of May 27, I told the NSC Principals' meeting that Ayad Allawi now had the firm support of at least sixteen members of the Governing Council. Even more important, according to Brahimi, he was acceptable to Ayatollah Sistani. "But it's still difficult for Brahimi to appoint him because of Allawi's previous contacts with the CIA. And he finds neither Pachachi nor Ghazi ideal. On the other hand, Brahimi hasn't been able to come up with any other credible Sunni presidential candidates."

What I left unsaid was the fact that Washington had criticized the CPA for months for not identifying more non-Baathist Sunni leaders, but that Brahimi, an internationally respected Sunni Arab nationalist, was encountering the same difficulties that we had. The difficulties reflected a structural fact of Iraq's political life: any Sunni with political ambitions had either joined the Baath Party, been killed, or forced into exile. Credible Sunni political leaders were just thin on the ground. I suspected that the Iraqis themselves would face the same problem when they put together their own government.

"But there *is* good news. We have agreement on at least twenty-five ministers," I said. "And the Governing Council has also agreed to dissolve itself."

The next day I met alone with a much subdued Ibrahim Jaafari. "Mr. Ambassador," he said, "over the past year we have had many meetings and talked about a lot of things. Now I have to ask you, as a friend, for your advice. What should I do?"

"You've served Iraq well," I said. "Every Iraqi leader now has a responsibility to help his country. The next eight months will be crucial, so I encourage you to accept one of the vice presidencies."

He did not accept outright, but I chalked him up for the job.

Later that day, Pachachi arrived, dressed in his customary dark diplomat's suit. He was outraged at Sheik Ghazi. "I can't understand how Ghazi could have gotten so much support," he said. "He's still so young, whereas I am known throughout the country and around the world."

I agreed that I knew of no other Iraqi who had worked harder for his country since Liberation.

This led Pachachi to a description of his first diplomatic post: Washington in April 1945, where he had arrived only six days before President Franklin Roosevelt died. There he had married the Iraqi ambassador's daughter. Obviously, he was appealing for my intervention to grant one last decorative medal to complete his long service. But as I saw him to my door, I offered only vague assurances that things would come out all right in the end.

When Blackwill and I went to the Governing Council that afternoon to discuss some administrative details, we were told that the members had just unanimously approved Ayad Allawi as their candidate for prime minister. The room was jammed with members and staff, all in a jovial mood. Somewhat surprised by the Council's speedy decision, I congratulated Allawi and said I was sure that he and all his colleagues agreed that every serious political leader should support the new Iraqi interim government.

But as often was the case, this seemingly smooth progress was deceptive.

•　　•　　•

The next morning Brahimi, Blackwill, and I met with Ayad Allawi to review a list of ministers we had prepared. Before we started offering jobs we needed to know if there were any of them that Allawi wouldn't accept.

The new prime minister wanted a few changes, which inevitably altered the overall cabinet balance in various ways: north versus south; Sunni, Shia, and Kurd; men and women; and, of course, the exiles versus the "internals." So for the last time, we worked through what I had earlier described as a game of three-dimensional tic-tac-toe. And we agreed on which of us would inform the candidates, with Allawi reserving the most important calls for himself. I would call the other new ministers and all the outgoing ministers to thank them for their service.

Allawi promised to explain to Talabani that the Kurds could not have both Foreign Affairs and Defense, which had been the last ultimatum we'd heard out of Sulaymaniya.

And so it went. A few steps forward. Several more backward.

A few hours later, Brahimi returned and announced over an espresso that he'd encountered a "real problem" with Ghazi. I reminded him of Bremer's Iron Rule of Iraqi Politics, that no two of the three major groups would ever be tranquil at the same time. In the past twenty-four hours, only the Kurds had been grumpy, so it was inevitable that either the Sunnis or the Shia would break loose soon.

And now we had a problem with the Sunnis. Brahimi had called Ghazi and told him that he'd finally decided that Pachachi would be president and asked the young sheik to withdraw his own candidacy. According to Brahimi, Ghazi had been "fine" with this decision, saying, "Adnan is like my uncle." But within minutes Ghazi had called back shouting that Pachachi was telling everyone who'd listen that he only intended to stay in office three months and would then resign in favor of Ghazi. Ghazi found this "insulting." Under these circumstances, he had told Brahimi that he refused to withdraw his candidacy. When Brahimi reached Pachachi, the old politician professed ignorance of the matter and said he could call on Ghazi to straighten out any misunderstanding.

"You know these guys, Mr. Ambassador," Brahimi said. "Can you sort it out so we can go ahead with the new government?"

I agreed to see if perhaps Ghazi could be persuaded to become a minister of state or Iraq's ambassador to Washington.

Once more unto the breach.

I arranged to meet Ghazi in his sunny, well-appointed GC office. His mood was anything but sunny. He said he felt "betrayed by Pachachi," a man to whom he still felt close.

"It's a tragedy that the two of you have fallen out," I said. "You've both given so much to this country in the last year." I floated the alternate two jobs at Ghazi.

Ghazi found the first suggestion distasteful. "I'm a leader in one of Iraq's most important tribes," he said, "and we generally prefer to stay with our people. As for the embassy job, frankly, I'm a simple man who isn't cut out for diplomacy. Besides, my wife and children live in Saudi Arabia."

The meeting ended with Ghazi's vague suggestion that we leave the matter of the presidency to the Governing Council, where he was clearly collecting votes, to make the decision.

When I saw Pachachi in his office down the hall a few minutes later, he refused to believe Ghazi's protest that he was not seeking the presidency. He said he had gone down to Ghazi's office to make amends only to be told that Ghazi would not receive him. "Certainly, Sheik Ghazi has some support among the Council Kurds and Shia," Pachachi said. "But I have the support of the entire country. And anyway, why should the Kurds and Shia be deciding who the Sunnis pick for president?"

On returning to my office, I found that the Shia also had fallen out of line, which meant that all three components were in motion. Abdul Aziz Hakim had called Dick Jones to insist that Dr. Adel be one of the vice presidents. This was "absolutely essential." His fallback was Adel for minister of interior (the same two positions I had told Adel two nights earlier we could *not* assign to SCIRI). Then Adel had called Brahimi insisting on the vice presidency. Being finance minister was just a "technical" job, which did not exploit his ability to deal with all facets of Iraqi society. Brahimi pushed Adel to accept Finance, and I agreed to back him up.

That afternoon I made a series of calls on serving ministers who were going to continue in the next government. I then made my farewell calls on the outgoing ministers, a painful business because I had to inform them that they would not have positions in the new government.

Sunday, May 30—a day devoted to the presidency—was tragicomic. Bob Blackwill expressed his concern that Pachachi's obvious passion for the job meant that he foresaw an activist presidency, which was not what the TAL had intended. Executive power would go to the prime minister, as in most parliamentary republics.

And now the Governing Council was threatening to vote on the presidency themselves. Condi Rice had told us that either Pachachi or Ghazi was acceptable to the U.S. government, so our concern was to avoid a messy public confrontation between the two men. Meanwhile Brahimi was still looking for other Arab Sunni candidates for the presidency, and Allawi came up with a couple of names we agreed to vet.

Wearily, I got in my armored SUV and drove through the blowing dust for another meeting with the GC. Using my best stagecraft, I innocently let drop that Brahimi and the CPA were considering candidates for the presidency other than Ghazi and Pachachi. Through staff-level contacts, we let it be known that several of these candidates were ex-officers in Saddam's army. This news set off the predictable alarums among the Shia, who preferred a Sunni they knew to ones they did not. And it forestalled a Council vote, at least for that day.

Barzani asked to see me alone after the meeting. In a small room beside the GC conference room, over hot tea, he said he had an idea. "Why don't we offer the presidency to Pachachi and have him turn it down?" This was an idea Brahimi had hit on several days earlier, and which I had encouraged him to pursue. So I told Barzani to give it a try, too.

Egos would be satisfied and honor upheld.

But time was running out.

Blackwill and I went to Talabani's house in Baghdad for a stormy meeting in which the Kurd accused Bob of "going back on the deal" made two days earlier about the divisions of ministries. Once more we went through the familiar litany: how we supported the Kurds and what an important role they had played in liberating Iraq. Calmer, Talabani eventually accepted a suggestion we had made several days earlier. He agreed to propose his associate Barham Saleh for deputy prime minister. We said we would see if Allawi would buy it. When he did, we thought at least we had the Kurds in line.

Late that night at the palace, we decided to delay the announcement of the new government by twenty-four hours to give us time to sort out the presidency.

Early the next morning, May 31, Dick Jones, the Governance Team, Blackwill, Richmond, and I met to review the bidding. We had pretty well shuffled the Shia and the Kurds into the deck of the new Iraqi interim government, but the presidency was still wide open.

We spent several hours on the choreography for the new government's presentation the next day. The plan was to offer the presidency to Adnan Pachachi. We'd heard no more about Barzani's efforts to arrange for him to decline the post.

The plan also included that Brahimi issue a statement at 9:30 the next morning announcing the appointment of the president, the two vice presidents, and the prime minister. Brahimi and Allawi would then present the full cabinet to Iraq and the world that afternoon. But before the presidency announcement, we needed to break the news to Ghazi to persuade him to retire gracefully from the field.

After another long day calling new ministers and saying "thanks" to outgoing ones, I phoned Condi Rice at 2:00 A.M., Tuesday, June 1, to bring her up to date. I told her I thought we had identified a strong cabinet, with good people for the key posts we cared about most—prime minister, interior, defense, and finance ministers. I also said that we intended to offer Pachachi the presidency in a few hours.

Our meeting that morning with Sheik Ghazi was very difficult. Ghazi entered the office in his finest white robes, looking very much the Arab head of state. Brahimi, in a dusty well-cut European business suit, led the discussion, noting that he had consulted about the presidency widely across the country. "And I have concluded on the basis of these discussions that Adnan Pachachi should be president."

Ghazi stared at us without speaking. Brahimi told Ghazi that we both appreciated the enormous work that he had done for his country and asked him for one final sacrifice—that the sheik permit Brahimi to announce to the press that Ghazi had removed his candidacy.

The sheik's jaw was clenched and his eyes veiled. He began speaking with a calm that quickly unraveled. Pachachi, he said, whom he used to consider an uncle, had "betrayed" him by attacking him personally and denigrating his family. Pachachi had even accused Ghazi of being in league with Chalabi, a "pernicious lie." Ghazi shook his head. "He has hurt me deeply."

He protested that he had never sought the post, but over the previous weeks had received support from friends and tribes and from people around the world.

While agreeing that Pachachi had not always behaved admirably, I added that we all had to recognize his patriotism, too. And all good Iraqis had the duty to help the interim government succeed. "Sheik Ghazi," I said, "the way for you to carry out that duty is to withdraw gracefully this morning before the Governing Council meeting convenes." Ghazi dismissed this suggestion with a wave of his hand. "I can never withdraw," he concluded firmly.

Then Brahimi noted that Pachachi had tried to visit Ghazi to make amends for any misunderstanding and reminded the sheik that "in our culture" the younger man had the obligation to receive the elder and accept his apology. Ghazi rejected this as well.

"It's just too hard. He has hurt my honor," he said with mounting emotion. Ghazi had probably told his wife and teenage children that he would soon be the president of Iraq. And he had certainly spread the good news among his tribe. He was now on the verge of being overcome by emotion.

Quietly, I repeated the importance of his supporting the new Iraqi government for the next critical months. But the sheik kept protesting that he could never support Pachachi after the hurt he had done "to my heart." He could support the new government and prime minister, but not the president. He vowed to return to politics one day and fight anyone in Pachachi's party "wherever I find them."

Finally it was clear there was no more we could accomplish and we saw Ghazi out. Brahimi and I agreed that he would call Pachachi and ask him to become president. Meanwhile I would make my way over to the Council building for a meeting with Barzani to break the news to the Kurds, who had been openly in support of Ghazi throughout.

At the GC building, David Richmond, Scott Carpenter, Meghan, Roman, and I met with Barzani in a side room. Before we could start, Meghan put a letter from Talabani in my hand. He was locked away in his Council office and his letter insisted on reopening the ministerial decisions. I sent word back to Talabani that the cabinet was closed.

Turning to Barzani, I told him we'd chosen Pachachi. This made the Kurd furious.

"I can't understand what Brahimi is doing! Last night it was arranged that Pachachi would be offered but decline the position. That was my arrangement with Brahimi. If this is the way things will be, I'll have to . . ."

Yet another open-ended Kurd threat. *What the hell else is going to happen today?* I asked myself.

Just then my military aide handed me a cell phone. It was Brahimi.

"Astonishing news," he said. "Pachachi has declined the position. I'm dumbfounded and don't know what got into him. What do we do now?"

Richmond suggested that we simply announce the cabinet and leave the name of the president open for a few more days. I vetoed this. "We've got to close the whole deal now or it will all unravel."

Speaking again to Brahimi, who was still holding on the line awaiting my answer, I asked him to offer the job to Ghazi "and pray to God he accepts it."

Never a dull day in Baghdad, I thought, looking at the astonished expressions on our team's faces. "Well, guys, this is one for the 'lessons learned.' And you're all young enough to take advantage of the lessons. As for me, I've decided that if anyone ever asks me to do this again, I'm busy that week." All we could do was share a laugh with Barzani at the bizarre turn of events.

One of Pachachi's aides explained that the old man had watched a stream of negative comments about him on television the night before and had woken up this morning and changed his mind. He was now locked in his house, talking to his wife in Abu Dhabi on the telephone.

Brahimi called back ten minutes later to say that Ghazi had accepted and was on his way to the GC building. I reached him by phone. "Congratulations, Mr. President," I said. "You must have prayed mightily to have turned things around so quickly."

He laughed, voice mellow. "God *is* great, Ambassador."

That afternoon, Lakhdar Brahimi, Sheik Ghazi al-Yawar, and Dr. Ayad Allawi presented the new Iraqi interim government to the assembled press and to the world.

Chapter 14

SOVEREIGN IRAQ

■ BAGHDAD
JUNE 2004

The interim government was another huge milestone. But I suspected that we'd have plenty to keep us busy over the next four weeks.

Much of my time would be devoted to passing as much of the CPA's collective knowledge of Iraq's governance, economic situation, and security as I could to Prime Minister Ayad Allawi, who faced the difficult task of shepherding the country from the return of sovereignty to the scheduled January elections. The CPA also would have to undertake last-minute political work in June to see to it that all sides would honor the Transitional Administrative Law as the interim constitution.

And security remained a big problem. The insurgency in Baghdad and in the Sunni Triangle was intensifying as the terrorists and insurgents saw Iraq moving to democracy. The standoff in Fallujah threatened to flare into open warfare. In the south, the Mahdi Army had been greatly weakened, but Muqtada himself remained at liberty.

In this period, I also wanted to say farewell to many Iraqis who had worked so hard, under such difficult—and often dangerous—conditions to realize Iraq's future of hope.

My first job was to help Pachachi, who was leaving to join his wife in Abu Dhabi, depart Iraq with dignity. Given the important role he had played in producing the interim constitution and the emotional roller coaster of the past few days, I wanted to pay my respects to the elder statesman. Accompanied by Scott Carpenter and David Richmond, I flew out to the airport on June 2 to say goodbye. When we greeted each other in the VIP room there, Pachachi was in a good mood. "I'm convinced that I did the right thing," he said. The presidency should unify, not further divide Iraqis. Over the past two days, he had been attacked in the media for his long-ago membership in the Baath Party. So he had concluded that his serving as president would have been disruptive to the new government. "There was a real possibility that some would have boycotted the ceremony yesterday."

"What will you do now?"

"My party will continue to prepare for the elections next year," he said calmly.

We spoke of the need for the new government members to pull together, and I noted that my impression from a year of traveling around the country, talking to thousands of Iraqis, was that the sectarian divides that had dominated Iraqi politicians on the Governing Council were much less pronounced among average Iraqis.

"It was a tragedy that Saddam destroyed the middle class, the reservoir of moderation, and drove wedges among the people," Pachachi agreed.

"But you've done much to repair that damage, Mr. Pachachi." I said that at the previous day's final GC meeting, I had recognized his contribution by describing him as "Abu-TAL" ("Father of the TAL"). "The Bill of Rights is your lasting legacy to Iraq. I hope the rights and protections will get embedded in the permanent constitution."

I told him I hoped we could meet again in Washington. I promised to cook a good meal for him and his wife. "I'll be deeply offended if I hear that you've come to town without contacting me."

He seemed touched by the invitation and said he would take it up. We chatted briefly about our preferences for classical music until it was time for him to leave.

As he crossed the sun-blasted tarmac, Pachachi struck me as a distinguished elderly Iraqi statesman who had emerged from a crisis with his spirits diminished but his pride intact.

On the way to our helicopter for the short flight back to town, I commented to David Richmond, "Politics is blood sport, all right." I'd often told New York business friends, who prided themselves on being tough guys in tough professions, that if they wanted to test their mettle, they should try a truly rough town, Washington.

That was before Baghdad.

The next day, Generals Abizaid and Sanchez and I met with Prime Minister Allawi at his office to consult on a letter Allawi would send the United Nations about the resolution the UN Security Council was debating, which would endorse the Iraqi interim government and define the security responsibilities of the Coalition after June 30. The resolution would also highlight the role of the United Nations in Iraq's ongoing political process.

When the generals left, Allawi and I had the first in a series of regular daily briefings. I wanted to be sure that he became as "read in" as possible during the next four weeks.

Our staff had put together a thick book covering more than four dozen subjects, including the training of Iraqi security forces, establishing Iraq's monetary policy (including ways to fight inflation), continuing local government reform, setting the Iraqi government budget for 2004 and 2005, fighting corruption, beefing up intelligence services, tightening border controls, negotiating Iraq's debts, deciding the future of state-owned enterprises, diversifying Iraq's economy away from overdependence on oil . . . and more and more.

Lifting the heavy book in his big hand, Allawi glanced at the calendar, as if measuring the number of pages against the days remaining in the month. "We're meeting again tomorrow, aren't we, Ambassador?"

"Every day until I leave and as often as you want."

Over the next weeks, we would meet more than thirty times. Our meetings were usually in two parts: first a briefing by a Senior Adviser—oil, electricity, etc. Then the prime minister and I would have time alone to discuss more confidential matters.

The following night I hosted a dinner for the former Governing Council. Most members attended, including the new president and the prime minister, a graceful gesture from them to their also-ran former colleagues. But all was not Fanta and roses. Just before dinner, Emad Dhia handed me a copy of Ayatollah Sistani's tepid endorsement of the new government. In the last sentence, he noted ominously that next year's elected national assembly "would not be bound by the TAL." "This'll be trouble," I told Dhia. And trouble wasn't long in arriving. At the dinner, one of Barzani's colleagues pulled me aside with "an urgent message" (*were there any other kind?*) from Barzani expressing his unhappiness that the current draft UN resolution did not contain any reference to the TAL.

The man launched into another tiresome complaint about the long-suffering Kurds—and how if they "were not satisfied," they would have to reconsider their entire posture toward the new government. Frankly I was fed up with *all* the political posturing.

"It would be rash and irresponsible for the Kurds to pull out now," I told

Barzani's man. The Kurds had gotten more from the political process than any other party over the past four months, thanks to our efforts.

"Perhaps," he said, but "the street" in Kurdistan was insistent.

I shook my head. "That," I said, "is what leaders are for—to explain to their people what is possible."

The question of whether the TAL should be referred to in the UN resolution posed a dilemma. On the one hand the Kurds insisted. On the other an explicit endorsement of the TAL risked propelling the Shia into revolt against the new government and the TAL. At the same time, I knew Sistani wanted the UN to approve the political timeline laid out in the November 15 Agreement and the TAL.

To tighten the screw a turn, that night Sistani sent me a new message saying that if the TAL was mentioned in the UN resolution, he would have to issue another statement. I contacted Steve Hadley, suggesting President Bush endorse the TAL in his regular weekly radio address. And I suggested we have the UN resolution endorse the concept of federalism, which the Kurds wanted, and the timetable for the January 2005 elections, as a way to thread the needle between the Kurdish and Sistani demands.

Is the whole month going to be like this?

At the morning intel briefing on June 5, there was good news from Najaf. The briefers announced that "Muqtada's people" had pulled out of the Shrine of Ali the night before and Iraqi police had entered. With Muqtada and his band out of the shrine, that crisis was defused—temporarily. But only temporarily. And my view of Muqtada had not changed since he first burst on the scene a year earlier. Now an Iraqi government would have to deal with him.

But the situation in Fallujah was troubling. Reports indicated that the Fallujah Brigade continued to disappoint the Marines' hopes that the brigade would help bring order to the city.

"We're being salami-sliced out there," I told Dick Jones.

Two days later, Prime Minister Allawi smiled at me across his conference table. "Massoud Barzani called this morning," he said, "with good news on the UN resolution."

Barzani was now content that, while the draft resolution would not explicitly mention the TAL, it would refer to federalism and Kurdish rights. And, as I'd hoped, he was pleased that President Bush had endorsed the TAL in his Saturday radio address.

"I now consider the matter closed," Allawi said.

Thank God, I thought. *One problem resolved.*

We moved on to discuss Muqtada. I told the prime minister that I regretted that we were leaving this issue unresolved and that his government would have to figure out how to deal with the man. He responded that Iraqi police should not try to arrest Muqtada before June 30. When I raised the broader issue of the insurgency, Allawi said that he favored opening some kind of talks with insurgents.

I briefed him on the approaches we had had from alleged insurgents after Saddam's capture. We'd pursued each of them to no avail, "but it's definitely worth a try."

On June 8, UN Security Council Resolution 1546 was unanimously adopted. It welcomed the Iraqi interim government as a "new phase in Iraq's transition to a democratically elected government." It also contained an explicit endorsement of the timeline established in the TAL and of elections by January 31, 2005. Attached to the resolution were letters from Allawi and Secretary Powell that defined the role of the Coalition Multinational Force.

That afternoon, Dia brought a more conciliatory message from Ayatollah Sistani. He was "pleased" with the outcome in the holy cities, with the new government and prime minister, and that the UN resolution did not explicitly mention the TAL, and that it had endorsed the timetable for elections in January 2005. "My dialogue with Ambassador Bremer over the past year," he concluded, "has been very useful, and I hope it will continue."

Though the ayatollah had refused to meet occupation authorities, over the previous fourteen months he and I had exchanged more than three dozen messages through various intermediaries. And I, too, had found them to be "very useful."

The countdown clock was ticking. We had a little over two weeks left before divesting sovereignty and I would leave Iraq. So I began quietly discussing the protocol and security involved in the transfer. Because the latest intel revealed "strong indications" of major terrorist attacks planned for Wednesday, June 30, there was a risk that security would become the tail that wagged the dog. The whole situation would have to be planned and watched very carefully.

As I went through the long list of issues with the prime minister, I also wanted to say goodbye to many of the Iraqis I'd worked with over the past fourteen months. On June 13, I paid a farewell call on Vice President Ibrahim al-Jaafari, who offered another marvelous meal, the centerpiece of which was, as usual, *fesinjan*. Jaafari was in his high-octane flight mode, holding forth on a cascade of topics, hardly stopping for breath—the Greek scholars, Hitler, Stalin, Saddam, George Washington, and John Adams—all the while speculating on the future of the new Iraqi cabinet.

I congratulated him on agreeing to serve as vice president. "I know it was not an easy decision for you, Mr. Vice President. But you've done the right thing for yourself and for your country." As I left his house, I reflected that Jaafari was still the most popular politician in the country. He was an Islamist, but proudly spoke of his unveiled wife, herself also a medical doctor, and their three daughters.

One of our major objectives had been to establish checks and balances in government to counter the historic experience of centralized one-man rule in Iraq. Two days after I said goodbye to Jaafari, two senior Iraqi officials asked to pay farewell calls to express their appreciation for this effort.

First, Dr. Sinan Mohammed Rida al-Shabibi, the governor of the Central Bank, whom I had appointed in July 2003, came in to thank me for making the bank independent and for freeing interest rates. "These steps are vital for Iraq to recover its economic strength—and to eventually find stability," he concluded.

Two hours later, he was followed by Chief Justice Medhat al-Mahmoud, who appreciated our work to reestablish the rule of law in Iraq. He was grateful that I had signed an order making the courts independent of the government. "And on a more personal note, I'm particularly grateful that you doubled judges' salaries," he concluded with a big smile.

Later that morning we received reports of multiple sabotage attacks on Iraq's strategic southern pipelines. By early afternoon, the extent of the damage became clear. The forty-two-inch pipeline linking the southern oilfields with the Daura refinery and the Mussayib power station had been cut. The twelve-inch line from the Kirkuk-Two field in the north was still under repair from earlier sabotage.

An hour later, I got a report that the forty-eight-inch pipeline connecting the main South Oil Company field to Al-Faw and the offshore loading terminals had also been hit around noon southwest of Basra. The line was described as "split and spewing oil."

Intel reports had indicated terrorists planned a wave of attacks meant to peak on June 30 and that these attacks would include major sabotage of oil infrastructure.

It's started already. We have to think seriously about security on June 30.

My farewell call on Baghdad's Ayatollah Hussein al-Sadr required the most intense security. Frank Gallagher insisted that I not travel to his house again at night. "The last time you went for dinner," Frank explained, "we had a grenade thrown at us."

I arranged to visit the cleric for lunch. Even so, Frank wasn't happy to take me in daylight given the steady flow of intelligence suggesting increased attacks. So this time he laid on seventeen extra Humvees to cover our convoy's route, ordered all three Blackwater helicopters—each with two "shooters"—to fly just above our motorcade, and arranged with the military for a couple of Apache choppers to fly on our flanks and F-16 fighter bombers to fly top cover. It wasn't the best way to say goodbye to a quiet and dignified friend.

The ayatollah greeted me warmly in his book-lined study. Over tepid orange sodas, then lunch, and finally steaming tea, the conversation covered everything from the role of religion, to the importance of family everywhere, to the development of Iraqi democracy, to the need for more guns for the police.

Toward the end, the ayatollah looked me in the eye and explained what Liberation had meant to him. During Saddam's time, the Mukhabarat often came to his house in the night to take him away for questioning and torture.

"Mr. Ambassador, for years, I found it difficult to sleep for fear they would come and kill me in my sleep. Now we are free and I sleep like a baby."

Later on June 17, I heard a surprising idea in a call from Rice.

"The president is interested in trying to 'wrong foot' the opposition by doing the transfer of sovereignty a couple of days early," she said.

"Not a bad idea," I concurred, "assuming Allawi agrees." The insurgents certainly wouldn't expect this. "But there are two conditions," I insisted. "We have to keep this secret until the last minute or we'll just trigger the terrorists to move early." Secondly, I stressed that an early transfer had to be preceded by several days of relative calm. "It can't look as if we are scuttling out of here, Condi." She agreed and I said I'd take it up with Allawi.

The next day, I raised the matter with the prime minister, citing the mounting intelligence about terrorist attacks timed for June 30. He concurred and approved the two conditions I'd discussed with Rice, and we agreed to fix the exact date for the transfer in about a week.

On Saturday, June 19, it was time to say goodbye to many of the Iraqi women we had worked with over the past year to promote women's rights. I hosted a lunch for representatives of the most important women's groups in Iraq and for the new government's female ministers and deputy ministers. They appreciated the work we had done and were particularly pleased with the 25 percent goal for women in the parliament to be elected in January.

"I'd better be careful when I tell my wife that I had lunch today with fifty women," I joked.

When the laughter faded, one sophisticated lady retorted, "Much better than lunch with one."

The next day, Judy Van Rest, one of the CPA's most energetic political officers, briefed Allawi on our democracy-building program. I first explained to the prime minister why I had given such a priority to this effort. I noted that democracy involves a lot more than just holding elections. So I had allocated almost $750 million from the American and Iraqi budgets. Much of the program was meant to build the institutions and organizations that formed what we Westerners call "civil society." After decades of tyranny, Iraqis desperately needed these "social shock absorbers" I had first mentioned to the president more than a year before.

"Prime Minister," Judy explained, "we are establishing these institutions all over Iraq." She explained that our provincial offices had midwifed the birth of dozens of human rights centers, nongovernmental organizations, legal associations, even PTAs. We had funds to set up Women's Centers in all eighteen provinces, nine in Baghdad alone. We had also earmarked hundreds of millions from the Iraqi budget to support voter registration and education and to conduct the January elections.

"This is splendid work," Allawi said. "I hope some funds might be available to establish an independent think tank. If Iraq is to become a modern country, we'll need such institutions, which can help the Iraqi people learn about the basics of democracy."

We finished our efforts to deal with the knotty problem of the parties' militias in June with the passage of a law that the Iraqi interim government quickly endorsed. The act banned all militia that were not in the process of entering government security services, retirement, or training for civilian life. We also created a Veterans Administration to oversee the registration and reintegration of militia as well as ex-army personnel.

We had no assurance that the militia agreements David Gompert had negotiated would hold. But given that our alternative was to use force against all
these groups, including our allies the Peshmerga, we felt that we had negotiated
about as good a deal as possible. At least we were leaving the Iraqis with a
chance to bring militias under control. But would the new Iraqi government be
able to enforce the law and implement the transition and reintegration agreements?

On June 22, with only six days to go, I spent the day outside Baghdad. First I
flew to Kirkuk with President Ghazi, David Richmond, and a large press contingent. Ostensibly, this was another farewell visit. In reality, we wanted to address some of the severe tensions still gripping the city.

The new minister of displacement and migration, Pascale Warda, a Christian woman from the region, joined us. Her ministry would have a major role in
resolving the damage that thirty-five years of forced resettlement had done to
Kirkuk. After difficult negotiations with the Kurds, the TAL had postponed the
resolution of Kirkuk's final status. But the Kurds continued trying to reclaim
lands there, each Kurdish political party vying to outdo the other. Kirkuk was a
tinderbox and we would be lucky if it didn't explode before the January elections.

One concept the CPA had encouraged was establishing and endowing a
Kirkuk Foundation to promote projects reaching across the various ethnic communities. I designated $50 million from Iraq's national budget and persuaded
the Kurds to put up another $50 million. With this endowment, and a decent
multiethnic board, the foundation should be able to implement several worthy
projects every year. But as with so much in Iraq, this would depend on those
communities deciding to cooperate with one another. And that in turn would
require them to get away from the zero-sum approach to all matters.

After announcing the foundation to town notables in Kirkuk we choppered
to a small landing zone in a soccer field near Massoud Barzani's mountain retreat.

As I got off the plane, Barzani greeted me with an enthusiastic proposal that
we ignore the schedule. "You can't leave Iraq without giving me the chance to
show you the beauty of Kurdistan. That way I'll be sure you'll bring your wife
back here one day."

We drove north for two hours, at last entering a shady gorge. Driving beneath
a cliff face, our SUV was misted from the sparkling waterfalls rushing from
crevices and holes all across the limestone above. This felt like a different coun-

try. There were restaurants and teahouses along the various streams, and to judge by the Tuesday afternoon trade, they were doing a good business. My sharpest memory is of a grizzled old mountaineer standing by the roadside as we passed.

"Massoud," he shouted, "hang Saddam!"

The crowd along the shoulder of the road broke into cheers.

At a late afternoon private meeting with the prime minister on June 23, we agreed to try to transfer sovereignty on Monday, June 28 . . . provided the security held up.

But the next day opened with four mortar attacks at 5:45 A.M., one killing an Iraqi worker just inside the palace grounds. The blasts echoed across the Green Zone.

At that morning's intelligence briefing General Barbara Fast said that intelligence reports suggested that terrorists were coming into Baghdad from the west and the south, to conduct car bombings and other attacks on June 30. If violence stepped up in the next few days, however, we would have to cancel the early-transfer maneuver because it would seem as if we were being driven out.

After that meeting, I went to bid goodbye to Dr. Sayyid Mohammad Bahr al-Uloum at his office.

The lively white-bearded cleric was in a cheerful mood.

"You have more gray hair today than when you arrived a year ago, Mr. Ambassador," he laughed.

"You're a keen observer, Sayyid," I said. Pointing to hair on my right temple, I said, "These gray hairs are from Sunnis. The ones on the back of my head are from the Kurds, and these here, on top, come from Shia like you."

He chuckled. When I added that if he thought it had been difficult to deal with Americans running the government, "wait until you have to deal with Iraqis," the imam roared with laughter.

"I have a proposition for you, Mr. Ambassador. I will forgive you all your mistakes if you will forgive me all mine."

"Agreed, Sayyid."

I would miss this man, too.

•   •   •

At noon, we reopened the Baghdad stock exchange, which operated only two hours, but set a record for number of shares traded. *Once secure, this country will be a tremendous economic success.*

Security in the run-up to our planned early transfer continued to be a concern. On Friday, June 25, I was again awakened by the Giant Voice blaring: "Take Cover! Take Cover!"

Seconds later, I was running barefoot down to the villa's shelter when a heavy mortar round hit the Green Zone.

The first reports indicated no casualties or damage, but would we have the quiet few days we needed for the early transfer?

Later that afternoon, I asked Brigadier General Scott Castle, the CPA's general counsel, to accompany me to my regular meeting with the prime minister. Scott summarized our policy in preparing the more than one hundred laws enacted over the past year. "We've been conservative, Prime Minister," he said, "respecting Iraqi laws whenever possible—amending them only as necessary to create a legal structure within which democracy and a free-market economy can flourish." We had taken a narrow "surgical" approach rather than replacing Iraqi statutes with Western ones.

Iraqi lawyers served on his staff, Scott added, and we had consulted regularly with other Iraqis—attorneys, professors, and businessmen. The concerned Iraqi ministries had been closely involved in identifying necessary reforms and reviewing the draft laws. These were also carefully coordinated within the U.S. government, with the International Monetary Fund, the World Bank, and with the British and Australian governments. All legal boundaries under international law and UN resolutions had been respected.

"It was a very meticulous and exhaustive process," Scott concluded.

I added that we had tried to modernize Iraqi commercial law to make Iraq competitive and to help Iraq develop a robust, diversified private sector.

"General Castle, I can see that your work hasn't been easy," Allawi said. "Under Saddam, Iraq had many laws, but no lawfulness."

On leaving, we presented him with bound volumes of the new Iraqi laws in Arabic and dozens of additional proposed reforms for the new government to consider. This body of law—a solid framework capable of supporting Iraq's rebirth—represented tens of thousands of hours of work.

•   •   •

On Saturday, June 26, I had just fallen asleep when the first of several mortar rounds hit near the Green Zone for the third day in a row. Shuffling down the corridor, I checked the luminous face of my watch. Five minutes past midnight.

Daylight revealed that the attacks had done no harm inside the palace grounds. But they were probably signs of things to come. At that day's intel briefing, General Fast reported indications that the insurgents were planning to capture a city—perhaps Ramadi or Baquba—on June 30.

They want to wound the new government before it takes its first steps.

In the afternoon, we received unexpected word that Muqtada's spokesman had apparently announced some kind of a "cease-fire" against Coalition forces.

"This is the second piece of good news about Muqtada in a week," I told General Sanchez.

We'd recently heard credible reports that Muqtada was trying to rally Iraqis against the terrorists.

"Whatever happens in the south," I said, "we're not going to stop offensive operations against Muqtada in Sadr City. We're not going to get ourselves drawn into a Fallujah-type 'solution' there."

"I concur, sir," Sanchez said.

At a morning meeting with Allawi on Sunday, June 27, behind the closed door of his office, I reviewed options for the early transfer. Time was very short.

"We hope it can be tomorrow," I said. "But that will depend on maintaining a relative level of calm today."

"I understand. And I agree," he replied. I said that I would contact the prime minister again at the end of the day after we had been able to see how security had gone.

Meanwhile the British staff at CPA seemed to have picked up a rumor about the early transfer of sovereignty. I reminded David Richmond that if the story leaked, "all bets are off."

"Well," he said, "I've received instructions from London to speak directly to Allawi about the proposed transfer. They want to assure themselves that he indeed wants to do it tomorrow."

"Go ahead and see the PM, David," I said somewhat coldly. I was not pleased that his government would think I was twisting Allawi's position.

Later that morning, I met privately with Sanchez. "We're thinking of possibly transferring sovereignty tomorrow," I said, "but it'll depend on keeping things relatively quiet today." So I asked the general to take a survey of his military commanders at 6:00 P.M. to see how the day had gone. "We'll get together again at 6:15 to hear your report and then I'll check with the president."

I had one more farewell to make in the short time remaining. I needed to go back to Al-Hillah. Almost fourteen months earlier, my first visit outside Baghdad had been to the mass gravesite that held the remains of thousands of Iraqis killed by Saddam's henchmen and thrown into a huge open pit.

But instead of returning to the site on this trip, I spent several hours visiting again with one of the most remarkable Iraqis I had met, Sheik Sayyid Farqat al-Qizwini.

When I'd first met this tall, black-turbaned imam a year before, he had thanked the U.S. for liberating Iraq and had spoken of wanting to turn Iraq into "America's fifty-third state." He had just taken possession of a mosque Saddam built in Al-Hillah and had told me of his dream to turn it into a university to study and teach democracy.

Now I discovered that he'd done it, with the enthusiastic support of the CPA and Mike Gfoeller. First the sheik showed me through a photo exhibit of the mass graves in the former mosque's hall. It was to remind everyone, he said, of the "Old Iraq." The photos were powerful—women digging frantically in the dirt, one holding pictures of her three sons killed by Saddam and whose bodies she could not find. Dozens of skulls had been cut open by Saddam's ghouls to see the effects of chemicals used on the victims.

Sheik Qizwini had also transferred seventy-five unidentified bodies from the gravesite and buried them in neat rows in front of a monument with a plaque, which had inscriptions from the Torah, the Koran, and the Bible.

Standing in bright sun alongside these "tombs of the unknown" were a dozen living heroes, men and women who had resisted Saddam during the 1991 uprising. Two had been young boys, hauled off with their families, then shot and dumped in the mass graves. Somehow they had survived by feigning death. After dark they had crawled out of the pits and escaped into neighboring villages. I was barely able to hold back tears as I shook their hands.

Next we visited the New Iraq. The key organization was Qizwini's "Regional Democracy Center." This included a local radio station, "the Voice of Independent Democratic Iraq." He had opened an Internet café where students, most of them theologians, were attentively studying the screens on the twenty-five computers the CPA had provided. They were searching the Web for information about the many aspects of democracy. I was also introduced to a score of *abaya*-shrouded women studying and writing about women's rights and human rights.

At the end of the visit I made a brief statement to the accompanying press. "I remember meeting Sayyid Qizwini a little more than a year ago. He told me then of his dream to establish a democracy center. That dream has come true."

I added that there were still people who doubted that overthrowing the tyrant Saddam had been beneficial. There were others who considered a peaceful and democratic Iraq to be nothing but a dream.

My message to both groups of people is simple:

Come to Al-Hillah.

Come and see the mass graves and say that it was not noble to overthrow Saddam.

Come and see the democracy center and say that Iraqis cannot build a pluralistic society.

If it is a dream, it is a dream shared by millions of Iraqis.

That evening General Sanchez reported that we'd had only nineteen incidents countrywide, versus almost forty daily before.

I met again with Allawi.

"Prime Minister," I told him, "I can confirm that we intend to go ahead with the transfer tomorrow . . . subject to final approval of my government."

I called Condi Rice in Ankara, where she was with the president at a meeting of the heads of state of NATO. "We've had a few quiet days, Condi. No leaks. We should be able to transfer tomorrow."

She sighed. "Now the Brits have raised doubts. They're wondering if it will look like we're bailing out. The president and Blair will discuss it at dinner at 9:30 tonight and I'll brief you afterward."

At about midnight, Rice called.

"Blair is okay with a transfer tomorrow," she said.

"Good. I've asked Rick Sanchez to give me an update on the overnight situation at 7:45 in the morning," I told her.

"Let's talk at 7:55 A.M. then, Jerry," she said. "We'll make the decision then.

As I was working my way through a stack of documents that night, Colonel Norwood brought disturbing news.

"Sir," he said, "a C-130 taking off from Baghdad airport has been attacked with small-arms fire. One DOD civilian aboard killed."

Frank Gallagher was standing beside Scott in the doorway, looking grim.

Over the past week, my security detail had become increasingly concerned about how to get me out of the country alive. For more than a year, I had almost always flown C-130s into and out of Iraq. The C-130s were equipped with flares to throw off most—but not all—heat-seeking surface-to-air missiles. And several times, these had been triggered on planes I was flying on. Now Gallagher was concerned that even though there would only be a few hours between the transfer of sovereignty and my departure, the terrorists might have time to prepare a missile attack on any departing C-130s.

I called for Brian McCormack. "I want you to work one of your magic-trick plans with Frank Gallagher, Rick Sanchez's staff, and the Station and get me out of here tomorrow, preferably in one piece."

I returned to the garish, echoing villa and packed my bags, hoping that it would be my last night there. Only my immediate staff was aware that Monday would be the day. Most were planning to leave with me on Wednesday via a C-17 to Germany.

We'll all drink a cold beer in Washington was as much a mantra as a wish.

■ MONDAY, JUNE 28, 2004

Sanchez briefed Dick Jones and me on overnight events. "Only a few isolated incidents," he said. "Looks like they're waiting for Wednesday."

As agreed, I called Condi Rice in Ankara at 7:55 A.M. to say "All systems are go" for transfer today at 10:00 A.M.

"I'll inform the president that we're proceeding," she said.

Now that it was certain we would leave today, I sent the president my final report. In this letter, I noted that Iraqis were delighted to be free and that over the past year had shown a huge thirst for the individual freedoms made possible by Liberation. I recounted how a student from the University of Baghdad had said to me, "We had been living in a dark room for decades. You have come and opened a window onto a bright world beyond."

The Coalition had done its best to establish the principle of government responsible to the people and committed to the rule of law. We had embedded the concepts of balance of power in government and respect for minority rights in the TAL. I admitted that political reality in Iraq had unfortunately made it impossible for us to carry out the many necessary economic reforms, particularly cutting subsidies. On the other hand, I drew his attention to our efforts to combat corruption, cautioning, "It will take years for these institutions to reverse the tide."

While noting the damage Saddam's reign had done to Iraq's infrastructure, I wrote, "The regime's most devastating impact was on the psychological infrastructure of the Iraqi people." For decades they had lived in that dark room where they had been taught to trust no one. Given the numbing brutality of day-to-day life, "building a society of trust will be a huge undertaking."

I admitted disappointment that we had not been able to establish a secure environment. "The insurgents have proven better organized and more difficult to penetrate than we had expected. Terrorists from Al-Qaeda and Zarqawi have decided to make Iraq the front line in their evil struggle. Because a democratic government is anathema to these men, there will be more violence in the months ahead." I said that our immediate emphasis should be on training professional leaders for all the Iraqi security forces. "We must emphasize the quality of the leaders more than the quantity of the followers."

Nonetheless, "We can take a measure of satisfaction that we acted responsibly as temporary custodians of Iraq's sovereignty this past year." I concluded that as a result of the president's courage and the Coalition's efforts, "Iraq has before it a path toward a better future. It is a future of hope for all Iraqis, a future where Iraqis can say what they want, study what they will, travel as they please, and pursue the daily joys of work, family, and faith which we in America have been privileged to enjoy for centuries."

At about 9:00 A.M., June 28, the CPA's strategic communications office sent word to the media that Prime Minister Allawi and I would have comments for the press at the government building at 10:00 A.M.

When the correspondents arrived at the former Governing Council building, our staff collected everybody's cell phones, so that they could not report the event real time, or immediately after, to allow me to leave Iraq first.

At 9:55, David Richmond and I climbed into our armored SUV for the mile ride to the government building. There were quite a few press gathered in the outer hallway.

We passed into the prime minister's office, where he and I had met so often in the past month. Allawi had invited President Ghazi and Deputy Prime Minister Barham Saleh to attend. We sat and made small talk with Chief Justice Medhat al-Mahmoud until the reporters entered the room. They were held behind a rope line, and were apparently unaware of what was about to happen.

Realizing how interested the president would be in the event, Condi Rice had asked Brian McCormack to set up an open phone line to Liz Lineberry on her staff in Ankara, where the president and NATO heads of state were sitting around a large table listening to each other's speeches. Rob Tappan, head of the CPA strategic communications division, was posted just outside Allawi's office and relayed a running commentary on events to Brian, who in turn passed it along to Liz.

After things quieted down a bit in the office, I stood, opened a blue Morocco leather folder that Brian had cadged from someplace, and read out a letter that I had signed that morning, formally transferring sovereignty to the Iraqi people and their government. It concluded, "We welcome Iraq's steps to take its rightful place of equality and honor among the nations of the world."

With some emotion, I handed this folder to the chief justice. The Iraqis were beaming broadly and so was I.

In Ankara, Condi Rice heard from Brian that the deed was done. She scribbled on the back of a piece of paper. "Iraq is sovereign. Letter was passed from Bremer at 10:26 A.M., Iraq time." She gave the note to Secretary of Defense Rumsfeld, who was sitting directly behind President Bush. He leaned over and handed the note to the president.

The president showed the note to Tony Blair, seated next to him, and scrawled across it, "Let Freedom Reign!"

Allawi and Ghazi escorted David Richmond and me to our car. Shaking hands in farewell, I said to Allawi, "You have your country now. It's in your hands. Take good care of it."

Back at the palace, word was out that we'd made the transfer, and there was a huge crowd in the hall outside my office, many cheering, and some in tears. Rick Sanchez was waiting in my office with a flag of CJTF-7 for me, signed by him, his commanders, and senior staff. I invited him to join me in the hall to say goodbye to the civilians and military milling around out there. We shook all the hands and then I went down to the marble entrance for the last time and climbed back into my car for the short trip to our landing zone.

The military had laid on two Chinook helicopters to accommodate the press, our staff, and luggage. Prime Minister Allawi had designated the deputy prime minister to see me off.

For the last time, and again in the sweltering heat of a Baghdad summer, I took off from the Green Zone for the twenty-minute flight to Baghdad Airport. The Chinooks landed behind several camouflaged C-130s, one of which was designated to fly me out of Iraq. Our party moved into the cool VIP room to greet the last of many congressional delegations, this one led by California Republican Congressman Duncan Hunter, chairman of the House Armed Services Committee and a staunch supporter of the liberation of Iraq. He congratulated me on the transfer and after a few minutes, I was told the press had formed by the C-130 to photograph my departure.

The deputy prime minister and I made our way across the blazing tarmac to a West Virginia Air National Guard C-130. After shaking his hand, I followed several of my security men up into the plane, pausing at the top step to wave a final farewell to the deputy PM.

Then the press was escorted back into the holding room in the terminal.

The C-130 crew closed the door behind me and Frank Gallagher and I waited in the hot plane for fifteen minutes until the press had left. Then we crawled up and over the plane's fully loaded cargo bay, and ran down the tailgate ramp. We dashed fifty yards across the baking tarmac to a waiting Chinook, where my small personal staff—Scotty Norwood, Sue, Brian, and Dan—were already belted in. The Chinook took off at once and flew for five minutes to another area of the airport where we deplaned, and immediately boarded a small U.S. government jet. I took one last look at Iraq, and we left.

On the flight to Jordan, Sue handed me a letter that had come in that morning. It was from a young Baghdad schoolgirl and was translated into English. "You have given us a new life. We are very pleased and we offer our love to those who want good for us. We thank them and thank you for this wonderful deed."

Gazing at the stark brown desert below, I thought back on my farewell address to the nation, which I had videotaped for broadcast the night of my departure.

Don Hamilton, Dan Senor, and I had worked for several weeks on the text. I wanted a speech that was highly personal, telling Iraqis how I felt about their country's future.

My wonderful Iraqi-born interpreter, Muean Aljabiry, suggested that I end the speech with a few stanzas in Arabic by a famous Iraqi poet, Ibn Zuraiq al-Baghdadi. He rehearsed me on these lines for days before I recorded the speech, which would be broadcast the day I left the country.

There were passages that I knew I would remember my entire life.

I leave behind a country very different from what it was a year ago. Iraq today is a very much better country, though much work remains to be done to bring about a future of hope for all Iraqis . . .

The days of the tyrant are over. Justice will prevail—the justice you have prized in the Land between the Two Rivers since the time of Hammurabi . . .

Today, Iraq is united, not by forced loyalty to a tyrant, but by a shared vision of freedom for every single Iraqi—man or woman, Arab, Turkman or Kurd, Sunni or Shia, Christian or Muslim . . .

Our soldiers came to Iraq for no purpose except to depose a tyrant, to help reconstruct the country and to establish order until you could do it yourselves. They have sought nothing for themselves. Our soldiers will stay only as long as the Iraqi government wishes. And when they leave, they will take nothing with them but their dead.

The future of Iraq belongs to you, the Iraqi people. We and your other friends will help. But we can only help. You must do the real work . . . You Iraqis must now take responsibility for your future of hope . . .

A piece of my heart will always remain here in the beautiful Land between the Two Rivers, with its fertile valleys, its majestic mountains and its wonderful people. As an historian I have come more deeply to respect Iraq's proud history. Living here, I have come to see why for thousands of years Mesopotamia has been the cradle of so much that is best in all of mankind . . .

And I ended with the poetry stanzas delivered in Arabic:

I bid farewell to a moon in Baghdad
That rises over the skies above Al-Karkh.
Although wishing to part with life's serenity instead.
And the Baghdad moon appealed as well
That I should not say goodbye.
But needs, at times
Have greater ways of compelling.

Mabruk al-Iraq al-jadeed . . . Congratulations to the New Iraq . . .
Aash al-Iraq! . . . Long live Iraq!

After a ninety-minute flight, we landed at the military airport in Amman, Jordan. I called Francie, who by now had seen news reports of the early transfer of sovereignty.

"I'm safe and free," I said. "And I'm coming home."

AFTERWORD

Since the events described in this book, there have been significant developments in Iraq's struggle to build a new nation with a future of hope.

Defying terrorists and pundits alike, Iraqis by the millions voted in the country's first truly democratic elections in January 2005. Who can forget the moving image of thousands of Iraqi men and women waving their purple-stained fingers in pride? Nothing could better illustrate the thirst for self-government felt by the vast majority of the Iraqi people. Fully 31 percent of the deputies elected were women, one of the highest percentages in the world (and twice that in the U.S. Congress).

The terrorists and other antidemocratic forces recognize the threat to them posed by self-governing Iraqi citizens. And so they have stepped up their attacks on the very people they seek to rule. The terrorists will not succeed because the Iraqi people and their allies will not allow it.

Recently, voices have been heard in America calling for the withdrawl of our forces or for setting a clear deadline for their return to the U.S. This would be an historic mistake, only serving to encourage the terrorists to wait us out before renewing their attacks. It would signal a defeat for America's interests, not just in Iraq, but in the wider region. Terrorists everywhere would take heart.

What is at stake is far more than Iraq's future, for the elections in early 2005 stirred democratic winds throughout the region. It is in America's interest to fan those winds because responsible self-government is the best long-term antidote to the hatred and warped vision of the terrorists.

President Bush, addressing the United Nations in September, put the case very clearly, "Either hope will spread or violence will spread, and we must take the side of hope."

Finally, a personal message to the men and women of America's armed forces: During my time in Iraq, I was constantly impressed by your courage and steadfast dedication. You liberated Iraq from Saddam's tyranny and then helped the Iraqi people reclaim their country, whether by fighting the insurgents and terrorists or by rebuilding schools and orphanages. You, and Iraqis of all sects and ethnic backgrounds, have paid a very high price in this fight. Hard as the job has been, you can take comfort in knowing that you have done a noble thing.

But there is no quick, easy path to renewing a society like Iraq's, recovering from decades of brutality. We must honor your sacrifices by showing the patience and determination to finish the job.

Acknowledgments

It is difficult, writing a book, to know where to begin to thank the people without whose help it would not have been possible.

I suppose the best place is to begin at the beginning and to thank my wonderful agent, Marvin Josephson. It was he, on a visit to Baghdad, who first suggested that I write this book. So readers disappointed that I have followed his advice should take their grievance to Marvin.

To me, however, Marvin was a gift. I thank him for his help identifying a publisher and willingness to give sound advice on the book as the writing proceeded. And I am further indebted to him for suggesting that I engage Malcolm McConnell as my collaborator on the project.

My sincere thanks to Malcolm for his extraordinary energy and insight. He came to the project with the perfect background—former diplomat, experienced author, and sensible man. Malcolm is an excellent writer and has become a good friend. He also brought to bear his secret weapon, his wife, Carol. She somehow succeeded at the near-hopeless task of keeping us organized.

Alice Mayhew lived up to her reputation as one of the country's best and most experienced editors. I am deeply grateful for her constructive and thoughtful comments on the structure and content of the book. She also mobilized the considerable resources of the publisher, Simon & Schuster. I particularly want to thank Tom Pitoniak for his perceptive copyediting and Serena Jones for her indefatigable support.

The story told here would not have been possible without the heroic men and women of the American armed forces and my former colleagues in the Coalition Provisional Authority.

These civilians, all of them volunteers, served in a stressful and dangerous environment, working 18–20 hours a day to help the Iraqi people reclaim their country. It was the most extraordinary group of dedicated individuals I have ever worked with. I thank them from the bottom of my heart.

I note with great sadness that my close friend and invaluable counselor, Hume Horan, died before this book was published.

My special thanks to former colleagues who helped me with the research on this book and who gave—sometimes rather freely—their advice on how to improve it. Wherever I have fallen short of their high standards, I myself am to blame.

Thanks to you: Muean Aljabiry, Rodney Bent, Scott Carpenter, Scott Castle, Christina Estrada, Mounzer Fatfat, Matt Fuller, Peter Gibson, Bob Gifford, David Gompert, Tom Foley, Reuben Jeffery, Dick Jones, Roman Martinez, Brian McCormack, Don Hamilton, Clay McManaway, Peter McPherson, Scotty Norwood, David Oliver, Meghan O'Sullivan, Chris Ross, Ed Schmults, Dan Senor, Walt Slocombe, Gene Stakhiv, Hugh Tant, Gary Vogler, and Alex Zemak. Your contributions to this story, both before and after we left Iraq, were remarkable.

A very special thanks to my long-time colleague and friend Sue Shea. Following an unfathomable calling, she came to Baghdad on a moment's notice to work for me—yet again. Somehow, through the tensions and chaos of life there, she brought a measure of calm and organization.

My thanks to my children and their spouses. They set aside misgivings they might have had about the dangers inherent to my mission and showed me, in a hundred ways over the fourteen months, how love can conquer distance.

Finally, to Francie: wife of thirty-nine years, loving mother of our children, experienced author, wise counselor, and love of my life. Her steadfast courage throughout the long months of this story was just the latest example of her strength and faith. God bless you, Francie!

Index

Photo Credits

About the Authors

Ambassador L. Paul Bremer III, a career diplomat, was the Presidential Envoy to Iraq from May 2003 to June 2004. During his twenty-three years at the State Department, he served on the personal staffs of six secretaries of state and on four continents. In the 1980s, he was Ambassador to the Netherlands and Ambassador at Large for Counter Terrorism. After leaving government, he was Managing Director of Kissinger Associates. In December 2004, George W. Bush awarded Bremer the Presidential Medal of Freedom for his service in Iraq.

Malcolm McConnell is a former Foreign Service officer and the author or co-author of numerous books. He collaborated with General Tommy Franks on his No. 1 bestselling memoir, *American Soldier.*